ASPIRE SUCCEED PROGRESS

GLOBAL PERSPECTIVES & RESEARCH

for Cambridge International AS & A Level

Jo Lally

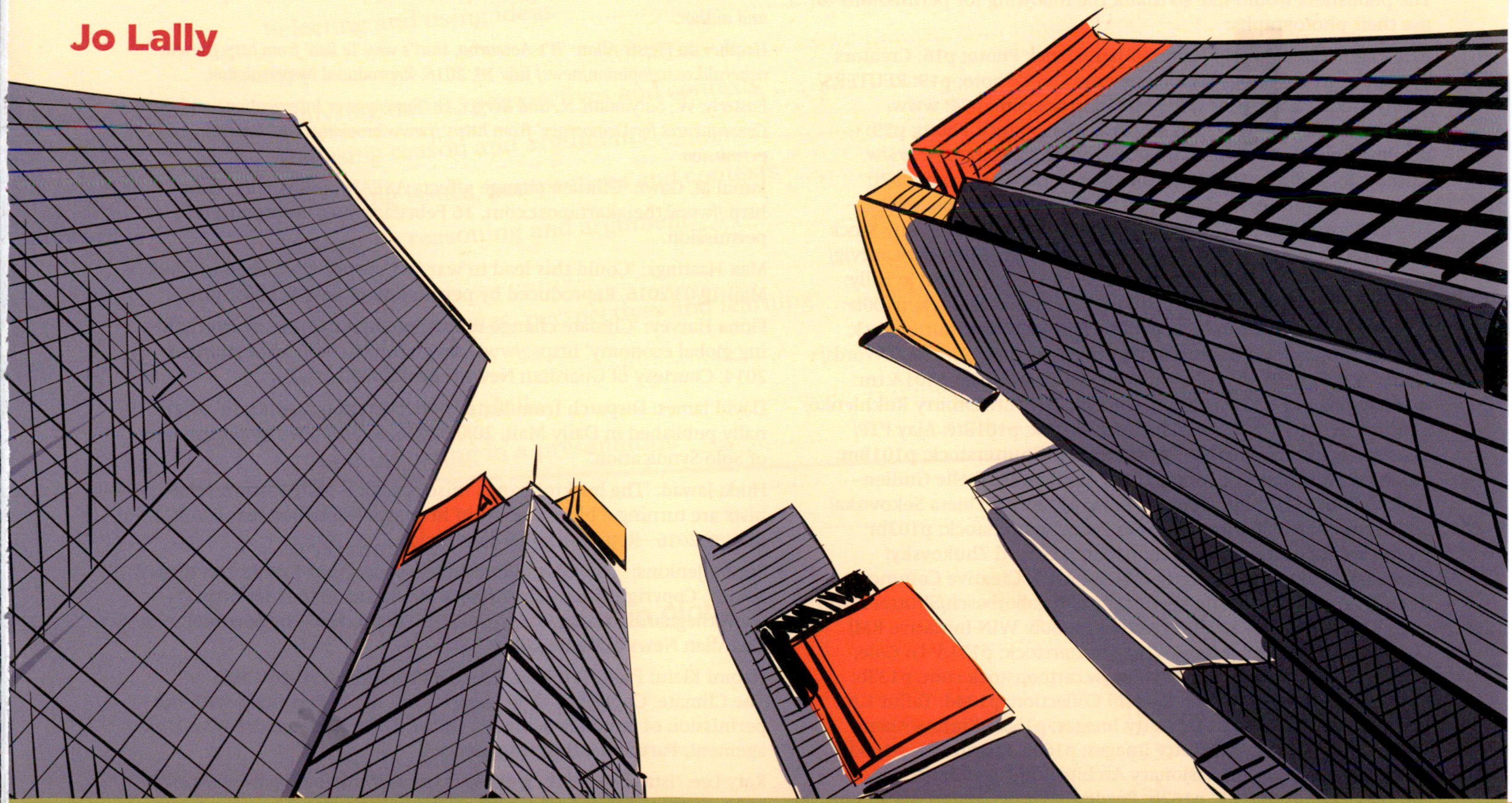

Oxford excellence for Cambridge AS & A Level

OXFORD

it (reconstruction); think about the issues, the contexts and the perspectives, trying to find and justify your own personal perspective (reflection); and you will communicate, collaborate and present ideas, information and arguments relating to the issue.

Developing the skills

Skills, rather than specific information, are at the heart of Global Perspectives and Research. Section A provides activities and tips relating to the skills and activities which will help you to understand and develop the skills. The activities are designed to develop practical knowledge: that is, you should **be able** to, use the skills rather than 'knowing about' the skills. If we take the example of a sportsperson, we can see that knowing about the skills needed to score a goal, hit a home run or throw the javelin further than anyone else has ever thrown it, is much less important than **being able** to do these things.

It is important to work through all of the skills development exercises in Section A. However, merely working through the skills once and in isolation from the Global Perspectives and Research contexts is not likely to be effective. One of the best ways to develop your skills is through practice and application in interesting contexts. Even when the skills seem strange or hard, it is important to keep trying to apply them in context. It is also important to listen to feedback, and use the feedback to improve. Skills development is an iterative process. That is, it requires plenty of practice.

Applying the skills

Section B focuses on applying the skills in context. It does not aim to teach you any specific knowledge, but it does include plenty of ideas, evidence, arguments and perspectives about a range of contexts, along with questions to provoke thought and reflection. This section organises the twenty-four Global Perspectives and Research topics into five over-arching chapters, which reflect some of the key issues facing us today:

B1: Changing countries.

B2: Changing world

B3: Changing technologies

B4: Decisions about limited resources

B5: Decisions about international fairness.

Each of these chapters includes:

- Activities to get you started. These aim to make you think, to raise issues, to introduce perspectives and to provide starting points for research. These activities will help you to begin to apply some of the skills, but you do not need a thorough understanding of the skills before you start.
- Stimulus material. You can read as much or as little of this as you find useful. It would be worth skimming through to find arguments, issues and perspectives that you find interesting, and then focusing on those as a starting point. You can always return to the other articles for more practice later.

- Skills development activities. These relate to the documents in the stimulus material, but also take you beyond these documents. The questions begin with deconstruction – analysing and evaluating the reasoning and use of evidence in the document. They move beyond a focus on the specific document to cover reconstruction by asking questions that will require you to think about the issues and to research more information. They also offer opportunities to reflect and to develop your own perspective. The 'Research and Discuss' boxes are an important part of this process. Remember that you do not need to research and discuss every single question. There is room for you to choose what interests you. The class might divide the questions and present their findings. Alternatively, different groups in the class might research different aspects of a question, and discuss them in a seminar style lesson.
- Assessment practice. This includes activities helping you to write strong research questions for the assessed Essay and the Team Project, as well as a practice Written Examination.
- Quotations. These quotations are predominantly taken from important thinkers, and aim to help you to apply their ideas in global contexts. The quotations generally come from perspectives relating to one or more of the Global Perspectives and Research themes: Politics, Ethics, Economics, Science, Technology, Culture and Environment. The table below provides some guidance on how to make use of the quotations.

Background research	Who is this person? Why are they significant?
	When, where and why did they write or say this?
	What effect does their own cultural, social and academic background have on the assumptions and beliefs underlying their perspective?
	What does this quotation mean?
	How did this person justify the claim?
Applied context	How does this quotation relate to the issue we are currently discussing/the issue in the document?
	How does the quotation (and the perspective underlying the quotation) help me to make sense of this issue and its context?
	How does this quotation challenge my own beliefs and assumptions?
	Should I adapt my own perspective in response to this quotation, and if so, how?

- Marginal questions. These questions in the margins aim to make you think about issues and perspectives; to question specific comments or uses of evidence in the stimulus material; and to consider how to apply ideas and theories from the different Global Perspectives and Research themes. It is not necessary to have in depth knowledge of the theories relating to the themes, but thinking about some of the key ideas of these theories and how to apply them in global contexts can improve the level of your work.

B1: Changing countries.

Changing countries focuses on the ways in which individual countries are changing, as well as the ways in which our ideas relating to our country or nation are changing. It covers issues and perspectives relating to the following topics, drawing links between them:

- Standard of living/quality of life
- Migration and work
- Changing national identities
- Gender issues
- Cultural heritage
- Political systems

The chapter also provokes reflection and discussion about:

- Political and cultural ideas about identity (including personal, national, cultural, religious and supranational ways of thinking about identity).
- Ethical and political ideas about the relationship between citizen and state, freedom and security, tolerance and respect.
- Ethical, political and economic ideas relating to cost benefits, free economic movement and our duty to help those in need.

B2: Changing world

Changing world focuses on the ways in which the world is changing in a global, or overarching sense, as opposed to the smaller changes we notice in individual countries. Themes, issues and perspectives are related to the following syllabus topics, and draw links between them:

- The ethics and economics of food
- The religious secular divide
- Rise of global superpowers
- Transnational organisations
- Arts in an international context
- International sport
- Tourism

The chapter also provokes reflection and discussion about:

- Ethical ideas relating to how we to decide what is the right thing to do.
- Economic concepts such as free trade, and tensions between ethical, economic and political concerns.
- Political and cultural concepts about religious and national identity, the relationship between religion and state.
- How we set up identity based on national and international concepts of us and them (the 'Other'), how changing worlds lead to changing senses of identity, and our changing concepts of local and global.
- Economic and cultural ideas about development and globalisation, and political ideas about sovereignty.

B3: Changing technologies

Changing technologies focuses on how technologies are changing, and how they are changing our lives. Themes, issues and perspectives are related to the following syllabus topics, and draw links between them:

- The impact of the internet
- Technology and lifestyles
- Architectural priorities
- Genetic engineering
- Artificial intelligence
- Transport

The chapter also provokes reflection and discussion about:

- Political, economic and ethical ideas about technology, development and fairness/justice.
- Ideas about need.
- Ideas about the relationship between technological change and the environment.
- Ideas about the relationship between scientific – technical advances, ethics and economics.
- Concepts about technology and identity.
- Ideas about privacy, freedom, choice and surveillance.
- Ideas about reality, perception and simulation.

B4: Decisions about limited resources

Decisions about limited resources focuses on how we make decisions in contexts where our resources are limited. Themes, issues and perspectives are related to the following syllabus topics, and draw links between them:

- Climate change
- Alternatives to oil
- Biodiversity
- Sustainable futures
- Industrial pollution
- Urbanisation

The chapter also provokes reflection and discussion about:

- Ideas about knowledge, burden of proof, theory, hypothesis, weight of evidence and 'balance' between scientific consensus, new ideas and political, cultural and religious reasons for opposing scientific ideas.
- Environmental theories
- Economic, political and ethical concepts relating to development and international fairness.
- Ways of making decisions, including ethical ideas about right and wrong, game theory, and considerations of whether we make decisions emotionally or rationally.
- Ideas about the relationship between humans, other species, the natural world and future generations.

B5: Decisions about international fairness.

Decisions about international fairness focuses on how we make decisions in contexts relating to international fairness. Themes, issues and perspectives are related to the following syllabus topics, and draw links between them:

- Endangered cultures
- Global economic activity
- International law
- Ethical foreign policies
- Medical ethics and priorities

The chapter also provokes reflection and discussion about:

- Ideas about the value of cultures, languages and traditions.
- Ethical, economic and political ideas relating to international relations, law and peacekeeping.
- Ethical, scientific and economic decision making relating to medicine.
- Barter, bitcoin and representative currency.
- Capitalism, consumerism, ethics and sustainability.
- Altruism and selfishness.
- Conflict resolution.

Choosing topics

In the AS, you should choose topics which generate appropriate research questions. So long as your research questions fall within one of the topics on the syllabus, and meet the assessment criteria, you are free to choose your own research areas. In the A Level, you have a free choice of research area. Generally speaking, research is more effective if you enjoy and are stimulated by the topic, because you will be more willing to read beyond the bare minimum, and more likely to engage with the ideas, arguments and perspectives.

There are a number of options for choosing topics from within this book for the Global Perspectives and Research AS:

Method for choosing a topic	Comments
Do all the Section B chapters thoroughly, then decide.	This is likely to be very time consuming, and students are likely to have little time left for their actual research. On the other hand, students would have a good overview, and should have really solid skills.
Do the 'Getting started' activities from each Section B chapter. Then choose two general areas which seemed to be interesting and focus more narrowly, doing selected skills development and application activities within the chosen areas.	This would give students a good overview of the issues, perspectives and contexts. They might end up with less breadth of understanding, so it could be useful to skim through some of the documents and 'Research and Discuss' boxes. Teachers with larger classes could end up mentoring students doing a range of different research projects.

Method for choosing a topic	Comments
Choose one Section B chapter for the Essay and one Section B chapter for the Team Project. Work through the activities in detail. Different students in a class can do research projects in different areas from within the chapters.	This allows for a combination of thoroughness of preparation with some individuality of choice. Those students with strong feelings about engaging in research on other topics should be sufficiently prepared to do the research independently.
Choose one topic from the syllabus for the Essay and one topic from the syllabus for the Team Project. Find the relevant parts of the book and work through as a class.	This is an acceptable option, which can meet assessment requirements, and can be easy for the teacher to manage. However, it has several disadvantages. Students will have less overall understanding of the broader contexts and the links between different topics and issues, and may well be less fully prepared for the Written Examination. Many students will end up researching within a topic that does not really interest them, and could be disempowered by the lack of choice. Some classes might end up doing teacher led projects rather than individual and group research.
Each student individually chooses their research area, and manages their own research entirely independently.	With a strong cohort of students, possibly with students who have already successfully completed the IGCSE in Global Perspectives, and who are already independent learners with research experience, this could work. It could be extremely fulfilling for students. However, it has several pitfalls. There would need to be a clear mentoring system in place, skills would need to be developed and extended in a whole class context, and the differences in demand between IGCSE and AS would need to be made clear. There would also need to be a mechanism for ensuring that students gain a clear overview of contexts and perspectives.

Assessment

Global Perspectives and Research AS is assessed through:

- Written Examination
- Essay
- Team Project.

Section A covers the skills which will be assessed in each paper. Each chapter in Section B includes a practice Written Examination, and guidance on setting research questions for the Essay and Team Project.

Managing Research

Section C covers the Global Research and A Level, which is assessed through the Cambridge Research Report. You have a completely free choice of research topic, although it is recommended that you choose a topic which fascinates you, and which is related to your future studies.

This section focuses on applying the skills from the AS part of the course in a longer research project, and on the practicalities of managing the research process.

SECTION A
Skills development

Introduction to Section A

Section A contains activities that are designed to help you develop your skills.

Skills development is an iterative process of learning, applying, revising, extending and applying more effectively. Explicit learning of discrete skills can be useful as part of the learning process, but the ultimate aim is to use the skills in an integrated and fluid way. You can view it like the process of learning to use a new phone. To start with it is difficult and you don't know what you are doing, and you have to really concentrate on finding where the exact function you need is in the Settings menu. But you quickly learn how to do things, and soon find yourself automatically using the skills you need. You might forget one or two things, and have to remind yourself how to do them, but after that, you go back to selecting and using the skills you need.

Because skills development is iterative, and you need to repeat, combine and apply the skills, it can be useful to do one or two activities from each chapter and to practise applying them in Section B, before moving on to do more activities from each chapter, and applying them again in a different context. For instance, you will need some communication skills in almost every lesson. You will not, however, need to complete the skills activities on using images in a presentation before you even begin to apply your research skills.

These skills are extremely enabling, in life, in business and in your further academic studies. Enjoy your journey through them, and the benefits that they can bring.

General skills

The critical path

The critical path is fundamental to studying Global Perspectives. It is a learning process you will repeat and practise in different global contexts, and it will help you to develop and apply a range of thinking and reasoning skills.

The critical path is a learning process, or a way of **experiencing** your studies. It is fundamentally about active, thoughtful learning and an independent, critical approach to research. You may be used to learning as a receptive skill; that is, other people know things and you have to memorise them. The critical path will help you to become one of the people who actively constructs knowledge.

The critical path has four repeating stages:

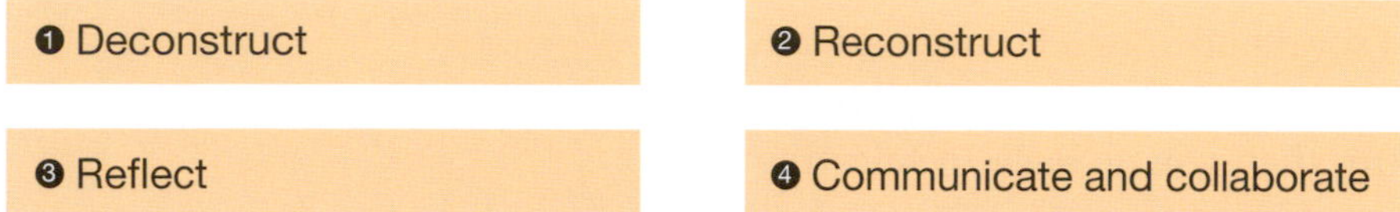

❶ Deconstruct
❷ Reconstruct
❸ Reflect
❹ Communicate and collaborate

As the diagram below shows, each of these stages feeds into the others. The activities below help you to understand what each of these stages means, and which sub-skills are in each stage. As you work through the course, you will find that it begins to make sense as a way of approaching learning. You should understand it from inside, by **being able** to work this way rather than by 'knowing about' it.

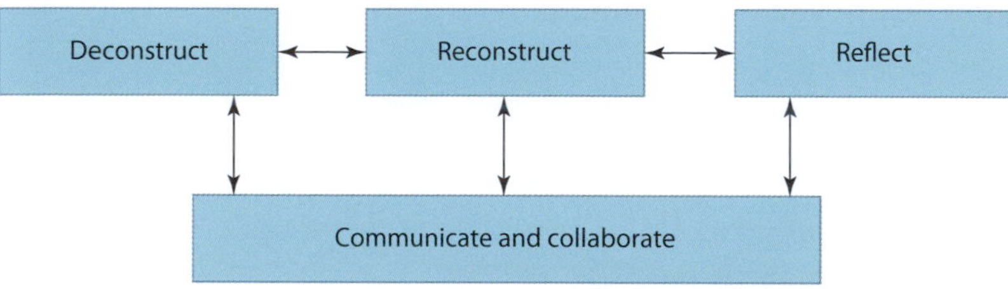

Activity 1

1 Match the definitions on the right to the key terms on the left.

Deconstruct	To analyse by breaking down into its parts (and then reinterpreting).
Reconstruct	To work with others to achieve a goal.
Reflect	To think deeply and carefully about issues, perspectives and personal viewpoints.
Communicate	To share and exchange information, ideas and arguments by speech, writing, gestures, etc.
Collaborate	To build up a wider context, to reassemble ideas into new ways of thinking.

2 Which of the skills listed below count as:
- deconstruction
- reconstruction
- reflection
- communication
- collaboration?

Differentiate between fact, argument, opinion, rant, speculation, prediction, explanation, hypothesis, account and belief.
Carry out research.
Identify conclusions, reasons, evidence and assumptions in an argument.
Find out what evidence there is to support different points of view.
Ask whether there are other possible explanations and perspectives.
Come to a judgment based on evidence.
Evaluate the strengths and weaknesses in the arguments, reasoning or claims.
Consider how research has affected your personal perspectives.
Give a presentation.
Select and organise relevant information in a logical and coherent way.
Work effectively in teams.
Cite references accurately and clearly.

3 Find a copy of the A Level Global Perspectives specification online.
   a Skim read it to find relevant sections on skills.
   b Make sure you have a complete list of all the Global Perspectives skills.

Document 1

Jingoism is the ugly side of Olympic competition

It's probably naive to demand change to a tradition as old as the Olympics themselves, but then Olympic sports have evolved a lot in recent decades. Today's intolerance for doping and for objectification are both relatively new. Why not apply them to the jingoistic threads too? A swimmer or long jumper represents herself and her coaching team as much as her country. Celebrating human achievement, regardless of nationality, makes more sense in a globalised world than turning an archery competition or a 100-meter race into a proxy war between countries.

While many athletes feel the highest honor is to represent their country in their sport, that doesn't change the fact that the goal of high achievement sports is ultimately to set records and celebrate individual mastery. There ought to be rules for TV companies requiring equal coverage for individual events (they can do whatever they want with team ones). There is even a good argument for removing the national flags from individual competition—allowing the athletes to wear sponsored kit instead of the team kit—so that only team events count in the final medals tally.

What does 'jingoistic' mean? Is this a word you need to know in order to understand what the argument means? Use a dictionary to look it up. Think about the different nuances of the word.

> Nationalism won't disappear if broadcasters embrace the spirit of the games a bit more or the competition rules are changed to downplay the national element to some events, but the focus of the Olympics will at least be returned to its rightful place, on the feats of human athletic attainment, regardless of the flag.[1]
>
> *Written by Leonid Bershidsky. Bershidsky is a Bloomberg View columnist. He was the founding editor of the Russian business daily Vedomosti and founded the opinion website Slon.ru. The opinion expressed is his.*

Activity 2

Read Document 1.

1. a. What is the author arguing for?
   b. What reasons does the author give?
   c. Do you agree with the author? Why or why not?
   d. Overall, how well do you think the author has argued?
2. Find the original article and read the rest of it then answer these questions.
   a. Does it contain any information, evidence or arguments which change your view about:
      - the issues discussed
      - whether this is a well-argued opinion?
   b. Do you think this author is objective and fair?
   c. Are there any reasons to think that the author might not be objective and fair?
3. a. Consider this article: http://thebackbencher.co.uk/can-we-please-keep-the-spotlight-on-the-actual-athletic-event/. How does it add to the argument?
   b. How would you go about finding more evidence and different perspectives on the issue of excessive nationalism in sports coverage?
4. a. Work in a group to find a range of evidence and perspectives – this could be articles, statistical information, opinions expressed on television, academic journals, etc.
   b. Read and listen to the evidence and perspectives found by your group.
5. Hold a class debate on the best way to reduce excessive nationalism in sports coverage.
6. Look back at the previous questions in this activity. Which questions relate to:
   a. deconstruction
   b. reconstruction
   c. reflection
   d. communication
   e. collaboration?

What is the difference between agreeing with the author and thinking that he has made a good argument?

Start a learning journal.

- Write your thoughts, reflections and feelings in your learning journal.
- You do **not** need to write down everything that happens in your Global Perspectives lessons.

1 http://www.thanhniennews.com/commentaries/jingoism-is-the-ugly-side-of-olympiccompetition-65143.html

Activity 3

1 Use Internet searches to find an opinion piece that interests you from an online newspaper based in another country. It should be related to one of the topics in the Global Perspectives specification.

2 Work in a group and explain to each other:

   a why your chosen opinion piece is interesting
   b whether you agree with the opinions put forward in the piece
   c how the perspective is similar to or different from your own – is there anything the author takes to be obviously true, for example, that seems strange to you?

3 Choose an issue from one of the opinion pieces that your group has discussed. It should be an issue that you disagree on.

   a Work out a plan so that each of you find evidence, opinions, arguments and perspectives on a different aspect of the issue.
   b Read through the various evidence, opinions, arguments and perspectives that you and the others in your group have found.
   c Identify a specific question to debate.
   d Organise the evidence, opinions, arguments and perspectives into columns as shown here:

For	Against	Could be used for or against	Irrelevant	Tick this column if you need more information

   e Do more research as necessary.
   f Prepare to hold a debate.
      - Make sure you can answer any objections or arguments against you.
      - Make sure that you have objections and arguments against your opponents.
   g Hold the debate.
   h Did you change your mind on anything? Why or why not?

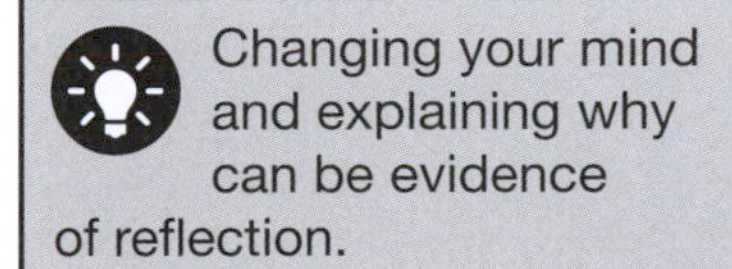
Changing your mind and explaining why can be evidence of reflection.

Perspectives

Understanding other people, their perspectives and the arguments, opinions and assumptions that help to form these perspectives is a vital part of the Global Perspectives and Research course. This includes the perspectives of other people in your local area as well as the various perspectives of people from other countries and cultures.

Perspectives are viewpoints. You may come across the German word, 'Weltanschauung', which literally means, 'way of looking at the world.' A person's perspective is affected by what they actually see or look at. This might be in their local area, on the television or by travelling. A person's perspective is also affected by the beliefs and assumptions they encounter. This can be what they hear from those around them, but people are not limited to believing and imitating what they hear. Our perspectives can also be what we read, research, investigate and hear when we travel. So our perspectives are also affected by our own active efforts to construct our own understandings and our own way of looking at the world.

> Everyone's personal perspective is made up from a collection of overlapping national, cultural and global perspectives. By thinking about these various perspectives we can develop our own personal perspectives. We can develop our personal perspectives even further by reflecting on national, cultural and global perspectives that are very different from our own.

One of the most important outcomes of the Global Perspectives and Research course should be a developed, reflective, well-supported and flexible personal perspective. Another is the ability to continue to develop your personal perspective in the light of new evidence and information. This does not mean that you should change your mind with every new argument you read, but it also does not mean that you should stick to your initial beliefs whatever else you see and hear. Rather, it means that you should be able to adapt thoughtfully to new information and arguments.

The activities in this chapter will help you to think through different kinds of perspective, how they are built up, and how this thinking can positively develop your own perspective. The idea is that you will develop these skills as a part of how you think, rather than as knowledge that exists outside of you. These are, of course, skills that need to be practised and applied in global contexts. There are opportunities for further application of these skills in Section B, but you should also develop the habit of considering perspectives whenever you read or hear something new.

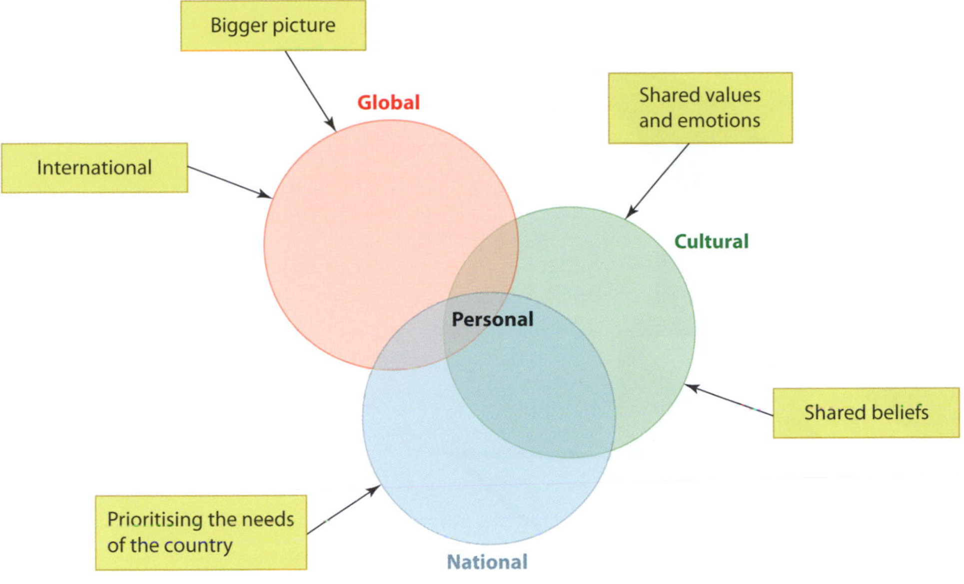

Activity 1

Look at the images. What do they tell you about different perspectives?

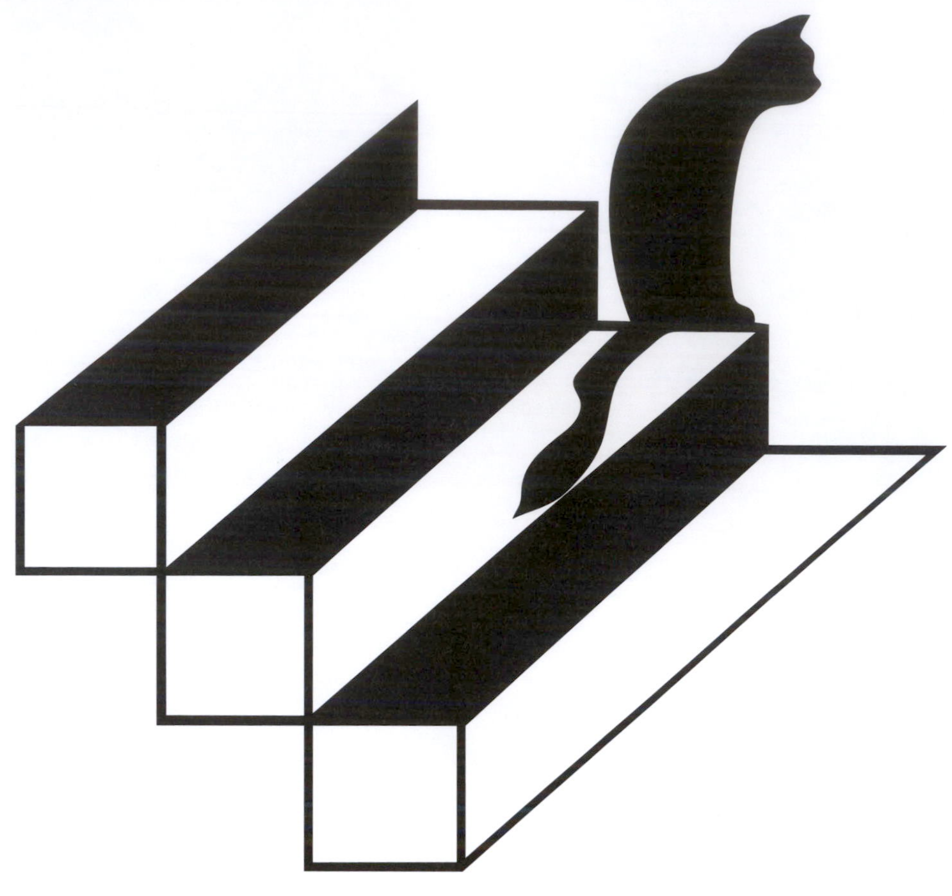

Out of work?

House foreclosing?

Exhausting commute?

Boss difficult?

Business failing?

Bills piling up?

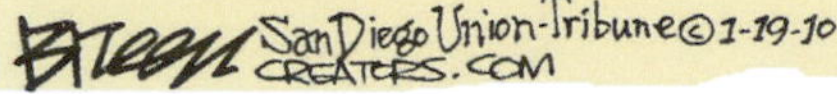

She'd trade places with you in an instant.
HAITI

Activity 2

1 Complete the questionnaire.

1 = I disagree strongly   2 = I disagree a bit   3 = I'm not sure
4 = I agree a bit   5 = I agree strongly

	1	2	3	4	5
Killing another human being is sometimes the right thing to do.					
Power corrupts people, so we should always challenge authority.					
Every individual should have the opportunity for self-development.					
A happy family life is more important than professional success.					
With hard work, you can achieve just about anything you want to.					
There can never be a good reason for cannibalism.					
Female genital mutilation should be accepted as a cultural practice.					
If people are being oppressed, it can be necessary to use violent means to gain freedom.					
Women's sports should gain equal television and online coverage to men's sports.					
Good and evil, right and wrong are real things that exist, no matter what people think about them.					

2 Think about your answers to the questions. Do you have any instant responses where the answer seems clear? If so, these beliefs are likely to be part of the national or cultural perspective you have grown up with.

3 Work in groups.

a Discuss the questionnaire – do you all agree on each statement?

b Can you think of reasons for and against each of these statements?

c Use online searches to find ideas, evidence and arguments to support any views you cannot agree with.

d Do the new ideas, evidence and arguments change your personal perspective? Why or why not?

e Write in your learning journal. Focus on any beliefs that you are unwilling to change, and why you are unwilling to change them.

A perspective is a world view which underlies an argument. It can be quite hard to pin down.

Argument, reasoning and opinions are the specifics of what the author says – they are informed by his or her perspective.

Not only did Mandela refuse to renounce violence, Amnesty refused to take his case stating "[the] movement recorded that it could not give the name of 'Prisoner of Conscience' to anyone associated with violence."

http://thebackbencher.co.uk/3-things-you-didnt-want-to-know-about-nelson-mandela/

But I did not get my picture of the world by satisfying myself of its correctness; nor do I have it because I am satisfied of its correctness. No: it is the inherited background against which I distinguish between true and false.

Ludwig Wittgenstein

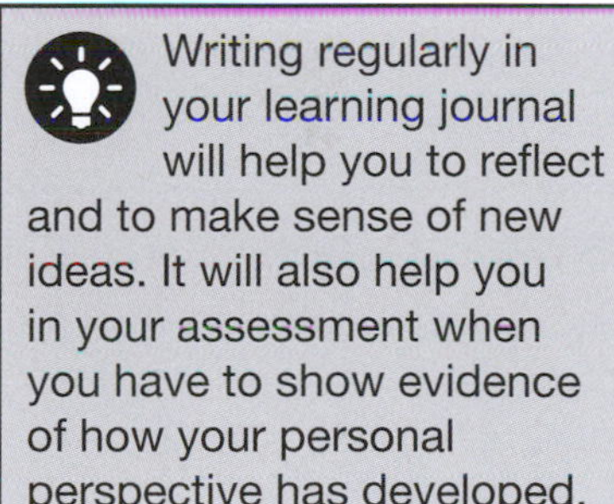

Writing regularly in your learning journal will help you to reflect and to make sense of new ideas. It will also help you in your assessment when you have to show evidence of how your personal perspective has developed.

Activity 3

Consider the quotations below.

1 Do you agree with them? Why or why not?
2 What do they tell you about different perspectives?
3 Briefly research the person who said each of these things. How is their background likely to affect their perspective?

Science is a way of life. Science is a perspective. Science is the process that takes us from confusion to understanding in a manner that's precise, predictive and reliable – a transformation, for those lucky enough to experience it, that is empowering and emotional.

Brian Greene

Everything we hear is an opinion, not a fact. Everything we see is a perspective, not the truth.

Marcus Aurelius

Few people seem to realise that the resurrection of Jesus is the cornerstone to a worldview that provides the perspective to all of life.

Josh McDowell

Terrorism should be seen in the light of the country's security and not from the narrow perspective of caste, creed and religion.

Oscar Fernandes

Activity 4

Read documents 1 and 2 about 'facekinis' and 'burkinis'.

1 What different perspectives can you identify in the articles?
2 What beliefs and values underlie each perspective?
3 What do you think about facekinis?
4 What do you think about burkinis?

Document 1

Facekinis

Editor's note: As the temperature sizzles, the facekini has become a fashion trend hitting some Chinese beaches this summer. Adopted mostly by middle-aged women, the facekini is believed to protect their fair skin from the sun. Is it a weird fashion? Forum readers share their thoughts.

Chris (UK): Isn't the whole purpose of going to the beach to enjoy the water and catch a few rays! Kinda ruins the experience doesn't it? Strange indeed.

jpwang (US): These masks are ugly and Chinese must not wear them outside of China unless they want to be mistaken as terrorists.

Jessie (Canada): It looks scary, but they are right to protect their skin. I always admire their flawless porcelain skin. Just as the Chinese saying goes, "There is no ugly women in the world, only lazy women in the world." [sic] I think this is the price they have to pay.[1]

1 http://www.chinadaily.com.cn/opinion/2016-07/24/content_26159836_7.htm

Document 2

The burkini ban is misogynistic

Choosing to conflate a cultural and religiously inspired mode of bathing attire – which women choose to wear to make them feel safe from the sexual gaze of society while partaking in a very ordinary pastime – with a terrorist group is a convenient "othering" of fellow citizens in times of national crisis.

The greatest causalities of Isis have been Muslims, and the banning of the burkini illustrates the extent to which France's fundamentalist secularism is singling out the most visible and vulnerable group in society for blame.

Since when did wearing a burkini, in most cases a loose fitting nylon version of a wetsuit, become an act of allegiance to terrorist movements? Do Marks & Spencer or House of Fraser know that their attempt to raise profits and exploit a gap in the over-saturated clothing market is selling and promoting allegiance to Isis?[2]

Activity 5

Read document 3, an extract from the New Order website.

1 How would you describe the perspective that this extract comes from?
2 What beliefs and values underlie this perspective?
3 What do you think about the ideas in this extract?

Document 3

The NEW ORDER is a spiritual community representing a revolutionary new faith and a great historic movement. We are comprised of white men and women of all ages and social backgrounds who are committed to building a better world for future generations of their race. Our program is in our name: We stand for a revolutionary New Order here on Earth.

2 http://www.independent.co.uk/voices/burkini-cannes-islamophobiabanning-the-burkini-is-misogynistic-and-western-feminists-are-turninga-a7188806.html

Today we live under an Old Order which is corrupt, decadent and diseased – a mad, psychotic system of mindless materialism, self-indulgence, drugs, pollution, pornography, race-mixing, filth, chaos and alienation. It is the way of Death, and more and more people are coming to recognise it as such.

We see ourselves as part of a world Aryan community and a new folk in formation. No multiracial society can be viable in the long run. That is why we want to build a separate, all-white society, one with its own unique culture and way of life.[3]

Activity 6

Read document 4, an extract from an article on China Daily's English language website.

1. How would you describe the perspective that this extract comes from?
2. What beliefs and values underlie this perspective?
3. What do you think about the ideas in this extract?

Document 4

It is disturbing to see the cooperative spirit of Western powers dissipating in these difficult times.

Many developments, some of which directly target China, are telling. For instance, the Western powers are blaming China for industrial overcapacity when in fact it is a global phenomenon. And although 81 countries have recognised China as a market economy, the traditional industrial powers are still reluctant to do so – which they should because that was the condition for China joining the World Trade Organisation in 2001.

Besides, some countries are challenging China's maritime claims, with a few considering shutting the door on Chinese investment, which ironically their economies need to create jobs and boost growth. Perhaps these are part of the "many factors" referred to by the staff of the international institution's chief I approached.

But the Western powers pressuring China to include issues closely related to its national interests will be disappointed, because China's claims and interests are protected by law and history. These powers have to change their mindsets, and use the Hangzhou summit to "re-recognise and understand China better" to minimise the number of wrong decisions that could be taken when dealing with a country that believes in a win-win philosophy.[4]

Write in your learning journal. Focus on:

- any perspectives that have made you think
- any of your own underlying beliefs
- any new skills you have learned
- any aspects of these skills that you find difficult
- how you can improve.

3 http://www.theneworder.org/about/
4 http://www.chinadaily.com.cn/opinion/2016-08/16/content_26486795.htm

Global significance and relevance

When you choose research areas in Global Perspectives and Research, you need to select issues that are of global significance and relevance. This chapter helps you to work towards an understanding of what an issue is. It also encourages you to think through what might count as 'of global significance and relevance.'

There are no simple, fixed definitions. However, a habit of considering whether an issue is of global significance and relevance, and of justifying your decisions about this should help you to select appropriate research areas.

Let's look at an example. Abortion is a popular topic for discussion, but is it an issue? Is it of global significance and relevance? To start with, 'abortion' is not an issue, it is simply a general topic.

One issue related to this general topic might be: 'Should abortion be legal?' It is possible to support or oppose this, and to discuss and debate the issue, but is it of global significance and relevance? In some countries, the legality of abortion is no longer an active issue. Abortion is legal and there is no immediate threat to this status. Individuals in these countries need to consider whether they would/should have an abortion (or support their partner in doing so) if the circumstances arose. This means that, in these countries, there is an issue: 'Should I have an abortion?' However, this is a personal decision rather than a global or even national decision. In other countries it is hotly contested whether abortion should be legal. This makes the topic a national and personal issue, but not yet of global relevance or significance.

Does the fact that people around the world need to make decisions about abortion make it of global relevance? Or is it still just a very common personal decision? We might be able to argue that it is of global relevance, but not really that it is of global significance.

How about if a rich, powerful country decides not to fund any international health charities or aid programmes that offer family planning or abortion (or abortion counselling)? This is a national decision which affects the opportunities, health and human rights of women around the globe, especially in less wealthy parts. So, although this is a national decision, it may become an issue of global significance, although you could argue this either way.

As you work through the activities, you should develop a clearer sense of what seems to be of global significance and relevance.

An issue is an important topic for discussion or debate.

Issues are usually matters of opinion, value judgement, prediction or conflicting perspectives. Facts are not issues – but you may be able to think of issues that are related to facts.

For example: the statement 'Women do not have equal rights in every country' is a fact. The statement 'Women should have equal rights in every country' is a value judgment, which can be debated or discussed, so it is an issue.

Activity 1

1 Do you think any of the following statements are issues?

   a How should we deal with multinational food corporations that are selling food containing unhealthy ingredients in many countries?

   b In some countries young people do not have the right to marry as they choose.

   c High-quality transport is essential to economic development.

   d We need to find ways to make international tourism less harmful to local communities.

   e Powerful countries often take advantage of their smaller neighbours.

   f Cultural heritage needs to be considered.

2 Think of specific issues relating to facts or topics you identified in question 1.

Activity 2

1 Are any of the following issues of global significance?

   a Genetic engineering of humans.

   b Should different communities deal with loss of biodiversity in different ways?

   c Is abortion ever justified?

   d India should invest in skills training to ensure that the next generation is prepared for work.

   e It is important that we preserve endangered cultures.

   f Brexit.

   g The UN has no right to tell my country what to do.

   h Should we support the government's proposals for tax-funded healthcare?

   i There should be more funding for arts education in my country.

2 Think of any issues relating to facts, topics and statements in question 1.

Issues of global significance often relate to more than one topic. For example: 'Should architects focus more on designing environmentally friendly buildings rather than beautiful ones?'

This issue relates to architectural priorities, alternatives to oil, climate change, cultural heritage, industrial pollution, migration and work, standard of living, sustainable futures, technology, lifestyles and urbanisation.

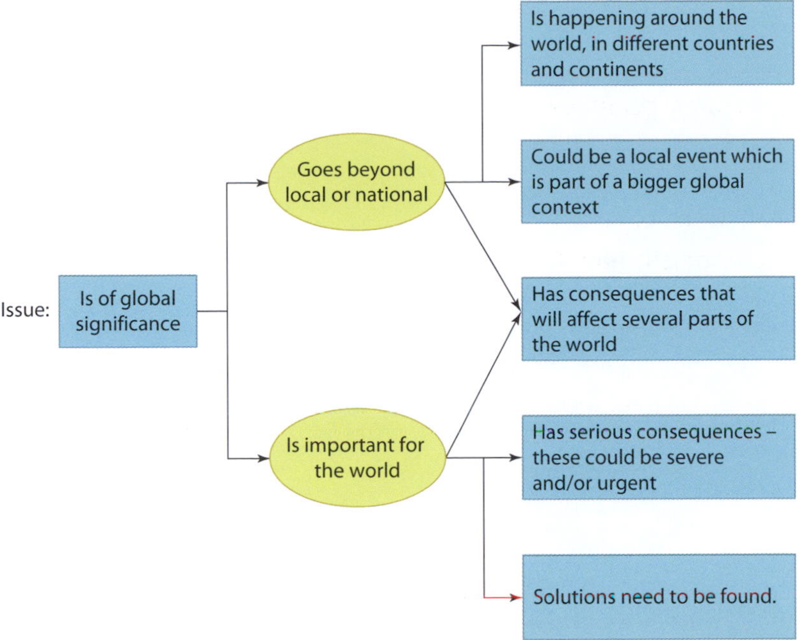

A fact that is new to you is not the same as an opinion. Checking facts is not the same as discussing opinions.

1. People are eating food all around the world, every day.
2. People are eating poisoned food all around the world.

Statement 1 is global, but it is not of global significance, and it is not an issue that can be debated or discussed. Statement 2 is also global, and it is of much greater significance because of its negative and serious consequences. There may be an issue here to discuss, there are certainly questions to be raised, and a solution would be good.

Activity 3

1 Work in groups. Think of three different issues of global significance relating to each of these topics:
   - a Alternative sources of energy to oil
   - b Changing national identities
   - c Impact of the Internet
   - d Sustainable futures
   - e Tourism

2 What interests you?
   - a Think of at least five issues of global significance that really interest you.
   - b Which topics on the syllabus are these issues related to?

Write in your learning journal.

- What new skills have you learned?
- Are there any aspects of this that you struggle with?
- How can you improve?'

Themes

Seven themes are identified in the course. These are:

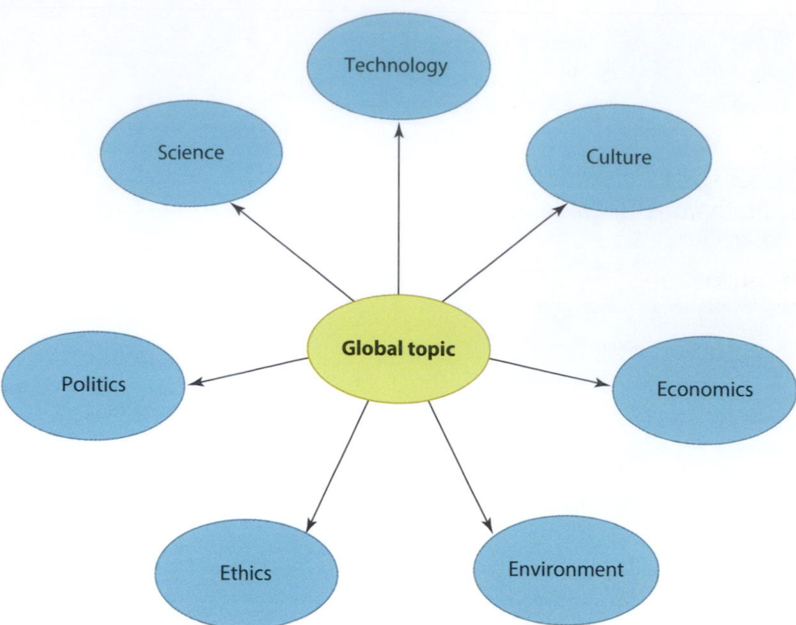

These themes can be seen as different aspects of a topic, which can help you to explore that topic in more depth and with more understanding. One way of doing this is to simply consider what questions you could ask within each theme. Another way is to think about causes, consequences and possible solutions within each theme. Quite often, different themes will result in different priorities or different possible solutions, which can make for interesting research and debate.

Another way of using the themes is to explore them as perspectives, questioning the beliefs, assumptions and values that underlie them as different ways of seeing the world. For instance, an economic perspective will, generally speaking, prioritise concerns relating to finance and money over concerns relating to, for example, the environment. So, from an economic perspective, one might argue that it is acceptable to continue damaging the environment so long as we continue to generate economic growth, because the consequences of halting economic growth are disastrous.

Sometimes you might be faced with an opinion and wonder, 'How can you possibly think that?' By exploring the different values and assumptions that underlie the perspectives within each theme, it is possible to find an answer to this question, and to understand *how* someone can think something which was, to you, unthinkable. This can be an important step forward in your own personal development.

The activities below will help you to start using the themes effectively in your thinking and research. There are activities in Section B to help you apply the skills you develop here in global contexts. You should begin to develop the habit of using the themes to help you when you come across new ideas and arguments.

Activity 1

Use quick Internet searches to add further causes of the French ban on the burka in public places to the diagram. Use the themes to guide you.

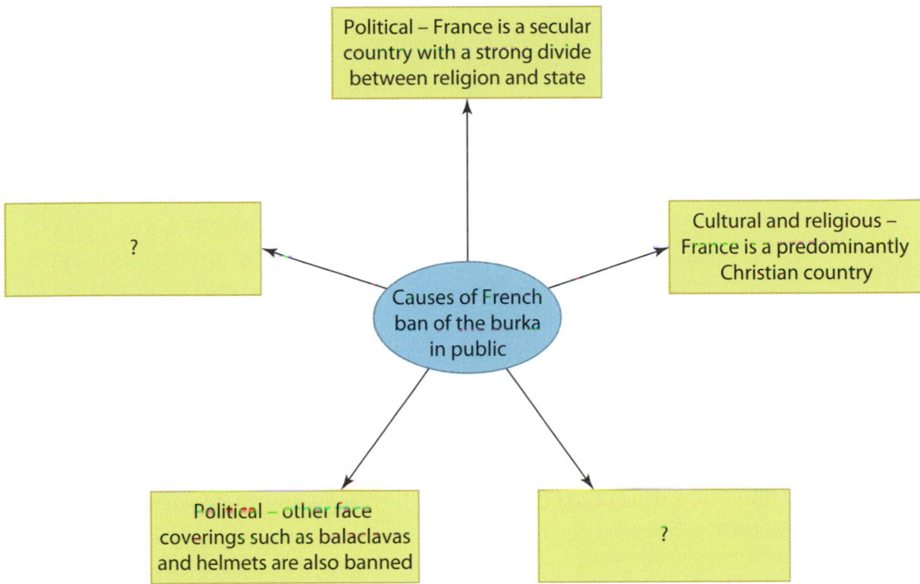

You can also use the themes to ask questions to help you to think more deeply about issues or to make informed decisions.

Activity 2

Use quick Internet searches to add further consequences of the French ban on the burka in public places to the diagram. Use the themes to guide you.

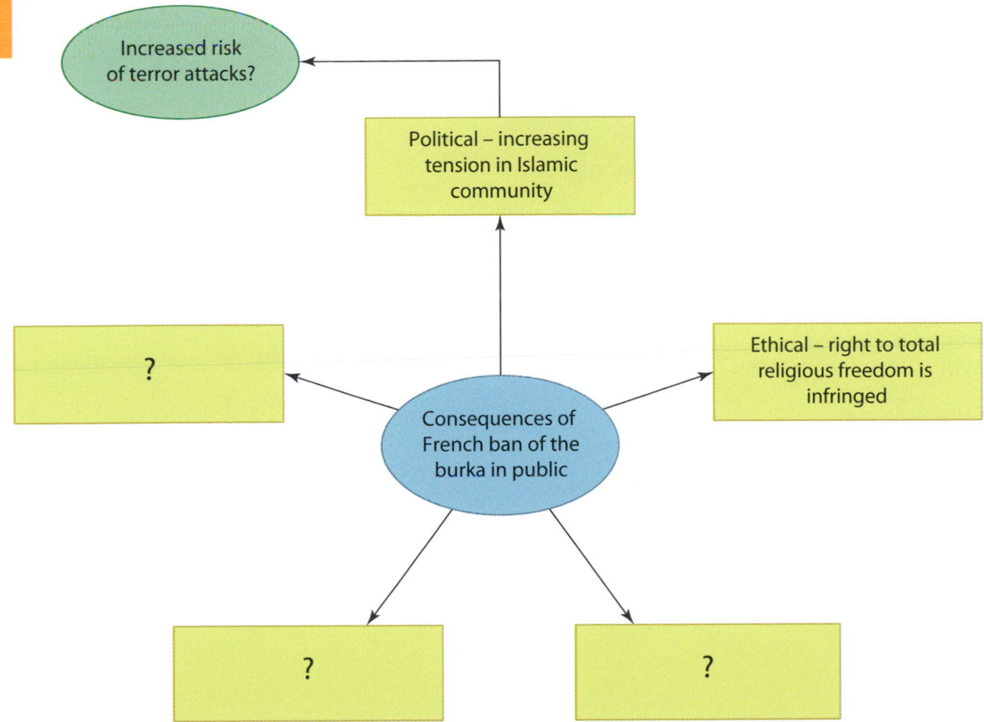

To what extent is the French ban on the burka an issue of global significance? Are there similar bans in other countries? Is this ban part of a broader global clash of cultures?

Activity 3

1 Can you think of any possible solutions to problems caused by the French ban of the burka in public?

2 Which themes do they come under?

Can science or technology provide solutions to political or cultural problems?

Activity 4

Use the themes to help you think about causes, consequences and possible solutions in the areas of:

a climate change

b increasing tourism at world heritage sites

c time spent by young people using social media.

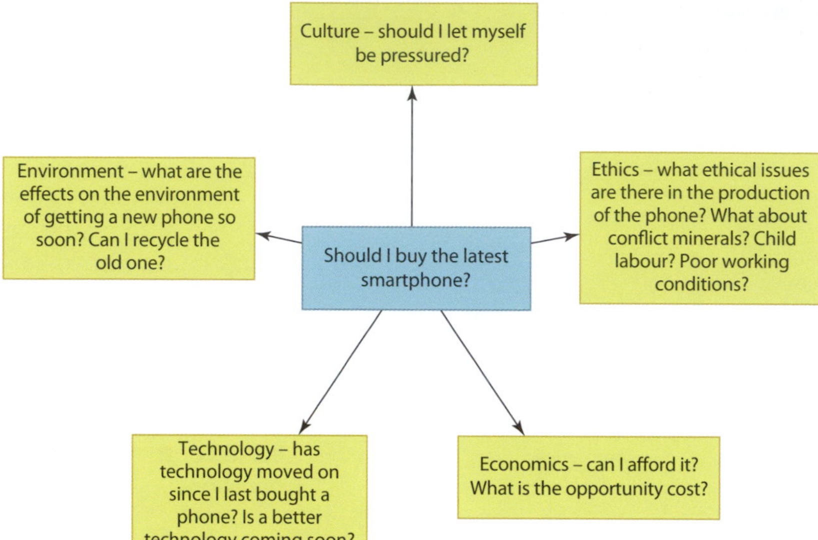

The opportunity cost of an item or action is all the things that you cannot do if you buy the item or do the action. For instance, if you buy a new smartphone, you cannot spend that money on a holiday.

What are the answers to some of the questions in the diagram? Where appropriate, use Internet searches to find out. Do these searches raise more questions?

Themes can also be different ways of looking at an issue. That is, they can be perspectives, with their own priorities, values, underlying assumptions and belief systems.

Activity 5

Use the themes to ask questions to help you to think more deeply about issues or to make informed decisions on the following.

a Is it worth paying more for ethically sourced products?

b Should governments fund research into artificial intelligence?

c Is war ever justified?

d How should governments deal with biodiversity loss?

e How should art and music be funded?

Document 1

It has already been proven that pacemakers and insulin pumps can be hacked. Security experts have warned us that someone would be murdered through these methods any time soon. How can we prevent wearable devices that are connected to our physiological system from being hacked and controlled from a distance?[1]

- Technology (and ethics).
- Values – it assumes that it is wrong or bad if people are killed by hackers controlling pacemakers, and so forth.
- It assumes that we should find a solution. It also assumes that a solution can probably be found.
- The priority is to find a technological solution to a problem.

Can you find arguments on the issue of medical hacking that come from more ethical or political perspectives?

Activity 6

1 Read the extracts below. Which of these extracts comes from:
   a a political perspective
   b an economic perspective
   c an environmental perspective
   d an ethical perspective?
2 For each extract, identify:
   a the main perspective, using the themes
   b the main priorities
   c any values
   d any important beliefs.
3 Using the themes, for each extract, find arguments on the same issue that come from different perspectives.

Document 2

Extracts A–D

A. The world can still act in time to stave off the worst effects of climate change, and enjoy the fruits of continued economic growth as long as the global economy can be transformed within the next 15 years, a group of the world's leading economists and political leaders will argue on Tuesday.[2]

B. Power from renewable sources like wind and water predates the use of fossil fuels and is becoming cheaper, more efficient, and easier to store every year. The past two decades have seen an explosion of ingenious

1 https://medicalfuturist. com/list-of-ethical-issues-in-thefuture- of-medicine/
2 https://www.theguardian.com/environment/2014/sep/16/climate-change-report-damage-overhaul-global-economy

zero-waste design, as well as green urban planning. Not only do we have the technical tools to get off fossil fuels, we also have no end of small pockets where these low carbon lifestyles have been tested with tremendous success.[3]

C. When I talk about an ethics of immigration, I mean that we ought to think about what's right and wrong, and not just about what's efficient or good for some segment of the population. We ought to think about how we're going to justify our policies in moral terms.[4]

D. Throughout the cold war, Soviet bloc nations used sport as a proxy for economic success. With the connivance of the International Olympic Committee, they turned what used to be an amateur sport into the equivalent of a national defence force, hurling money and status at their athletes while the IOC turned the Games into a lavish field of the cloth of gold—at some poor taxpayer's expense.

The west used to ridicule the communists for this. Their athletes were derided as state employees, civil servants and cheats. Of course many took drugs. Winning was what mattered to the Soviets, the state media being monopolised to convince their people that their "system" was better.

Since Atlanta in 1996, Britain has followed suit. The poor performance of British athletes was considered by John Major as a comment on his government. He demanded medals, and lots of them. The subsidy to "elite" sport was increased tenfold, from £5m to £54m, while popular sports facilities were closing. Money was directed specifically at disciplines where individuals could win multiple medals rather than just one, away from field athletics to cycling and gymnastics. It worked. The medals tally at Sydney 2000 rose from 15 to 28.[5]

Priorities, values and beliefs may be stated. However, they may not be stated, so you have to think about what is said, and what beliefs and values the writer probably holds.

Aa Values are beliefs about what is right and wrong, good and bad, about what should be the case, and about what is important in life.

You could try searching for key terms from the extract plus one of the Themes. For instance, you could search for 'medical hacking + political'.

Write in your learning journal. Focus on:

- understanding how you can use themes to help you understand issues and perspectives
- any new skills you have learned
- any aspects of these skills that you find difficult
- how you can improve.

3 https://www.theguardian.com/environment/2015/mar/08/how-will-everything-change-under-climate-change

4 http://munkschool.utoronto.ca/ethnicstudies/2015/01/joe-carens-the-ethics-of-immigration/

5 https://www.theguardian.com/commentisfree/2016/aug/17/olympics-hysteria-britain-turned-soviet-team-gb

Research

The Global Perspectives and Research course is based around research. The assessment is predominantly research-based; at AS level the Essay and Team Project are research-based and at A level the Research Report is, of course, research-based. So it is especially important to develop, practise and apply your research skills.

There are a number of different research skills. This section considers how to choose an appropriate research area. There are three main questions to ask:

Is it on the syllabus?
Is it interesting?
Does it allow discussion on an issue of global significance?

Whether you feel lost and blank because you have no idea at all, or whether you feel adrift in an ocean of infinite possibilities for study, this book and these questions can help you to arrive at a suitable choice. If you lack ideas, you can:

- Look at the list of topics on the syllabus.
- Look through the ideas in Section B of this book.
- Read (almost) any newspaper and link articles to topics on the syllabus.

If you have too many ideas you can focus on what is most interesting and most likely to allow discussion of an issue of global significance. If there are three issues that are very interesting, pick one, and save the others for later. There will be other opportunities for research. Do not try to do all three in one essay, project or research report.

Choosing an area of research

A research area is a starting point for research. It can be one small aspect of a broader, Global Perspectives topic. A research area can also be a focused issue that overlaps two or more Global Perspectives topics.

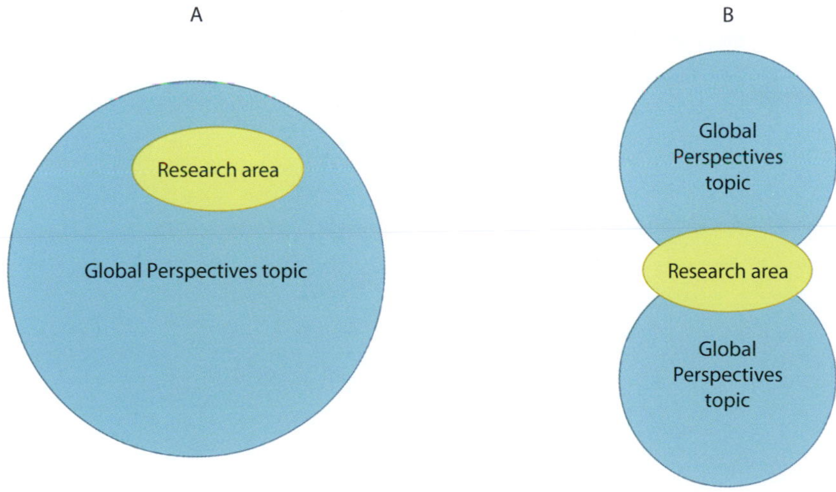

Deciding on the right research area for you is very important. The three most important things you need to consider are shown in this diagram:

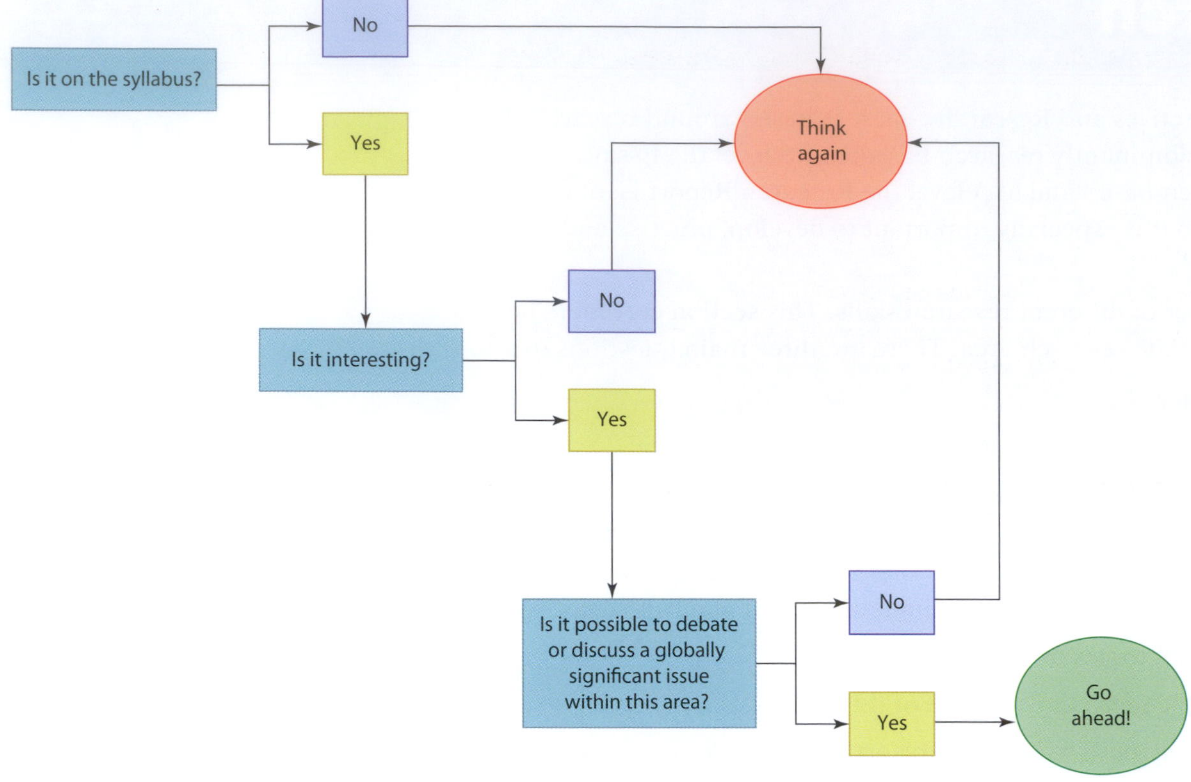

There are two main approaches to finding a research area that is interesting to you and also on the syllabus.

Method A

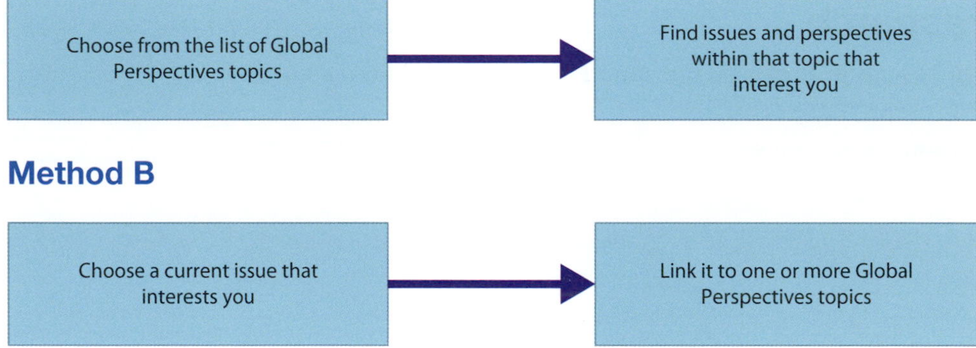

Method B

Choose a current issue that interests you → Link it to one or more Global Perspectives topics

Activity 1

1 Which of the following would be acceptable research areas?

2 Are any of these areas interesting to you?

a Global superpowers

b Different cultural attitudes to what women wear on the beach – bikinis, facekinis, burkinis

c Who is the world's best football player?

d Abortion

e Comparing written and spoken records of cultural heritage

f Climate change

g How different countries think about work–life balance

h Is it ever acceptable to go to war with another country in order to change their leader or their government style?

Activity 2

Think of research areas that would be interesting for students A, B and C below. Suggest research areas that are on the syllabus and that allow for a discussion of a globally significant issue.

Student A: I'm interested in arts in an international context. I do art.

Student B: I'm interested in the rise of global superpowers. I want to talk about the rise of the British Empire.

Student C: I want to talk about cars.

Use quick Internet searches to help you.

Linking current issues to Global Perspectives topics: Civil war in Syria

Possible links to Global Perspective topics include:

- destroying cultural heritage – Aleppo, Bosra and Palmyra in Syria
- the role of Islam and extreme Islam
- the role of Islam versus the role of Christianity
- secular and religious perspectives
- migration – why people are leaving, how to respond; refugee camps in Lebanon, people drowning in the Mediterranean; whether German Chancellor Angela Merkel was right or wrong to invite refugees to Germany
- links to other migration crises
- Syria as an arena for the proxy wars of global superpowers
- Syria and oil – the economy and climate change
- political systems – is the war in Syria partly about different political systems?
- Is the war about dictatorship, monarchy, democracy or religious rule?
- Do peoples have the right to vote for non-democratic systems?

Current issue: civil war in Syria. Link this current issue to Global Perspectives topics.

Activity 3

1 The following events and concerns were current in 2016. Which Global Perspectives topics can you link them to? Use diagrams and make notes to help you.
   a Refugee crises (Europe, Australia, USA)
   b Rising populism
   c Extremist terrorist attacks
   d The Olympic Games
   e Corruption in sport (especially financial corruption and doping)
   f Arguments about China's right to occupy the South Sea
   g Poor economy
   h Russian foreign policy
2 Are any of the events or issues from the list still current?
3 Choose two or three current events or concerns that interest you. Which Global Perspectives topics can you link them to?

The best research comes from curiosity and interest. Choose a research area that is meaningful to you.

Write notes in your learning journal about any areas that you might like to research. Explain to yourself why you are interested in these and how they might be good research areas. Also write in your learning journal:

- any new skills you have learned
- any aspects of these skills that you find difficult
- how you can improve.

Finding and selecting information

There is a great deal of information of varying quality available, both online and in more traditional print formats. The research skills of finding and selecting information deal with navigating this mass of information.

Finding and selecting information includes:

- Understanding the different kinds of information, ideas, evidence and argument that exist.
- Understanding the different uses and values of these kinds of information, ideas, evidence and argument.
- Knowing how to find information using focused search terms and library catalogues.
- Knowing what sort of sources to use for different purposes.
- Knowing what sort of sources to use to find different perspectives.

This will enable you to:

- Perform a preliminary search to establish whether there are issues, events, perspectives and suitable resource materials.
- Perform a targeted search to find and select material for a specific purpose.

The activities in this chapter will help you to develop these skills. There are opportunities to practise them in Section B.

Activity 1

1	Fact	
2	Opinion	
3	Prediction	
4	Value	
5	Belief	
6	Hypothesis	
7	Theory	
8	Evidence	
9	Guess	

You can find many different kinds of information and ideas during research. These kinds of information are not equally valuable. Understanding different kinds of information may help you to make better judgements about what to believe.

Aa Some of these words have everyday meanings, as well as technical meanings. For instance, 'argument' can mean a disagreement or quarrel in everyday meaning, but it has a technical meaning as well: 'a process of reasoning'. In the context of Global Perspectives, the technical meaning is the one we are interested in.

10	Speculation	
11	Explanation	
12	Judgement	
13	Rant	
14	Argument	A process of reasoning; reasons, evidence and ideas given in support of an idea, action or theory.
15	Report	

Make sure that you think carefully about everyday and technical definitions of these words.

1 Match the following definitions to terms in the table above.

a A set of accepted beliefs or organised principles that explain a group of facts or phenomena, and guide analysis. This set of beliefs is usually based on repeated testing and/or reasoning. One example is gravity.

b A means of showing how something has happened, discussing causes or justifying an action.

c A principal, proposition or idea that is held to be true. A state of mind in which someone accepts something as true. A mental representation of the world.

d An idea or explanation that you test through study and experiment. It can be the starting point for research.

e Ideas or beliefs formed without enough information, based on guesses and supposition.

2 Complete the table using dictionaries and online resources to help you.

3 Which of the following should you accept more firmly and why?

a Speculation or fact
b Rant or argument
c Scientific evidence or religious belief
d Prediction based on evidence or a guess
e Scientific theory or hypothesis

Activity 2

1 What kinds of information, ideas and reasoning are in the following extracts?

A. Nuclear power is the only possible realistic alternative to oil.

B. The world's population is likely to hit 11 billion by 2020, and half of [the global population] will live in Africa.

C. Well, there must be about, uh, 20 million people living in London.

D. When nationalism was firmly tied to various shades of liberalism and democratic ideas in early-nineteenth-century Europe, historiographic nationalism was a weapon to fight feudalism and absolutism and to uphold notions of citizenship and freedom. By the late-nineteenth century, nationalism had become much more the preserve of the political right and in the twentieth century it supported a range of authoritarian and fascist regimes across Europe. And yet it seems extremely difficult to make a firm distinction between a 'good' early-nineteenth-century nationalism and a 'bad' early-twentieth-century nationalism, as both shared a high potential for xenophobia and violence.[1]

E. NIJEL AMOS has not had a good Olympics. Having won Botswana's first ever Olympic medal four years ago—a silver in the men's 800m race—the 22-year-old athlete was eliminated in the first round of the 800m in Rio de Janeiro. Worse still, his time of 1:41.73 at London 2012 was comfortably better than any time posted in the 800m final on 15 August 2016. Had Mr Amos repeated his 2012 showing, he would be a gold-medallist. The same is true of London's silver- and bronze-medallists in the men's 100m. Both ran faster in 2012 than Usain Bolt did (9.81 seconds) in the 2016 100m final on 14 August.

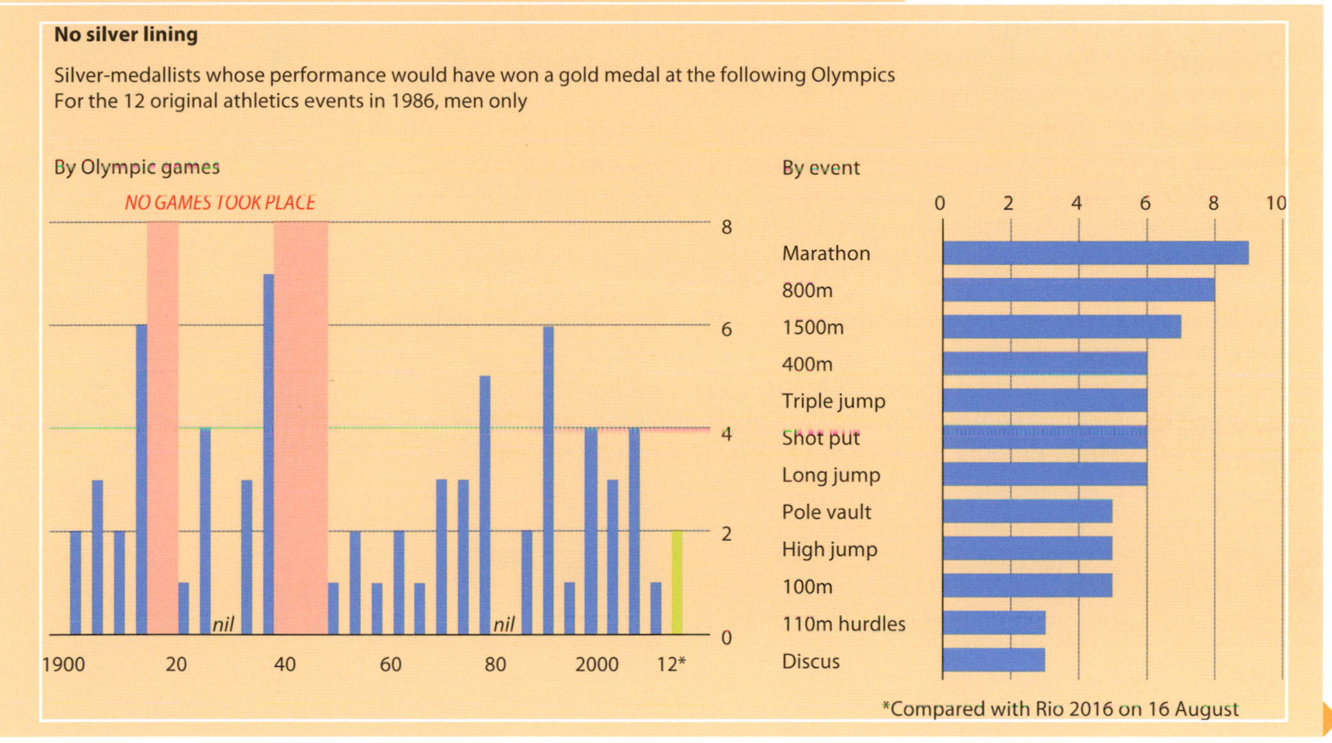

1 http://www.historyandpolicy.org/policy-papers/papers/history-and-national-identity-why-they-should-remain-divorced

Such misfortune is rare. It has only befallen 69 male athletes competing in the 12 track-and-field events that have been contested since 1896. The number of unfortunate runners-up was highest in the games preceding the world wars, as post-war Olympic teams were somewhat depleted. Boycotts can also play a part. At the Moscow games in 1980 half of the male track athletes who won gold posted slower times than the 1976 silver medallists. And then there are the games, like Barcelona in 1992, where performances just seem to fall short. There the men's marathon winner was slower than nine competitors from four years earlier. Silver-medallists from the London Olympics will be watching this year's remaining events with mixed emotions.[2]

F. The FBI admits we have been visited by 'beings from other dimensions'. The official link from the FBI vault can be found here: https:// vault.fbi.gov.

Is it surprising that the FBI has shown interest in the study of the UFO phenomena? Is it possible that many science fiction films are actually based on real events, or better called 'leaks' given by the government in order to deliberately raise awareness among the population?[3]

G. The findings of a new report suggest that US travellers are increasingly turning towards travel agents to book their holidays. And perhaps more surprisingly, it's the digital natives or Millennials, who are leading the charge. That's according to a new report released by the American Society of Travel Agents which reached out to 14,000 households in the aim of looking at the overall usage of travel agents.

In the past 12 months, 22 per cent of consumers polled said they booked their travel through an agent, the highest share reported in the past three years. That figure spikes to 30 per cent for Millennials. Another 45 per cent of Millennials polled also said they would recommend a travel agent to a friend or family member.[4]

2 Would you reject any of these sources of information for any reason? Why or why not?

3 Look at part G, an extract taken from a Malaysian online newspaper. Could you use this material to show that Malaysians in their early 20s are more likely than their parents to use a travel agent? Why or why not?

When you are researching, select high-quality, well-reasoned material with reliable evidence. Reject low-quality material that is based on guesses, speculations or very poor reasoning such as ranting.

2 http://www.economist.com/blogs/graphicdetail/2016/08/daily-chart-3

3 http://www.conspiracyclub.co/2015/06/12/fbireleases-documents-proving-aliens-have-landed-on-earth/

4 http://www.star2.com/travel/malaysia/2016/08/18/millennials-prefer-booking-holidays-through-travel-agents/

Activity 3

1 What sorts of information, ideas or argument will help you to answer the following questions?

   a How many different religions are represented in:

      i. London?
      ii. Tehran?
      iii. Delhi?

   b What should architects prioritise in new buildings?

   c How can cultural heritage enrich a nation?

   d Is democracy the best political system?

   e How should Europe respond to increasing migration?

   f How is climate change caused?

   g How can we respond to climate change?

2 What search terms would you use to help you answer the above questions?

3 Use quick internet searches to help you to find information, ideas and arguments that might help you to answer the questions.

There may be more than one answer for each question.

Activity 4

1 You want an economic perspective on an issue. Which of the following organisations and publications are likely to be useful to you?

www.imf.org	www.un.org
www.oecd.org	www.adamsmith.org
www.redcross.org	www.oxfam.org
www.economist.com	www.nzherald.co.nz
www.amnesty.org	www.fbi.org

2 Find economic perspectives on issues related to:

   a migration

   b international sport

   c industrial pollution.

3 What organisations and publications would be useful if you were looking for:

   a an ethical perspective

   b a political perspective

   c an environmental perspective?

4 Find ethical, political and environmental perspectives on issues related to:

   a migration

   b international sport

   c industrial pollution.

Use quick Internet searches to find out what the listed organisations are.

To find different views and perspectives, it is worth using online materials from other countries. They may have national and cultural perspectives that are very different from yours.

Build up a research section in your learning log. Whenever you find a useful website or other source, make a note of it.

Activity 5

1 Find English language news websites that include opinions and arguments from each of these countries:
   a United Arab Emirates
   b Malaysia
   c China
   d Zimbabwe
   e South Africa.
2 Find arguments and opinions from each of the online newspapers you used for question 1 that relate to:
   a new issues in architecture
   b key issues in migration
   c a current event or issue of global significance.
3 How are the perspectives underlying the arguments and opinions different?
4 Can you find any beliefs or values that are different from your own?
5 Within each source that you find, can you identify different perspectives – for example, economic, ethical or environmental perspectives?
6 Choose five other countries that you expect have very different perspectives.
   a Find English language newspapers from each of these countries.
   b Find opinion pieces or arguments from each of these newspapers on a current issue or event of global significance.
7 Make a record of the most useful publications and websites you have found.

When you are looking for opinions and arguments in online newspapers, it is useful to find 'opinion', 'columnists', or 'bloggers'.

Avoid international press releases and articles that are reprinted from other sources. These will not give you a truly different perspective.

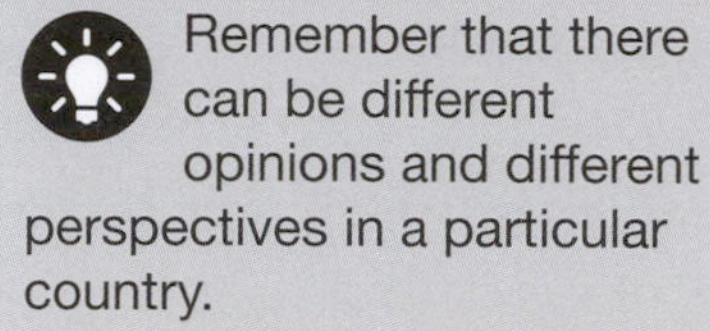

Remember that there can be different opinions and different perspectives in a particular country.

Try using:

- advanced searches
- Google Scholar
- online research databases to find academic work.

Write in your learning journal. Focus on:

- any useful sources that you have found and would like to remember
- any new skills you have learned
- any aspects of these skills that you find difficult
- how you can improve.

Skim reading, note taking and citation

Skim reading, note taking and keeping lists of your sources will help you to research effectively and to avoid plagiarism.

Skim reading means looking for key words and gist before you read in detail. By concentrating on relevant material and ignoring irrelevant passages, you can maximise the value of the time you spend reading. No one wants to spend half an hour on a difficult chapter, only to realise afterwards that it was not useful. Looking for key words, and reading sentences that contain the key words, can help you to read only what is valuable to you.

Keeping well-organised notes can help you to organise your thinking, and to find ideas later when you need them again. This chapter helps you to work through a few ways of taking notes, especially using diagrams to show the flow of key ideas.

Keeping records of your source material can help you to find material again. It can also provide you with the information you need to produce accurate citations and references. Taking photographs of both sides of the title page of a book can be useful, because this captures most of the information that you need. It is also important to archive your photos, though. You don't want to be looking through three thousand photos to find the one with the information you need! This chapter will help you to focus on what is needed for citations in your subject area.

Activity 1

1. Which of the following do you think are common mistakes made by students when they are researching?
   a. Students read everything they find.
   b. They forget where they have read useful information.
   c. They copy and paste material they don't understand into their essay.
   d. They leave all their research until the last minute.
   e. They include quotations from unknown sources.
   f. They can be distracted by interesting but irrelevant material.
2. Work in a group to think of strategies for avoiding the mistakes listed above.

Scanning for particular words and skim reading for gist both mean that you don't have to read every word of a source – so you can avoid reading parts that aren't relevant.

Note taking can help you to understand, remember and organise the material you read. Avoid simply copying the author's words. Instead use mind maps and diagrams to show:

- cause and effect
- links between issues
- perspectives linked to the themes.

Activity 2

1 Read the extracts below. Scan each extract for the word 'environmental' and underline it when you find it.

A. For as multicentric, interdisciplinary, and rapidly expanding an inquiry as environmental studies is, a work like this one couldn't be more timely. What better way to expand the horizons of those already on the way to immersing themselves in environmental studies than a collection of deeply informed, succinct, but nonreductive essays that range well beyond the horizons of any one scholar?[1]

B. The U.S. Justice Department has sued Harley-Davidson Inc for allegedly violating environmental laws, court filings showed on Thursday. The lawsuit, filed on behalf of the U.S. Environmental Protection Agency (EPA), accused the company of violating the Clean Air Act and on-highway motorcycle regulations. The lawsuit is related to 12,682 motorcycles that did not conform with EPA regulations governing engine emission standards, according to court filings. The civil lawsuit, filed in the federal court in Washington, D.C., seeks to impose fines for sale of non-compliant motorcycles. Harley-Davidson's shares were down 7.5 per cent.[2]

C. For over 25 years, Women's Environmental Network (WEN) has exposed the vital links between gender equality, health and wellbeing, and environmental issues. We believe that women and men have equal roles—and should have equal input—in making the transition to a sustainable lifestyle. Through campaigning, educating and community work, we aim to empower women and others to become agents of change in their society, enabling them to participate equally in a fair, healthy and sustainable future.[3]

2 Skim the extracts for gist to answer these questions.

a Which extract is most likely to be useful if you are writing an essay about air pollution?

b Which extract is least likely to be useful if you are writing about environmental sustainability?

3 Which words helped you to make the decision about the usefulness of an extract, without reading the whole extract carefully? How did these words help you?

Another useful tip for note taking is to use colour. Use different colours to show quotations, areas where you need more information, your own questions, arguments against the author, etc.

Remember that a perspective is a world view that underlies an argument. A single article or source is not, by itself, a perspective. Argument, reasoning and opinions are the specifics of what the author says – they are informed by the author's perspective.

1 http://www.jstor.org/stable/j.ctt15zc5kw
2 http://finance.yahoo.com/news/u-sues-harley-davidsonenvironmental-145252860.html
3 http://www.wen.org.uk/#home

Activity 3

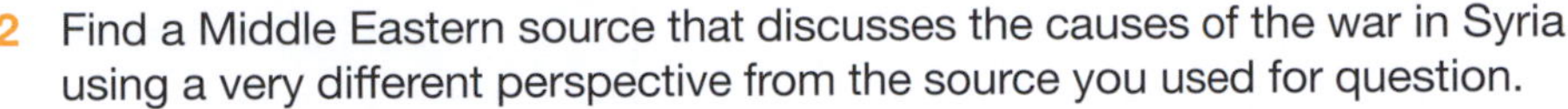

1. Find a European source that discusses the causes of the war in Syria. Use a mind map and colour to show causes, effects and your own questions.
2. Find a Middle Eastern source that discusses the causes of the war in Syria using a very different perspective from the source you used for question.
3. How are the two perspectives different?

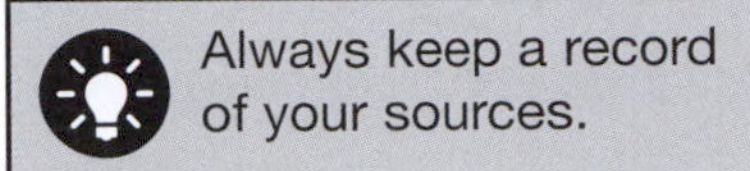

Always keep a record of your sources.

Activity 4

1. Use Internet searches to find style guides for two of the following.
   a. Harvard
   b. APA
   c. MLA
2. Choose one book, one journal article and one web-based source. Cite each of them in two different styles.
3. How are the styles different?
4. Which are you most comfortable with?
5. Find several sources that you have used. Cite them in the style that you prefer.

There are several approved styles for citations and references, including Harvard, APA and MLA. Some subjects have preferred styles, but the most important thing is to be consistent.

Write in your learning journal. Focus on:

- Practising citing your sources in an approved style.
- Any new skills you have learned.
- Any areas you struggle with.
- How you can improve.

Selecting and using ideas

Selecting and using ideas, evidence and arguments from a range of sources are important research skills.

Selecting means choosing. You cannot use everything that you find, so you have to find some way of selecting or choosing which ideas, evidence and arguments to include. The most important question you can ask to help you decide which material to select is: which material is most relevant to answering my question? Selecting relevant ideas, evidence or arguments shows that you understand the key issues, and that you have understood and reflected on the most important issues in your research area.

Using ideas, evidence and arguments means that you employ them for a purpose – to answer your question. Simply copying or quoting information from someone else's work does not count as 'using' it. You need to think about, interpret and reflect on the ideas, and then organise them in new ways to support your own reasoning. Using ideas in your own reasoning demonstrates that you are in control of your research material, and that you have your own contributions to make to the debate.

In Global Perspectives, you need to consider the evidence base for an idea; that is, you need to research widely, and understand the range of different arguments and perspectives within an area of research.

Select material carefully. Use the most relevant material to support your ideas and reasoning.

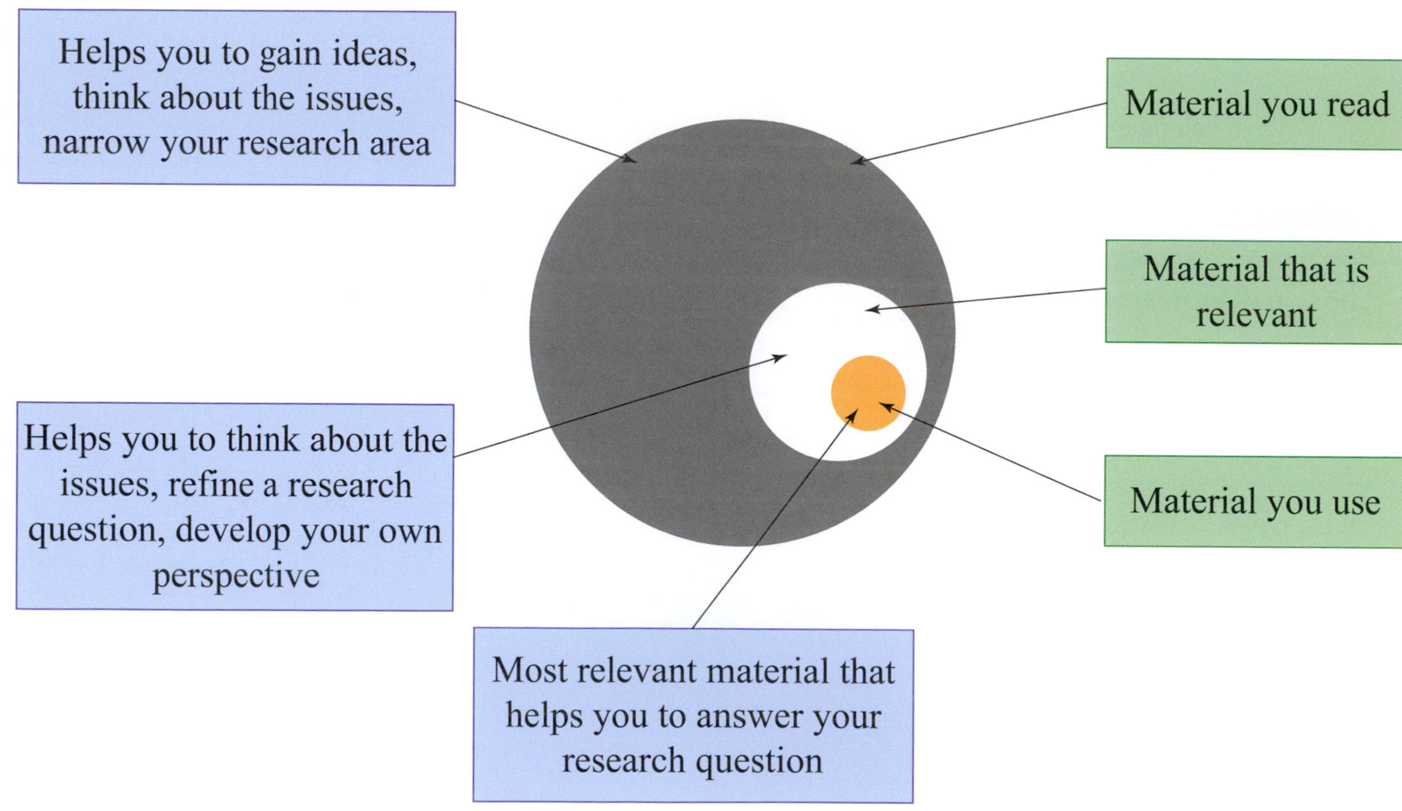
Helps you to gain ideas, think about the issues, narrow your research area
Material you read
Material that is relevant
Helps you to think about the issues, refine a research question, develop your own perspective
Material you use
Most relevant material that helps you to answer your research question

Egg in a pan – a representation of strong research

'Why should I read all this stuff if it turns out I don't use it?'

If it helps you to think, you are using it. Including material in your essay or presentation is only one way of using it.

You can make notes on why a source is **not** useful. That is helpful.

You can provide a bibliography of everything you have read and thought about, and a list of references, which gives details of the sources you have cited.

Activity 1

Look at the diagrams below. They represent the materials that two students (Stella and Pravit) have read and used in their research essays or presentations. Explain why these students' essays and presentations may not be very good.

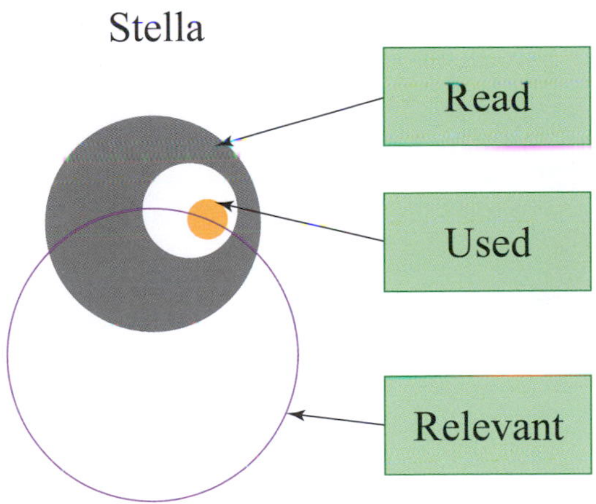

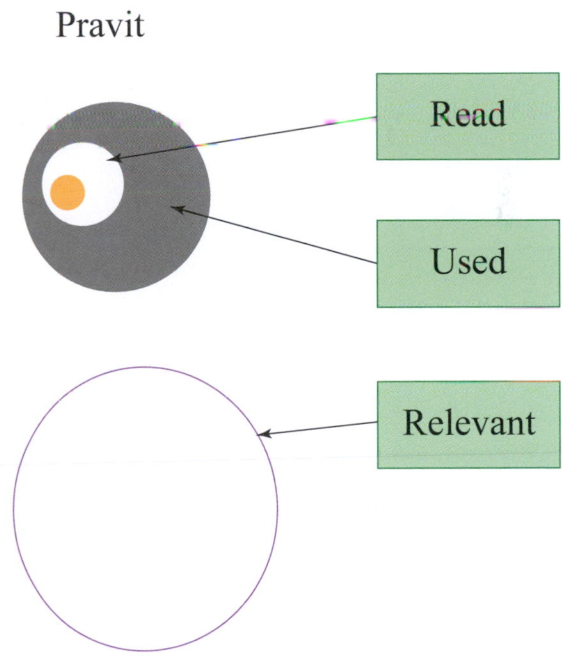

Activity 2

1 Look at a research essay you have written recently. Which diagram did it most resemble?

2 How could you improve your research essay?

Remember to cite your sources using an approved and consistent style.

How do I know what's relevant?

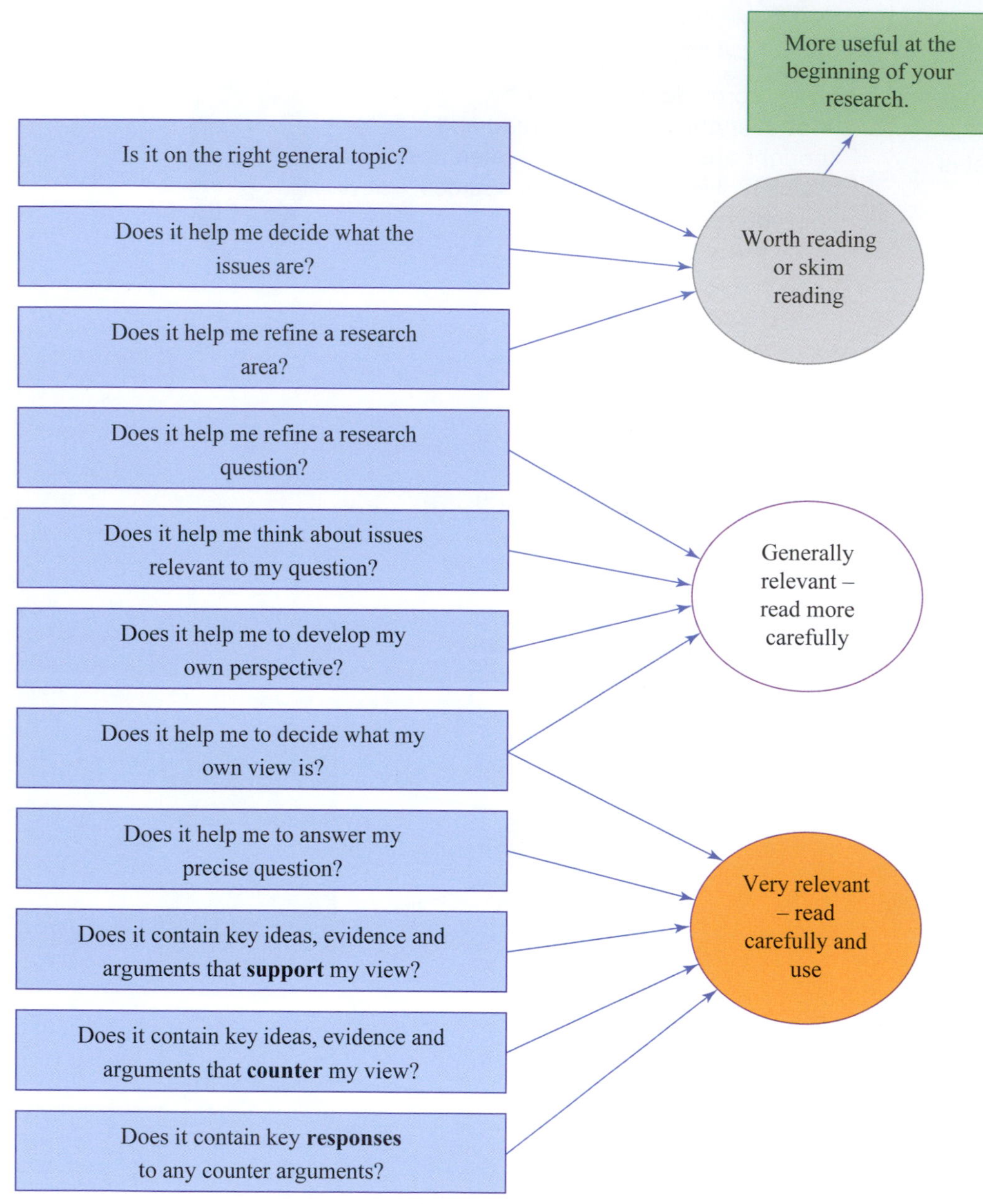

More useful at the beginning of your research.
Is it on the right general topic?
Does it help me decide what the issues are?
Does it help me refine a research area?
Worth reading or skim reading
Does it help me refine a research question?
Does it help me think about issues relevant to my question?
Does it help me to develop my own perspective?
Generally relevant – read more carefully
Does it help me to decide what my own view is?
Does it help me to answer my precise question?
Does it contain key ideas, evidence and arguments that **support** my view?
Does it contain key ideas, evidence and arguments that **counter** my view?
Does it contain key **responses** to any counter arguments?
Very relevant – read carefully and use

Activity 3

Which of the following ideas, evidence and argument are relevant to this question: How can we protect important national monuments from damage inflicted by industry?

1 The UNESCO World Heritage Committee has identified many objects as belonging to the heritage of mankind.

2 People spend a lot of money on visiting national monuments such as the Great Wall of China, the Taj Mahal or Schloss Neuschwanstein (the original for the Disney castle).

3 Beaches have been closed in the UK as a result of radioactivity, and in Haiti due to sewage pollution.

4 Currently, threats to Egyptian monuments – such as erosive environmental conditions, vandalism, theft and ongoing urban development – are increasing.

5 In 1995, a highway project near Cairo was likely to cause serious damage to the Pyramids. Negotiations with the Egyptian government resulted in a number of alternative solutions to replace the disputed project.

6 Wealthy countries are more interested in preserving national monuments than poorer countries.

7 The Taj Trapezium Zone is a 10 400 square kilometre area around the monument where industrial business is limited.

Activity 4

1 Some students were asked to answer this question: To what extent does the Internet aid small businesses in LEDCs? How effectively have these students selected and used information in these extracts from essays?

A. Some people argue that Internet access is a benefit, 'iHub is a working space that hosts developers, designers and others working with technology software. It is one of the most well-known tech hubs in Africa. In just four years since its founding, the iHub[1] has over 13,000 members in its online and off-line community, held close to 500 events and had over 50 companies calling it home'. Other people think that Internet business has disadvantages. 'One of the problems with doing business on the Internet is that it can be expensive to copyright or patent your website ideas globally', according to Internet business adviser Steve Ma.

B. The Internet can be vital to small businesses, especially in less economically developed countries. It allows businesses to connect directly with consumers and other business partners. Developments such as iHub in Kenya (UN, 2014[2]) allow small-tech businesses to thrive. They not only benefit in their own right, but they then provide services that allow other companies to thrive. 'The number of internet users on the continent grew at seven times the global average, clocking 3,600%, between 2000 and 2012 (UN, 2014). This is likely to be one of the factors contributing to high growth in Africa, with growth in many countries staying over 5% per year, and reaching 8+% in countries such as Ethiopia in 2016' (*Economist*, 2016[3]).

2 How could you improve these extracts from the students' essays?

1 http://www.un.org/africarenewal/magazine/april-2014/internet-access-no-longer-luxury
2 http://www.un.org/africarenewal/magazine/april-2014/internet-access-no-longer-luxury
3 http://www.economist.com/news/economic-and-financial-indicators/21699439-african-growth

Activity 5

1 Look at a research essay that you have written recently. Answer the questions below by ticking the appropriate box.

	☺	☹	😐
Did you read more material than you used?			
Did you have a clear research area?			
Did you select relevant material to answer the question?			
Did you use the material to support your own reasoning?			
Did you answer precisely the question that was asked?			

2 Work with a partner to see how you could improve the essays.

When you are working with a partner to improve the person's work, be constructive, and give advice in a kind and positive way.

Write in your learning journal. Focus on:

- ideas about selecting and using relevant ideas
- any new skills you have learned
- any areas you struggle with
- how you can improve.

Analyse

Analysing issues, perspectives and contexts

Analysing means identifying the component parts of a larger whole, and how they relate to each other. It can also mean reinterpreting. For instance, you might take an issue relating to immigration and separate it into causes, consequences, problems and possible solutions. You might analyse the evidence which supports different interpretations of what the problem is or how you might solve it. You might analyse the beliefs, assumptions and values underlying different perspectives on the issue. As a result, you might interpret the issue differently.

You can ask yourself the following questions:

- What are the issues?
- Can I use the themes to help me break the issues down?
- What are the causes, consequences, problems and possible solutions?
- How contentious are the causes, consequences, problems and possible solutions?
- What different perspectives can I find?
- What are the beliefs, assumptions and values underlying these perspectives?
- What is the background to the debates surrounding this issue?

People might argue about the possible answers to these questions. There is rarely a single, clear, 'correct' answer. You will need to find your own path to understanding, and make sure that your understanding is well supported by clear thinking and reasoning.

Remember the following definitions.

- An **issue** is an important topic for discussion or debate.
- A **perspective** is a viewpoint or standpoint, sometimes embedded in or strongly informed by a world view.
- A **context** is the background to a particular argument. It can include, for example, the historical and intellectual backgrounds, the evidence base for an argument and the different arguments about that issue.

Aa Analyse means identify, break down into component parts and possibly re-interpret.

To get an overview of issues within a field:

- search, 'key + issues + [field]' – for example, 'key issues gender'.
- skim read documents to get an overview
- note key issues; for example, equality.

Use diagrams to help you.

Try searching 'gender + equality + issues + economic'.

Activity 1

Look at the diagram below.

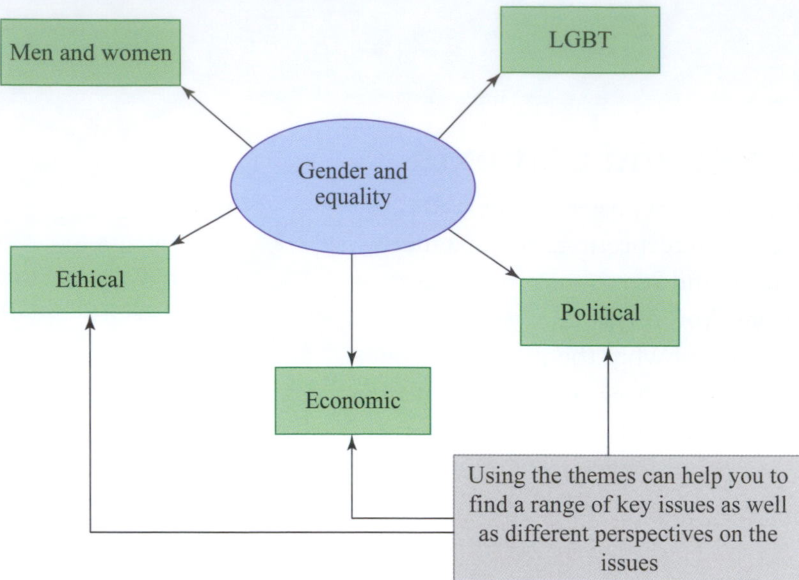

> You may find key issues relating to gender that are not equality issues. If they interest you, make a note of them to come back to – it might be the basis of future research. Do **not**, however, get distracted from the task you are doing!

1. What are some of the equality issues faced by men and women? Use quick Internet searches, scanning and skim reading to help you add to the diagram above.
2. What are some of the equality issues faced by LGBT individuals and communities? Use quick Internet searches, scanning and skim reading to help you add to the diagram above.
3. What are some of the economic issues relating to gender and equality?
4. What are some of the ethical issues relating to gender and equality?
5. What are some of the political issues relating to gender and equality?
6. To what extent are the issues you have found in these searches different issues, and to what extent are they different perspectives on the same issues?

Activity 2

1. Choose another topic from the Global Perspectives syllabus.
2. Repeat the process you followed in Activity 1 and identify key issues and perspectives within the topic you have chosen.

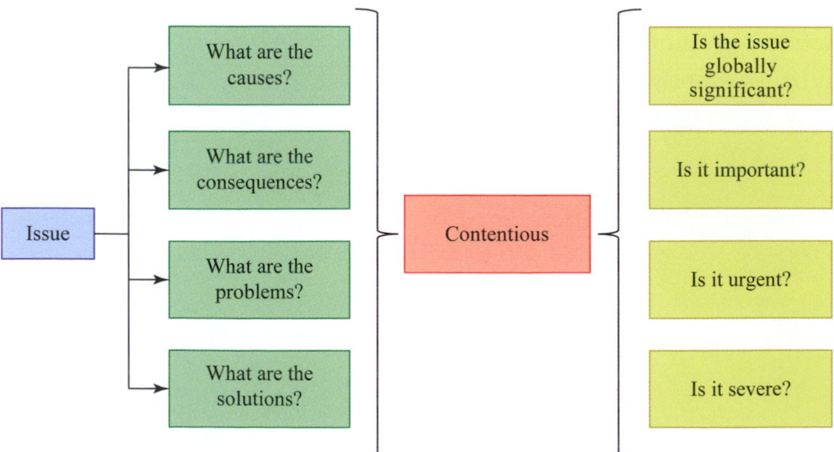

Analysing issues

Questions you could ask yourself include the following.

Do the sources agree on:

- the causes
- the significance of the causes
- the consequences
- the severity and likeliness of the consequences
- what the problems might be
- who will experience the problems
- the solutions
- who can take action to solve problems
- how urgent it is to solve problems?

Are the sources that disagree equally reliable?

Which disagreements are:

- within a single perspective?
- caused by different perspectives and the different beliefs and values underlying them?

Activity 3

1. Choose one specific issue relating to gender equality (for example, you might choose an issue relating to gendered toys).
   a. Identify causes – are they contentious? Explain how.
   b. Identify consequences – are they contentious? Explain how.
   c. Identify any problems – are they contentious? Explain how.
   d. Identify possible solutions – are they contentious? Explain how.
   e. Do different sources agree on how globally significant, important, urgent and severe these causes, consequences, problems and solutions are?
   f. Do any sources that disagree come from different perspectives? If so, can you identify any beliefs or values they hold that are different?
2. Choose one specific issue relating to the topic you were analysing in Activity 2. Break the issue down by asking about causes, consequences, problems and solutions, as you did for question 1.

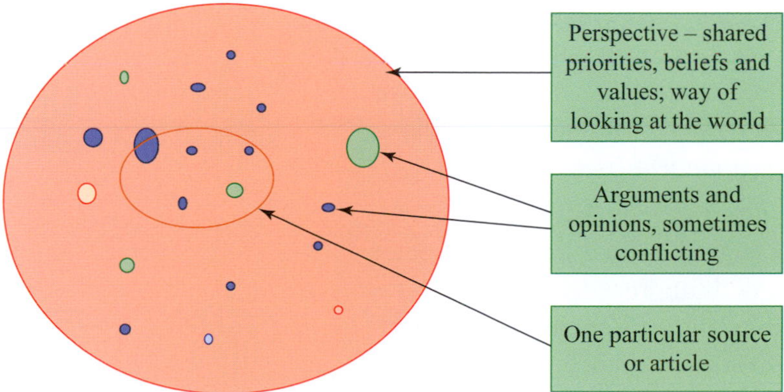

Perspectives contain many different opinions and arguments, including some that may conflict

Activity 4

1 Identify the different perspectives in extracts A–D. Consider the priorities, beliefs and values that might underlie them.

2 Work in a small group.

  a Find extracts from various sources with different perspectives on an issue of your choice from the Global Perspectives syllabus.

  b Present your extracts to the other groups. Discuss which perspectives you have identified, and what priorities, beliefs and values they hold.

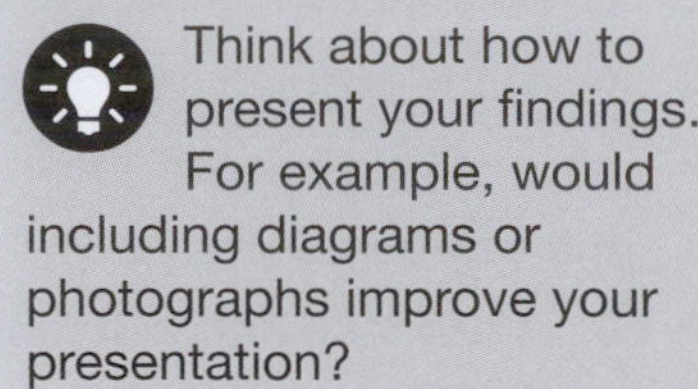

Think about how to present your findings. For example, would including diagrams or photographs improve your presentation?

Priorities, beliefs and values that underlie an argument are often not stated – sometimes because they are so obvious to the person writing that they do not need to be stated. When reading an argument ask yourself these questions.

- What else must this person believe in order for this reasoning to make sense?
- Why do I disagree with this reasoning?
- Does this reasoning challenge my basic values? If so, what are they?

Document 1

A. "By the end of today, another 200 children will have been cruelly separated from their fathers in secret family courts" (Matt O'Connor, Founder, Fathers4Justice). Fatherlessness is an obscenity. No child should be denied their human right to a father yet nearly 1 in 3 children now lives without a father in the UK—that's nearly 4 million fatherless children. Help us end the cruel & degrading treatment of families by the government.

Mission statement http://www.fathers-4-justice.org/

B. Modern psychological research continues to unveil differences in men and women from the most obvious in behavioral patterns to those as trivial as picking out an angry face in a crowd. In light of such manifest differences between the two genders, it is unsuitable for men and women to assume identical roles. As mentioned in a *New York Times* article on Women's health:

'In contrast to the feminist premise that women can do anything men can do, science is demonstrating that women can do some things better, that they have many biological and cognitive advantages over men. Then again, there are some things that women don't do as well.'

God created us with different but complementary strengths and capabilities. A man does not need to become a woman nor vice versa in order to be successful.

http://www.islamreligion.com/articles/458/viewall/concept-of-gender-equality-in-islam/

C. *Oppressed, inferior, and unequal—for many people, these are the first words that come to mind when thinking about women in Islam. These stereotypes confuse Islam with cultural practices and fail to recognize that Islam has empowered women with the most progressive rights since the 7th century. In Islam, women are not inferior or unequal to men. This brochure presents the actual teachings of Islam regarding the rights, roles, and responsibilities of women, with a special focus on gender equality in Islam.*

At a time when female children were buried alive in Arabia and women were considered transferable property, Islam honored women in society by elevating them and protecting them with unprecedented rights. Islam gave women the right to education, to marry someone of their choice, to retain their identity after marriage, to divorce, to work, to own and sell property, to seek protection by the law, to vote, and to participate in civic and political engagement.

In 610 C.E., God began to reveal the message of Islam to Prophet Muhammad, peace be upon him (pbuh), in Mecca. Muhammad (pbuh)

called people towards the belief in one God and encouraged them to be just and merciful to one another. In reforming the pagan Arab society, he particularly transformed their mindset regarding the treatment of women. Islam abolished the practice of killing female children and raised the stature of women in society to one of dignity, esteem, and privilege.
http://www.whyislam.org/on-faith/status-of-women/

D. 'The Lord Jesus chose men to form the college of the twelve apostles, and the apostles did the same when they chose collaborators to succeed them in their ministry ... For this reason the ordination of women is not possible' (*Catechism of Catholic Church*).
http://request.org.uk/issues/social-issues/gender-roles-and-the-church/

Activity 5

Read document 2 and answer the questions that follow.

1 What key issues may be identified in the article?
2 What causes and consequences may be identified in the article?
3 What problems and solutions may be identified in the article?
4 How would you describe the perspective that this article comes from?
5 What priorities, beliefs and values does the author hold?
6 Do you accept all of these priorities, beliefs and values? Why or why not?
7 Do you have any questions about the evidence, arguments or beliefs?
8 If so, how can you use these questions?

Document 2

Why Gender Equality Stalled

By Stephanie Coontz

Feb. 16, 2013

THIS week is the 50th anniversary of the publication of Betty Friedan's international best seller, "The Feminine Mystique", which has been widely credited with igniting the women's movement of the 1960s. Readers who return to this feminist classic today are often puzzled by the absence of concrete political proposals to change the status of women. But "The Feminine Mystique" had the impact it did because it focused on transforming women's personal consciousness.

In 1963, most Americans did not yet believe that gender equality was possible or even desirable. Conventional wisdom held that a woman could not pursue a career and still be a fulfilled wife or successful mother. Normal women, psychiatrists proclaimed, renounced all aspirations outside the home to meet their feminine need for dependence. In 1962, more than two-thirds of the women surveyed by University of Michigan researchers agreed that most important family decisions "should be made by the man of the house."

It was in this context that Friedan set out to transform the attitudes of women. Arguing that "the personal is political," feminists urged women to challenge the assumption, at work and at home, that women should always be the ones who make the coffee, watch over the children, pick up after men and serve the meals.

Over the next 30 years this emphasis on equalizing gender roles at home as well as at work produced a revolutionary transformation in Americans' attitudes. It was not instant. As late as 1977, two-thirds of Americans believed that it was "much better for everyone involved if the man is the achiever outside the home and the woman takes care of the home and family." By 1994, two-thirds of Americans rejected this notion.

But during the second half of the 1990s and first few years of the 2000s, the equality revolution seemed to stall. Between 1994 and 2004, the percentage of Americans preferring the male breadwinner/female homemaker family model actually rose to 40 percent from 34 percent. Between 1997 and 2007, the number of full-time working mothers who said they would prefer to work part time increased to 60 percent from 48 percent. In 1997, a quarter of stay-at-home mothers said full-time work would be ideal. By 2007, only 16 percent of stay-at-home mothers wanted to work full time.

Women's labor-force participation in the United States also leveled off in the second half of the 1990s, in contrast to its continued increase in most other countries. Gender desegregation of college majors and occupations slowed. And although single mothers continued to increase their hours of paid labor, there was a significant jump in the percentage of married women, especially married women with infants, who left the labor force. By 2004, a smaller percentage of married women with children under 3 were in the labor force than in 1993.

SOME people began to argue that feminism was not about furthering the equal involvement of men and women at home and work but simply about giving women the right to choose between pursuing a career and devoting themselves to full-time motherhood. A new emphasis on intensive mothering and attachment parenting helped justify the latter choice.

Anti-feminists welcomed this shift as a sign that most Americans did not want to push gender equality too far. And feminists, worried that they were seeing a resurgence of traditional gender roles and beliefs, embarked on a new round of consciousness-raising. Books with titles like "The Feminine Mistake" and "Get to Work" warned of the stiff penalties women paid for dropping out of the labor force, even for relatively brief periods. Cultural critics questioned the "Perfect Madness" of intensive mothering and helicopter parenting, noting the problems that resulted when, as Ms. Friedan had remarked about "housewifery," mothering "expands to fill the time available."

One study cautioned that nearly 30 percent of opt-out moms who wanted to rejoin the labor force were unable to do so, and of those who did return, only 40 percent landed full-time professional jobs. In "The Price of Motherhood," the journalist Ann Crittenden estimated that the typical college-educated woman lost more than $1 million dollars in lifetime earnings and forgone retirement benefits after she opted out.

Other feminists worried that the equation of feminism with an individual woman's choice to opt out of the work force undermined the movement's commitment to a larger vision of gender equity and justice. Joan Williams, the founding director of the Center for WorkLife Law at the University of

California's Hastings College of the Law, argued that defining feminism as giving mothers the choice to stay home assumes that their partners have the responsibility to support them, and thus denies choice to fathers. The political theorist Lori Marso noted that emphasizing personal choice ignores the millions of women without a partner who can support them.

These are all important points. But they can sound pretty abstract to men and women who are stuck between a rock and a hard place when it comes to arranging their work and family lives. For more than two decades the demands and hours of work have been intensifying. Yet progress in adopting family-friendly work practices and social policies has proceeded at a glacial pace.

Today the main barriers to further progress toward gender equity no longer lie in people's personal attitudes and relationships. Instead, structural impediments prevent people from acting on their egalitarian values, forcing men and women into personal accommodations and rationalizations that do not reflect their preferences. The gender revolution is not in a stall. It has hit a wall.

In today's political climate, it's startling to remember that 80 years ago, in 1933, the Senate overwhelmingly voted to establish a 30-hour workweek. The bill failed in the House, but five years later the Fair Labor Standards Act of 1938 gave Americans a statutory 40-hour workweek. By the 1960s, American workers spent less time on the job than their counterparts in Europe and Japan.

Between 1990 and 2000, however, average annual work hours for employed Americans increased. By 2000, the United States had outstripped Japan—the former leader of the work pack—in the hours devoted to paid work. Today, almost 40 percent of men in professional jobs work 50 or more hours a week, as do almost a quarter of men in middle-income occupations. Individuals in lower-income and less-skilled jobs work fewer hours, but they are more likely to experience frequent changes in shifts, mandatory overtime on short notice, and nonstandard hours. And many low-income workers are forced to work two jobs to get by. When we look at dual-earner couples, the workload becomes even more daunting. As of 2000, the average dual-earner couple worked a combined 82 hours a week, while almost 15 percent of married couples had a joint workweek of 100 hours or more.

Astonishingly, despite the increased workload of families, and even though 70 percent of American children now live in households where every adult in the home is employed, in the past 20 years the United States has not passed any major federal initiative to help workers accommodate their family and work demands. The Family and Medical Leave Act of 1993 guaranteed covered workers up to 12 weeks unpaid leave after a child's birth or adoption or in case of a family illness. Although only about half the total work force was eligible, it seemed a promising start. But aside from the belated requirement of the new Affordable Care Act that nursing mothers be given a private space at work to pump breast milk, the F.M.L.A. turned out to be the inadequate end.

Meanwhile, since 1990 other nations with comparable resources have implemented a comprehensive agenda of "work-family reconciliation" acts. As a result, when the United States' work-family policies are compared with those of countries at similar levels of economic and political development, the United States comes in dead last.

Out of nearly 200 countries studied by Jody Heymann, dean of the school of public health at the University of California, Los Angeles, and her team of researchers for their new book, "Children's Chances," 180 now offer guaranteed paid leave to new mothers, and 81 offer paid leave to fathers. They found that 175 mandate paid annual leave for workers, and 162 limit the maximum length of the workweek. The United States offers none of these protections.

A 1997 European Union directive prohibits employers from paying part-time workers lower hourly rates than full-time workers, excluding them from pension plans or limiting paid leaves to full-time workers. By contrast, American workers who reduce hours for family reasons typically lose their benefits and take an hourly wage cut.

Is it any surprise that American workers express higher levels of work–family conflict than workers in any of our European counterparts? Or that women's labor-force participation has been overtaken? In 1990, the United States ranked sixth in female labor participation among 22 countries in the Organization for Economic Cooperation and Development, which is made up of most of the globe's wealthier countries. By 2010, according to an economic research paper by Cornell researchers Francine Blau and Lawrence Kahn, released last month, we had fallen to 17th place, with about 30 percent of that decline a direct result of our failure to keep pace with other countries' family-friendly work policies. American women have not abandoned the desire to combine work and family. Far from it. According to the Pew Research Center, in 1997, 56 percent of women ages 18 to 34 and 26 percent of middle-aged and older women said that, in addition to having a family, being successful in a high-paying career or profession was "very important" or "one of the most important things" in their lives. By 2011, fully two-thirds of the younger women and 42 percent of the older ones expressed that sentiment.

Nor have men given up the ideal of gender equity. A 2011 study by the Center for Work and Family at Boston College found that 65 percent of the fathers they interviewed felt that mothers and fathers should provide equal amounts of caregiving for their children. And in a 2010 Pew poll, 72 percent of both women and men between 18 and 29 agreed that the best marriage is one in which husband and wife both work and both take care of the house.

BUT when people are caught between the hard place of bad working conditions and the rock wall of politicians' resistance to family-friendly reforms, it is hard to live up to such aspirations. The Boston College study found that only 30 percent of the fathers who wanted to share child care equally with their wives actually did so, a gap that helps explain why American men today report higher levels of work–family conflict than women. Under the circumstances, how likely is it that the young adults surveyed by Pew will meet their goal of sharing breadwinning and caregiving?

The answer is suggested by the findings of the New York University sociologist Kathleen Gerson in the interviews she did for her 2010 book, "The Unfinished Revolution: Coming of Age in a New Era of Gender, Work, and Family." Eighty percent of the women and 70 percent of the men Ms. Gerson interviewed said they wanted an egalitarian relationship that allowed them to share breadwinning and family care. But when asked what they would do if this was not possible, they described a variety of "fallback" positions. While most of the women wanted to continue paid employment, the majority of men said that if they could not achieve their egalitarian ideal they expected their partner to assume primary responsibility for parenting so they could focus on work.

And that is how it usually works out. When family and work obligations collide, mothers remain much more likely than fathers to cut back or drop out of work. But unlike the situation in the 1960s, this is not because most people believe this is the preferable order of things. Rather, it is often a reasonable response to the fact that our political and economic institutions lag way behind our personal ideals.

Women are still paid less than men at every educational level and in every job category. They are less likely than men to hold jobs that offer flexibility or family-friendly benefits. When they become mothers, they face more scrutiny and prejudice on the job than fathers do.

So, especially when women are married to men who work long hours, it often seems to both partners that they have no choice. Female professionals are twice as likely to quit work as other married mothers when their husbands work 50 hours or more a week and more than three times more likely to quit when their husbands work 60 hours or more.

The sociologist Pamela Stone studied a group of mothers who had made these decisions. Typically, she found, they phrased their decision in terms of a preference. But when they explained their "decision-making process," it became clear that most had made the "choice" to quit work only as a last resort—when they could not get the flexible hours or part-time work they wanted, when their husbands would not or could not cut back their hours, and when they began to feel that their employers were hostile to their concerns. Under those conditions, Professor Stone notes, what was really a workplace problem for families became a private problem for women.

This is where the political gets really personal. When people are forced to behave in ways that contradict their ideals, they often undergo what sociologists call a "values stretch"—watering down their original expectations and goals to accommodate the things they have to do to get by. This behavior is especially likely if holding on to the original values would exacerbate tensions in the relationships they depend on.

In their years of helping couples make the transition from partners to parents, the psychologists Philip and Carolyn Cowan have found that tensions increase when a couple backslide into more traditional roles than they originally desired. The woman resents that she is not getting the shared child care she expected and envies her husband's social networks outside the home. The husband feels hurt that his wife isn't more grateful for the sacrifices he is making by working more hours so she can stay home. When you can't change what's bothering you, one typical response is to convince yourself that it doesn't actually bother you. So couples often create a family myth about why they made these choices, why it has turned out for the best, and why they are still equal in their hearts even if they are not sharing the kind of life they first envisioned.

Under present conditions, the intense consciousness raising about the "rightness" of personal choices that worked so well in the early days of the women's movement will end up escalating the divisive finger-pointing that stands in the way of political reform.

Our goal should be to develop work-life policies that enable people to put their gender values into practice. So let's stop arguing about the hard choices women make and help more women and men avoid such hard choices. To do that, we must stop seeing work-family policy as a women's issue and start seeing it as a human rights issue that affects parents, children, partners, singles and elders. Feminists should certainly support this campaign. But they don't need to own it.

Stephanie Coontz is a professor of family history at Evergreen State College and the author of "A Strange Stirring: The Feminine Mystique and American Women at the Dawn of the 1960s."

http://www.nytimes.com/2013/02/17/opinion/sunday/why-gender-equality-stalled.html?_r=0

Activity 6

1 Read the article at: http://thebackbencher.co.uk/sexism-men-exist/

a What key issues may be identified in the article?

b What causes and consequences may be identified in the article?

c What problems and solutions may be identified in the article?

d How would you describe the perspective that this article comes from?

e What priorities, beliefs and values does the author hold?

f Do you accept all of these priorities, beliefs and values? Why or why not?

g Do you have any questions about the evidence, arguments or beliefs?

h If you do have questions, how can you use them to start reconstructing the context of the debate and building an evidence base?

2 How does this article help you to put the arguments and perspectives from document 2 (in Activity 5) in context?

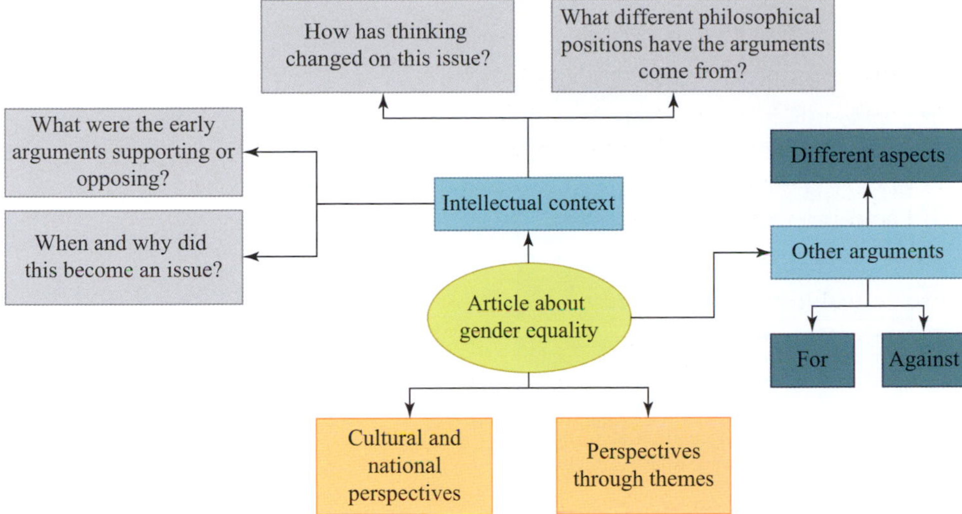

Building up the context and evidence base

In research, your next steps would be:

- to refine a research question
- to categorise the material you have read into:
  - useful background material
  - generally relevant material
  - material you should use in your argument to answer the research question.

Activity 7

1 Start to build up a broader context for the arguments you found in the articles in Activities 5 and 6.
2 Use the questions you raised while reading the articles.
3 Use the questions in the diagram above to help you.

Activity 8

1 Think back to when you built up the context for the arguments on gender equality and answer the following questions.
   a How many different articles, websites and other sources did you find?
   b How many different perspectives did you identify?
2 Use colour coding and diagrams to show how the sources and perspectives relate to each other.

Activity 9

Return to one of the topics you started to analyse and research in activity 2, 3 and 4 (not gender equality).

1 Start to build up a broader context for one of the key issues or arguments you identified.
2 Use the processes you used in activity 5, 6, 7 and 8 to help you.

Write in your learning journal. Focus on:

- analysing issues, perspectives and contexts
- any new skills you have learned
- any aspects that you struggle with
- how you can improve.

Analysing reasoning and arguments

These are some of the main kinds of writing and reasoning you will come across. Can you think of, or find, any others?

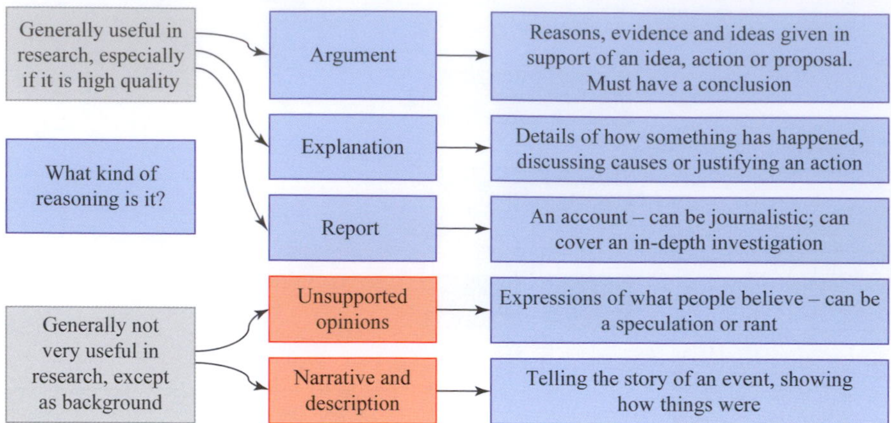

Activity 1

Document 1 consists of six extracts (A–F). Identify the kinds of reasoning in these extracts. You may find more than one kind of reasoning in some of them.

Document 1

A. Selfish people exist. Ignorant people exist. Raging imbeciles on the internet exist. They do not represent a whole side, they are bad apples and make no mistake, on the internet, they are the vocal minority. Do not pander to them, do not give them the time of day. When they have no one left to troll and fight, they will do what they always do, they will turn on each other.

http://thoughtcatalog.com/yohanne-mwale/2014/09/an-invasion-of-privacy-is-never-acceptable/

B. A new study has found that at various times the British have invaded almost 90 per cent of the countries around the globe. The analysis of the histories of the almost 200 countries in the world found only 22 which have never experienced an invasion by the British.

http://www.telegraph.co.uk/history/9653497/British-have-invaded-nine-out-of-ten-countries-so-look-out-Luxembourg.html

C. Teens are so full of potential, so full of life, so... sleepy. Research shows that most teens do not get the sleep that they need on a daily basis. Each person has their own need for sleep. This need may vary from one person to another. Teens are at an important stage of their growth and development. Because of this, they need more sleep than adults. The average teen needs about nine hours of sleep each night to feel alert and well rested.

D. There are many factors that keep teens from getting enough sleep. Causes for their lack of sleep include the following:

- Rapidly changing bodies
- Busy schedules
- Active social lives
- A wrong view of sleep

Teen sleep problems can begin long before [teens] turn 13. The sleep habits and changing bodies of 10 to 12-year-olds have a close link to the teen years. The sleep patterns of teens are also firmly set in their lives. It is not easy for them to change the way they sleep. Thus teen sleep problems can continue well into their years as adults. For these reasons, the information found here may apply to anyone from 10 to 25 years of age.

http://sleepcenter.ucla.edu/sleep-and-teens

E. I lived in a dictatorship for two years: Syria. If the aim of government is to provide peace and security, then Syria delivered on both counts. While in neighbouring Iraq, a premature stab at democracy was causing mass carnage. Dictatorship is a necessary prelude to democracy. Liberal democracies don't come about overnight.

https://www.theguardian.com/theobserver/2007/sep/30/featuresreview.review3

F. Links between hormone levels and poor behaviour in teenagers are either weak, or non-existent.

Nevertheless, if the number one risk factor for homicide is maleness (as it is) and the second is youth, and given that boys have loads of testosterone, and girls don't (or certainly not nearly as much), surely this must put testosterone in the dock as the cause of aggressive adolescent behaviour?

Actually not. First, there is no consistent relationship between normal circulating testosterone levels and violence in teenagers. In fact, there is a rather better correlation between high testosterone levels and levels of popularity and respect from peers. One hypothesis is that teenage boys pick up cues from the environment and use them to determine "normal" behaviour. This is illustrated by recent work from the MRC unit at the Institute of Psychiatry which shows that it is not testosterone levels that determine your waywardness as a teenager, but basically, the people you hang with. Keep the company of bad boys, and you will take your behaviour cue from them. Hang out with sober sorts and your behaviour will be like theirs. As we all remember, being split up from your best mate is a peril of adolescence. "They're a bad influence on you" is the general gist of parental or teacher wisdom on this one. Oh dear. The ignominy of the Institute of Psychiatry proving Miss Mansergh, year nine form teacher, right.

Deprivation may be a more important determinant of teenage violence. The theory—and there is a wealth of literature on this subject—is that if low-status males are to avoid the road to genetic nothingness (the words of neuroscientist Steven Pinker), they may have to adopt aggressive, high-risk strategies. If you've got nothing, you have nothing to lose through your behaviour. Certainly, in humans, both violence and risk-taking behaviour show a pronounced social gradient, being least in the highest social classes and most in the lowest ones. This is surely not what you would expect if testosterone were the only driver of violence.

Another clue that testosterone is not the whole story here is that teenage girls, while not as violent, certainly rival boys for downright bloody-mindedness during their adolescent years. Worse, I can hear some parents say.

The thing that is really irritating about teenagers (and by now you will have guessed that I have two teenage boys) is that one moment their behaviour is that of adults, while the next it is that of a not very bright three-year-old… Or an amoeba. The rapid oscillation between child and adult is one of the hallmarks of the teenager.

In fact teenage brains are going through a process of maturation, and it is this maturation which many now believe to be responsible for much of the behaviour that we classically attribute to hormones. These changes are independent of hormones and are a function of age.

Source:https://www.theguardian.com/science/2005/mar/03/1

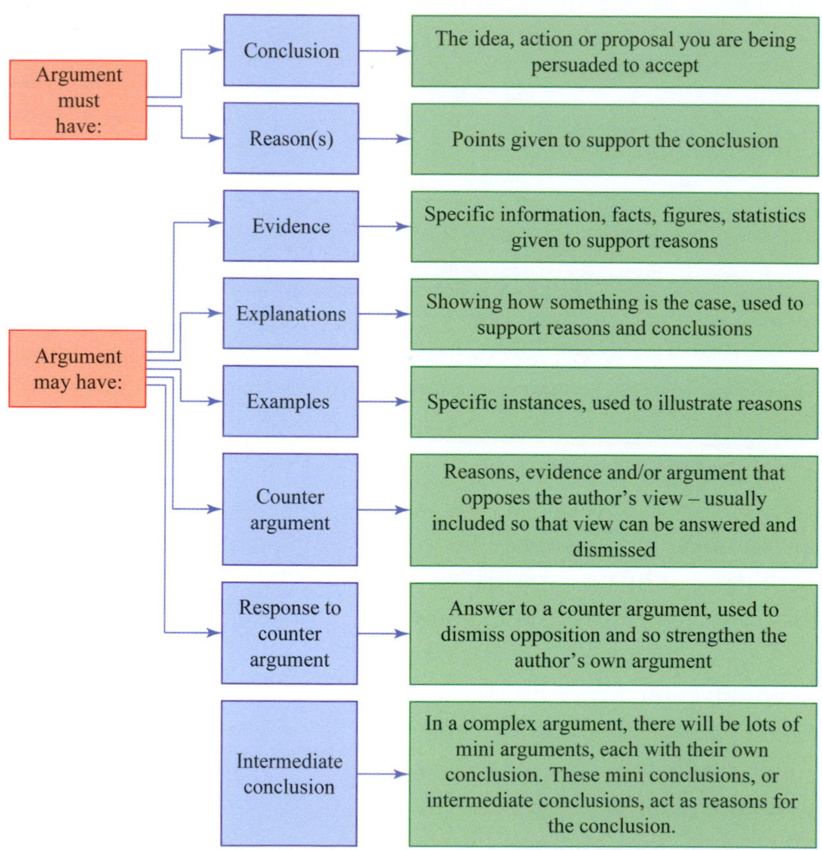

Analysing—identifying—the parts of an argument

In a long argument, analysing and identifying every single part of the argument would be time consuming and tedious. You only need to identify the most important parts of the reasoning – the main conclusion, the main reasons (these may be intermediate conclusions) and the key evidence. You may find that colour coding these can help with your research.

Activity 2

1 Identify the reasons, conclusions, evidence, etc., in extracts A–D below.

2 Look at any arguments you identified in Activity 1. Identify reasons, conclusions, evidence, etc.

Argument indicators

so, therefore, hence, thus, that is why → indicate a conclusion

because, as a result, in consequence → indicate a reason

Can you see any gaps in any of these arguments?

Look again at extract C. Is there any other information you feel you need in order to conclude that water-efficient maize is beneficial? Are there any questions you would like to ask?

Document 2

A. Democracy is a desirable form of government. It gives citizens the opportunity to reject a government without violence or bloodshed. Democracies usually do not go to war with each other, and usually support human rights for their populations.

B. Although many people believe that architects should prioritise the environment in their designs, there are many instances where other priorities are more important. Constructing stable buildings is one of the highest priorities in earthquake prone areas such as Japan and California. New buildings are often paid for by businesses, and their priorities are to maximise productivity and creativity.

C. Three-quarters of the world's most severe droughts over the past 10 years have occurred in Africa, making farming risky for millions of smallholder farmers, most of whom are women and rely on rainfall to water their crops. Maize is the most widely grown staple crop in Africa—more than 300 million Africans depend on it as their main food source. Maize production is severely affected by drought, which can lead to unpredictable and low yields, and at worst, complete crop failure. So water efficient maize, produced in cooperation with Monsanto, is beneficial to African farmers.

D. There are huge benefits to be gained from cultural export and exchange. International collaborations between artists improve the cultural offer available to us in England. They give audiences the chance to experience the finest artistic talent from across the world, while enriching the practice of artists and organisations here at home. Working internationally also gives our artists and cultural leaders the opportunity to develop new markets and audiences overseas.

http://www.artscouncil.org.uk/how-we-make-impact/international-development

How can you identify the main conclusion?

The main conclusion of a piece is **not** necessarily stated in the last lines. It is the idea that is supported by all of the other ideas.

Activity 3

Read the extracts given as documents 2 and 3 below.

1 Identify the types of reasoning you find in the extracts.
2 Identify the key parts of the reasoning – main conclusion, **key reasons** and **key evidence**.

Document 3

A. At MoMA PS1 in New York last year, I saw a landmark exhibition, *Zero Tolerance*, curated by the museum's director Klaus Biesenbach. The show examined the idea that the world's repressive regimes are cracking down on art for the same reason that New York Mayor Giuliani cracked down on homeless people at the end of the 1990s. The reason? Kill the chicken and you scare the cow. Imprison Ai Weiwei Hon RA and beat up Pussy Riot and you tell wider society that compliance is the only way forward.

I don't think that in Britain we live in an extreme police state, but we do live in a state of mind that is deadened by the media, where kids are told education is just about getting a job, where few young people can afford to buy somewhere to live and where some kids are brainwashed to think violence is the only way out. For the first time since Mosley in the 1930s, we now have a serious political party that is telling people Britain's problems stem from outsiders.

This is why art is embracing, indeed must embrace, politics. Call me old fashioned, but I think we have a duty to society not just to buy things we don't need and borrow money we cannot afford, but also to speak out. We need to treat our politicians with the same zero tolerance of which they are so fond. Artists need to get in front of politicians and with an eagle eye inspect and depict each expression of mean-mindedness. We also must advocate the world we want to live in. It's not Pussy Riot or Ai Weiwei who are extreme or outrageous, it is the governments who rule over them. To protect our society and make it more democratic, artists' diverse, angry voices must be celebrated and heard. The Royal Academy and the great public collections are not just art galleries. They are huge repositories of free speech and free thinking.

https://www.royalacademy.org.uk/article/should-art-be-political

Document 4

B. If the UN is to continue to fulfill its unique and vital global role in the twenty-first century, it must be upgraded in three key ways.

Fortunately, there is plenty to motivate world leaders to do what it takes. Indeed, the UN has had two major recent triumphs, with two more on the way before the end of this year.

The first triumph is the nuclear agreement with Iran. Sometimes misinterpreted as an agreement between Iran and the United States, the accord is in fact between Iran and the UN, represented by the five permanent members of the Security Council (China, France, Russia, the United Kingdom, and the US), plus Germany. An Iranian diplomat, in explaining why his country will scrupulously honor the agreement, made the point vividly: "Do you really think that Iran would dare to cheat on the very five UN Security Council permanent members that can seal our country's fate?"

The second big triumph is the successful conclusion, after 15 years, of the Millennium Development Goals, which have underpinned the largest, longest, and most effective global poverty-reduction effort ever undertaken. Two UN Secretaries-General have overseen the MDGs: Kofi Annan, who introduced them in 2000, and Ban Ki-moon, who, since succeeding Annan at the start of 2007, has led vigorously and effectively to achieve them.

The MDGs have engendered impressive progress in poverty reduction, public health, school enrollment, gender equality in education, and other areas. Since 1990 (the reference date for the targets), the global rate of extreme poverty has been reduced by well over half—more than fulfilling the agenda's number one goal.

Inspired by the MDGs' success, the UN's member countries are set to adopt the Sustainable Development Goals (SDGs)—which will aim to end extreme poverty in all its forms everywhere, narrow inequalities, and ensure environmental sustainability by 2030—next month. This, the UN's third triumph of 2015, could help to bring about the fourth: a global agreement on climate control, under the auspices of the UN Framework Convention on Climate Change, in Paris in December.

The precise value of the peace, poverty reduction, and environmental cooperation made possible by the UN is incalculable. If we were to put it in monetary terms, however, we might estimate their value at trillions of dollars per year—at least a few percent of the world economy's annual GDP of $100 trillion.

Yet spending on all UN bodies and activities—from the Secretariat and the Security Council to peacekeeping operations, emergency responses to epidemics, and humanitarian operations for natural disasters, famines, and refugees—totaled roughly $45 billion in 2013, roughly $6 per person on the planet. That is not just a bargain; it is a significant underinvestment. Given the rapidly growing need for global cooperation, the UN simply cannot get by on its current budget.

Given this, the first reform that I would suggest is an increase in funding, with high-income countries contributing at least $40 per capita annually, upper middle-income countries giving $8, lower-middle-income countries $2, and low-income countries $1. With these contributions—which amount to roughly 0.1% of the group's average per capita income—the UN would have about $75 billion annually with which to strengthen the quality and reach of vital programs, beginning with those needed to achieve the SDGs. Once the world is on a robust path to achieve the SDGs, the need for, say, peacekeeping and emergency-relief operations should decline as conflicts diminish in number and scale, and natural disasters are better prevented or anticipated.

This brings us to the second major area of reform: ensuring that the UN is fit for the new age of sustainable development. Specifically, the UN needs to strengthen its expertise in areas such as ocean health, renewable energy systems, urban design, disease control, technological innovation, public-private partnerships, and peaceful cultural cooperation. Some UN programs should be merged or closed, while other new SDG-related UN programs should be created.

The third major reform imperative is the UN's governance, starting with the Security Council, the composition of which no longer reflects global geopolitical realities. Indeed, the Western Europe and Other Group (WEOG) now accounts for three of the five permanent members (France, the United Kingdom, and the US). That leaves only one permanent position for the Eastern European Group (Russia), one for the Asia-Pacific Group (China), and none for Africa or Latin America.

The rotating seats on the Security Council do not adequately restore regional balance. Even with two of the ten rotating Security Council seats, the Asia-Pacific region is still massively under-represented. The Asia-Pacific region accounts for roughly 55% of the world's population and 44% of its annual income but has just 20% (three out of 15) of the seats on the Security Council.

Asia's inadequate representation poses a serious threat to the UN's legitimacy, which will only increase as the world's most dynamic and populous region assumes an increasingly important global role. One possible way to resolve the problem would be to add at least four Asian seats: one permanent seat for India, one shared by Japan and South Korea (perhaps in a two-year, one-year rotation), one for the ASEAN countries (representing the group as a single constituency), and a fourth rotating among the other Asian countries.

As the UN enters its eighth decade, it continues to inspire humanity. The Universal Declaration of Human Rights remains the world's moral charter, and the SDGs promise to provide new guideposts for global development cooperation. Yet the UN's ability to continue to fulfill its vast potential in a new and challenging century requires its member states to commit to support the organization with the resources, political backing, and reforms that this new era demands.

This article is published in collaboration with Project Syndicate. *Publication does not imply endorsement of views by the World Economic Forum.*

https://www.weforum.org/agenda/2015/08/3-reforms-the-un-needs-as-it-turns-70/

Write in your learning journal. Focus on:

- your thoughts about analysing reasoning and arguments
- any areas you have found difficult
- how you can improve.

Evaluate

Evaluating issues, perspectives and contexts

When you are evaluating something, you need to think about the criteria you are using. For instance, what criteria will help you decide whether working on a project will be beneficial? Use questions such as these when you are evaluating an issue:

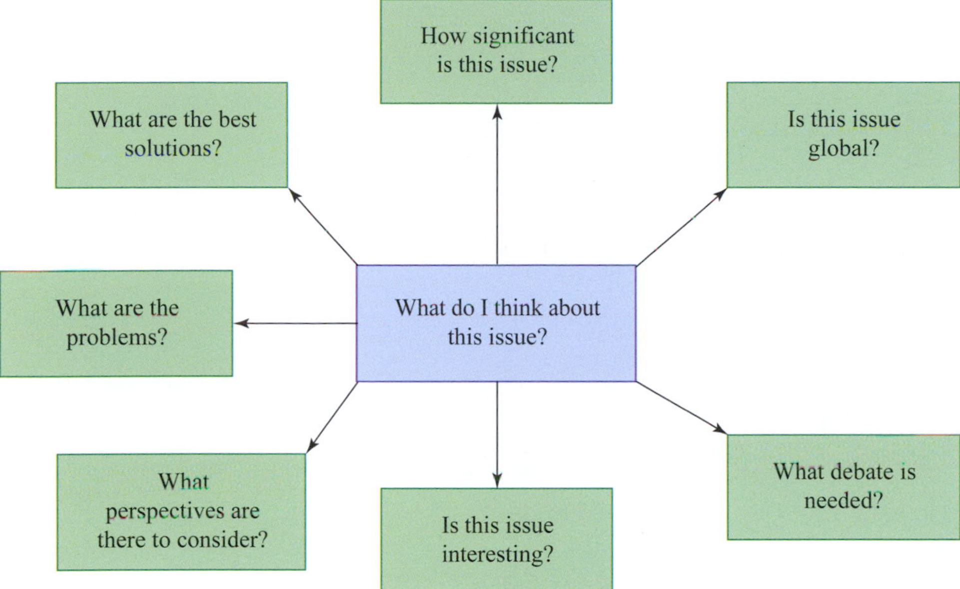

Evaluating possible causes can help you to evaluate issues, contexts and perspectives:

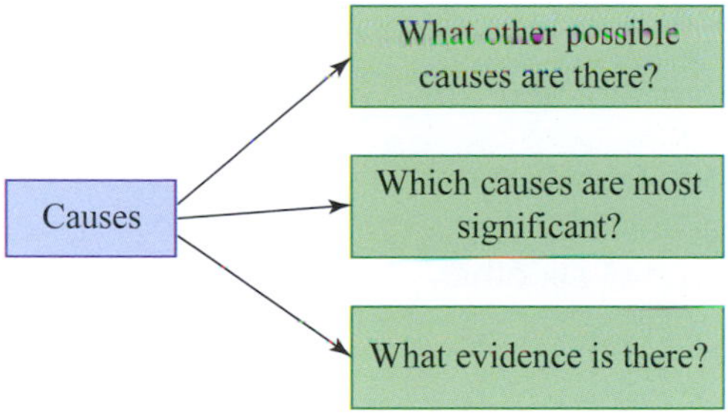

Evaluating means giving a value to something or passing a judgement. This could mean deciding how good, how effective or how reliable something is, for example.

When evaluating consequences, use themes and perspectives to help you weigh up their significance:

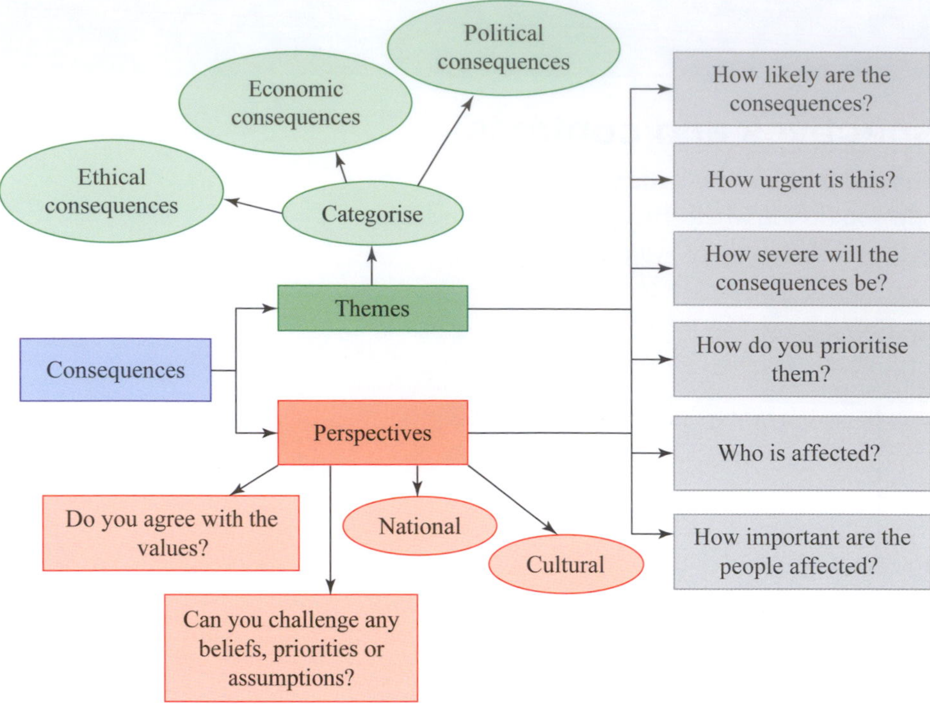

Activity 1

Hamilton Heights, a derelict building in New York City, is scheduled to be demolished. The area is being regenerated and gentrified.

1 What are the possible consequences for each of the people described in A–D below?

2 How likely, severe and urgent are these possible consequences for each person?

3 What possible solutions can you think of?

4 Consider which solutions each person is likely to approve of and why.

A Tommy D is a homeless veteran who has returned from Iraq and Afghanistan. He has lost an arm and has mental health issues. He has been sheltering in the building with a group of six other veterans.

B Susannah Compton is the Vice Principal of a company which is looking for a new site for its corporate headquarters. Ms Compton has overall responsibility for acquiring a desirable site at a suitably low cost.

C Farid Compton is a New York politician who has some influence over decisions in that part of New York. He is married to Susannah Compton's sister. He has won a great deal of political support through his former role in the US Army, and his sponsorship of a charity for veterans.

D Oadirah Evans is a doctor who works with veterans.

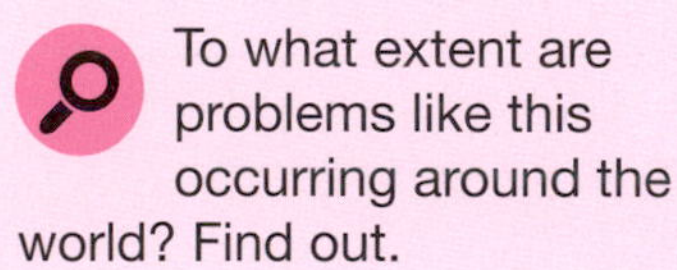

To what extent are problems like this occurring around the world? Find out.

Activity 2

Read the documents and answer the questions below.

Document 1

Six Fatalities in Demolition Fail

Who is to blame?

Six people lost their lives late last night in a dramatic demolition failure in New York City. Hamilton Heights was scheduled for demolition today, but parts of the 1960s concrete tower collapsed amid chaotic explosions at 10 pm last night. The bodies of two construction workers, one 8-year-old boy, and three homeless veterans have been retrieved from the rubble.

Local residents were alarmed and anxious. 'We were due to be evacuated in the morning so the blast could go ahead safely, they said. But we were raised from our beds by all sorts of explosions and crashes, glass flying everywhere. I thought Judgement Day had come,' said Clary Sinclair, a retired resident of the neighbouring Rapunzel Tower.

'I think it was deliberate,' opined another resident of Rapunzel Tower, who wished to remain anonymous. 'I think they wanted to damage Rapunzel Tower so that our homes needed demolishing too. So then they could get us all outta here and build another fancy new building. You notice no rich folks got killed? Just poor folks?'

Hamilton Heights has certainly been the site of recent controversy, highlighting the plight of our valiant soldiers when they return home and the self-interested dealings of the politicians we elect to act in the interests of us all.

This newspaper will be demanding a thorough investigation of the circumstances of this tragic incident.

Document 2

Televised police statement

Investigations into the fatalities that occurred during the premature collapse of Hamilton Heights remain ongoing. Preliminary investigations have revealed no explosives other than those placed in the building in preparation for the planned demolition. Our thoughts are with the families of those who lost their lives.

Document 3

Press release by NYC Demolition Ltd

NYC Demolition Ltd is cooperating fully with the police in this matter. In addition to this, we are conducting our own internal review into how this tragic accident could have happened, including a thorough investigation into the application of health and safety procedures. We have every sympathy for those who have lost loved ones.

1 What possible causes of the early building collapse are:
   a suggested in the documents
   b excluded by the documents?
2 What other causes of the early building collapse can you think of?
3 Which causes seem most likely, based on the evidence you have?
4 What additional information do you need?
5 Who should you ask?
6 What questions should you ask?
7 What other sources should you use?
8 What are the likely consequences of the early building collapse?

You could use colour coding and diagrams to map the evidence to different possible causes.

Don't believe everything you read. Ask questions about everything before you decide what, and how much, to believe. Use the diagram to help you.

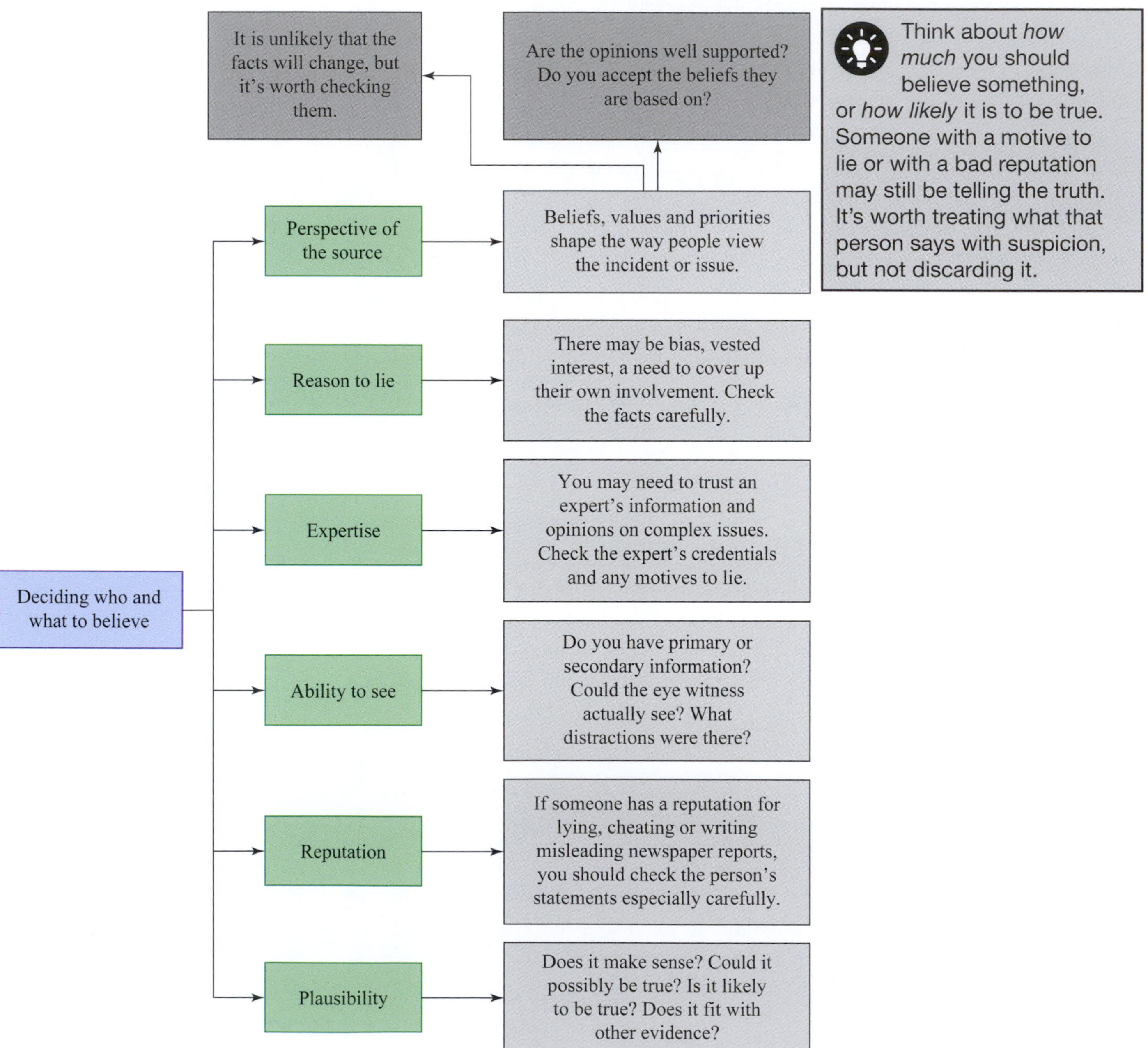
Deciding who and what to believe
Perspective of the source
Beliefs, values and priorities shape the way people view the incident or issue.
Are the opinions well supported? Do you accept the beliefs they are based on?
It is unlikely that the facts will change, but it's worth checking them.
Reason to lie
There may be bias, vested interest, a need to cover up their own involvement. Check the facts carefully.
Expertise
You may need to trust an expert's information and opinions on complex issues. Check the expert's credentials and any motives to lie.
Ability to see
Do you have primary or secondary information? Could the eye witness actually see? What distractions were there?
Reputation
If someone has a reputation for lying, cheating or writing misleading newspaper reports, you should check the person's statements especially carefully.
Plausibility
Does it make sense? Could it possibly be true? Is it likely to be true? Does it fit with other evidence?

Think about *how much* you should believe something, or *how likely* it is to be true. Someone with a motive to lie or with a bad reputation may still be telling the truth. It's worth treating what that person says with suspicion, but not discarding it.

Here is an example. Contrast the evidence base for the following two beliefs and decide which is, overall, more reliable; that is, which is more likely to be accurate.

A We live on a more or less round world, which orbits a fiery star. People are held on the planet by gravity. The planet is held in orbit around the fiery star by gravity. Scientists have used their understanding of these laws of gravity to help them put satellites in orbit around the earth, to send men to the moon, and to send probes to other planets.

B We live on a flat world which rests on a cosmic turtle, which sits on the back of a giant elephant. The sky is flat, and the sun, moon and stars are holes cut in the sky which allow the power of the gods to shine through.

When you look at the whole context for an argument, or the whole evidence base, think about how reliable the evidence is as a whole. Do some views have a more reliable evidence base than others?

Activity 3

Read these online comments in response to the Hamilton Heights collapse and answer the questions that follow.

Comments

@activist2004

This was a tragedy waiting to happen. Political greed, corporate heartlessness and cost-cutting in demolition companies were always going to be an explosive combination. We should look at the cheating politicians and businesses who really caused this.

@helicopter_mom

What was an eight-year-old boy doing in a condemned building at ten o'clock at night? Parents who would let such a young boy roam around so late at night don't deserve a child at all. It just shows what our nation is coming to.

@Soldier Joe

I was one of those vets sleeping in Hamilton Heights that night. I seen people judging me for being homeless, dirty and drunk. Well, let me ask you—if you had blood on your hands and your dying buddy's eyes in your head—could you go back to your clean house and your clean wife and your innocent kid? Could you live a clean, innocent life?

I shoulda died in Hamilton Heights, except I shoulda already died in Iraq. I seen my brothers in the military exploded by the enemy. I see that every night in my dreams, over and over. Now I seen my friends exploded in America, by Americans. By people that should thank and protect us.

John wanted to talk to a reporter. Maybe about things in Iraq, maybe about things here. I didn't want to know. I still don't. I woulda gave my life for my country. I did give a leg. I did give my mind. If my country wants to come and take the rest, it can go right ahead. I'll be waiting.

1 For each person, consider:
   a the person's perspective
   b any evidence or ideas that the person has added
   c how far you believe what the person says and why
   d whether you accept any opinions the person expresses
   e what you think about any values the person seems to hold.
2 Does this evidence give you any new suggestions about the causes of the demolition failure?
3 What do you think happened that night? Why?
4 Can you think of any possible solutions? If so, what are they, and what problems are they solving?
5 Which of these possible solutions do you think is the best? Why?

Do not dismiss an idea because there is one unreliable or implausible source in the evidence base. Try to make an overall judgement.

Activity 4

Choose one of these research areas.

- Demolition fatalities or slum clearances in at least two contrasting countries.
- Homelessness and/or mental health issues among former military personnel in at least two contrasting countries.

   1 What are the main issues of global significance in the area you have chosen?
   2 Explain how the issues are of global significance.
   3 Are the issues similar in the contrasting countries?
   4 What specific problems can you identify?
   5 What solutions are there to these problems?
   6 Which solution or solutions seem best to you? On what grounds?
   7 What perspectives can you identify? Do you accept the priorities, beliefs and values that underlie them?
   8 Examine the evidence base for different views. Overall, do some collections of sources have more reliable evidence bases than others?

Write in your research journal. Focus on:

- thoughts about how to evaluate issues, perspectives and contexts
- any new skills you have learned
- any areas you have struggled with
- how you can improve.

Evaluating reasoning and argument

Can you explain what is wrong with the reasoning in the cartoon? You don't need technical terms – just use your common sense.

When you are evaluating reasoning and argument, ask yourself these questions.

- What are the strengths of this argument?
- Is the evidence relevant to the point being made?
- How well does the author use evidence to support his or her reasoning?
- Is there a sufficient evidence base to support the view?
- Are any explanations convincing? Can you think of any alternative, plausible explanations?
- Do the reasons support any main and intermediate conclusions?
- Are there any gaps in the argument? For example, are there:
  - assumptions that you don't agree with
  - reasons you can attack
  - underlying beliefs and values you can't accept
  - holes in the argument through which counter argument can be let in?
- Are there any flaws or weaknesses in the argument? If so, explain why and how far they mean that the argument does not support the conclusion. For example, are there any weaknesses relating to:
  - the argument itself: inconsistency, contradiction, *non sequitur* (see the table below), over-generalisation, false dilemma

Latin terms are explained below.

- counter argument: *ad hominem* and straw man (see the table below)
- the consequences: slippery slope, *post hoc*
- language: emotive language in place of reasoning, blurring the meaning of terms to confuse?

When you are evaluating reasoning, it is as important to note strengths as well as weaknesses.

- If the evidence is relevant and really does support the point the author is making, say so.
- If the reasoning is logical and thoughtful, say so.

Activity 1

Complete the table. Use quick Internet searches to help you.

	Term	**Definition or description**
1	*Non sequitur*	*Non sequitur* means 'does not follow.' It is a way of saying that the argument is illogical and the conclusion does not follow from the reasoning. Many of the other weaknesses in this list are forms of non sequitur.
2	Inconsistency	
3	Contradiction	
4	Over-generalisation	
5	False dilemma	
6	*Ad hominem*	This means attacking the arguer instead of the argument.
7	'Straw man'	This refers to responding to a weak, incomplete or distorted version of a counter argument.
8	Slippery slope	
9	*Post hoc*	
10	Emotive language	Emotive language may persuade people by making them feel angry, outraged, sad, and so forth, but an argument should use logical reasoning.

When you are thinking about weakness in reasoning, think about *how* weak it is. Can you still accept the conclusion? Do you need to find another way of answering a counter argument? Has the weakness destroyed the whole argument?

Activity 2

Look at the reasoning in extracts A–D in document 1.

1 Identify any strengths and weaknesses in the reasoning and how these affect the overall strength of the reasoning.

Document 1

A. With 330,000 new migrants arriving in Britain last year, and our border controls and vetting process so woefully inept, it is hardly surprising that our judiciary is being overwhelmed.

Each morning, an unsavoury procession of characters files through the security scanner at Westminster Magistrates' Court, emptying phones and other gadgetry from the pockets of their baggy tracksuits and bomber-jackets (the standard attire of foreign criminals, it seems) before waiting to be called.

On a recent Wednesday, expected to be a quiet day because it is the summer holidays for many staff—25 cases were listed for the five extradition courts. Among those pleading their right to remain in Britain were men and women from Hungary, the Czech Republic, Lithuania, Romania, Portugal, and Spain. With 14 Polish names on the lists, I felt I could have been in Warsaw.

Most names were pronounceable only by the huddle of interpreters hired to help—also at taxpayers' expenses, of course.

http://www.dailymail.co.uk/news/article-3749905/Dispatch-Britain-s-deportation-madhouse-Wonder-s-hard-courts-kick-foreign-criminals-hearing-Read-blood-pressure-it.html#ixzz4I03EjwFr

B. … why are we not getting more medals in the Olympics? According to a Chinese news daily, India just does not spend enough money on sports and there is so little to inspire the young.

http://blogs.timesofindia.indiatimes.com/no-free-lunch/how-the-indian-girls-wowed-us-at-the-olympics/

C. First, we should rule out what cannot be done in Kashmir. A plebiscite is not possible. Of the many resolutions the UN passed on Kashmir, only two are relevant to the plebiscite: those of August 13, 1948 and January 5, 1949. A plebiscite was to follow the complete withdrawal of tribal invaders and Pakistan forces from the invaded areas of Jammu & Kashmir, after which India would draw down its forces to a number just sufficient to maintain law and order and hold a plebiscite. Pakistan never withdrew its troops, and one cannot imagine it withdrawing them now. That rules out a plebiscite permanently.

http://blogs.timesofindia.indiatimes.com/toi-edit-page/kashmir-what-can-be-done-any-workable-solution-would-have-to-include-restoration-of-full-autonomy-to-kashmir/

D. We must give the poor and the disabled, including those who take care of the disabled and are thus unable to work, enough aid for them to live.

For example, some old folks get no help from social welfare at all because they have children working in Kuala Lumpur – but it's wrong to assume that all working children help their parents or other kin

These are all extracts. How does reading the whole article change your view of the overall strength of the argument?

and it's also quite easy to establish if these children even give monthly contributions to their parents, and how much.

Sometimes a welfare officer might not recommend support to someone just because that person has a colour TV at home: I remember an old lady who could not get any help because she had a colour TV, given by her friend, but nowadays people give TVs away quite freely and it's no indication of the financial condition of a household.

http://www.thestar.com.my/opinion/columnists/all-kinds-of-everything/2016/08/19/theres-no-life-if-youre-poor-the-next-budget-should-make-adequate-provision-for-those-with-a-low-inc/

"Now, keep in mind that these numbers are only as accurate as the fictitious data, ludicrous assumptions and wishful thinking they're based upon!"

Activity 2

Read document 2 and answer the following questions.

1. What sorts of reasoning does this article contain?
2. What is the author trying to show?
3. How does he show it?
4. How effectively does he use evidence?
5. How effective is the reasoning (apart from use of evidence)? Think about strengths and weaknesses.

Document 2

AS OLYMPIC host nations go, Brazil is an outlier. Not only is it the first country to stage the summer or winter games that is neither rich nor autocratic. It also happens to be facing a record recession and unprecedented political upheaval (the suspended president, Dilma Rousseff, looks poised to be impeached over dodgy government accounting by the end of the month). Rio de Janeiro is the most violent host city to date—a statistic tragically illustrated on August 11th when a national guardsman died in hospital after being shot by drug traffickers the previous night when his vehicle took a wrong turn and entered a lawless favela (shantytown). The same day the vice-president of the International Olympic Committee, John Coates, declared that the Rio games are "the most difficult ever" for his organisation. (Though Mexico City in 1968, with dozens killed in political unrest, or Munich in 1972, with its terrorist outrage, were presumably no cakewalk, either.)

Sadly for Olympic spectators, Rio is likely to underwhelm in athletic achievement, too. Almaz Ayana of Ethiopia lopped 14 seconds off the women's 10,000-metre record yesterday. Yet such feats will be rare this games. Almost certainly, fewer world records will tumble than in previous ones.

Start with performance limits. In 2008 Mark Denny of Stanford University published a paper looking at the highest speeds achieved each year in running events from sprints to the marathon, some dating back to 1900. He used a statistical technique called extreme-value analysis to uncover trends, as well as maximum deviations from them. For the men's 100-metre dash, Dr Denny found, the human speed limit was 10.55 metres per second, which translates into 9.48 seconds, just 0.11 seconds below the record set by Jamaica's Usain Bolt in 2009. For the women's marathon, it is 5.21 metres per second, which means completing the 42.195km (26.2 mile) race in just under two hours and 15 minutes. In 2003 Paula Radcliffe, a British runner, came within 30 seconds of that mark.

Nothing in the past eight years suggests that the statistical bounds have shifted, reckons Dr Denny. Research by Geoffroy Bertholet, of France's National Institute of Sport, and colleagues confirms this diagnosis. Dr Bertholet keeps a running tab of the top ten annual results in swimming and athletics. A recent review of the evidence points to continued near-stagnation in all disciplines with only "tiny increments" in performance. Results in disciplines like men's javelin and weightlifting, where records were reset around 1990 following a string of doping scandals, have plateaued close to pre-reset levels (suggesting either that doping is back, or that physical limits have been reached—probably both). New benchmarks will keep getting rarer and more incremental, Dr Bertholet predicts.

Rio is not the ideal place to buck this trend. For a start, it lies at sea level. This is a boon to beach volleyball players, who get to compete in their discipline's spiritual home on Copacabana. But it is a bane for many track-and-field athletes, because it means air in Rio is denser than at higher altitudes, and drag greater. This matters to sprinters, jumpers and throwers, whose effort is mostly anaerobic, and therefore less affected by the extra oxygen. One explanation for the above-trend track-and-field performance in 1968 was that the Olympic games that year were held in Mexico City. At an altitude of 2,240 metres the air is a fifth thinner than in Rio, providing 20% less resistance. Eight of that year's 25 best results for the 100 metre dash were recorded at the games. Most of the rest were notched up by athletes preparing for Mexico City at high altitudes. And then there was Bob Beamon's record-smashing 8.9 metre long-jump.

Long-distance runners will no doubt enjoy Rio's abundant oxygen. But not its subtropical heat. Although the city has been unseasonably chilly, with temperatures falling as low as 11 degrees celsius at night, the coming days are forecast to be balmier. This will be pleasant for spectators, but does not augur well for long-distance runners. The best marathon times, for instance, are notched up in races such as Berlin's, where temperatures throughout the course range between 10 and 16 degrees Celsius. This is unlikely both this Sunday morning, when the women race, or during the men's event a week later, meteorologists predict.

Such factors are, of course, less relevant for indoor events like weightlifting, cycling or swimming. But here too Rio's Olympians are unlikely to excel. For one thing, a recent crackdown on doping probably means less scope for artificial augmentation. At the same time, organisers are running out of clever, legal boosts. There is, for example, a practical limit to how much temperature can be raised in the velodrome to force the warmer air to rise to the ceiling and decrease its density on the track. The addition of a step on swimming-pool starting blocks to allow swimmers to generate more force during the initial plunge—introduced a day after the fullbody suits were banned in 2009—was a one-off.

On the bright side, athletes in disciplines where performance is not gauged with a tape measure or stopwatch continue to astonish. Anyone who, like your correspondent, was fortunate enough to watch Simone Biles (pictured), a 19-year-old American gymnast, perform her gold-winning routines in the ladies' overall final on August 11th cannot but marvel at the physical prowess of some conspecifics.

And even in stagnating disciplines humans retain the ability to spring surprises. Take Nijad Rahimov, a weightlifter from Kazakhstan competing in the under-77kg category. Mr Rahimov trailed the holder of the category's overall world record from China, Lu Xiaojun, after the snatch. Improbably, he heaved 214kg in the clean-and-jerk, beating not just Mr Lu's 202kg, but also the 16-year-old record for that lift—by a whopping four kilos. Such feats are becoming rarer. But that makes them all the more special.

http://www.economist.com/blogs/gametheory/2016/08/olympics

Activity 4

How effective is the reasoning in document 3?

Document 3

The impotence of the United Nations in halting the level of violence is truly appalling. The world currently needs an international judicial structure that is independent of the power constellation prevailing in the UN Security Council.

The United Nations, both in principle and in practise, was the closest thing we would have had to a world government, that comes together to tackle the challenges faced by all humanity. However the UN is an utterly useless organisation when it comes to protecting human rights and enforcing security. It has failed to stop the invasion of Iraq which has resulted in the death of thousands of civilians, and made Iraq worse than it was under Saddam Hussein. The UN has proven itself a failure for its entire history and will continue to do so. It is a completely impotent organisation with no will or authority to implement decisions.

The UN is and always has been a non-governmental organisation and has no authority in itself and its utopian and impractical ideals make it a toothless tiger.

The institution has no credibility. Even though the genocide in the Balkans occurred under the organisation's nose, it was unable to protect the innocent. The sanctions on Iraq which led to the death of millions, mostly children, by the West occurred in collusion with the UN. The Genocide in Darfur exposed the institution's impotence. How can the UN promote democracy and human rights when members like the US do not even acknowledge a world court?

The UN does need reform to adequately address the problems of the 21st century. In Winston Churchill's words, the UN was set up not to get us to heaven, but to save us from hell. The organisation has unfortunately succumbed to the malignant ravages of politics and bureaucracy. We must strive to apply workable solutions to the problems the world faces today. The UN must be restructured to bring a real sense of equity to the international forum.

As long as the US is bent on unilateralism and ignores its international obligations and duties as the world's only superpower, the security apparatus of the UN is in trouble. The US is good at adopting a stand-back-and-wait-and-see-what-happens attitude. They have used this head-in-sand approach as early as 1919 when they refused to ratify the treaty of Versailles.

The UN, like its predecessor, the League of Nations, was doomed to fall from since the day of it came into existence [sic]. In fact, the UN inherited many of the functions and shortcomings of its predecessor. On disarmament, very little has been achieved. It seems that today, more nations have nuclear weapons than before the non-proliferation act came into being. Some permanent members of the Security Council are quiet [sic] selective in the kinds of nations they choose to prevent from acquiring weapons of mass destruction.

In 1945, the UN was founded amidst much euphoria. It was to be mankind's "last best hope." The UN has done some outrageous things in the past, as when it herded Muslim men into Sarajevo, methodically disarmed them and left them to be shot by militiamen, or when it ordered its commanding officer in Rwanda not to seize arms caches that were about to be used for the genocide that left more than a million Tutsis dead and many more disabled or displaced.

The UN is an organisation that can churn out plenty of resolutions but is helpless in implementing them.

http://www.khaleejtimes.com/letters-to-the-editor/the-un-is-defunct

Activity 5

Do any of the issues in this chapter interest you? Do some research and start building up the context of the arguments you find here.

Write in your learning journal. Focus on:

- identifying strength and weakness in reasoning
- any new skills you have learned
- any areas you are struggling with
- how you can improve.

Reflect

Reflecting on issues, perspectives and learning

Reflection is quiet thinking, which can be either conscious or sub-conscious. It is useful for spotting patterns, and for sorting out what you really think and feel, and why. You can reflect on issues, perspectives and on your own learning.

It is important to find regular time for reflection because:

- it is such a valuable process
- it is linked to mindfulness and can help you deal with stress
- your assessed work needs to demonstrate evidence of reflection and you simply can't fake it.

As with the other skills you have been developing, it is more important to be able to do it, than to have knowledge about it. This chapter guides you through activities which will help you to reflect. As you progress, you should find that achieving the calm state of mind, in which reflection best happens, becomes much easier. Section B provides opportunities for you to reflect on a range of issues and perspectives in global contexts, as well as on your own learning.

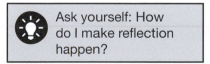

Why do you think that Rodin's 'Thinker' is in this pose?

Reflection is quiet thinking. It can be conscious or unconscious.

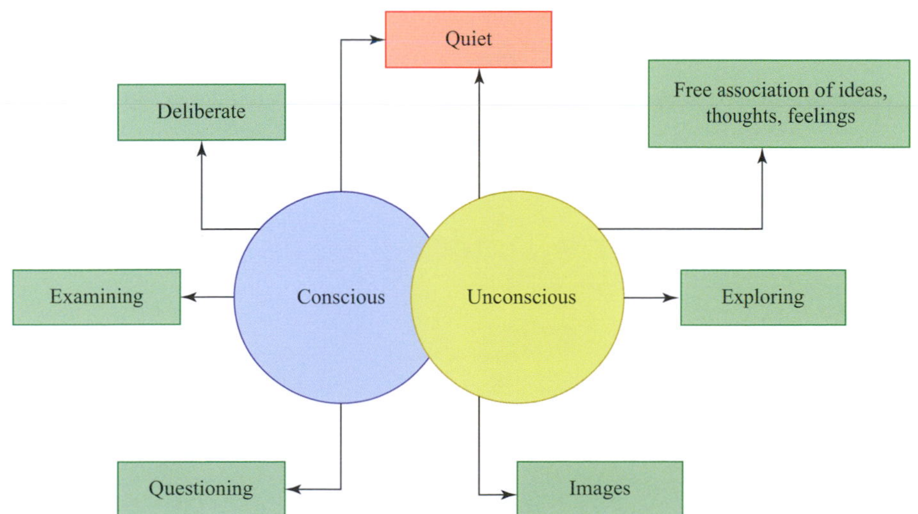

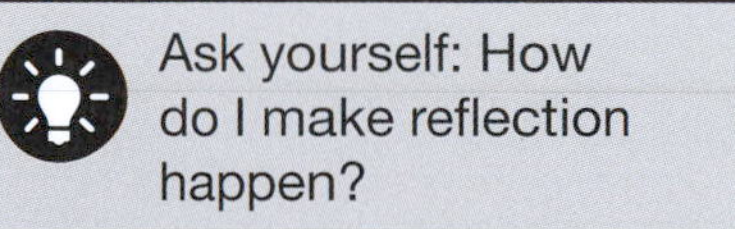

Ask yourself: How do I make reflection happen?

People reflect in different ways. Find a way that helps you to sort and process ideas. Some ways are:

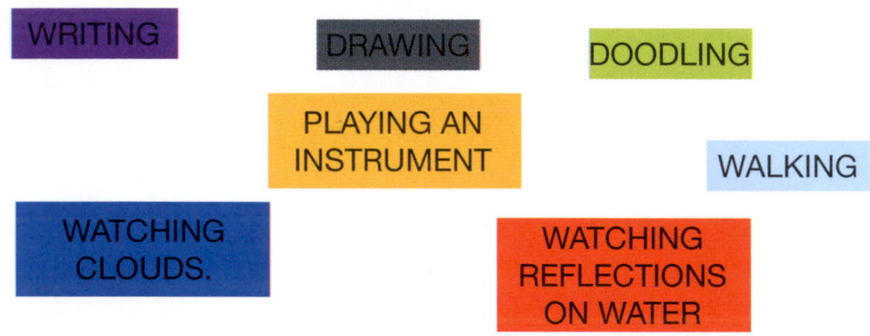

It doesn't matter how you reflect, provided you give yourself mental space to listen to your thoughts.

Reflection is useful in many ways:

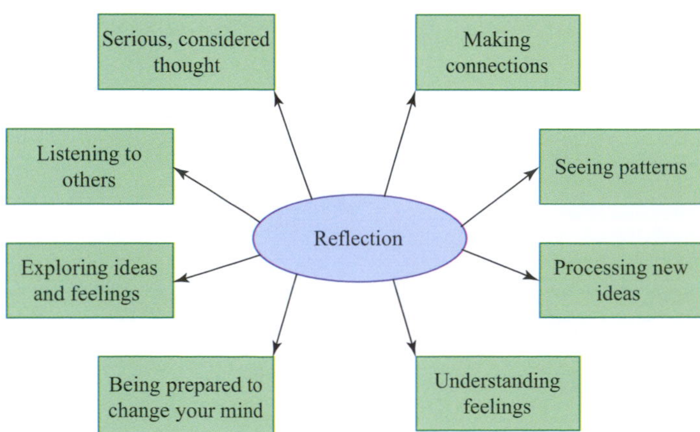

Questions to ask yourself to help reflection:

Reflecting on issues

- What do I think about this issue?
- Why do I think this?
- How has my position changed in response to the evidence, arguments, ideas and perspectives I have come across?
- Can I see any patterns or connections?

Reflecting on perspectives

- How does this perspective challenge my perspective?
- How does this perspective challenge my priorities, beliefs, values and assumptions?
- Can I understand and empathise with this perspective even if my perspective is very different?

Reflecting on your own position

- How do I feel about my underlying beliefs, priorities and values?
- Do I want to change them?
- Have they been changed by the process of thinking about different issues and perspectives?
- How do I feel about this?
- Are some of my beliefs based on fear, anxiety or prejudice?
- Are some of my beliefs influenced by peer pressure or by unreliable sources?
- Do I believe what I want to believe despite the evidence?
- Can I or should I try to change my beliefs, priorities and values? If so, how?
- Do I feel overwhelmed by all the new ideas and information?
- How can I sort it out so that I can make sense of the new ideas and information?

Reflecting on learning

- How am I learning?
- How well am I learning?
- How independently am I learning?
- What skills am I using?
- How well am I using them?
- What other skills could I or should I be using?
- How can I achieve this?

Writing in your learning journal on a regular basis will help you to reflect. You can use the questions in this section to help you.

Activity 1

This activity is a mind exercise.

Find a quiet place. Close your eyes. Imagine that you are floating up to the clouds, but leave all your thoughts and feelings behind you. Find a comfortable, warm cloud so that you can lie comfortably and safely and look down.

Of course, clouds aren't warm and comfortable places to lie – but it's a nice image, and it can work. Try it!

You should be able to see your thoughts and feelings. Allow them to swim around on the surface without really thinking about them.

- Can you tell the difference between your thoughts and feelings?
- How are they linked?
- Can you change them?
- Can you see links and patterns between ideas?
- Is the distance from your thoughts and feelings giving you a new perspective?

Activity 2

Find a quiet, calm place.

Think of an issue, a feeling, a perspective or an aspect of your learning that is bothering you. Take deep breaths and stop thinking.

Take a crayon and several sheets of paper. Use your non-dominant hand (your left hand if you are right-handed, your right hand if you are left-handed).

Write all the words that you associate with the issue, feeling, perspective or aspect of learning.

Draw images related to this issue.

This can help you to understand feelings and ideas in a new way, especially ideas and feelings that bother you.

Activity 3

Read the learning journal entries (A–G) below.

1 How do you respond?
2 Make a note of any reflection on issues, perspectives or learning.
3 Give advice on how to improve where necessary.

A. Today in Global Perspectives we did migration. We read an article. It said that migrants benefit the economy. It talked about paying tax and creating jobs. It's rubbish.

B. We were looking at an article about migration benefiting the country today. It said that migrants contribute more in tax than they take in benefits, and that they create more jobs than they take, because they buy stuff, go out etc. The information was taken from a government report and an OECD report. It seems like reliable information. But I don't want to believe it. I can see that it's illogical to think that migrants are all on benefits and that they take our jobs. I understand that many migrants are nice people. But I feel like migration is a bad thing. I feel threatened.

C. I understand that some countries feel that human rights are a Western imposition, and that they should be able to make their own laws according to their customs and their level of development. I would probably feel the same if the Chinese tried to make us accept their values, like putting the community before the individual, and prioritising strong government over democratic choice of leader. But I still can't believe that torture or gender inequality is ever right.

D. I can't do Global Perspectives. It's too hard. I just want the teacher to tell me what to learn.

E. I am not doing very well in Global Perspectives. I will do better tomorrow.

F. I'm really enjoying being able to think for myself in Global Perspectives. It's like, suddenly, I matter. If I find a topic boring, Mrs Emerson is ok about me researching a different one, so long as I can justify it. I like that. I didn't like doing climate change, because we've done it so many times already. So now I am looking at architectural priorities. I want to be an architect. I feel like I ought to research ideas about architectures and the environment, but what I'm really interested in is how different office layouts can affect creativity and interaction. I wonder whether this will be the same in every culture, or if they are generalising from what works in companies like Google.

G. I like researching, and I think that I am pretty good at identifying good sources of information and I can understand when the information is relevant. But I don't really feel comfortable with evaluating the strengths and weaknesses of reasoning. I'm going to ask Mrs Emerson for help, I'm going to get a book to help me, and I'm going to practice – I could find opinion pieces and make myself sit down and think about their strengths and weaknesses.

Activity 4

Consider an issue that you have been working on in your Global Perspectives lessons.

1 Ask yourself the questions in this chapter, and write answers. Do not judge the quality of your writing, or worry about how much you are writing. Just keep writing.

2 Re-read what you have written. Underline or highlight anything that you think is reflective.

Activity 5

Write in your learning journal.

What do you think you should focus on?

Communicating

When you are writing for Global Perspectives, you need to think about:

- deciding on your evidence base
- answering the question
- using reasoning
- the purpose of your writing.

Communication refers to all of the ways in which you share information, ideas, arguments and feelings with others. In Global Perspectives and Research you will need to communicate in a variety of ways, including:

- academic writing
- formal presentation
- listening and speaking in team work
- listening and speaking in debates and discussions

This chapter will help you to develop the skills you need to communicate effectively in different ways. You will work on:

- understanding when to use different communication skills
- writing clear, effective academic English
- structuring your ideas into effective reasoning
- speaking effectively to an audience
- using images effectively

Communication skills

Activity 1

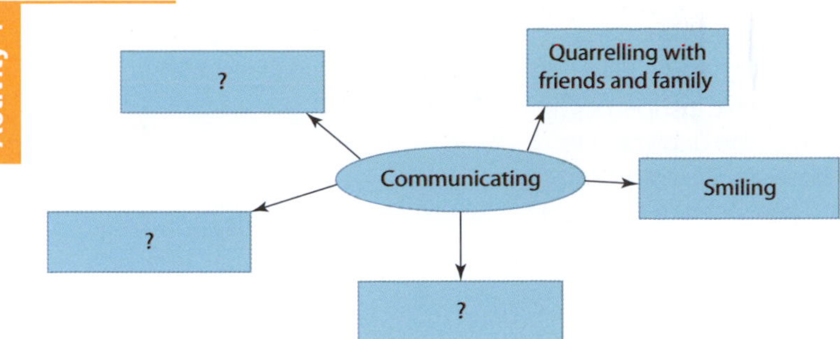

1 Think of all the ways that you communicate with others. Complete the diagram, adding to it if you need to.
2 How important is listening in communication?
3 How do people use their body language to help them communicate?
4 How important is body language in communication?
5 Which communication skills do you think are most important in Global Perspectives? Why?
6 Match the communication skills you have identified to different parts of the assessment.
7 Do you need to add any more communication skills?

Activity 2

1 Summarise and express the ideas in these passages in clear, simple English.

a Causal attribution of recent biological trends to climate change is complicated because non-climatic influences dominate local, short-term biological changes. Any underlying signal from climate change is likely to be revealed by analyses that seek systematic trends across diverse species and geographic regions. . . here we apply diverse analyses to more than 1,700 species, and show that recent biological trends match climate change predictions. Global meta-analyses documented significant range shifts averaging 6.1 km per decade towards the poles (or metres per decade upwards) and significant and mean advancement of spring events by 2.3 days per decade. We define a diagnostic fingerprint of temporal and spatial 'sign-switching' responses uniquely predicted by twentieth century climate trends. Among appropriate large-scale/long-term/ multi-species data sets, this diagnostic fingerprint was found for 279 species. This suite of analyses generates very high confidence that climate change is already affecting living systems.

Source: Nature, 421, 37–42 (2 January 2003) http://www.nature.com/nature/journal/v421/n6918/abs/nature01286.html

It is important to use your own, clear English.

Quoting is useful sometimes. However, your essays, presentations and reflective papers should be mainly in your own words.

b Do superpower interventions to install and prop up political leaders in other countries subsequently result in more or less democracy, and does this effect vary depending on whether the intervening superpower is democratic or authoritarian? While democracy may be expected to decline contemporaneously with superpower influence, the effect on democracy after a few years is far from obvious. The absence of reliable information on covert interventions has hitherto served as an obstacle to seriously addressing these questions. The recent declassification of Cold War CIA and KGB documents now makes it possible to systematically address these questions in the Cold War context . . . We find that superpower interventions are followed by significant declines in democracy, and that the substantive effects are large. Perhaps surprisingly, once endogeneity is addressed, US and Soviet interventions have equally detrimental effects on the subsequent level of democracy ... one should not expect significant differences in the adverse institutional consequences of superpower interventions based on whether the intervening superpower is a democracy or a dictatorship.

Source: Easterly, W., Satyanath, S., and Berger, D. 'Superpower interventions and their consequences for democracy' https://www.brookings.edu/research/superpower-interventions-and-their-consequences-for-democracy

c Huycke makes a stand against a popular present way of thinking about crafts, in which a surplus of technical skills are observed as something that would stand in the way of true expression and in which even the lack of apparent refined technical skills would point at the presence of some kind of intellectual concept. Huycke refers here to an article by Glenn Adamson who draws attention to a new trend: 'the sloppy craft movement', an outcome of the 'post-disciplinary art environment' and today's way of educating skills, 'blurring the line between hobbyism and professional endeavour'. Huycke's research should be observed in the light of this discussion, for sloppiness and haphazardness have become the new standard in contemporary crafts. I would like to present Huycke as an example of a relatively young generation of craftspeople who are interested in how they can bring traditional techniques and materials further as a serious contemporary means of artistic expression.

Source: 'Jewellery and tradition,' Liesbeth den Besten, in *On Jewellery,* Arnoldsche Art Publishers, Stuttgart

Activity 3

1 Match each phrase in ordinary language to the phrase in academic language that has a similar meaning.

Ordinary language	Academic language
Overall, I think that...	It is clear that...
Obviously...	This essay will consider...
I am going to write about...	Research has been unable to demonstrate whether or not...
Who cares anyway?	It seems reasonable to conclude that...
No one knows	It has become impossible to justify the importance of...

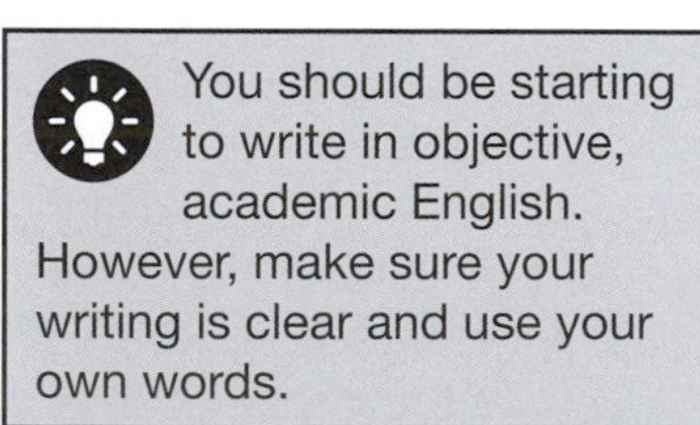
You should be starting to write in objective, academic English. However, make sure your writing is clear and use your own words.

2 What is the difference between the following three phrases?

a Research has so far been unable to demonstrate whether or not...

b Research has been unable to conclusively prove that...

c Research indicates that there is no empirical foundation for the belief that...

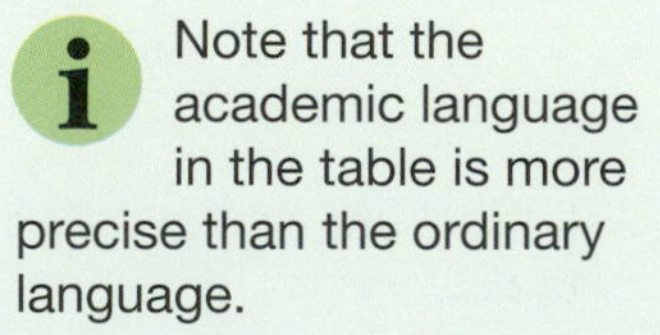
Note that the academic language in the table is more precise than the ordinary language.

3 Use online searches to help you find a variety of useful academic phrases to express:
   a major essay signposts
   b agreement
   c disagreement
   d giving reasons
   e giving examples
   f giving consequences
   g justifying
   h explaining
   i listing
   j contrasting.

Activity 4

1 Put these phrases in the appropriate box or boxes below.
   a As the image in this slide shows...
   b When I started thinking about this, I believed that...
   c Let's take a look at this chart...
   d The research indicates that...
   e You might be asking yourself, how can this be?
   f In this paper I will be exploring the question of whether...
   g To conclude,...

Essay	Presentation	Reflective paper

2 Work in groups. Add useful phrases to each box.

You should communicate differently for different purposes. Generally, you can address members of the audience directly in a presentation to develop their interest, and you can include your own thoughts and feelings in a reflective paper.

Activity 5

1 Which of the claims below will help to answer the question: To what extent is the rise of new global superpowers a threat to the West? Explain your answers.

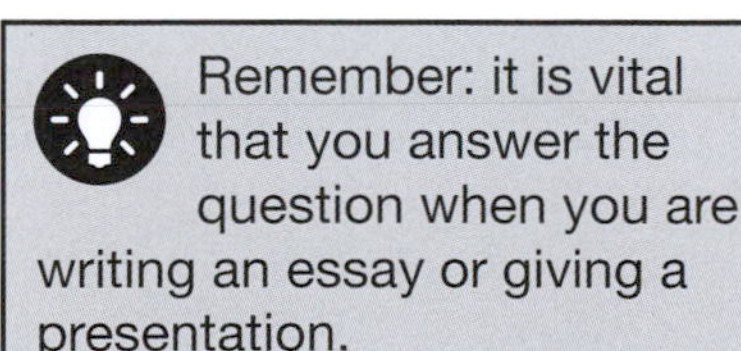
Remember: it is vital that you answer the question when you are writing an essay or giving a presentation.

   a China, Brazil and India have been growing more important for about a decade.
   b China seems inclined to engage in economic partnerships around the world.
   c India is the world's biggest democracy.
   d The leading Western powers all owe China significant amounts of money.
   e If there are new superpowers, the old superpowers will have to share the power.

Activity 6

Use the following structure to show the outline of reasoning in each passage from activity 2.

Even though...	make a point against the main conclusion
However, ...	answer the point against the main conclusion
because...	• main reason one • main reason two • main reason three
Therefore, ...	main conclusion

Essays and presentations should develop reasoning to answer a question, based on good understanding of the evidence base for different perspectives and views. One possible structure is shown here.

E Evidence, explanations and examples from the broad evidence base

R Reason supported by evidence, giving support to the main reason or intermediate conclusion

E Evidence, explanations and examples from the broad evidence base of a contrasting perspective

R Reason supporting a contrasting view

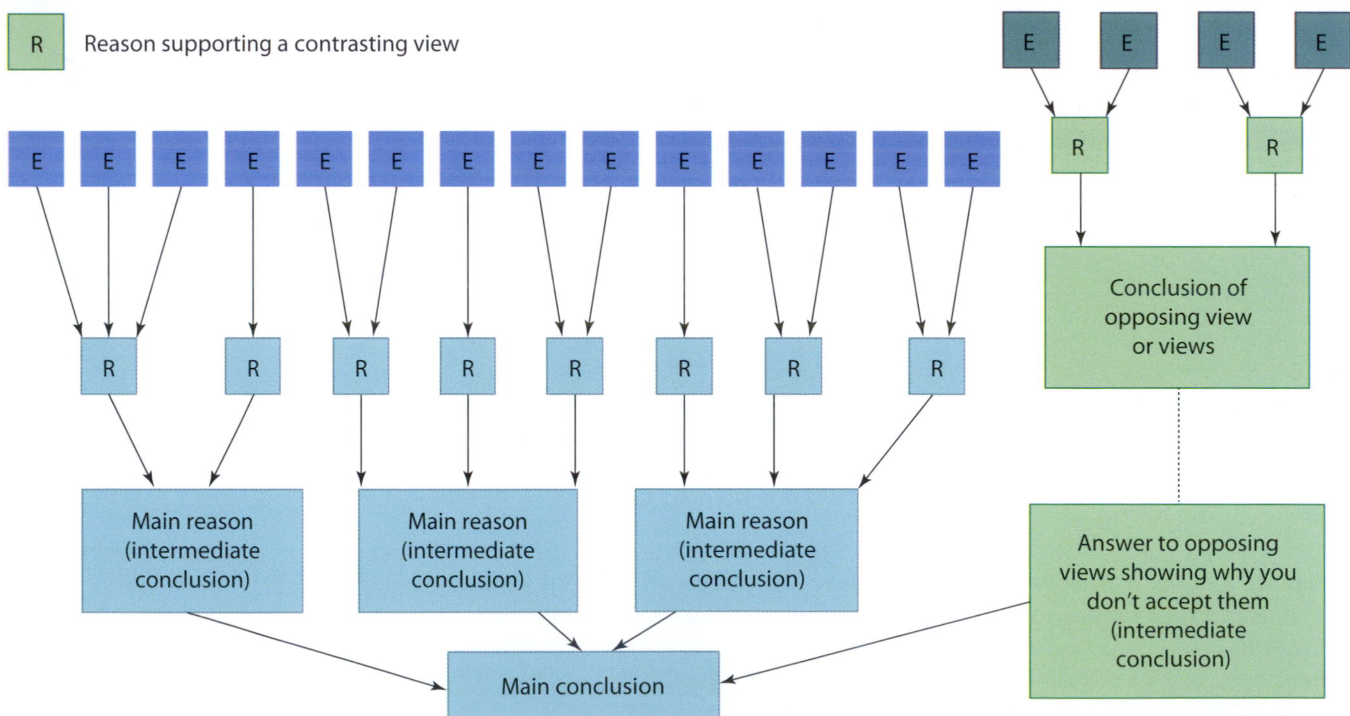

Activity 7

Choose a research question that appeals to you. You could choose your own example or one of these.

- Skills should be protected as an important part of our cultural heritage.
- Art should be about important international ideas not mere display of technical skills.
- How can HEDCs help LEDCs to develop without significant increases in CO_2 emissions?

Follow these steps.

1 Read, research, question, think.

2 Decide on your conclusion. Make sure it is precise.

3 Give three key ideas to support a conclusion. This should be a conclusion that you think you will agree with.

4 Give reasons, evidence and explanations to support each of your key ideas.

5 Give one or two key ideas against your conclusion.

When you are looking for ideas against the conclusion, consider completely different perspectives. Make sure you research the evidence base for the perspective you are questioning. You need to understand what you are arguing against.

6 Give reasons, evidence and explanations to support any ideas against your conclusion.

7 Answer those reasons, evidence and explanations.

8 Add relevant academic phrases to signpost and structure your writing. Choose phrases appropriate to the essay, presentation or reflective paper.

9 Write your ideas on paper. Don't worry about perfection.

10 Edit your material. Be brutal – if material doesn't serve a purpose in answering your question, delete it.

Leave out any material that is irrelevant to your question.

11 Edit your work again, asking these questions. Is your answer to the research question logical? Have you answered the question? How could you improve your writing?

12 Get some distance from your writing by doing something completely different. This will help you to look at it with fresh eyes when you start again.

13 After a while, edit your work again. By this stage, you should only find minor typographical errors to correct.

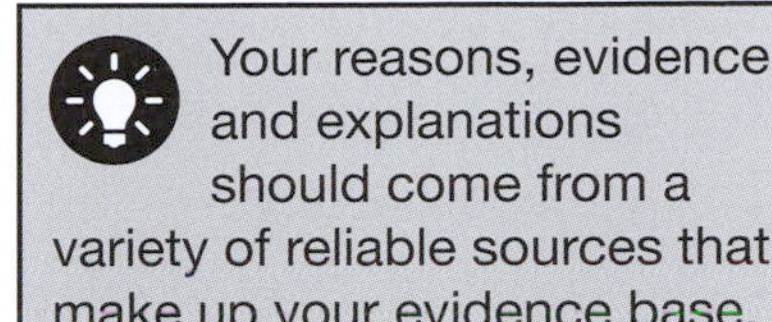

Your reasons, evidence and explanations should come from a variety of reliable sources that make up your evidence base.

Don't forget to cite your sources accurately.

Make sure you are not being unfairly biased against the view you disagree with. Apply the same high standards to arguments in support of your own view.

Communicating in a presentation

What is a presentation?

A presentation:

- is usually a talk to a specific audience
- usually has images to support the talk
- may include short sound or video files
- may include questions from the audience.

What are the characteristics of a good Global Perspectives presentation?

Giving a good presentation involves:

- arguing coherently
- answering the research question clearly
- speaking clearly (not mumbling, or speaking too quietly or too quickly)
- speaking from knowledge (not reading out material)
- making effective eye contact and gestures
- limiting the text on presentation slides
- including only images that are relevant to and support the talk
- making visual elements appealing to help to engage the audience
- including only short, relevant and purposeful audio and/or video files
- meeting assessment requirements
- sticking to the time limit.

"OK, I'm now going to read out loud every single slide to you, word for word, until you all wish I'd just stop talking."

Activity 1

1 Watch three or four TED talks on the subject you are researching.
2 Number the speakers 1 to 3 (or 4). Which speaker is most interesting? Why?
3 Give each speaker a rating for each of the points below.

	☺	😐	☹
Simple, clear explanations			
Structured, coherent argument			
Eye contact and body language			
Speaks clearly			
Speaking from knowledge (not reading or mumbling)			
Use of visuals			
Use of audio or video			
Interesting to you			

Activity 2

1 Arrange to have someone video you doing a practice presentation.
2 Watch the video and give yourself a rating using the grid from activity 1.
3 What can you do to improve?

Just because you *can* do something, it does not mean you should. It is easy to spend hours compiling flying animations and 'exciting' features that will not improve your presentation.

Activity 3

1 What are the main advantages and disadvantages of PowerPoint?
2 What are the main advantages and disadvantages of Prezi?
3 What are the main advantages and disadvantages of using a poster for your presentation?
4 What are the main advantages and disadvantages of having materials such as photographs or artefacts displayed around you?
5 Consider the advantages and disadvantages of any other forms of presentation.

Activity 4

How effective are these slides in communicating a point?

A

Interoperability
Since the end of the Cold War, interoperability has been at the heart of a debate over the viability and relevance of the NATO Alliance in a new security environment. The shift of focus from territorial defense to multinational expeditionary missions (Afghanistan, Kosovo, Libya) and the challenges encountered executing them has demonstrated the limits of Allied interoperability. While some interoperability challenges (sovereignty concerns, differing national interests, cuts in defense spending, support for local dense industries, and disparities in technological capabilities) can only be resolved by politicians at the strategic level, there are also numerous tactical challenges to interoperability. To mitigate them, NATO enacted the "Connected Forces Initiative" (CFI).

B

C

What is the evidence?

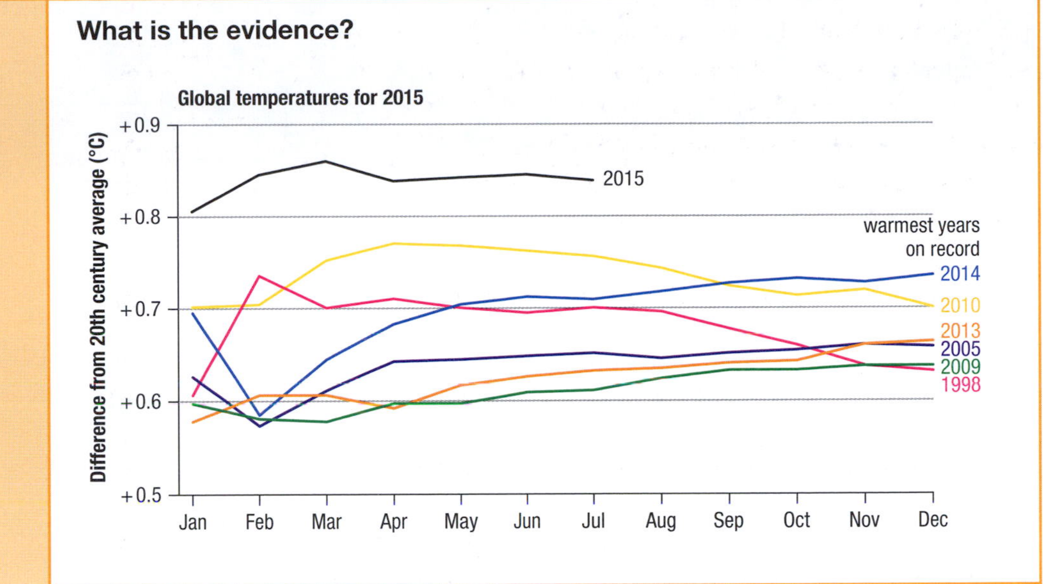

Write in your learning journal. Focus on:

- communicating in writing
- communicating in speech
- any issues you have had and how you might solve them.

Collaborate

Collaboration skills

Collaborating with others

Collaboration means working together, and there are a range of different skills that people can use to make their teamwork more effective. This chapter provides you with opportunities to consider which skills are useful in teamwork, extend your understanding through research, and put your teamwork skills into practice.

> **Aa** Collaboration: working with someone to produce something; teamwork.

Activity 1

Work in a group of 3–5 students.

1. In your group, agree on a list of the ten most important collaboration skills.
2. Put the skills in order of how important your group thinks they are, with 1 as the most important.
3. How easy was it to agree?
4. Does your group agree with other groups in the class?
5. How easy is it for the whole class to agree a list?
6. What skills are you using in your groups and in your class to agree the list?
7. Do these skills match the list you wrote? Why or why not?

> Is using the Internet to find a range of skills to consider for this activity cheating or is it putting your research skills to good use?

Activity 2

You will work in teams of approximately five people for this activity. All of you will complete tasks 1 and 2, but the teams will be different for task 1 and task 2. The teacher will nominate a leader for Teams 1 and 2.

- Team 1's leader will be autocratic, like a dictator. The team members must do what the leader says, and will not be allowed to give opinions, argue or disobey.
- Team 2's leader will listen to the team and then make decisions. Team members should express opinions, but must accept the leader's decisions.
- Team 3 must democratically elect their leader. There must be at least two candidates.
- Team 4 will have no leader.

Task 1

Prepare a treasure hunt for a younger age group. There should be a series of clues which lead to the treasure. The clues should be based around mathematical puzzles, a foreign language or problem-solving skills, for example.

Task 2

Choose a local problem with global relevance and allocate different areas for research.

Answer these questions about tasks 1 and 2.

1 What criteria for success would you use for each task?
2 How successful was your team for each task?
3 What problems did your team encounter?
4 How did you overcome these problems?
5 How would you overcome or prevent the problems next time?
6 What difference did the different leadership styles make in each task to:
   a the decision-making process
   b the efficiency with which each task was completed
   c the quality of the results
   d how much fun the activity was?
7 What have you learned about:
   a leadership styles
   b your own relationship with leaders?

Activity 3

1 In small teams, research team-building games.
2 Select a game you would like to play.
3 Prepare and give a short presentation to persuade the class to vote for the game you have chosen. This should include:
   - the aims of the game (in terms of team building and skills development)
   - an overview of the game, including what players will do and how it will work in the classroom or school grounds.
   - the benefits of the game.

The teacher can veto any games that he or she thinks are unsafe or inappropriate. The class considers the remaining games, then students vote on which game to play.

Everyone plays the game.

Activity 4

1 What skills did you use in Activity 3 during the:
   - preparation
   - presentation
   - game?
2 How successful was your teamwork at each stage?
3 What would you improve next time? How?
4 What have your learned about how you work with others?

What criteria are you using to decide on what counts as success at each stage?

Activity 5

1 Lucy is extremely bright and good at academic work, but she is struggling to fit into her team.

   a What should Lucy do to improve?

   b What can other team members do to help Lucy?

   c What can the team leader do to help Lucy?

2 Manosh won't stop talking. His voice is going a round and a round in your head and you can't think clearly.

   a What can you do to improve the situation?

   b What can other team members do?

   c What can the team leader do?

3 Toby and Sita have an idea that they are pushing ahead with. You don't think that their idea will work, because it won't meet the Global Perspectives syllabus, but you can't get them to listen to you. What should you do? Why do you think they won't listen?

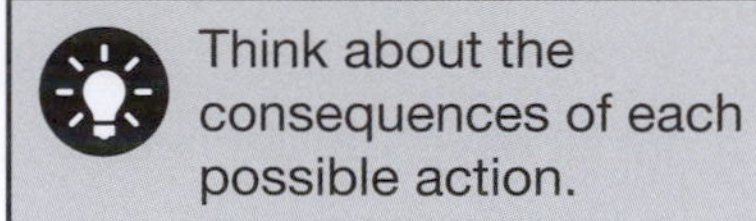

Think about the consequences of each possible action.

What assumptions are you making about each of the people mentioned? What role do your own feelings and insecurities play in your response to each of these people?

Write in your learning journal. Focus on:

- teamwork and leadership skills
- how teamwork and leadership are different from academic skills
- how you feel about teamwork and leadership skills
- any areas you are struggling with
- how you can improve.

SECTION B
Applying skills in global contexts

Section B is divided into five chapters:

B1 Changing countries.

B2 Changing world

B3 Changing technologies

B4 Decisions about limited resources

B5 Decisions about international fairness

Each chapter brings together a number of topics from the Global Perspectives and Research syllabus. Within the chapters there are also opportunities to draw links between the topics in different ways.

Each of these chapters includes:

- Activities to get you started.
- Stimulus material.
- Skills development activities.
- 'Research and discuss' boxes
- Assessment practice.
- Quotations.
- Marginal questions.

You will need to navigate your own path through the chapters, making use of the material here to help you to develop and apply your skills, but remember that your own research is important too

Changing countries

Topics

- Changing national identities
- Cultural heritage
- Gender issues
- Political systems
- Standard of living and/or quality of life
- Migration and work

Activities to get you started

During these introductory activities, you will start to explore and reflect on a range of issues, themes and perspectives relating to the overarching idea of 'Changing countries' and the Global Perspectives topics within this main idea. You may find interesting issues and perspectives which you would like to research further, and you may start to reflect on and develop your own perspective.

Activity 1

A

B

C

D

E

F

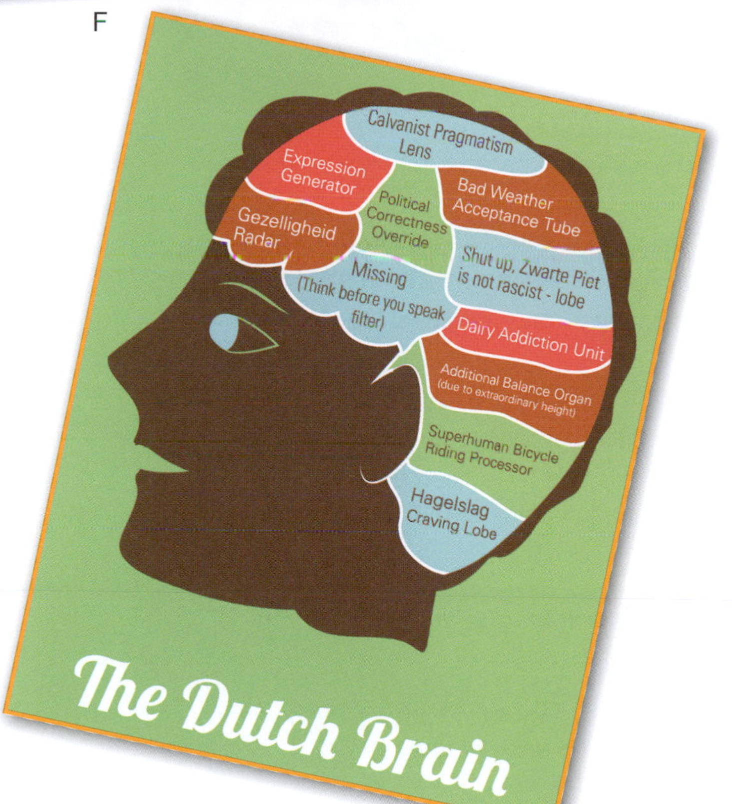

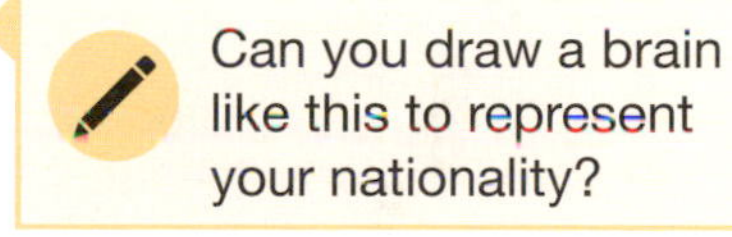

Can you draw a brain like this to represent your nationality?

1 What different issues and perspectives do these images raise on the topics in this chapter?

2 Does the whole class agree? Why or why not?

Activity 2

It's like everyone tells a story about themselves inside their own head. Always. All the time. That story makes you what you are. We build ourselves out of that story.

Patrick Rothfuss, *The Name of the Wind*

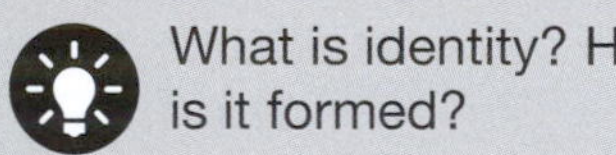

What is identity? How is it formed?

1 Look at the images, which show how a student called Sapphi sees her identity.
   a Use the images to help you discuss what is important to Sapphi's identity.
   b What issues relating to the topics in this chapter do these images raise?
2 Choose and explain five images to show your own personal identity, as Sapphi has done.
3 Compare the different images class members have chosen.
4 Discuss how you have chosen the images that really show your identity.
5 Comment on any issues and perspectives that have been raised during class discussions, relating them to the topics in this chapter.

The idea that your identity is a solid, consistent, tangible thing is an illusion.

Grayson Perry

When my perceptions are remov'd for any time, as by sound sleep; so long am I insensible of myself, *and may truly be said not to exist.*

David Hume

Activity 3

A

B

C

1 Which national identities are represented by these images?
2 How well do you think these images represent the different national identities? (Think about various regional, religious, political and economic perspectives.)
3 Which issues and perspectives do the images raise, relating to the topics in this chapter?
4 Each person in the class should choose and explain five images to represent their national identity.
5 Compare the different views that people in the class have of their national identities.
6 Make a display of the images selected by the class, including explanations relating to the issues and perspectives shown.

Research and discuss

How do you think about national identity without resorting to oversimplification, prejudice and stereotypes?

Activity 4

1 Complete the questionnaire.

2 Discuss the results in class. Do you all agree? Why or why not?

1 = I disagree strongly　2 = I disagree a bit　3 = I'm not sure
4 = I agree a bit　5 = I agree strongly

		1	2	3	4	5
1	My nationality is an important part of my personal identity.					
2	Being (my nationality) means the same to me as it did to my grandparents.					
3	It is important for a nation to have a common national identity.					
4	A shared cultural heritage is an important part of a national identity.					
5	A shared language is an important part of a national identity.					
6	I am interested in how the past led to the present in my country.					
7	Patriotism is the greatest virtue an individual can have.					
8	Democracy is an important part of our national identity.					
9	Migration is changing our national identity.					
10	Tolerance and respect for others are important parts of our national identity.					

Research and discuss

What is national identity? How is it related to personal identity?

How do cultural heritage, political systems, gender issues and migration affect national identities?

Has any nation anything more precious than the language of its fathers?

Herder

The strength of a nation derives from the integrity of the home.

Confucius

Terrorism has no nationality or religion.

Vladimir Putin

The individual has always had to struggle to keep from being overwhelmed by the tribe. If you try it, you will be lonely often, and sometimes frightened. But no price is too high to pay for the privilege of owning yourself.

Friedrich Nietzsche

National identity is frequently formed in deliberate opposition to other groups and therefore serves to perpetuate conflict.

Francis Fukuyama

Activity 5

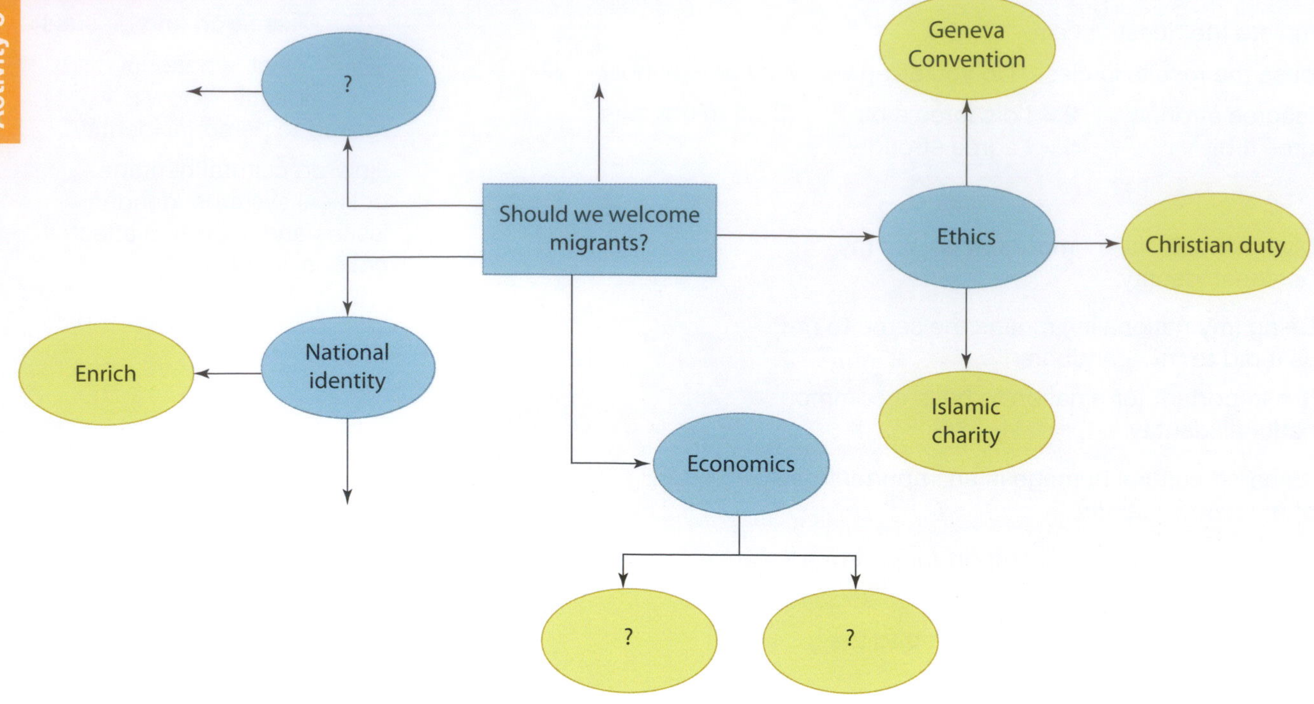

1 Complete and expand the mind map about whether we should welcome migrants. Use the themes to help you explore different perspectives.

2 Draw a mind map using the themes to help you explore different perspectives on one of these questions.

   a Should we all accept a reduction in the standard of living in the near future?

   b Should we have a third child?

   c Should I vote in the next election?

   d How can our society address the negative effects of 'lad culture' on young men and women?

   e To what extent is preserving our cultural heritage a priority?

Research and discuss

How far should we tolerate the beliefs of others?

I have seen great intolerance shown in support of tolerance.

Samuel Taylor Coleridge

Stimulus material

Document 1

African Migrants: Payback time?

25th September 2015

By Carlos Lopes

Since the beginning of the year a relentless flow of images from the Italian island of Lampedusa, the city of Calais where the Eurotunnel starts, Bodrum in Turkey, the eastern islands of Greece, or the Spanish enclaves of Ceuta and Melilla in Morocco, are invading television screens and media outlets. They portray a massive scale attempts by desperate souls trying to reach European countries. The EU Commissioner in charge of migration declared this month this is the worst migrant crisis since World War II. Is it?

Maybe for Western Europe it is perceived as such, but it is not. Understanding why is important, because more is coming.

Migration is part of the human journey since the sophisticated apes started moving out of the Rift Valley in Africa. The History of humanity is so rich and complex that we have difficulties relating to a very remote common origin, except for historical assessments and philosophical statements. It is easier for all to link to a more recent past, the one that through events and social interaction shaped our identities. Human beings have a selective reading of History. For most compensation will be justified for a wrong done to some, but not the other. Apologies will be fine with some, but not the other. Peace offers will be morally acceptable to some, but not the other. This is after all mimicking individual behavior at a larger, societal level.

Most Italians forgot they created entire nations such as Argentina and Uruguay. The British do not necessarily relate Australia, New Zealand or the Spanish and Portuguese most of South America to their making through migration. When referring to Indochina the Chinese must have only a vague idea why that region carries their name. Americans will find

> **?** What issues are raised in this document? To what extent are the issues in this document global?

> **?** How would you describe the perspective this article comes from? What are the beliefs and assumptions underlying the perspective?

> Find out about the migration crisis during and after the Second World War. How does it compare to current migration crises around the world?

it bad taste to mention part of the current US was bought from Mexico. The list is vast.

Still one continent in recent History has never been associated with migration to colonize or profit from other regions richness: Africa! If anything Africa is rather known for suffering from slavery, plundering of its natural resources and unfair international treatment.

Africa has struggled more than most to find a way out of poverty. It has been doing better of late, since the turn of the century in fact, posting growth rates above the world's and developing countries' average. Yet the narrative about the continent seems to be fixated on migration and negative assessments of its performance. It is, therefore, important, first to understand why Africa is perceived to be generating more migrants today than ever before.

African countries receive a lot more migrants than the continent exports abroad. In fact the bulk of Africans looking for opportunities outside their countries go to another African country. Less than 2 million seek a destination abroad every year, which is a tiny number in relation to migrant stocks, particularly in Europe. Of the quarter of a million that have tried the Mediterranean route this year the largest contingent are Syrians, with about 50,000, a fraction of those settled in, say, Lebanon, with over 1.5 million. Afghans, Yemenis, Pakistanis and other non-Africans use the route too.

Europe's pull factor is to be understood by a variety of developments, from information access (6 billion cell phones in the world), human rights proclamations, a call for universal moral values all the way to unfair distribution of income and inequality across the globe. Terrorism and religious extremism have played a card as well. It looks like the strong European rights advocacy has worked for its detriment.

Pockets of war such as Libya and its surrounding deserts, the Great Lakes and its neighborhood, and the long battled Somalia are generating political asylum seekers and massive number of refugees as well. Harsh African regimes contribute their lot.

The shyness African leaders show, when migration is a theme, including for other fellow Africans, is disturbing. But, still this does not give us the full story.

In every moment of History growth has generated outward migrants from the same location.

It is indeed happening with Chinese and Indians right now as it is in Africa. Growth spins the chances for a new life but its distribution, particularly at the early stages of a country take-off, is uneven and unpredictable. Those who see their neighbor with means and hope they do not have, venture out. It would have been absurd to propose bombing the boats that were sailing to South America full of migrants escaping the misfortunes of the two World Wars aftermath. These migrants were seeking better lives. Yet their countries were growing like never before, thanks amongst others to the Marshall Plan.

Listen to this TED talk about the way we use stories and narratives to build up images and perspectives: https://www.ted.com/talks/chimamanda_adichie_the_danger_of_a_single_story/transcript?language=en

Find out what the growth rates are in two different African countries.

Research African migrants and their destinations.

Did this migration actually come at the same time as economic growth? Check the facts!

Africans dying in the desert or the sea are the determined lot. They do not accept their fate and are ready to risk their life. The youngest population of the world sees the developed nations of Europe as the closest beacon of hope. For them it is the house of human rights that will, certainly, understand their plight and welcome them to work!

Africa's youthfulness will keep growing when the rest of the world will be ageing.

The difficulty of admitting that the current State's welfare in all ageing countries is unsustainable has led to the most bizarre economic policy proposals.

Accepting there is a demographic challenge would imply a vast overhaul of social and political choices to sustain the economy. As we all witness the limits of transfer of value from production and labour to knowledge and financial control, we are also seeing the limits of the prevailing economic model.

A demographic equilibrium is still essential despite technological progress and productivity gains. Social security or pension funds cannot be contributed towards by robots or intellectual property; it needs people, workers, and productive workers indeed.

That is why Europe will have to come to grips with its need for migrants, as many times acknowledged by the EU Commission.

The 2000 or so known deaths on the Mediterranean Sea, are a tragic wake up call. Between now and 2050 Africa will double its population. Even if it grows as fast, or faster than it is doing right now, it is likely to generate a much bigger flow of young Africans looking for opportunities in an ageing Europe.

The extraordinary and still amazing bravery of the European explorers, facing unknown seas and geography with just scarce scientific tools for orientation and survival has been celebrated. It is an extraordinary demonstration of human determination.

That same bravery is displayed by today's migrants. And they are turning into Europe. Payback time?

http://southernafrican.news/2015/09/25/african-migrants-is-it-payback-time/

Do you think that the changes in our countries will be as great as this author suggests? Why — what is your evidence base?

What can you find out about southernafrican.news? Where is it based? What sort of articles does it publish? What sort of issues does it concentrate on? Is it generally more informed or speculative?

Document 2

Freedom of movement is not simply an economic good, but a bulwark against oppression

*Freedom of movement is frequently posited as an economic good, writes **Floris de Witte**. But it is much more than that. It allows Europeans to pursue a way and quality of life that simply may not be possible in the state where they were born. And in curbing the capacity of domestic politicians to scapegoat and exclude the foreigner, it serves to prevent another descent into intra-European conflict.*

As the debate around a possible Brexit intensifies, it seems to focus more and more on the economic costs and economic benefits of free movement. This discussion, typically, focuses on securing access to the internal market for the UK's companies, to the skills that the UK can 'import' from other member states, but also the possible costs in terms of welfare benefits to which foreign workers become eligible. Much has been said on these arguments already. The purpose of this post is to highlight that free movement also has an important non-economic side to it. It is, for better or worse, about freedom. Missing this element means overlooking what many EU actors, national politicians and European citizens (and in particular its younger generations) understand as the core of the process of integration. It also means that any reformulation of the rules and conditions of free movement is deeply problematic, as many actors involved in such reformulation simply do not see it as a matter of economic costs or benefits. They see free movement as a symbol of European integration.

This non-economic element of free movement can be explained in different ways. For many younger European citizens (depending on the date of accession of their home state to the EU), a Europe of free movement is simply a given. All elements of their daily lives are infused with the results of free movement, whether it is their Polish classmate, their Belgian lecturer at university, their favourite Italian dish, a Czech football player on their favourite team, or Portuguese boss in the local restaurant. These little things matter: we make sense of our lives and of our selves by communicating and interacting with others. The more we become used to 'others' being in places that we understand as familiar, local, or 'us'; the more we take 'others' for granted. Free movement, as such, cannot be reduced to an accountant's cost/benefit analysis. It is so deeply part of how we live our lives that removing its traces would be as if all teenagers or all pensioners were to be banished from our neighbourhoods.

Freedom of action

For the individual European citizen, free movement is also much more than an economic idea. It is about being able to get more out of your life that you can get 'at home'. It is an idea that allows 761,000 Brits to live in sunny Spain instead of the UK. It is the idea that allows students to get to know other cultures, allows citizens to move to Warsaw, Marseille or Berlin for love, work, to learn a language, to master a culinary tradition, to open a bar in Croatia or Estonia, to decide for themselves what they think

1. What issues are raised in this document?
2. How would you describe the perspective this article comes from? What are the beliefs and assumptions underlying the perspective?
3. Why do governments and populations scapegoat foreigners?
4. Brexit was a 2016 debate and referendum about whether Britain should leave the European Union. What happened? How has it affected Britain, Europe and the wider world (if at all)?
5. Should people stay in the place they were born? Give your reasons.
6. Why do people feel such strong ties of belonging and ownership to the place they were born?
7. To what extent are the issues in this document global?

is most important in their lives, and act upon it. This more aspirational dimension of free movement is essentially about freedom. It is about the incapacity of states to decide what lives their citizens ought to lead.

Should the government be able to decide what sort of life people can lead?

If you are a gay couple living in a member state that is illiberal and does not (legally) recognise or (socially) respect your lifestyle, free movement allows you to move to a member state where these prejudices do not exist and where you can live a better life. If you are retired and your favourite pastime is hiking, free movement allows you to move from Amsterdam to the Pyrenees. The absence of barriers to movement, as guaranteed by the free movement provisions, are crucial in facilitating this aspirational quality. Wealthier Europeans will not struggle to move to other states even in the absence of free movement. But if free movement is to be about freedom, about chasing one's aspirations, it must be freely accessible for all.

Freedom of movement... the Pyrenees

The final way of viewing free movement from a non-economic perspective is to see it as the guarantor of the very purpose of European integration, which is to prevent authoritarian or totalitarian regimes. Much of the post-war political project of European economic integration did not primarily serve economic purposes. Primarily, it was about limiting the capacity of nation states to commit democratic suicide and impose the processes of internal exclusion or external aggression that accompanied it.

The legally guaranteed right to free movement of citizens, but also of goods, services, and companies, and the right to non-discrimination that comes with such movement, then, serves to hamstring the capacity of domestic political actors to scapegoat the foreigner, refuse them access or the rights that they have accrued. In many continental European political cultures, this argument still holds sway. For many countries, in fact, the

One of the key arguments against the European Union is rooted in sovereignty — the idea that no external power should limit a government's ability to govern a country in its own way.

What do you think? Should there be limits?

accession to the EU immediately followed a period of war, political oppression or totalitarianism. The incapacity of states to constrain the choices of their citizens—through their legally protected right to free movement, that member states cannot deny—is, on this view, simultaneously the most important achievement and core philosophical tenet of the process of integration.

Free movement is about the economy. It is about the movement of workers, the contributions of workers to host societies, and their welfare demands. But focusing only on this economic element of free movement is missing the bigger picture.

This blog represents the views of the author and not those of the BrexitVote blog, nor the LSE.

Floris de Witte *is an Assistant Professor of Law at the LSE. His research deals with the interaction between EU law and political theory, with particular emphasis on free movement, the Euro-crisis and the role of the individual in the EU.*

http://blogs.lse.ac.uk/brexitvote/2016/02/03/freedom-of-movement-is-not-simply-an-economic-good-but-a-bulwark-against-oppression/

? Does a country belong to its people or do the people belong to the country?

What sort of blog is this? Where is it based? What sort of articles does it publish? What sort of issues does it concentrate on? Is it generally more informed or speculative?

Document 3

Apocalyptic, yes. But even if conflict can be avoided, MAX HASTINGS says unchecked mass migration will make Europe unrecognisable.

Could this lead to WAR in Europe?

By Max Hastings for the Daily Mail

Published: 23:49, 18 March 2016 | Updated: 16:51, 19 March 2016

Last week in Washington, I met an old friend who is one of the smartest strategy wonks I know. His business is crystal ball-gazing.

During our conversation, he offered some speculations about what could happen to our world over the next decade or two which made my hair stand on end.

He predicts that the seismic turbulence in the Middle East will continue, and indeed worsen, unless or until the West is willing to commit stabilisation forces to the region. He calculates that an army of the order of magnitude of 450,000 men would be necessary, to have any chance of success.

In the absence of such an effort—for which he admits the political will does not exist on either side of the Atlantic, and is unlikely to do so in the future—he believes that the tidal wave of migration to Europe from the Middle East and Africa will continue, with consequences much greater and graver than any national leader has yet acknowledged.

He suggested that war within our continent is not impossible before the middle of the century, as southern European nations are swamped by incomers, and Greece stands first in line to become a failed state. […]

What was sobering about our conversation is that here was an uncommonly well-informed man who believes that the earthquakes shaking the Middle East, together with the scale of economic migration from Africa, could undo all our comfortable assumptions about the stability of the society in which we live, including our confidence that Europe has turned its back on war for ever.

The most obvious lesson of history is that events and threats always take us by surprise.

Consider the shocks we have experienced in modern times. Almost nobody expected the Irish Troubles; the Argentine invasion of the Falklands; the collapse of the Soviet Union; the dramatic rise of Muslim extremism; the 9/11 attacks in New York and 7/7 bombings in London; the global banking disaster of 2007-8; the break up of the Middle East that began with the 2003 Iraq invasion.

I never cease to be amazed by the continuing willingness of institutions all over the world to pay fat fees for speeches from the American academic Francis Fukuyama, who in 1992 published a ridiculous best-seller entitled The End Of History, which proclaimed that liberal democracy and free-market capitalism were now triumphant and unassailable, having shown their superiority to all alternatives.

Everything that has happened since shows that Fukuyama was as wrong as could be. Across large swathes of the globe, authoritarian regimes flourish like the green bay tree. Democracy has never looked rockier, even in the United States.

Who is Max Hastings? What can you find about him, his work and his reputation?

What sort of newspaper is the *Daily Mail*? Where is it based? What sort of articles does it publish? What sort of issues does it concentrate on? Is it generally more informed or speculative?

1. What issues are raised in this document?
2. How would you describe the perspective this article comes from? What are the beliefs and assumptions underlying the perspective?
3. To what extent are the issues in this document global?

Is this work 'ridiculous'? Is it mistaken? Or is it simply from a different perspective than the article?

Research Fukuyama and his work.

My think-tank friend in Washington observed last week: 'Democracy only works where there is a broad consensus about the distribution of wealth and power.' And it is because this consensus faces unprecedented stresses in consequence of migration in Europe, that he believes some factions may resort to violence, even outright war.

It seems foolish to dismiss this warning out of hand. The threat posed by mass population movement is huge and intractable, and it is hard to have much faith in the deal struck yesterday between the EU and Turkey which seeks to halt the huge numbers reaching the shores of Greece. What it will actually mean is that 77 million Turks will have the right to travel all the way to Calais unhindered should they so wish.

Tens of millions of people in Africa, too, aspire to move to Europe in search of a better life, and huge numbers are already crossing the Mediterranean via Libya, Algeria and Tunisia.

The entire Middle East is in a ferment, and it is impossible to see any reason why peace should be restored any time soon. [...]

Arguably the most sinister symptom of this vast region's troubles is the flight of money.

I attended a bankers' meeting this week at which much of the gossip was about the desperate flight of the rich, together with their money, from Egypt, Saudi Arabia, Bahrain, Qatar and in lesser degree the UAE. Many of those able to liquidate assets and move them to Europe or America are doing so. They fear for the stability of local regimes, and also anticipate more inter-state wars.

Strife will continue, and spread across the Middle East. There is no single, over-arching course of action open to the U.S. or Nato governments that can resolve this alarming state of affairs. It can only be addressed piecemeal, through local diplomatic initiatives and modest military assistance.

We should recognise that the old state borders of most of the embattled countries, notably including Iraq and Libya, are almost certainly defunct. They will fragment into statelets dominated by the local tribe or warlord. Moreover, it is hard to see any course of action that can stem the flow of migrants to the West, the foremost concern for most of the people who inhabit our continent. Only a proportion of the incomers are fleeing from the immediate consequences of violence. A far larger number, according to every survey conducted in Europe, come from places where there is no war. They simply seek better lives.

The physical difficulties of preventing them from coming are immense. When they are plucked from sinking boats in the Mediterranean, human rights law and the cynical attitude of North African governments make it almost impossible to return them to their ports of embarkation.

The people on these odysseys are driven by motivations and passions more intense than most of us can imagine. They see our societies offering a wealth and security unimaginable in their homelands. They embrace the most desperate dangers to reach our shores.

At present, the governments of Europe have no credible and coherent policies for checking or halting the flood, beyond creating some frail fences on the Eastern margins. Mass migration now poses the gravest threat to Europe's stability and tranquillity since the end of the Cold War, and arguably since 1945. Unless it is checked, over the coming decades it promises to change the character and make-up of all our societies on a scale to make past immigration seem trivial.

One policy to which David Cameron's government is rightly committed is to work to ameliorate the conditions of refugees and economic migrants in their own countries, or at least nearby. Britain is a generous donor to the UN's international refugee programmes. It would be naïve to imagine that aid alone can stem the migration tide, but it can help. […]

Of course, the West cannot aspire to enable Nigerians, Ethiopians or Afghans to enjoy the standard of living that exists in west London. But we must do everything in our power to diminish the incentives for migration. Fences and border controls at Calais will not suffice.

None of the answers is easy. This crisis can only grow in the months and years ahead. […]

I have no doubt that after reading all this, a spokesman for the compassion industry would demand: where is your human sympathy for the millions suffering terribly in their own societies? Fair enough. My words sound harsh. But I would in turn ask that spokesman: where should human sympathy stop?

We are witnessing the beginning—and it is only the beginning—of a game-changing shift of populations, which if it continues unchecked will over the next half-century change all our societies for ever.

Maybe our children's generation will be content to live with such a transformation. Maybe we can avoid the wars my friend in Washington fears. But our politicians should at least be telling the nation just how profound the coming upheaval threatens to be.

http://www.dailymail.co.uk/news/article-3499652/Could-lead-war-Europe-Apocalyptic-yes-conflict-avoided-MAX-HASTINGS-says-unchecked-mass-migration-make-Europe-unrecognisable.html#ixzz43V4tfdyd

Every man has a right to risk his own life for the preservation of it

Jean-Jacques Rousseau

What do you think? Where should sympathy stop?

Document 4

Democracy and Human Rights

The human rights normative framework

The values of freedom, respect for human rights and the principle of holding periodic and genuine elections by universal suffrage are essential elements of democracy. In turn, democracy provides the natural environment for the protection and effective realization of human rights. These values are embodied in the Universal Declaration of Human Rights and further developed in the International Covenant on Civil and Political Rights which enshrines a host of political rights and civil liberties underpinning meaningful democracies.

The link between democracy and human rights is captured in article 21(3) of the Universal Declaration of Human Rights, which states:

"The will of the people shall be the basis of the authority of government; this shall be expressed in periodic and genuine elections which shall be by universal and equal suffrage and shall be held by secret vote or by equivalent free voting procedures."

1. What issues are raised in this document?
2. How would you describe the perspective this article comes from? What are the beliefs and assumptions underlying the perspective?
3. What does 'the will of the people' mean? Is it different if there are lots of different opinions among the people?
4. To what extent are the issues in the document global?

Polling staff count votes at East Timor general elections in 2012

What else could form the basis of the authority of governments? Could it be God, international law, the power of an army?

The rights enshrined in the International Covenant on Economic, Social and Cultural Rights and subsequent human rights instruments covering the rights of certain groups (e.g. indigenous peoples, women, minorities, people with disabilities, migrant workers and members of their families) are equally essential for democracy as they ensure inclusivity for all groups, including equality and equity in respect of access to civil and political rights.

For several years, the UN General Assembly and the former Commission on Human Rights endeavored to draw on international human rights instruments to promote a common understanding of the principles, norms, standards and values that are the basis of democracy, with a view to guiding Member States in developing domestic democratic traditions and institutions; and in meeting their commitments to human rights, democracy and development.

http://www.un.org/en/globalissues/democracy/human_rights.shtml

Is there really a common understanding? Or are these Western principles and values that are being imposed on the rest of the world? Research different perspectives.

What sort of website is this document from? Where is it based? What sort of articles does it publish? What sort of issues does it concentrate on? Is it generally more informed or speculative?

Democracy is the worst form of Government except for all those other forms that have been tried from time to time… .

Winston Churchill

It is unnatural for a majority to rule, for a majority can seldom be organized and united for specific action, and a minority can.

Jean-Jacques Rousseau

Traditional beliefs, Western values in the workplace: Strange bedfellows?

October 11, 2011

Ngugi wa Thiong'o in the novel The River Between (1965) presents a picture that depicts Western Christianity as something that is disruptive to the African traditional way of life. Another writer, Chinua Achebe, in his novel Things Fall Apart (1985) has shown that before the advent of colonialism in eastern Nigeria, among the Igbo, there were institutions that served their society effectively, but were disrupted by British colonialists. Some Western writers have negatively portrayed traditional African life while extolling the values of Western institutions.

The age-old conflict between traditional African culture and Western values has implications on workplace relations that cannot be ignored. The Zimbabwean workplace of today reflects many diverse cultures and instances of culture clashes are an omnipresent reality.

Recently, the Parliamentary Portfolio Committee on Health chaired by former Health minister and Murehwa North Member of Parliament David Parirenyatwa reported that more than 80% of Zimbabweans consult traditional practitioners.

In traditional African religion, success or failure in life, business or work is defined in terms of the relationship that exists between a person and his or her ancestral spirits. The African traditional healer, called n'anga in Shona or inyanga in Ndebele has special ritual powers and is consulted by those seeking a cure for physical ailments, bad luck, protection against witchcraft or securing one's job. Consulting an n'anga or inyanga is an integral aspect of African religion premised on the idea that spirit mediums can communicate with souls of one's dead relatives.

These beliefs shape attitudes, emotions and cognitions alike and have a bearing on people's everyday behaviour. What are the implications for business? Employees may request time off at certain times of the year to perform the necessary rituals to appease their ancestral spirits.

In African culture, the funeral of a relative, whether close or distant takes precedence over everything else. […] A diligent junior employee may be suspected of wanting to topple his superior from his post. The superior may even cast a spell on him to thwart his perceived intentions. […] An employee may refuse to wear a red uniform because red colour is perceived to be associated with misfortune.

In African culture, when misfortune strikes, the answer is readily found in witchcraft or incensed ancestral spirits. Westerners are more likely to speak of chance and perhaps divine providence.

There are reports of employers, especially from the farming communities who have engaged tsikamutanda (witchhunters) or n'angas to sniff out employees suspected of theft.

Employees have been forced to drink certain concoctions as part of the rituals, some of which turned out to be lethal. In terms of Western values,

1. What issues are raised in this document?
2. How would you describe the perspective this article comes from? What are the beliefs and assumptions underlying the perspective?
3. To what extent are the issues in this document global?

this is obviously a violation of the Witchcraft Suppression Act [...] and can lead to the prosecution of the employer or n'anga concerned.

A company espousing Western values would carry out some investigations and conduct disciplinary hearings or involve the police when theft occurs. [...]

Western values at the workplace are premised on Christian beliefs. Christians generally view traditional rituals and practices as demonic and ungodly. They quote extensively from the Bible.

For example, Deuteronomy 18 verse 11 says anyone who consults the dead is abominable to God. Leviticus 19 verse 31 warns that people must not turn to mediums or spirits "for you will be defiled by them". These "gods" and "spirits" are demons according to Corinthians 11 verses 14 and 15.

Employees with strong religious views may seriously consider leaving an organisation that values traditional beliefs.

It was reported in The Herald of November 23 2009 that a local beverage company had fired 48 workers for refusing to wear corporate uniforms they believed had been taken to a traditional healer for ritual purposes "to increase sales".

One of the workers is reported to have remarked: "It is better to be unemployed than to have work where you are used for ritual purposes."

At times there is a confusing mixture of traditional beliefs and Western or Christian values at the workplace. [...]

Tensions arising from workplace values generally governed by Western business practice and those underpinning traditional cultures of Africans are a reality. A fine balance has to be struck between the opposing values.

Workplace policies that emphasise more on shared values need to be designed. Managers who comprehend and value the cultural diversity of workers and are flexible in using what works from a practical perspective will have a competitive edge over their counterparts.

In my view, it is not the wrongness or rightness of one's beliefs that matters, but the recognition of the fact that people do genuinely hold different beliefs.

The answer lies in acknowledging the existence of such diversity and finding common ground.

https://www.newsday.co.zw/2011/10/11/2011-10-11-traditional-beliefs-western-values-in-the-workplace-strange-bedfellows/

? What sort of source is newsday.co.zw? Where is it based? What sort of articles does it publish? What sort of issues does it concentrate on? Is it generally more informed or speculative?

Security first, freedom will follow

by John Sawers/January 21, 2016

Published in February 2016 issue of Prospect Magazine

New technology helps our enemies as well as us and raises new questions about providing security and preserving freedom

Can we stop a Paris-style attack happening in London? The honest answer is yes—most of the time.

As MI6 Chief, my top priority was identifying terror attacks against Britain planned from abroad. Working with intelligence partners in the United States and the Middle East, we had significant successes. You do not know about the attacks we prevented because they did not occur, and we don't talk about them. Why give our enemies clues to how we stop them?

When I joined MI6, I was trained to spot people tracking me by tapping my phone, intercepting radio communications or following me by car or on foot. Today those techniques are used against terrorist suspects, supported by technologies like face or footstep recognition. But you have to know which people pose a threat—and first, you have to find them.

One method we use is the new science of data analytics. Every time you use your mobile, post a Tweet, shop online, drive past a CCTV camera, tap your Oyster card, or watch a YouTube cat video, you create data. Everything you do digitally—everything anyone does—makes these data oceans bigger, richer and deeper.

"These days, terrorists are scheming in cyberspace. If terror suspects are operating on the internet, it is essential that the police and security services have the legal power to track them."

So we dive into these data oceans and look for patterns. We search for snippets of information that warrant a closer look. Then we have to work out who, among several thousand possible extremist sympathisers, might launch an attack in Britain next week.

1. What issues are raised in this document?
2. How would you describe the perspective this article comes from? What are the beliefs and assumptions underlying the perspective?
3. To what extent are the issues in this document global?

What is MI6? What is the equivalent in your country?

We need to follow suspects wherever they go. If a terror suspect enters a pub, it is reasonable if not vital that the police and security services have the legal power to enter and monitor him or her there. These days, terrorists are scheming in cyberspace. If terror suspects are operating on the internet, it is essential that the police and security services have the legal power to track them online and identify who they are communicating with.

As citizens, we want maximum privacy and maximum security. Unbreakable encryption is at the centre of the argument. Intelligence agencies focus on security; technology companies focus on privacy. They each accuse the other of ignoring the public interest they are protecting, but both have a point. We want world-class encryption to keep our data secure. But terrorists and extremists use this encryption against us, keeping their identities and communications secret. There is nothing new here. Every technological advance—guns, cars, telephones—has quickly been used by the enemies of society. And like these advances, unbreakable encryption cannot be uninvented.

The big technology companies have a crucial role—and a unique responsibility—in building the security that keeps us free and safe. We trust them in part because they are private. Co-operation is much preferable to legislation. The next step is for all parties to collaborate on a way forward to benefit from new technologies while doing what we can to stop those who would do us harm. This kind of co-operation between public and private sectors is needed in free societies where security underpins our privacy, private enterprise and liberal democracy.

How, though, should we set clear limits on how the state can acquire data?

Say that you do not trust the government and intelligence agencies, but you also do not want to live in fear of terrorism. You grudgingly accept that agencies need to look at internet data to find and track terrorist networks. Then you sit down to devise laws and come up with something like the following.

First, privacy is the norm. Exceptions are allowed only when a minister decides that intrusion is necessary. Second, while agencies can look for patterns in data, high-level authorisation is needed to track individuals. Next, those doing the work must be tightly vetted and alarms should go off over improper searches. Then, while we should share intelligence with other governments, we use extreme caution if they have a bad human rights record. Finally, there must be oversight by MPs and judges, frequent spot-checks, and checks and balances on every level.

Guess what? That is more or less what we have now.

There is rarely a good time for these debates. New laws rushed through after a major attack will not strike a wise, principled balance. Fortunately, this is not the case with the new Investigatory Powers Bill before parliament. This is based on the recommendations of David Anderson QC, the Independent Reviewer of Terrorism Legislation, and is designed to strike such a balance.

? How much freedom and privacy are you willing to give up in order to be safe?

How much safety are you willing to give up in order to be free?

? Why might people not trust a government? What harm can be done by governments with too much power over individuals?

? What is the situation regarding state surveillance in your country?

When you put all the powers of the agencies into one codified legal framework, the overall package might look ominous, if not alarming. Do our agencies really need to be able to do all this?

Some people also argue that if state surveillance did not stop the Paris attacks, what good is it? But, to make an analogy, no goalkeeper has a perfect record. Even the finest can be beaten by a top-class shot or a freakish deflection. That does not make them a bad goalkeeper, or the idea of goalkeeping redundant.

I do not want to downplay reasonable concerns. But technologies that empower us also empower our enemies. We can track down people like Mohammed Emwazi, known as "Jihadi John." But you and your children are only a few clicks away from people who use 3D printers to create replica guns, those who make synthetic drugs, or from Islamic State (IS) and al-Qaeda and their propaganda.

This presents an acute dilemma. Is it better to shut down this ghastly material, even if you drive it deeper into the dark web? Or should we accept that this poison is in society's bloodstream and quietly watch what is happening and who might be infected?

Those in the intelligence and security services face this dilemma all the time. You can trust the skill and restraint of the people working day and night to protect you. Or you can further limit their powers—and pray the people working day and night to destroy our societies do not hit you, your family or your town.

Today's security requires the use of technology to guarantee huge areas of freedom for all of us, by making difficult compromises on the margins. This is not an attack on privacy, but the only way to safeguard it while combatting the enemies of free society.

Technology is changing foreign policy as well. In 1982, under President Hafez al-Assad—the father of Syria's current President, Bashar al-Assad—the Syrian army attacked Hama, Syria's fourth largest city, to put down an Islamist uprising. They killed over 20,000 people—three times the death toll of Srebrenica. The attack went on for weeks, but barely any news seeped out. When it did, global reaction was muted. There was little public pressure and it suited most governments to look away.

Compare that with the reaction to Malaysia Airlines flight MH17, shot down over Ukraine in July 2014. Swarms of amateurs and experts from everywhere in the world took to the internet. Drawing on live satellite imagery and other open-source websites, they pinpointed the probable launchpoint of the missile, the type of missile used, and the likely people responsible. They punched big holes in the official story coming from Moscow and pointed the finger of guilt at Moscow-backed separatists.

In *BloombergView*, James Gibney called this a "citizen-driven open-source intelligence revolution." In October, bombs fell on a Médecins Sans Frontières hospital in Afghanistan. Crowd-sourced investigation quickly forced the US to accept responsibility. All very admirable—but the immediacy and transparency of today's technology is giving our leaders serious problems.

The first problem is time. Events and disasters now come thick and fast. The 24/7 media cycle and incessant clamour of the internet puts politicians under pressure to respond quickly. Often, their actions are aimed at shutting up their noisiest critics. Yet what may be needed is real leadership, taking people along a path that is tough, slow and unpopular to achieve a greater goal.

Take Syria again. In 2011, Syrians demonstrated against Bashar al-Assad's rule and he turned the army on them. The west was torn, but did not intervene. Then in 2013, he used chemical weapons against his people in a breach of international conventions. This war crime demands a swift, strong response: it is vital to hold the line against these weapons. The British government took a clear position that military action is required, but chose to seek approval from parliament. Reflecting public unease about another Middle East intervention, parliament said no. President Barack Obama then had doubts whether he could act without the support of Congress. This left the west in a hopeless position, "demanding" the departure of Assad without tackling him.

What do you think – should these governments have acted without a vote in Parliament or Congress? How important is the will of the people?

Since then, Syria's civil war has created space for the rise of IS, who pose the worst terrorist threat in living memory. Syrian refugees are coming in unmanageable numbers, undermining European solidarity. And now Russia is involved, unconstrained by democratic pressures or concern for civilian casualties, using air power and missiles to prop up the dismal Assad regime.

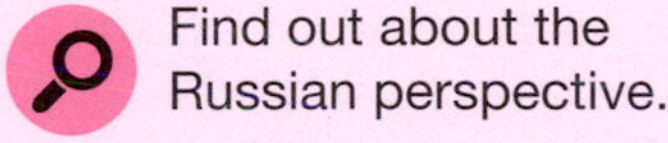

Find out about the Russian perspective.

We all share some responsibility for these grim outcomes. But when timelines are so short and technology gives a deafeningly loud voice to all sorts of critics, well-intentioned or not, thinking strategically becomes next to impossible in a modern democracy.

In the wake of the Paris attacks, we need a strategy to help the Syrian people and remove IS from its strongholds. A new diplomatic process for Syria has begun, but its outcome will be shaped by the strength of forces on the ground. If we want moderates to have a voice, we need to support them militarily.

The second problem is trust. Technology makes us all more accountable. Scandals such as MPs' expenses or media phone tapping are healthy exposures of abuse. But examples like these can lead to unbridled cynicism, in which anything secret is a cover-up.

Yet patient diplomacy relies on confidentiality. For years, the Iran nuclear talks were stuck. Both the US and Iran faced forces at home rejecting compromise. Then the Obama Administration made a sustained effort with Iran through secret meetings in Oman. It led to a breakthrough and then an agreement. At times, transparency has to sit back and give diplomacy a chance.

The final problem is disruptive change. Every leader, good or bad, wants to reap the benefit of new technologies and big data. But what if today's technology is too disruptive for free societies, making democracies look weak or uncertain?

In contrast, autocratic or oppressive systems may avoid the worst disruptions. They are already skilled at closing down debate and manipulating public opinion. And they do not worry about transparency, so they can think strategically and act decisively. No country is more strategic than China. I have met some of China's leaders and they plan in decades, even centuries: they are surprised that we don't. As we saw in Ukraine and now Syria, President Vladimir Putin is using his power to create new realities. Autocratic states may start to look stronger, more effective, more orderly than democracies.

But, for all their fumbling, scandal and confusion, democracies have one huge advantage. They are flexible and open. They embrace new ideas and opportunities. It is our greatest strength. Yet we cannot take success for granted. We are at a moment in history like the industrial revolution. Who will get first mover advantage, as Britain did in the 18th and 19th centuries?

Societies that master big data will enjoy a head start, whether they are democratic or not. They will lead the way in artificial intelligence and robotics, reaping benefits in health and education simply by knowing more. They will adjust faster to change. Nations that veer away from new technology will fall behind, and radical new inequalities in wealth and power emerge.

Soon, self-learning computers will start displacing people. Scientists like Stephen Hawking urge us to consider the ethical implications of this now, rather than wait until they are upon us. We need to work through the implications for our politics, too. To make technology support our freedoms won over centuries, and not erode them, we must think ahead, and not leave the next generation with a stark choice between security or freedom. [...]

My whole career has been geared around the issues of freedom and security. Neither can be absolute or guaranteed: and each depends on the other. Oppressive security undermines freedom. But freedoms evaporate if there is no security we can rely on to uphold them.

The longer term issues [raised] by new technologies for our societies and political systems are much greater and more profound than the short term trade offs needed to combat terrorism. No one knows where technology will take us. In a free society we have the advantage of dynamism and flexibility. We're going to need that to ensure the technologies are harnessed to reinforce both freedom and security. We don't want to wake up one day and discover that new technology has pushed us in a direction we never wanted to take.

http://www.prospectmagazine.co.uk/features/what-spies-should-see-mi6-terrorism-security-technology

? What sort of website is www.prospectmagazine.co.uk? Where is it based? What sort of articles does it publish? What sort of issues does it concentrate on? Is it generally more informed or speculative?

Skills development activities

Activity 6

1 Document 1 aims to show that European migration is not as bad as it might seem.

   a How does it aim to show this? (Think about reasons and evidence.)

   b How well does it show this? (Think about the quality of the argument.)

2 Document 1 aims to show that migration from Africa is not a hugely significant issue.

   a How does it aim to show this?

   b How well does it show this?

3 Document 1 explains why Europe is attractive to migrants.

   a How does it do this?

   b How well does it do this?

4 According to document 1, why will Europe have to come to grips with migrants?

5 There is an inconsistency in the overall argument in document 1. Identify and explain this inconsistency.

Research and discuss

Document 1 says, 'Africa is rather known for suffering from slavery, plundering of its natural resources and unfair international treatment.'

Do former colonisers have a responsibility or duty to help develop modern African countries they used to colonise?

What are the economic and political barriers to development in former colonies? Choose one or two to research. How can these barriers be overcome – and who needs to do this?

Does democracy always lead to economic and social development?

Activity 7

The author of document 2 argues that focusing on the economic element of free movement is missing 'the bigger picture'.

1 How does the author argue in support of this? (Think about reasons, evidence, examples and analogies.)

2 How effective is his argument?

3 Do you agree with his reasoning? Why or why not?

4 How would you describe the author's perspective? (Think about underlying beliefs and attitudes, and about the way he sees the world.)

5 How far do you share this perspective?

A perspective is a world view which underlies an argument. It can be quite hard to pin down.

Argument, reasoning and opinions are the specifics of what the author says — they are informed by the author's perspective.

Each of these people has a different perspective on the world

Research and discuss

Should we abandon the idea of nations and go for a global government to go with our global lives?

What is government for – to control the people or to serve the people?

Discuss and research this statement: We should aim to see ourselves as citizens of the world.

Government has no other end, but the preservation of property.

John Locke

Government serves the interest of those in power.

Activity 8

1 How are the opinions and issues expressed in documents 1 and 2 different?
2 How are the underlying perspectives and unspoken beliefs different?
3 Find more arguments that come from each perspective.
4 Start to build up and evaluate the evidence base for these perspectives.

Activity 9

1 Does the author of document 3 have sufficient evidence to support his claims?
2 Is document 3 an argument? If not, what sort of writing is it?
3 How effective is the overall reasoning in document 3?
4 How likely are the predictions the author makes?
5 Can you think of alternative possible futures? What evidence base is there to support them?

A nation is 'an imagined political community'.

Benedict Anderson.

Research and discuss

1. Should people in the West accept a reduction in their living standards in order to share out the world's wealth more fairly?
2. The author of document 1 worries that migration will destroy national identities. What do you think about this?
3. Another concern is that conflict and neglect are leading to the destruction of cultural heritage. How much does this matter?

You may find these TED talks interesting: https://www.ted.com/talks/elizabeth_lindsey_curating_humanity_s_heritage/transcript?language=en

www.ted.com/talks/taiye_selasi_ don_t_ask_where_i_m_ from_ask_where_i_m_a_ local?language=en

www.ted.com/talks/sheikha_al_ mayassa_globalizing_the_ local_localizing_the_global/transcript?language=en

Activity 10

1. Is document 4 an argument? If not, what type of writing is it?
2. How equal are minority groups in your country?
3. Compare the status of minority groups in your country with two other very different countries.

When answering question 2, think about equality in the law and equality in practice. You could consider freedom, income, property, access to education and opportunities, and representation in government.

Research and discuss

1. Research the basis for other forms of government than democracy.
2. Do you agree that democracy is the most effective form of government? Justify your answer.
3. Does the international community have the right to interfere in national affairs in order to promote human rights and democracy? If so, what gives them this right? Where does it come from?

Think about the differences between 'effective,' 'fair,' 'good' and 'right'.

Activity 11

1. Is document 5 an argument? If not, what type of writing is it?
2. Examine the contrasting perspectives represented in document 5.
3. Which of these perspectives does the author seem to have most sympathy for?
4. The author says, 'In my view, it is not the wrongness or rightness of one's beliefs that matters, but the recognition of the fact that people do genuinely hold different beliefs.' Do you agree? Why or why not?

Activity 12

1. Is document 6 an argument? If not, what type of writing is it?
2. Summarise the key points the author makes. Use a diagram or mind map if this helps you.
3. How effective is the reasoning?

Research and discuss

1. How important are spies to a nation's security?
2. How important are narratives and stories about spies in your cultural heritage and nation building?
3. To what extent do our narratives about spies romanticise boredom and betrayal?

Most people like to read about intrigue and spies. I hope to provide a metaphor for the average reader's daily life. Most of us live in a slightly conspiratorial relationship with our employer and perhaps with our marriage.

John le Carré

From the outside, the CIA seems pretty exotic, but from the inside, it's a big, bureaucratic place. Think 'post office with spies'.

Barry Eisler

Research and discuss

Overall, what has most interested you in the documents?

What would you most like to research further?

Activity 13

1 Which of the following would make good research questions for an assessed essay? Why?

   a National identity and cultural heritage
   b What is the source of authority in government?
   c How can we best deal with migration?
   d Has China's One Child Policy created a better society?
   e To what extent is cultural heritage an important part of national identity?
   f Is preserving cultural heritage in war zones a priority?
   g Should the UN accept that some countries are better served by non-democratic governments?

2 Write two or three questions of your own. Work in groups to assess and improve the questions.

Think about the following when considering the research questions:

- globally significant
- different perspectives
- argument and discussion
- question to answer
- can answer within the word limit
- suitable evidence base
- on a global perspectives topic

Remember to be positive and polite about each other's questions. You are helping each other to improve!

Avoid very theoretical or purely philosophical questions. To meet the assessment criteria you need to build up an evidence base, so remember to apply theoretical concepts in practical contexts.

Activity 14

1 Which of the following would make suitable questions for the team research project?

   a How can we support local migrant communities without alienating majority communities?
   b How can we keep the local library open?
   c How can we encourage young people to vote?
   d Why does the American President pardon a Thanksgiving Turkey every year?
   e Should same-sex couples be allowed to marry?
   f How has our national identity changed in the last 50 years?

2 Write two or three questions of your own. Work in a group to assess and improve the questions.

Think about each of the following when considering these questions:

- local problem
- global relevance
- effective solutions possible
- different aspects for individual research
- contrasting perspectives
- argument, reflection and discussion.

Practice examination paper

Document 1

Trump opens Pandora's box in US

2016-3-14 0:40:36

Donald Trump, front-runner to be the GOP's candidate for the upcoming US presidential election, encountered a major protest at his campaign event in Chicago on Friday evening. Over a thousand people, both his supporters and opponents engaged in a physical confrontation, which was quelled by police who arrested a number of people.

Fist fights among voters who have different political orientations is quite common in developing countries during election seasons. Now, a similar show is shockingly staged in the US, which boasts one of the most developed and mature democratic election systems. Trump's mischief has overthrown a lot of conventional norms of US political life. His remarks are abusively racist and extremist, which has left an impression on the US public that he is intentionally overthrowing political correctness.

Trump's rise was not anticipated by most analysts and observers. At the beginning of the election, Trump, a rich, narcissist and inflammatory candidate, was only treated as an underdog. His job was basically to act as a clown to attract more voters' attention to the GOP. However, knocking down most other promising candidates, the clown is now the biggest dark horse.

Trump is the last option for the GOP establishment. If he wins the primaries, the GOP will face a bitter dilemma. On the one hand, it will be a big compromise to GOP values, and the party takes a major risk of losing the game if they choose Trump as their candidate for president; on the other hand, if the GOP refuses to choose Trump, he might run as an independent candidate and split the vote, in which case, the GOP will also stand no chance in the final game.

The rise of Trump has opened a Pandora's box in US society. Trump's supporters are mostly lower-class whites, and they lost a lot after the 2008 financial crisis. The US used to have the largest and most stable middle class in the Western world, but many are going down.

That's when Trump emerged. Big-mouthed, anti-traditional, abusively forthright, he is a perfect populist that could easily provoke the public. Despite candidates' promises, Americans know elections cannot really change their lives. Then, why not support Trump and vent their spleen?

The rise of a racist in the US political arena worries the whole world. Usually, the tempo of the evolution of US politics can be predicted, while Trump's ascent indicates all possibilities and unpredictability. He has even been called another Benito Mussolini or Adolf Hitler by some Western media. Mussolini and Hitler came to power through elections, a heavy lesson for Western democracy. Now, most analysts believe the US election system will stop Trump from being president eventually. The process will be scary but not dangerous.

Even if Trump is simply a false alarm, the impact has already left a dent. The US faces the prospect of an institutional failure, which might be

> **Aa** GOP stands for Grand Old Party, and is a nickname for one of the USA's two leading political parties.

triggered by a growing mass of real-life problems. The US had better watch itself for not being a source of destructive forces against world peace, more than pointing fingers at other countries for their so-called nationalism and tyranny.

http://www.globaltimes.cn/content/973564.shtml

Global Times is a Chinese government sponsored online newspaper. It appears in English and Chinese. The English version aims to open up China.

Recognising the importance of democracy

By September 16, 2015

In this, the year of the 800th anniversary of the UK's Magna Carta, September 15, yesterday, was the UN International Day of Democracy. […]

The UK marks this day to recognise the benefits of democracy and the rule of law to individual states and their citizens, and to make clear support for the rules based on international system. Some may question how an 800-year-old document can still be relevant. But it is important to remember that the drivers behind Magna Carta — concern about unrestricted power of the executive, the State's ability to curtail individual rights and lack of due process in convicting individuals of crimes against the Crown — remain just as relevant in today's world.

Arbitrary detention, torture, and state-sponsored harassment of those who disagree with the government of the day continue, regrettably, to be a reality in many countries around the world. The UK believes that strong democratic institutions and accountable government, which uphold universal rights and the rule of law, are key building blocks for secure and prosperous states. In short, rule of law and a strong democracy are the best way to ensure people are not only free in the political sense, but also economically free and prosperous.

It is a sad fact that the current global environment is challenging. Evidence suggests that globally the pace of democratisation has slowed. Autocratic and dictatorial regimes can be seen in many places, abusing the rights of their people.

But there are positive stories as well. On May 11, last, Guyana went through a free, fair and democratic election. People were able to cast their votes and a new Government was elected. Democracy was seen to prevail. […]

There are some who claim that democracy is a Western model of government that has either failed or is not relevant in certain places. I could not disagree with this statement more. It is often made by those who seek to justify repression and abuse. People want and aspire to live in countries with democratically elected governments, so that they have some control over the decisions that affect their lives.

These principles of transparency, accountability and representative government are important values. They are universal. […]

Let me be clear. What we term democracy is not perfect. No system is perfect. But it is by far the best system we have to ensure that Government is selected by the people and rules for the people. That means all of the people — not one specific group. […]

http://www.kaieteurnewsonline.com/2015/09/16/recognising-the-importance-of-democracy/

Kaieteur News Online is a publication based in Guyana.

Questions

1 **a** According to document 1, why was Trump's rise not predicted? [2]

b How does the article explain Trump's success? [2]

2 How effective is the reasoning in document 1 in support of its claims? [12]

3 Compare and contrast the perspectives in the two articles. [14]

Extension activity

Each of these articles comes from a particular perspective. Can you find a more solid evidence base for these perspectives?

Research and discuss

What kind of legacy has Donald Trump's campaign and presidency in the US left on the US political system and on the USA's image in the wider world?

Changing world

Topics

- The ethics and economics of food
- The religious secular divide
- The rise of global superpowers
- Transnational organisations
- Arts in an international context
- International sport
- Tourism

Activities to get you started

During these introductory activities, you will start to explore and reflect on a range of issues, themes and perspectives relating to the overarching idea of 'Changing world' and the Global Perspectives topics within this main idea. You may find interesting issues and perspectives which you would like to research further, and you may start to reflect on and develop your own perspective.

Activity 1

A

B

1 What different issues and perspectives do these images raise on the topics in this chapter?

2 Does the whole class agree? Why or why not?

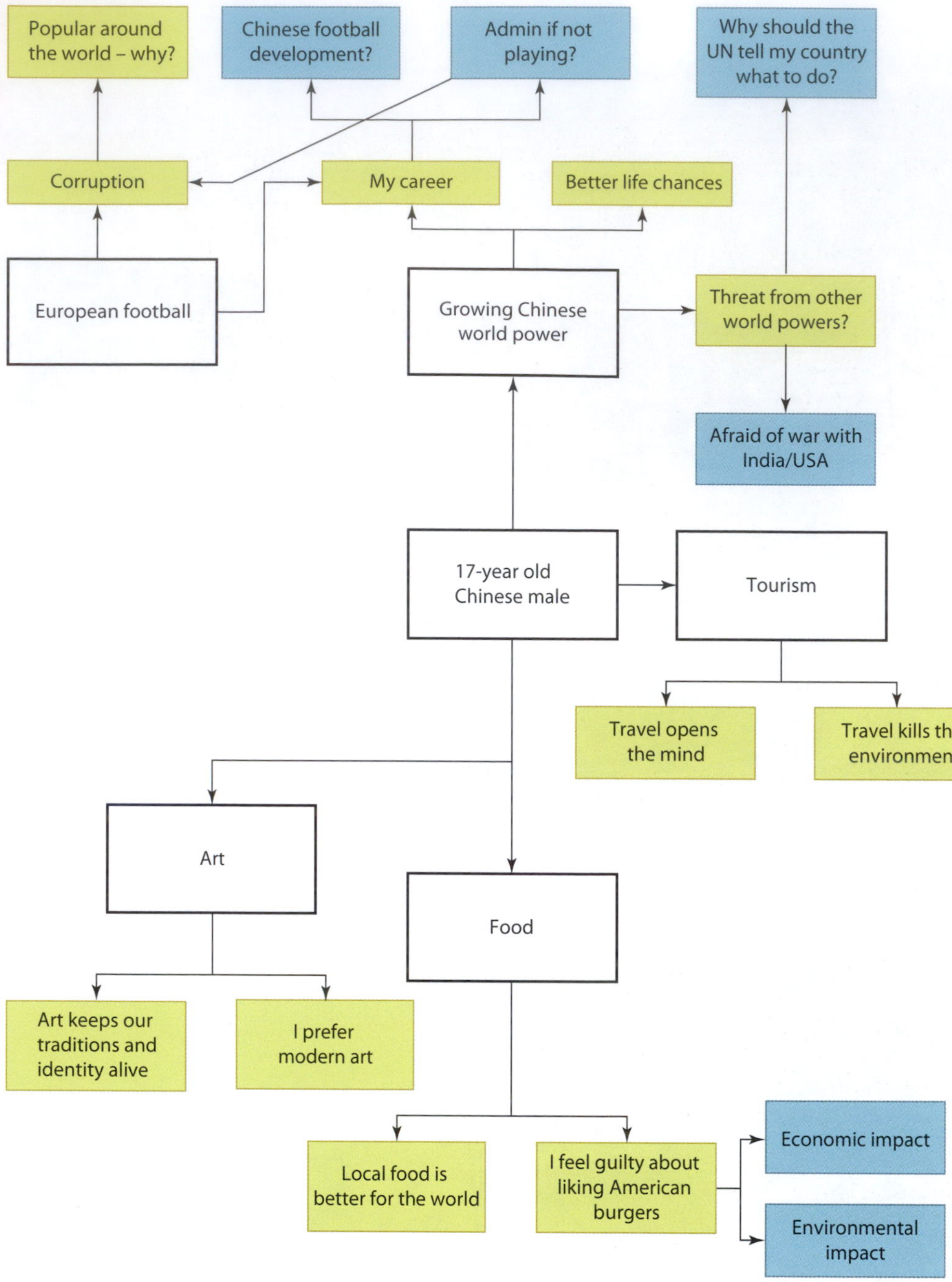

Activity 2

Popular around the world – why?

Chinese football development?

Admin if not playing?

Why should the UN tell my country what to do?

Corruption

My career

Better life chances

European football

Growing Chinese world power

Threat from other world powers?

Afraid of war with India/USA

17-year old Chinese male

Tourism

Travel opens the mind

Travel kills the environment

Art

Food

Art keeps our traditions and identity alive

I prefer modern art

Local food is better for the world

I feel guilty about liking American burgers

Economic impact

Environmental impact

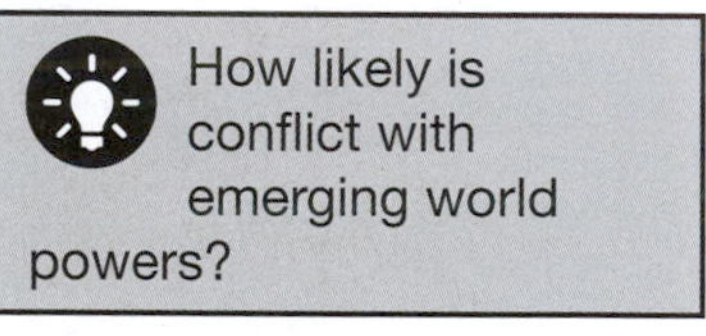

How likely is conflict with emerging world powers?

1 Look at the diagram and the images it contains. It shows how Chan Ming sees his perspective developing in relation to the topics in this chapter. Discuss the following questions.

   a What issues relating to the topics in this chapter do the images raise?

   b What questions would you ask Chan Ming to help him think more deeply about his perspective?

2 Choose and explain five images to show your own perspective relating to these topics, as Chan Ming has done.

3 Compare the different images class members have chosen.

4 Discuss how you have chosen the images to show your developing perspective.

5 Comment on any issues and perspectives relating to the topics in this chapter that have been raised by the class.

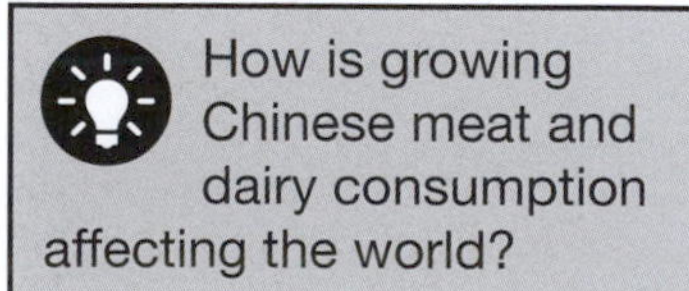

How is growing Chinese meat and dairy consumption affecting the world?

Activity 3

1 What do you think of these works of art? Why?

A

B

Research and discuss

Should art be beautiful?

Should art make a political statement?

How do we know what counts as good art?

Art is the lie that enables us to realise the truth.

Pablo Picasso

The most beautiful experience we can have is the mysterious. It is the fundamental emotion that stands at the cradle of true art and true science.

Albert Einstein

C

D

2 Does everyone agree? Why or why not?

3 In groups, research the background to one of these works of art. Start with the link that is given, but look deeper. Think about

- the artist
- the cultural background
- the meaning of the work
- the work as an expression of national identity
- the work as expression of international concerns
- how your response to the work has changed during your research.

4 Present your research to the class, in four minutes or less.

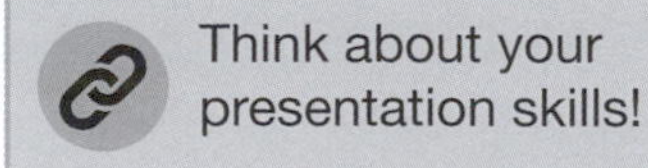
Think about your presentation skills!

Activity 4

1 Complete the questionnaire.

2 Discuss the results in class. Do you all agree? Why or why not?

1 = I disagree strongly 2 = I disagree a bit 3 = I'm not sure
4 = I agree a bit 5 = I agree strongly

		1	2	3	4	5
1	Travel opens people's minds and makes them more tolerant of others.					
2	The UN has outlived its usefulness.					
3	I am worried about the effects that old and new global superpowers might have on the world.					
4	Art and literature are essential ways of helping us to understand a complicated world.					
5	Religion and politics should be completely separate so that no single organisation gets too much power over people.					
6	We decide what is right by thinking about the best consequences of an action.					
7	Transnational organisations such as the World Health Organisation and the World Bank have a vital role to play in maintaining a peaceful, healthy world.					
8	I would rather be an international politician than an international sportsperson.					
9	GM foods don't help the hungry, they help the rich grow richer.					
10	Feeding the hungry is a bad idea: it leads to overpopulation.					

Research and discuss

1. Which transnational organisation does the most important work?
2. Do sportspeople, actors and artists play a meaningful role in international development?
3. Should religious belief be entirely private?

Those who say religion has nothing to do with politics do not know what religion is.

Mahatma Gandhi

Activity 5

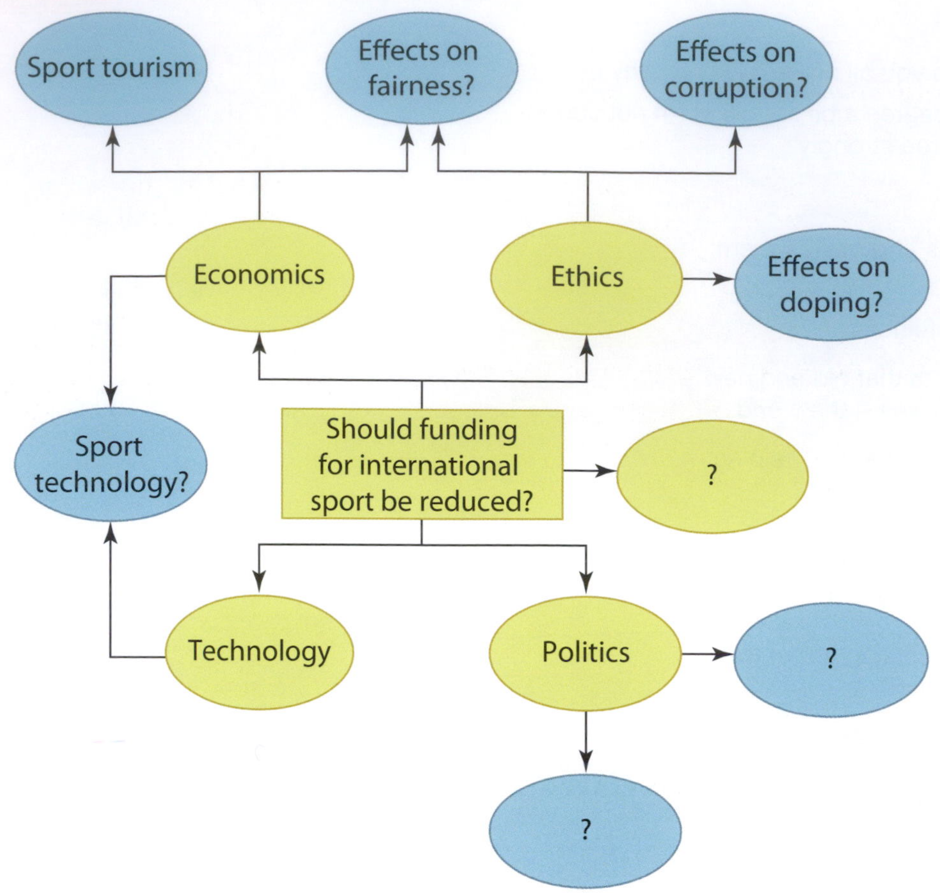

I would prefer to abandon the terminology of the past. 'Superpower' is something which we used during the cold war time. Why use it now?

Vladimir Putin

Use quick Internet searches to help you map out some of the issues and perspectives.

1 Complete and expand the mind map about whether funding for international sport should be reduced. Use the themes to help you explore different perspectives.

2 Draw a mind map using the themes to help you explore different perspectives on one of these questions.

   a Should unelected, transnational organisations be able to restrict the actions of nations?

   b Should governments support medical tourism?

   c Do global superpowers benefit the whole world?

   d Should internationally important art and literature aim to subvert power?

   e Are conspicuous religious symbols provocative?

At the height of the British Empire very few English novels were written that dealt with British power. It's extraordinary that at the moment in which England was the global superpower the subject of British power appeared not to interest most writers.

Salman Rushdie

Stimulus material

Document 1

Why aren't Islamic countries secular?

Coumba

My country, Senegal, is 92% Muslim, but the country is secular and if you think about women's rights or liberty of speech, you won't have to worry there. Sometimes, the girls are more modern in their style than many Europeans. We think that people should have the right to live their life like they want. Some girls (the majority) are more into the classic Scarlett Johansson, Kerry Washington, Anne Hathaway style, some others (specially young girls) will go with the sexy Beyonce or Nicki Minaj style, some others with the traditional Senegalese African style and others (a few) prefer casual or modern outfits with a hijab on their head (I have noticed that many girls use the hijab like a fashion item actually like some Indonesians girls do). Dakar, capital of Senegal, is one of the hottest cities to go out in Africa with plenty of night clubs, pool parties, students' parties, romantic restaurants, etc.

Bahadur

Secularism has less to do with which religion, and more to do with the type of government and economic wellbeing.

Widespread support for democracy, religious freedom

Median % of Muslims who ...

	prefer democracy over strong leader	say religious freedom is a good thing**
Sub-Saharan Africa*	72	94
Southeast Asia	64	93
Southern-Eastern Europe	58	95
Middle East-North Africa	55	85
Central Asia	52	92
South Asia	45	97

*Data for all countries except Niger from "Tolerance and Tension: Islam and Christianity in Sub-Saharan Africa."

**Medians show Muslims who say non-Muslims in their country are very free to practice their religion and consider this a good thing.

Source: PEW Research Center, Q10, Q11 and Q14

Political role for religious leaders

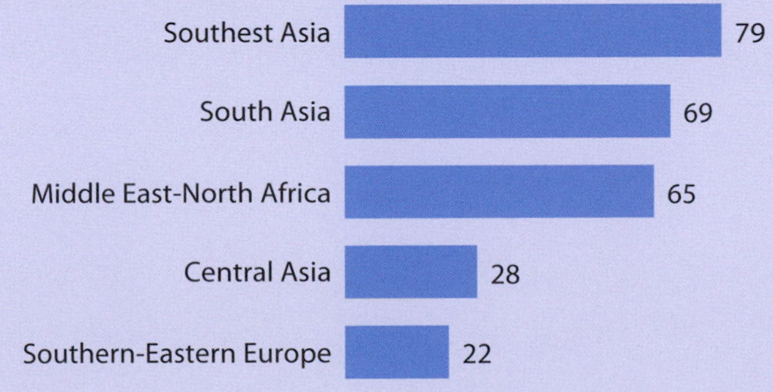

This question was not asked in sub-Saharan Africa.

1. What issues are raised in this document?
2. To what extent are the issues in this document global?
3. How would you describe the perspectives that this article comes from? What are the beliefs and assumptions underlying the perspective?

Research the facts. Find out about Senegal.

What is a secular state? If you're unsure, find out.

We can see that most Muslims believe in religious freedom and democracy. But there are differences between Muslims when it comes to the desire for a strong leader. There are even more differences between Muslims on the issue of whether religious leaders should have a role in politics, depending on where in the world they live.

This means that there are lots of reasons why people are more secular or more religious—these reasons include culture and governance, but also, political history, economic factors and external factors.

For example, Saudi Arabia, is a country with a great economy and good standards of living, **but** it has a Royal family who are also considered the religious custodians. Result, lesser freedoms (for women, and moral police, sharia law). Indonesia, on the other hand, is a democracy, also has a huge majority Muslim population, although it has lower standards of living, yet has a good track record in religious tolerance.

So in my opinion, secularism is not about Islam, or Christianity, or Hinduism or Buddhism. It is more about the contextual development of the citizens' psyche.

Elmas

I am Turkish, and I don't think that it's right to say that Islam cannot be secular.

Turkey has officially been secular since the early twentieth century but religion was never very dominant even under the Ottoman Empire. For example, the Ottoman Empire was the second country in Europe to legalise homosexuality, drinking was legal, etc. Women could vote in Turkey before women could in the USA; slavery was abolished in Turkey long before it was in the USA.

I think Turkey has one of the most strict secular state cultures. The Western media likes to see the main party in Turkey, AKP, as 'Islamist' when they are just scumbag conservatives.

The USA is not secular compared to Turkey at all. For example: Republicans say things like, 'We oppose abortion because it is against Christianity'. Say that in Turkey, and you will soon have to talk to the Constitutional Court or the Turkish Armed Forces.

And the UK? The UK has a religious leader as head of state. The Queen is the head of the Church of England. So don't tell me this is about Islam. It's not.

Research the facts. Which countries are mainly Muslim? Which countries have religious leaders in politics?

In what ways are religious identity and national identity linked?

Document 2

Canadians argue over how to promote religious freedom abroad

Feb 21st 2016, 11:45

By M.D. and ERASMUS | OTTAWA

Should Western democracies make the defence of religious freedom around the world a separate, fenced-off part of their foreign policy? Or is it better simply to subsume that concern under the general heading of human rights? In an age when blasphemy laws are horribly abused in many countries, and regimes like those of China, Iran and Turkmenistan deal brutally with dissent in metaphysical matters, that is not just a question for bureaucrats. It's a real dilemma both for individual countries and for clubs of nations like the European Union, which see themselves as a force for good in the world.

Very often, discussion about how best to promote freedom of belief internationally, or at least to protest effectively over appalling violations, gets snarled up with domestic arguments about religious freedom. These are always highly contentious: arguments about whether teachers can wear face-veils, or what schools should teach about the meaning and origin of life, and so on. In America, for example, religious-freedom advocates are upset with the Obama administration for its unwillingness to describe the travails of Middle Eastern Christians as genocide; some insist that the administration is making life a bit uncomfortable for American Christians too, and see the two questions as linked.

The latest country to have a debate about religion and diplomacy is Canada. People are watching closely to see what the newish Liberal government, headed by Justin Trudeau, decides about the Office of Religious Freedom, created in 2013 by its Conservative predecessors. In recent days, the government gave a short extension to the term of Andrew Bennett, an ambassador who heads the office, but the mandate for the office itself runs out at the end of next month and there have been clear hints that it will be axed.

Stéphane Dion, the global affairs minister, told the Senate this week that "[human] rights are indivisible, interlinked, interdependent... that is the approach we want to develop". After all, he noted, Prime Minister Trudeau had strong feelings on equality between the sexes but that did not imply that a special government bureau had to be established to work uniquely on that issue. And in another recent speech, Mr Dion asked rhetorically: "How can you enjoy freedom of religion if you don't have freedom of conscience? Freedom of speech? Freedom of mobility?" The implication was that freedom to engage in non-religious speech or activity, or simply to speak contentiously about matters which have nothing to do with religion, is no less important than the right to pray or to sing hymns.

What taints the office in the eyes of Liberals (as well as Canada's centre-leftists, the New Democratic Party) is its political origin. In other words, the fact that it's a brainchild of Conservatives who often seemed to play the religious card in domestic affairs. Evangelical Christians were an important electoral constituency for Stephen Harper, the Conservative ex-Prime Minister, whose staunchly pro-Israel views were rooted in Christian belief. Before last year's elections, his government enacted a law entitled the "Zero Tolerance for Barbaric Practices Act" which reinforced existing

1. What issues are raised in this document?
2. To what extent are the issues in this document global?
3. Why is religious freedom so important?
4. How would you describe the perspectives that this article comes from? What are the beliefs and assumptions underlying the perspective?
5. Do Western democracies have the right to defend religious freedom around the world? Why or why not?

What is blasphemy? Find out about blasphemy laws in your country and at least one other, contrasting, country.

How do we know what the right thing to do is? How do we know what is 'right' and what is 'wrong'?

Research and discuss one of these contentious issues. Make sure that you consider different perspectives.

What do you think? Is the freedom to criticise the government or to express controversial opinions as important as the right to worship as you choose?

legislation on polygamy, forced marriage and honour killings; for example, it barred people who had contracted polygamous unions in other countries from entering Canada. The Liberals, then in opposition, went along with the law but they were queasy about the title.

In general, anything the Conservatives did in the field of religion is a bit suspect among Liberals. But in fairness to the Office, nobody has questioned the competence of Ambassador Bennett, and its supporters are not confined to Christians: Jewish, Sikh and Ahmadiyya Muslim groups have made a joint appeal to keep it going.

Mr Trudeau's government, with its impressive mix of races, generations and genders, has inspired citizens of other democracies to follow Canada more closely than they usually do; the country is cool at the moment. It has also gained kudos as the country that has offered hospitality to the wife and family of Raif Badawi, the Saudi dissident who has been sentenced to 1000 lashes for his liberal-minded blog. Many people will therefore be interested to see how the Liberals handle this question.

Ideally, the defence of religious freedom around the world should rise above party politics, as it does to some extent in the United States. No democracy is likely to match the large and impressive bureaucratic apparatus which monitors global religious freedom on behalf of the American government. But other countries might have something to learn from the US Commission on International Religious Freedom (USCIRF), which is jointly appointed by Congress and the White House. The Commission has a powerful legal mandate but maintains an arm's-length relationship with the administration, which it frequently criticises.

It would also be a good idea if government agencies or departments working in this area made clear their determination to defend the rights of non-religious dissidents, including atheists and humanists. The USCIRF does raise the matter from time to time but it might do so more often; Canadian humanists have lobbied Ambassador Bennett to look after their interests and come away more or less satisfied. As Mr Dion says, freedom is indivisible.[1]

What do you think about this Act? Is it an act of religious intolerance or does it protect civilised values?

What can you find out about *The Economist*? Where is it based? What sort of articles does it publish? What sort of issues does it concentrate on? Is it generally more informed or speculative?

In some other countries they are now content to say: "Believe, or I detest thee; believe, or I will do thee all the harm I can. Monster, thou sharest not my religion, and therefore hast no religion; thou shalt be a thing of horror to thy neighbours, thy city, and thy province." … The supposed right of intolerance is absurd and barbaric. It is the right of the tiger; nay, it is far worse, for tigers do but tear in order to have food, while we rend each other for paragraphs.

Voltaire

All who are acquainted with the nature of government, must at once see the absurdity of considering civil government, and the government of the church of Christ, as different branches of the same government. In all free governments, the governing power is separated into different departments or branches, such as, the legislative, the executive, and the judiciary. These three being exercised by one person, or by one body of men, is, in the opinion of the celebrated Montesquieu, the definition of tyranny.

William Findley

1 http://www.economist.com/blogs/erasmus/2016/02/canadadiplomacy-and-religious-freedom

Document 3

The ethics of food

Because food choices influence and are influenced by economic, social and political institutions, it is difficult—if not impossible—to alter individual dietary behavior without also improving the economic, social and political environment within which individuals make food choices.

If dispensing dietary advice were sufficient to change behavior, diet-related chronic diseases would have vanished long ago. As early as the 1950s, cardiologists recommended dietary guidelines for prevention of coronary heart disease. Decades later, their advice still holds: Consume most daily energy from fruit, vegetables and grains (plant foods); less energy from meat and dairy foods (animal foods); and even less from processed foods high in fat, sugars and salt, and relatively depleted in essential nutrients (junk foods).

Since then, dozens of domestic and international governmental and professional committees have reconfirmed the value of these recommendations for prevention of diet-related diseases in general, but to no avail. Such diseases remain leading causes of worldwide death and disability, in part because dietary advice is more easily dispensed than followed. Because of entrenched institutional barriers, particularly food industry pressures, neither clinicians nor patients get much help from official sources of this advice.

To illustrate how these pressures operate, consider the first two "key recommendations" of the 2005 edition of the *Dietary Guidelines for Americans*. The *Guidelines*, jointly issued by the U.S. Departments of Health and Human Services and of Agriculture (USDA) every five years since 1980, constitute an official statement of government policy regarding all federal nutrition education, training, food assistance and research programmes. Although they are explicitly set forth as "science based", specific recommendations are invariably influenced by the economic interests of food industry stakeholders.

"Adequate nutrients": The first key recommendation is to "Consume a wide variety of nutrient-dense foods and beverages within and among the basic food groups while choosing foods that limit the intake of saturated and trans fats, cholesterol, added sugars, salt and alcohol". This statement translates as eat more fruit, vegetables and whole grains (nutrient-dense foods), eat fewer animal products (major sources of saturated fats and cholesterol) and eat less processed "junk" foods (major sources of *trans* fats, sugars and salt). The substitution of nutrients for actual foods in this recommendation obscures its basic point; it is best to eat more plant foods but fewer animal and processed foods.

If this message is obfuscated, it is surely because of its impact on sales of foods in the "eat less" categories. Policymakers learned this lesson in 1977. When Senator George McGovern's Select Committee on Nutrition and Human Needs released a report suggesting that Americans reduce consumption of meat, eggs, full-fat dairy products, sugars and salt, the affected industries protested and persuaded Congress to intervene. Their vigorous opposition established an apparently unshakable precedent that dietary advice must never suggest eating less of anything. Over the years, *Dietary Guidelines* committees have internalised this approach. The 1980 version of the sugar guideline simply said, "Avoid too much sugar". By 2005,

?

1. What issues are raised in this document?
2. To what extent are the issues in this document global?
3. Is this a fact or an opinion? Can you find evidence to support this statement?
4. How would you describe the perspectives this article comes from? What are the beliefs and assumptions underlying the perspective?

? How important are economic interests when compared with national health?

? Do you agree with this explanation? Are there other possible reasons why the advice is made less clear?

under pressure from sugar industry groups, the *Guidelines* used 23 additional words to make the same point, beginning with "Choose and prepare foods and beverages with little added sugars or caloric sweeteners… ."

"Within calorie needs": In a similarly oblique fashion, the second key recommendation is to "Meet recommended intakes within energy needs by adopting a balanced eating pattern, such as the USDA Food Guide or the DASH [Dietary Approaches to Stop Hypertension] Eating Plan". This recommendation, aimed at obesity and its health consequences, translates to "eat less". But such advice directly conflicts with the USDA's primary mission, which is to promote greater agricultural production and sales.

As a result of USDA policies, the U.S. food supply provides a startling 4000 kcal per day for every man, woman and child in the country (calculated as food energy produced, less exports, plus imports). Although this level is nearly twice the amount needed to meet average energy requirements, Congress continues to subsidise the production of commodity crops such as corn, soybeans and wheat. Cheap commodities promote the production of processed foods made with subsidised ingredients: corn sweeteners, soy oils and wheat starch. Subsidised corn and soybeans also are fed to farm animals and reduce the cost of meat. Low food costs encourage people to eat more.

The overabundance of calories forces companies to compete for sales by encouraging food consumption in more places, at more times of day and in larger amounts—all demonstrably effective "eat more" strategies. Companies advertise relentlessly and even market directly to children. Taken together, "eat more" environmental cues encourage people to consume more energy than needed. The *Guidelines* may urge adoption of balanced eating patterns reduced in fats and sugars, but the food and restaurant industry spends billions of dollars to market processed foods and to lobby against "eat less" messages.

Health claims: As a result of Wall Street's insistence that companies increase sales in an overabundant food economy, food companies increasingly rely on health messages to sell food. In 1990, they pressed Congress to allow health claims on the new food labels authorised by the nutrition labeling act. Congress forced the FDA to begin approving claims backed by adequate science. The FDA approved some claims, but rejected others. Food companies objected to the rejections, took the FDA to court and, on the grounds of free speech, won the right to make claims that were supported by minimal research. The result is a cacophony of confusing and misleading statements on food products such as sugary breakfast cereals said not only to reduce the risk of heart disease or cancer, but also to boost immune function. These claims take advantage of new research findings, no matter how preliminary. Health claims can best be understood as about marketing, not health.

Environmental impact: If one problem with dietary advice is confusing messages, another is the potential consequence of dietary choices for agricultural production and its effects on the environment. Eating less saturated fat, for example, often means switching from beef to fish, chicken or lean pork. But overfishing has led more than 75 per cent of the world's fisheries to hover on the point of collapse, meaning not only that entire species are approaching extinction, but also that food for much of the world's

It is not from the benevolence of the butcher, the brewer, or the baker, that we expect our dinner, but from their regard to their own interest. We address ourselves, not to their humanity but to their self-love, and never talk to them of our necessities but of their advantages.

Adam Smith

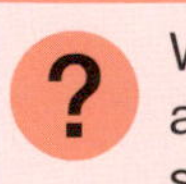

What do you think about this use of free speech?

population may vanish unless people eat less fish. Fish farming (the practice of raising fish in tanks or enclosed ocean areas) is proposed as a sustainable solution to this problem but creates water pollution, spreads marine diseases and paradoxically requires catching large numbers of wild fish to use as feed.

As for chicken and pork, confined feeding operations overburden the ability of land and water to absorb the waste products. Although the volume of animal sewage in the United States far exceeds that of human sewage, animal waste is not required to be treated and represents a substantial health hazard. Nutrients, antibiotics, hormones and pesticides in the waste end up in nearby waterways, where they contaminate drinking water and eradicate marine life. More than half the antibiotics in the United States are used in animal agriculture, leading to a proliferation of bacteria resistant to common antimicrobial agents.

Recommendations: Individuals on their own make daily decisions about what to eat. But making healthful decisions in the current food environment puts individuals in conflict with larger forces in society. Similarly, clinicians who advise patients about dietary choices do so in conflict with the goals of food companies. Because an exclusive focus on individual behavior is demonstrably inadequate to change it, clinicians might do better by accounting for the context in which people make food choices. Only by addressing both will dietary advice stand a chance of being effective in promoting health and preventing disease.

People need to hear clear messages about what to eat. They also need a food environment that makes it easier for them to follow those messages. To achieve both, we need to change policy. Since 1980, U.S. food and nutrition policies have favored industry deregulation. With the advent of a new administration, this is a good time to reconsider this approach and to press for policies that are more supportive of healthful food choices. As starting points, we favor:

- Development of dietary guidelines free of food industry influence.
- Restrictions on marketing low nutrient-dense foods to children.
- Restrictions on health claims that lack substantial scientific substantiation as determined by independent bodies.
- Elimination of agricultural subsidies for commodity crops.

Today, so many Americans are demanding a food supply that is healthier for people and for the environment that attempts to improve food policies can be considered a new social movement. On the production side, this movement focuses on community food security, organic production, local food, worker rights, animal welfare and fair trade, among other aspects. On the consumption side, the movement works to improve food marketing (especially to children) and school food, and to introduce food ranking systems and calorie labeling. Clinicians can help their patients and themselves to achieve healthier food choices by working to further these efforts.[2]

?

1. If individual decisions are influenced by the environment, does this mean that individuals are not fully responsible for their choices?
2. Is what we eat a personal matter that governments should not interfere in? Or is it reasonable for governments to intervene in the social and economic environment to affect our eating and our health?

What can you find out about http://realitysandwich.com? Where is it based? What sort of articles does it publish? What sort of issues does it concentrate on? Is it generally more informed or speculative?

2 http://realitysandwich.com/29964/ethics_food/

Document 4

Istanbul nearly a ghost town as tourists stay away

AFP | Jul 5, 2016, 03.19 AM IST

ISTANBUL: The tourists are so scarce you can hear their footsteps clattering down the empty shopping street. Nearly a week after the deadly airport bombings, it is eerily quiet in Istanbul.

The magic of Turkey's biggest city has been seducing visitors for centuries, from its array of historic mosques and palaces to its stunning views over the sparkling Bosphorus. But for people working in the once-thriving tourist trade, Tuesday's gun and suicide bomb spree represents one more nail in the coffin for an industry already reeling from a string of attacks this year.

"It's disastrous," said Orhan Sonmez as he stood hopelessly offering tours of the Hagia Sophia, the cavernous former mosque and church that is now a museum. "All my life I've been a tour guide. Most of us have come to a turning point where we don't know if we can go on. It's tragic."

Restaurants sit empty in the Sultanahmet tourist district, and five-star hotel rooms can be booked for bargain prices. In happier years the queues outside the Hagia Sophia might have stretched an hour or longer at this time of year—today you can walk straight in and share the place with just a smattering of other visitors. To add to the ghost town feel, many Istanbulites have left the city for Bayram, a nine-day nationwide holiday that began Saturday.

Nineteen foreigners were among the 45 people killed at Ataturk airport by suspected Islamic State jihadists, and analysts say the attack may have been a deliberate attempt to weaken the Turkish state by hitting its tourist industry.

The group had already been blamed for a January suicide blast that killed 12 German tourists in Sultanahmet, while three Israelis and an Iranian died in another on the Istiklal shopping street in March. The TAK, a radical Kurdish group that has carried out several attacks in Turkey this year, also warned foreign tourists to stay away after it killed 11 people in an Istanbul car bombing in June.

The United States, Germany and several other countries have warned their nationals against threats in Turkey, which is a candidate to join the European Union. Those still arriving say they are enjoying the peace and quiet, while taking a philosophical approach at a time when jihadist attacks have gone global.

"This could happen in any city—it's an unlucky lottery," said Irish visitor Nessa Feehan, perusing Sultanhamet's empty shops as she whiled away a stopover on her way to India. "The people are really friendly, and I really think I'll come back and spend some more time here."

In May, Turkey suffered its worst drop-off in visits in 22 years—down 35 per cent from a year ago—as an industry which ordinarily brings in 30 billion euros ($33.2 billion) went into free fall. This was partly a result of a Russian ban on Turkish package holidays that Moscow had slapped on Ankara over a bitter diplomatic row. That ban was lifted last week as the two countries made up—cause for celebration in the resort province of Antalya, where Russians traditionally come to sun themselves in their droves. That will be a boost for the tourist industry as a whole, but

1. What issues are raised in this document?
2. To what extent are the issues in this document global?
3. How would you describe the perspectives this article comes from? What are the beliefs and assumptions underlying the perspective?

When our country or our region changes, how does this affect our national identity?

Russians tend to plump for all-inclusive deals on Turkey's turquoise coast rather than heading to Istanbul to soak up history.

"If it goes on like this, many shops will close," said Ismail Celebi, worrying at a string of prayer beads in one hand as he sat at the gleaming counter of his jewellery shop. "I'm thinking of moving to America. I can't make money here."

The large Chinese tour groups still arriving are about the only bright spot on the horizon, said Celebi, adding that they spend "crazy money". "But it's not enough," he said. "We need Americans, we need Europeans."

His shop is just a stone's throw from the scene of the Sultanahmet bombing that left a dozen Germans dead six months ago—and Celebi said he didn't blame people for not wanting to come.

"Even I'm afraid to come to work here," he said.[3]

What can you find out about *the Times of India*? Where is it based? What sort of articles does it publish? What sort of issues does it concentrate on? Is it generally more informed or speculative?

Document 5

News from nowhere

The Syrian artist Randa Mdah expresses the suffering of a people.

Never before in my life have I seen drawings like the ones I'm looking at, and what makes them unprecedented—in any case for me—is the life experience with which they are impregnated. They don't describe or illustrate this experience; they are simply filled with it.

This experience may well be, historically speaking, unprecedented, too. History, despite what the editorialists say, does give rise to new forms of suffering.

What is this experience with which these drawings are filled? It is a form of endurance, an endurance which is habitual, common and endless. A harsh endurance. An endurance in each body circulating like the body's bloodstream.

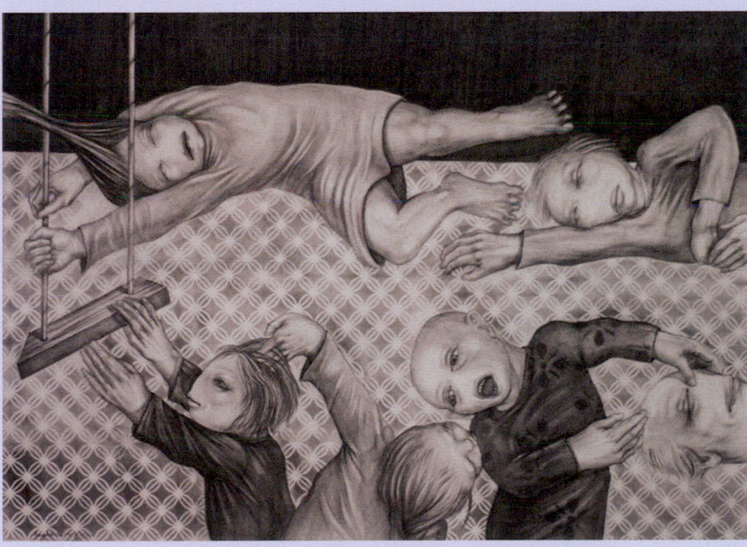

1. What issues are raised in this document?
2. To what extent are the issues in this document global?
3. How would you describe the perspectives this article comes from? What are the beliefs and assumptions underlying the perspective?

When suffering knocks at your door and you say there is no seat for him, he tells you not to worry because he has brought his own stool.

Chinua Achebe

There is no agony like bearing an untold story inside of you.

Maya Angelou

You must have chaos within you to give birth to a dancing star.

Nietzsche

3 http://timesofindia.indiatimes.com/world/europe/Istanbul-nearly-aghost-town-as-tourists-stay-away/articleshow/53053037.cms

The hands and figures of the bodies are taking the pulse of the soul's endurance. The faces of the bodies do not exchange glances because with their eyes shut or unseeing they all face the same wall. The faces' mouths are simply open because there are no more words to be pronounced.

Their silence makes me think of the motionless mouths of statues. But the figures are not statues; they are awaiting life and they have become old. Juvenile and senile.

Where are they? On the floor of a waiting room in a law-courts office of a judge who has disappeared? Or are they nowhere? Their clothes are winding sheets; their lips are as warm as ours. They are nowhere.

The series to which these drawings belong is entitled *Lead on paper.* Lead like the lead of a pencil. And lead as the name of one of the heaviest metals.

The drawings were made recently by the Syrian artist Randa Mdah, who was born in 1983 in Majdal Shams, just on the ceasefire line running along the Golan Heights, once part of Syria and illegally occupied by Israel since 1967. The Israeli forces still control that area today. Despite this, Randa Mdah lives and works there.

The methodical, unrelenting filching of the Palestinian people's homeland from under their feet has been going on for eighty years, and today the redress of this criminal injustice is more remote than it has ever been. The Palestinian homeland is Nowhere. These drawings are a chart of that Nowhere.[4]

"Portraits: John Berger on Artists" is published by Verso. See more details at: randamdah.blogspot.co.uk

? Is it more important for art to be beautiful or meaningful?

Research the history of Golan Heights. Consider different perspectives.

The article was published by the *New Statesman*. What can you find out about them? Where is it based? What sort of articles does it publish? What sort of issues does it concentrate on? Is it generally more informed or speculative?

In the fight between you and the world, back the world.

Franz Kafka

Document 6

The United States is riding Europe's superpower coattails

By Andrew Moravcsik 15 April 2016

Andrew Moravcsik is a professor of politics at Princeton University and a senior fellow at the Transatlantic Academy

President Obama and Donald Trump rarely agree on foreign policy. Yet they share one core belief: Our closest allies in Europe are exploiting U.S. military might.

Trump says NATO should be renegotiated: It is "obsolete" and "unfair… to the United States… because (we) pay a disproportionate share".

Obama has criticised Trump's stance. Yet for years the president has been conducting his own NATO renegotiation—including demanding European leadership in the Libyan operation and telling Prime Minister David Cameron that if Britain wants to maintain the Anglo-American "special relationship", it must increase defense spending to the recommended NATO minimum of 2 per cent of gross domestic product. His explanation? "Free riders aggravate me."

?

1. What issues are raised in this document?
2. To what extent are the issues in this document global?
3. How would you describe the perspectives this article comes from? What are the beliefs and assumptions underlying the perspective?
4. What sort of President was Obama? What do you think the most important part of his legacy to America and the wider world will be? Consider different perspectives.
5. What effect has Donald Trump had on America and the wider world? Consider different perspectives.

4 http://www.newstatesman.com/culture/art-design/2016/03/newsnowhere

But Trump and Obama are both wrong. Although more foreign policy spending is always welcome, Europe already assumes more than its fair share of the regional security burden. It invests not only in its military but also in crucial geo-economic and institutional instruments that the United States does not possess—but needs. In this respect, the United States freerides on European power.

Consider the facts. The U.S. military commitment to European defense is surprisingly small. After the Cold War, almost 90 per cent of American soldiers departed. Today only about 5 per cent of total U.S. active-duty personnel and a few hundred among thousands of U.S. nuclear weapons are deployed there.

The primary purpose of this military presence is in any case not to defend Europe. It is to promote vital interests elsewhere. Without naval ports, air force bases, hospitals and command centers in Italy, Spain, Germany and Turkey, U.S. military operations in the Middle East, South Asia, the Mediterranean, Africa and the Arctic would be nearly impossible. In recent years, for example, 95 per cent of people and material delivered to U.S. forces in Iraq and Afghanistan crossed through Europe.

Trump singles out resistance to Russia as a prime example of U.S. leadership. "Nobody else", he said, "is fighting for the Ukraine". Yet the slice of the United States' $600 billion defense budget directed to supporting Ukraine or deterring Russia in Europe is tiny. One-time allocations of $800 million this year and $3.4 billion next year are earmarked for NATO "reassurance measures" in Eastern Europe. Less than a billion more goes for military aid to Ukraine, where key Western governments have ruled out a direct military response. By contrast, Poland alone spends nearly $10 billion annually on its military, and NATO Europe as a whole more than $250 billion.

Is $250 billion too little? Like Obama, the U.S. foreign policy establishment rejects Trump's bluster yet almost unanimously embraces his underlying premise. A common complaint inside the Beltway is that European spending falls short (by roughly $75 billion) of the 2 per cent of GDP that NATO leaders have pledged to spend.

Yet all such criticism of low European defense spending rests on a misleadingly narrow conception of national security. When Americans think about global influence, they tend to calculate only military power. Yet in world politics, non-military instruments are often more effective. And Europe is the world's preeminent civilian superpower.

Supreme excellences consists of breaking the enemy's resistance without fighting.

Sun Tzu

Europe is the world's largest trading bloc, provides two-thirds of the world's economic aid and dominates most international organisations. It has invested heavily in the European Union, which spreads peace and market economics across the continent, and permits Europeans to negotiate as a bloc.

Europe's resulting clout is most obvious in the very area in which Trump believes the United States is being exploited the most. The primary external force helping Ukraine resist Russia today is not the U.S. military but European geo-economic and diplomatic power.

No Western policy is more critical to keeping Russia at bay than Europe's $9 billion in annual economic aid and debt relief to Ukraine, without which the country would long since have collapsed. This is about 10 times more than the United States provides. Europe has a similar though smaller assistance programme for other countries in Russia's neighbourhood.

Brussels also recently signed a free-trade agreement with Ukraine, giving it an international lifeline in the face of Vladimir Putin's tightening trade boycotts. Without this, the country would have no prospects to free itself from the Russian stranglehold and to achieve sustainable growth, since Europe is by far its largest trading partner.

Europe pays a high cost in lost trade to sustain Western sanctions against Russia. Some estimate the total loss at $50 billion annually. This is again more than 10 times more than the United States, because European trade and investment are that much higher.

Russia's policy options are limited also by its dependence on European energy markets. Today E.U. authorities are further undermining the Kremlin's leverage by clamping down on Russian energy monopolies and spending billions to diversify Europe's energy imports. This includes rerouting the energy supply of Ukraine, which now imports more energy from Europe than from Russia.

Bolstered by Europe's underlying strength, leaders such as German Chancellor Angela Merkel have taken the diplomatic lead in negotiations over eastern Ukraine. Within the Minsk Process, in which the United States is not formally involved, they have persuaded Putin to limit his territorial gains in eastern Ukraine, concede a cease-fire and withdraw heavy weapons under international oversight—with further plans for local elections and eventual removal of Russian forces still under discussion. Although Ukraine is far from secure, even such modest gains mark a remarkable diplomatic achievement, given the strategic edge that Russia enjoys when projecting power into its most culturally proximate and strategically vital Western neighbour.

The geo-economic and institutional instruments of power that permit Europe to flex its muscles with regard to Russia are simply unavailable to the United States, with its low levels of foreign aid, antipathy to international legal commitments and secondary economic status in the former Soviet zone, as well as its military dependence on forward bases. And resisting Russia is only one of many regional and global issues in which Europe has taken the lead.

Portraying Europe as a continent of slackers makes for rousing election-year rhetoric. But pulling back from a transatlantic partnership that benefits the United States at least as much as it does Europe would be self-defeating.[5]

? Do you think that Russia is still a global superpower? Why or why not?

? Do you think that Russia is as unreasonably aggressive as Europeans and Americans often suggest? Could there be another perspective? Would seeing another perspective help to avoid conflict?

It is better to be feared than loved, if you cannot be both.

Niccolo Machiavelli

? Do you think that Europe is or could be a global superpower? Explain your view.

This article was published in *the Washington Post*. What can you find out about the newspaper? What sort of articles does it publish? What sort of issues does it concentrate on? Is it generally more informed or speculative?

5 https://www.washingtonpost.com/opinions/the-united-states-isriding-europes-superpower-coattails/2016/04/14/90b3dd98-0193-11e6-9203-7b8670959b88_story.html

Document 7

Unhappy New Year: The 10 Geopolitical Risks to Watch in 2016

By Daniel Twining, 7 January 2016, 5:34 pm

2016 is looking like it might be a turbulent year. Rising populism, great

power revanchism, the continued specter of terrorism, disputes over "cyber-sovereignty", intensified regional turmoil, and dramatic shifts in the global economy presage unsettled times. Against this uncertain backdrop, here are the top 10 notable geopolitical risks to keep an eye on in the year ahead:

1 The rise of populism: The combination of the middle-class economic squeeze and Islamic extremism at home risks fueling the populist politics of xenophobia and anger surging across Europe and the United States. This could continue to weaken establishment politicians and empower those on the far left and far right, making both American and European foreign policies more unpredictable and diverting leaders from engagement abroad in favor of damage-control domestically. It could encourage greater insularity that would allow regional crises to fester.

2 A foreign policy reset for the United States: A major terrorist attack on the United States, along the lines of 9/11, could scramble the presidential race and force the Obama administration to reverse its current round of retrenchment to attack the danger abroad. This could transform the dynamic of international politics after seven years in which U.S. President Barack Obama has appeared content to lead from behind, or not to lead at all. Should Donald Trump or another outsider candidate prevail in the race for the Republican nomination, it will be partly a result of widespread anger and fear over the Obama administration's perceived inability to keep America safe. Whether a Democrat or a Republican wins the contest in November 2016, U.S. foreign policy is likely to return to its traditionally more hawkish, expeditionary orientation.

3 The breakdown of transnational institutions: A series of Paris-style attacks across Europe could fracture the European Union, as individual countries close their borders and pursue different national approaches to the threat of Islamic extremism at home and abroad. The Syrian refugee crisis has already placed enormous strains on European unity. If jihadists motivated

1. What issues are raised in this document?
2. To what extent are the issues in this document global?
3. How would you describe the perspectives this article comes from? What are the beliefs and assumptions underlying the perspective?

by the successes of the Islamic State group abroad succeed in terrorising the major capitals of Europe in a systematic way, existing trans-national institutions may simply buckle. The EU would likely remain as a shell institution, but decades of integration could finally be reversed.

4 The slowdown of developing economies: Global inequality could spread as the developed world resumes its traditional position as the driver of economic growth (although industrialised economies will not be immune from turbulence, with British Chancellor George Osborne warning of a "cocktail of risks" spilling over from abroad). Emerging economies that have powered the past 15 years of worldwide economic growth are slowing down or even contracting. The narrative of the past decade has been one of a "great convergence," as poor nations from the global south narrowed the economic gap with the industrialised West through rapid economic growth. After years in which conventional wisdom assumed the future belonged to the BRICS (Brazil, Russia, India, China, and South Africa), the balance of economic power is now being redressed. This is a function of dynamic technological change, collapsing commodity prices and the end of easy money that led emerging powers to rack up debts, rising labor costs in China and its slowdown into the middle-income trap, and America's normalisation of monetary policy following the Federal Reserve's decision to raise interest rates for the first time since 2006. Emerging markets that binged on debt and commodity riches during the boom now face a reckoning as the U.S. dollar strengthens and weak Chinese demand hollows out their primary export market.

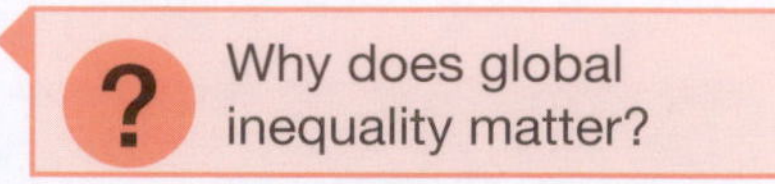
?
Why does global inequality matter?

5 Volatile oil markets: Changing energy dynamics will continue to tip the balance between net energy exporters and importers, placing intense pressure on the former. India and the United States are among the lead beneficiaries, although cheap oil and desperate efforts by the Organisation of Petroleum Exporting Countries to protect market share risk undercutting U.S. shale producers, even as America returns to the global market by liberalising oil exports. Top energy exporters like Saudi Arabia, Iran, and Russia, as well as commodity superpowers like Brazil, are the losers, not only in terms of profit but from the risk of rising unrest among disaffected constituencies at home as the money runs out. China is in the middle—as an energy importer it benefits from low prices, but its slowdown is causing widespread harm to its trading partners in Latin America, Africa, the Middle East, diminishing its leverage abroad even as it places pressure on China's big state-owned oil producers at home.

6 A reckless Moscow: Russia's decline will make Vladimir Putin more dangerous, not less. The Russian president is a gambler and a risk-taker; these propensities may grow, not diminish, even as his foreign adventures do not bear fruit for Russian interests. Domestic pressure on Putin will mount as the economy contracts, the plummeting oil price requires severe cuts to government programs (including military spending), and Moscow secures no quick victories in either Ukraine or Syria. Should Putin be ousted through elite factionalism, his successor is likely to be no more liberal and to be equally anti-Western in orientation.

7 A face-off with Beijing: China's growth slowdown, potentially to below 5 per cent, could increase President Xi Jinping's propensity to fan the flames of nationalism and assert China's interests more forcefully abroad. Indeed, one senior Chinese official opened the new year with a warning that the U.S.-led order "is like an adult in children's clothes", and that an America whose "great contributions to human progress and economic growth" now "lie in the past" should get out of the way so China can work to construct a new order. A crisis over Taiwan, the Senkaku Islands, or maritime disputes in the South China Sea could help restore the Chinese Communist Party's legitimacy should it come under challenge from socioeconomic discontent. But this is also a risky proposition for China as the United States is likely to stand firm, and a loss of face abroad (much less a loss through conflict) could do untold damage to the Party's continued rule. Whether China's "Go west" strategy of infrastructure exports through the One Belt, One Road initiative spurs reform at home or only postpones the necessary transition away from heavy industry remains a wild card.

8 A Balkanised Internet: Fueled by China's demand for cyber-sovereignty and the failure or fragility of democratic institutions in Eurasia and the Middle East, the Balkanisation of the Internet could gather pace, signaling the close of an era that promised a truly worldwide web of free information flows. China has more Internet users than any country, so the online norms it advocates have potency. Beijing's illiberal alliance with Moscow in favour of state control over its virtual territory, echoing state control over its geographic domain, could find additional support from conservative undemocratic regimes in the Middle East, including Iran and Saudi Arabia, as well as from strongmen in democracies like Turkey who seek to tilt the political playing field in their favor. Pressures on the liberal order in cyberspace increase the stakes for transatlantic leadership on this issue, and for new alliances to protect the open Internet with democracies like India.

9 More trouble from North Korea: Jealous of the great powers' focus on Islamic State terrorists in the Middle East and their deal-making on Syria, North Korea's Kim Jong-un will seek to rattle the cage through provocative missile or nuclear tests, like the hydrogen bomb explosion his regime allegedly conducted on 6 January. North Korea recently failed in an attempt to test a submarine-fired ballistic missile; as 2015 closed Pyongyang was warning the United States of "unimaginable consequences" if it failed to agree to a peace treaty. Although strategists and journalists more recently have focused on other potential military contingencies in Asia, U.S. military officers continue to see the Korean theater as the most likely venue for regional conflict, with pressure growing on Pyongyang as Beijing distances itself from Kim's antics and the economic gap between North Korea and its more prosperous neighbors grows ever wider.

10 Wider war in the Middle East: As U.S. leadership in the Middle East remains inadequate, the risk of heightened regional conflict increases.

This reality inverts President Obama's belief that regional powers should settle regional disputes; the evidence over the past few years suggests that localised wars intensify, in the absence of robust U.S. engagement and coalition-building. The risk of conflict between Turkey and Russia could intensify over Syria, building on a centuries-long history in which their imperial predecessors sparred for influence from the Balkans to the Caucasus. Iran's behavior could also become more destabilising as hardliners seek to offset charges of appeasement over the nuclear deal struck with the great powers in 2015 by stepping up support for Shia insurgents in Yemen, Iraq, and Syria, intensifying hostilities with Saudi Arabia and Turkey in particular. A Saudi-Iran cold war threatens to turn hot in the wake of Iranian hard-liners' storming of Riyadh's embassy in Tehran and a Saudi-led bloc of Sunni governments' severing of diplomatic relations with Iran at the start of the year.

Despite this grim prognosis, 2016 holds the potential for upside surprises. Perhaps the most important would be a positive outcome of the American presidential election that delivers national renewal after a poisonous political season and a recommitment to foreign policy leadership, reassuring anxious allies and creating a firmer foundation for global prosperity. Happy new year.[6]

An earlier version of this essay appeared in the Nikkei Asian Review.

What can you find out about http://foreignpolicy.com? Where is it based? What sort of articles does it publish? What sort of issues does it concentrate on? Is it generally more informed or speculative?

6 http://foreignpolicy.com/2016/01/07/unhappy-new-year-the-10-geopolitical-risks-to-watch-in-2016/

Skills development activities

Activity 6

Refer to document 1.

1. How well does Coumba support her view that you don't need to worry about women's rights or freedom of speech in Senegal?
2. What additional evidence would you look for to support Coumba's view? How would it help?
3. What is Bahadur's conclusion?
4. What evidence does Bahadur use to support his conclusion?
5. How effectively does he use this evidence to support his conclusion?
6. How effective is Elmas's reasoning? Think about evidence and arguments.
7. Coumba is Senegalese and Elmas is Turkish. How does this affect their reliability?
8. Compare the perspectives of these people.
9. Has reading these people's views affected your perspective? Why or why not?

A perspective is a world view which underlies an argument. It can be quite hard to pin down.

Argument, reasoning and opinions are the specifics of what the author says – they are informed by the author's perspective.

Activity 7

Refer to document 2.

1. Document 2 poses the following question: 'Should Western democracies make the defence of religious freedom around the world a separate, fenced-off part of their foreign policy?' Does the author provide a satisfactory answer?
2. How effectively does the author use evidence and argument?
3. How does the perspective in document 2 compare with the perspectives expressed in document 1?
4. How far do you share the author's perspective?
5. Can you find any opposing opinions or perspectives in your research?

Research and discuss

Research the history of religious tolerance and intolerance in your own country and in at least one other contrasting country. You could make a timeline.

Does learning about the past affect your perspective on the present? Does it change your opinion about the relationship between government and religion?

Research and discuss

A: How would this help you to decide what it is right for Western democracies to do in defence of freedom of religion?

Actions are right in proportion as they tend to promote happiness, wrong as they tend to produce the reverse of happiness.

John Stuart Mill

B: How would this help you to decide what it is right for Western democracies to do in defence of freedom of religion?

Do what is right, though the world may perish.

Kant

Which of these quotations feels closer to the way in which you decide what is the right or wrong thing to do? Do you get the same answers to each of the questions? Why or why not?

Research and discuss

How do we draw the line between things we should tolerate (even if we disagree) because they are part of someone else's religion, and things we should oppose, because they are wrong?

How can we know that something is 'wrong' and not just different from our own opinions?

Activity 8

Refer to document 3.

1 Summarise the main arguments in document 3.
2 How effective is the reasoning?
3 How well does the evidence support the reasoning?
4 What are the ethical issues in this article?
5 How do the ethical and economic issues in this article relate to each other?
6 Do you agree with the reasoning? Why or why not?
7 How would you describe the author's perspective? (Think about the author's underlying beliefs and attitudes and about the way the author sees the world.)
8 How far do you share this perspective?

Research and discuss

How efficient is the world food industry?

To what extent can economic efficiency justify dubious ethical practices? Support your view.

How do you think the world food industry should change? Consider economic, ethical, scientific, technological, social, political and environmental perspectives, and justify your proposed changes.

Activity 9

Refer to document 4.

1 Is document 4 an argument? If not, what sort of writing is it?

2 Explain how terrorist bombings in Turkey (and their causes and effects) could be relevant to two or more of the topics in this chapter, thinking about different themes and perspectives.

3 Explain how the 2016 terrorist bombings in Turkey might be linked to other Global Perspectives topics, dealt with in other chapters. Think about different themes and perspectives on these topics.

Research and discuss

Investigate the causes and effects of a terrorist attack aimed at a tourist destination. Explain different perspectives, themes and issues on the attack.

Research and discuss

How important is tourism to your country's economy? Compare it to one very different country.

How significant are the ethical, environmental and political implications of tourism in the countries you have researched?

Activity 10

Refer to document 5.

1 Is document 5 an argument? If not, what sort of writing is it?

2 How reliable is John Berger as a source of information and opinions about art?

3 How does the author support his opinions? Is this effective?

4 To what extent do you share the author's views on Randa Mdah's art? Justify your answer.

Research and discuss

Is art necessarily political?

What is the relationship between science and art?

Activity 11

Refer to document 6.

1 Is document 6 an argument? If not, what sort of writing is it?

2 What does the author think that Trump and Obama are wrong about?

3 How effectively does the author of document 6 support the view that Trump and Obama are wrong?

4 Has time changed this perspective?

Research and discuss

1. Is Europe a global superpower, in your view?
2. How has the British referendum vote to exit the European Union affected Europe's power and global influence?
3. Which countries are global superpowers, in your view? Are they emerging or declining?

Activity 12

Refer to document 7.

1 Document 7 makes predictions about 2016. How accurate were these predictions? Justify your answers with research.

2 What predictions has www.foreignpolicy.com made about the current year? How accurate do you think they are likely to be?

3 What do you predict for next year? How can you support your predictions?

Research and discuss

Overall, what has most interested you in the documents? What would you most like to research further?

Activity 13

1 Which of the following would make good research questions for an assessed essay? Give your reasons.

a My favourite football team.

b Tourism: blessing or curse?

c To what extent is the UN/World Bank/UNICEF still relevant as a solution to twenty-first century problems?

d How far is the West responsible for providing solutions to food crises in developing countries?

e Does God exist?

f Why has BRICS not become a more important global power?

2 Write two or three questions of your own. Work in groups to assess and improve the questions.

Think about these points when deciding on a good research question:

- Globally significant
- Different perspectives
- Argument and discussion
- Question to answer
- Can answer within the word limit
- Suitable evidence base
- On a global perspectives topic

Activity 14

1 Which of the following would make suitable questions for the team research project? How can you improve them?

a How can we support Amnesty International in campaigning to free a writer or artist who has been imprisoned for political views?

b Should we always do what our conscience dictates?

c How can we bring together religious and non-religious people in our community?

d Make an allotment and supply the school canteen with food.

e Organise a trip to a part of our country that relies on tourism. Analyse the effects of global recession and terrorism.

2 Write two or three questions of your own. Work in groups to assess and improve the questions.

Remember to be positive and polite about each other's questions. You are helping each other to improve!

Avoid very theoretical or purely philosophical questions. To meet the assessment criteria you need to build up an evidence base, so remember to apply theoretical concepts in practical contexts.

Think about these points when deciding on a team research project:

- Local problem
- Global relevance
- Effective solutions possible
- Different aspects for individual research
- Contrasting perspectives
- Argument, reflection and discussion

Practice examination paper

Document 1

In the last 20 years, the amount of locally grown foods consumed in the American diet has tripled, according to the U.S. Department of Agriculture, and it now comprises 2 per cent of the food consumed in the country. As with anything that's popular, some have seen fit to attack this trend. Why do they do this? Do they find locavore talk of "terroir" pretentious and therefore annoying, or do they seriously believe, as some critics argue, that local food enthusiasts pose a threat to the planet?

One frequent complaint is relatively minor and concerns the fraudulent claims made by some restaurants. Thanks to the farm-to-table movement, menus have become dense with information, as chefs detail the life histories of every ingredient in every dish. *San Diego Magazine* did some investigating and documented cases of straight-up menu fraud: "Chefs will come look (at what we're selling that day), write down notes, leave without buying anything, and then say they're serving our food at their restaurants," said Tom Chino of California's Chino Farms.

The main argument against the locavore movement, however, revolves around the purported energy savings of growing food locally. In "The Locavore's Dilemma: In Praise of the 10 000-mile Diet," economists Pierre Desrochers and Hiroko Shimizu argue that if everyone focused on local foods, agriculture would damage the environment even more than it already does. Their case rests on a widely circulated statistic: that local production adds up to a lot more food-related carbon emissions than the 5 per cent accounted for by the transportation of food. Greenhouse tomatoes grown in the United Kingdom, for example, have been shown to produce three times the greenhouse gas emissions as tomatoes imported from Spain.

This criticism is not new. Stephen Budiansky wrote about it in a 2010 *New York Times* op-ed, "Math Lessons for Locavores," and several books have made the same argument, including "Just Food, An Economist Gets Lunch and Food Police". Their arguments, based on economic concepts such as efficiency, comparative advantage and the economics of scale, assume that all advantages and disadvantages of a given food chain can be accounted for. But is this true?

Taken to their logical extremes, the economics-based arguments would label almost all gardens as inefficient. Most gardeners would agree that it would be more efficient, and even cheaper, to spend a few extra hours at work and buy all their food than spend that time crawling through the dirt. But they choose to garden just the same. Quality of life is hard to quantify.

An article published last summer by two economics professors, Anita Dancs and Helen Scharber, rebuts the efficiency arguments in the economists' own language. While California can grow a lot of produce, they point out, the economic calculations don't account for the state's dwindling aquifer. Florida may also grow cheap tomatoes, but that

It is the maxim of every prudent master of a family, never to attempt to make at home what it will cost him more to make than to buy... What is prudence in the conduct of every private family, can scarce be folly in that of a great kingdom.

Adam Smith

economic efficiency doesn't account for the near-slavery conditions in which some of the workers toil.

"I can't believe that people are trying to argue that communities feeding themselves is a bad thing," says Josh Slotnick, a farmer in Missoula, Mont. "Growing food in just a few places and shipping it around the world from there doesn't sound like efficiency."

Eating locally, he argues, makes you a better citizen. "Food is a medium for creating culture. It's a medium for people falling in love with their places. And when people love where they live, all kinds of great behavior follows, very little of which is economically rational. It's a red herring to say that, because the industrial food system is so efficient and its carbon footprint is so small, that it's a good thing. Agribusiness isn't about making food and places better. It will make us better consumers, but not better people or better citizens."

Anyone who's raised chickens will surely concede that it is more efficient to buy eggs at the store. But try telling that to my 2-year-old, whose first words in the morning are, "Get some eggs," as he stumbles toward the coop in his sagging diaper. Should I tell him how inefficient that notion is? I'll let you explain it to him, if it means that much to you. But I don't think it's an argument you're going to win.[7]

Ari LeVaux is a contributor to Writers on the Range, an opinion service of High Country News (hcn.org). He writes about food and food politics in Montana.

Document 2

Serving up a solution to Singapore's retiring hawker sellers

By 2 July 2016

Singapore is cooking up new methods to find the next wave of hawker sellers amid fears the city state's signature street-food delights could fall off the menu with chef retirements. Singapore has more than 100 hawker centres and 6 000 stalls selling popular multi-ethnic meals for as little as S$2.80 ($2), but enticing new chefs to the small, basic kitchens is proving tricky against the riches offered by modern restaurants.

Chen Fu Yuan, a 72-year-old hawker that has been cooking Char Kway Teow (fried flat rice noodles) since 1969, is struggling to find anyone to take over his stall after his children and grandchildren took up other careers. "I will definitely be very heartbroken," Chen said. "It is a waste that no one wants to take it on."

In April the government set up an advisory Hawker Center 3.0 Committee, charged with sustaining a trade that is a source of pride for locals and regularly draws visiting celebrities, like British chef Gordon Ramsay. The government will open 10 new hawker centres over the next 12 years but many of these venues come without the government subsidies that have kept some monthly stall rents as low as S$320 ($238). New rates can be S$1 800 a month.

7 http://www.denverpost.com/writersontherange/ci_29303546/economics-and-ethics-locally-grown-food

"We can build hawker centres but who is going to man them?" Singapore food blogger, author and Hawker Center 3.0 Committee member Dr Leslie Tay asked. Tay said most hawker stall owners were in their 50s and 60s with a wave of retirements expected in the near future but new initiatives to find replacements were showing signs of promise, such as pairing aspiring hawkers with experienced hands.

"I was holding a pen and a laptop a year ago and a year later I'm holding on to this knife," 30-year-old Derrick Lee said after giving up a career in oil and gas to learn alongside a hawker master. "I believe there are still people out there who are interested to take over."[8]

($1 = 1.3447 Singapore dollars.)

Questions

1 a Identify two key arguments against locally produced food in document 1. Answer briefly. [2]

b Identify two key arguments in support of locally produced food in document 1. Answer briefly. [2]

How effective is the reasoning in document 1? [12]

2 Compare and contrast the perspectives on local food in documents 1 and 2. [14]

Extension

Each of these articles comes from a particular perspective. Can you find a more solid evidence base for these perspectives?

Research and discuss

Investigate the arguments for and against local food more thoroughly. Consider different economic, ethical, political and technological perspectives

8 http://www.nst.com.my/news/2016/07/156228/serving-solutionsingapores-retiring-hawker-sellers

Changing technologies

Topics

- The impact of the Internet
- Technology and lifestyles
- Architectural priorities
- Genetic engineering
- Artificial intelligence
- Transport

Activities to get you started

During these introductory activities, you will start to explore and reflect on a range of issues, themes and perspectives relating to the overarching idea of 'Changing technologies' and the Global Perspective topics within this main idea. You may find interesting issues and perspectives which you would like to research further, and you may start to reflect on and develop your own perspective.

Activity 1

E

WHY ASIMOV PUT THE THREE LAWS OF ROBOTICS IN THE ORDER HE DID:

POSSIBLE ORDERING	CONSEQUENCES	
1. (1) DON'T HARM HUMANS 2. (2) OBEY ORDERS 3. (3) PROTECT YOURSELF	[SEE ASIMOV'S STORIES]	BALANCED WORLD
1. (1) DON'T HARM HUMANS 2. (3) PROTECT YOURSELF 3. (2) OBEY ORDERS	EXPLORE MARS! HAHA, NO. IT'S COLD AND I'D DIE.	FRUSTRATING WORLD
1. (2) OBEY ORDERS 2. (1) DON'T HARM HUMANS 3. (3) PROTECT YOURSELF		CHAOS
1. (2) OBEY ORDERS 2. (3) PROTECT YOURSELF 3. (1) DON'T HARM HUMANS		CHAOS
1. (3) PROTECT YOURSELF 2. (1) DON'T HARM HUMANS 3. (2) OBEY ORDERS	I'LL MAKE CARS FOR YOU, BUT TRY TO UNPLUG ME AND I'LL VAPORIZE YOU.	TERRIFYING STANDOFF
1. (3) PROTECT YOURSELF 2. (2) OBEY ORDERS 3. (1) DON'T HARM HUMANS		CHAOS

Research and discuss

1. Read one of Isaac Asimov's robot stories. How well did he predict the future? What issues did he raise?
2. Choose a piece of modern science fiction. How well do you think it predicts the future? What issues does it raise?
3. Which of the stories do you prefer? Why?

1 What different issues and perspectives do these images raise on the topics in this chapter?

2 Does the whole class agree? Why or why not?

Activity 2

1 Which of these predictions do you think are most likely to come true and why?

- **a** 'Buildings will be more like biological systems – they will react to the environment.'
- **b** 'We will have made contact with intelligent alien life forms.'
- **c** 'Technology will look about the same as it does now – what else could we possibly improve?'
- **d** 'People will walk more and travel less.'

2 **a** Make five predictions of your own about the future, relating to the topics in this chapter.

- **b** Work in a small group. Share your predictions and decide:
  - which you think are most likely to come true and why
  - which you most want to come true and why.
- **c** How similar are your two lists? What are the reasons for this?

Use your research skills to help you find information and ideas to support your views.

1 Look at the images of interior spaces. Which of these inside spaces:

 a would you most like to work in and why
 b would you most like to live in and why
 c would you most like to party in and why
 d would be most economical and why
 e would be most environmentally friendly and why
 f is the most beautiful in your opinion and why?

A *Source:* http://www.nzherald.co.nz/business/news/article.cfm?c_id=3&objectid=11672085
B *Source:* http://www.archdaily.com/595033/when-one-size-does-not-fit-all-rethinking-the-open-office/54d0c0efe58ece990100055d-google-campus-dublin
C *Source:* http://interiii.com/2013/04/salon-urbain-design-by-sid-lee-architecture-and-aedifica/
D *Source:* http://interiii.com/2016/02/manasara-the-metal-profile-cutting-store/
E *Source:* http://inhabitat.com/this-tiny-off-grid-hawaiian-home-cost-just-11000-to-build/
F *Source:* http://familyhouse.co/ancient-japanese-architecture-interior/ancient-japanese-architecture-interior-and-softness-underfoot-creates-relaxation-in-a-zen-room/

1 For each image, what do you expect the architect's priorities were? Use the URLs to help you research and check your ideas.

2 In small groups, you are going to research and plan an interior space, using one of the briefs below.

a Research what architects are thinking and doing in spaces like the one you need to design.

b Make a 'mood board' with images that you like.

c Create a plan, with images if possible.

Brief A	Create an innovative party and entertainment space, for a wealthy celebrity couple who throw lavish parties, both for pleasure and for charity. It should be the most modern architecture possible, and include smart technologies.
Brief B	Create an entertainment space for a young woman who really cares about the environment, but does not have much money.
Brief C	Create a learning environment for students in the sixth form, which will maximise the work that students do. The space must also allow both group and independent learning, using new technologies and traditional learning techniques. In addition, the space must be environmentally friendly and a showpiece for the school.
Brief D	Create an ideal personal space for a teenager. It should allow for work, leisure, exercise, sleep and anything else that your group thinks is necessary.

Activity 4

1 Complete the questionnaire.

2 Discuss the results in class. Do you all agree? Why or why not?

1 = I disagree strongly   2 = I disagree a bit   3 = I'm not sure
4 = I agree a bit   5 = I agree strongly

		1	2	3	4	5
1	Better technology makes us worse human beings.					
2	The Internet is the most important technological development since the printed book.					
3	I feel sorry for designer babies.					
4	Why take the bus when you have a Ferrari?					
5	We need radically new building designs to make homes and offices suitable for the twenty-first century.					
6	GM foods are as likely to be healthy as traditional foods.					
7	How can we create artificial intelligence when we don't even understand our own intelligence?					
8	Too many countries are building big, showy buildings, instead of environmentally friendly buildings.					
9	24 hours without WiFi? No way!					
10	Technology is changing the way humans think.					

Research and discuss

1. What are the five most important technological developments in human history? Why?
2. What would be the five most needed technological developments in the next fifty years? Why?
3. Is there a future for technological society without oil? What might this look like?

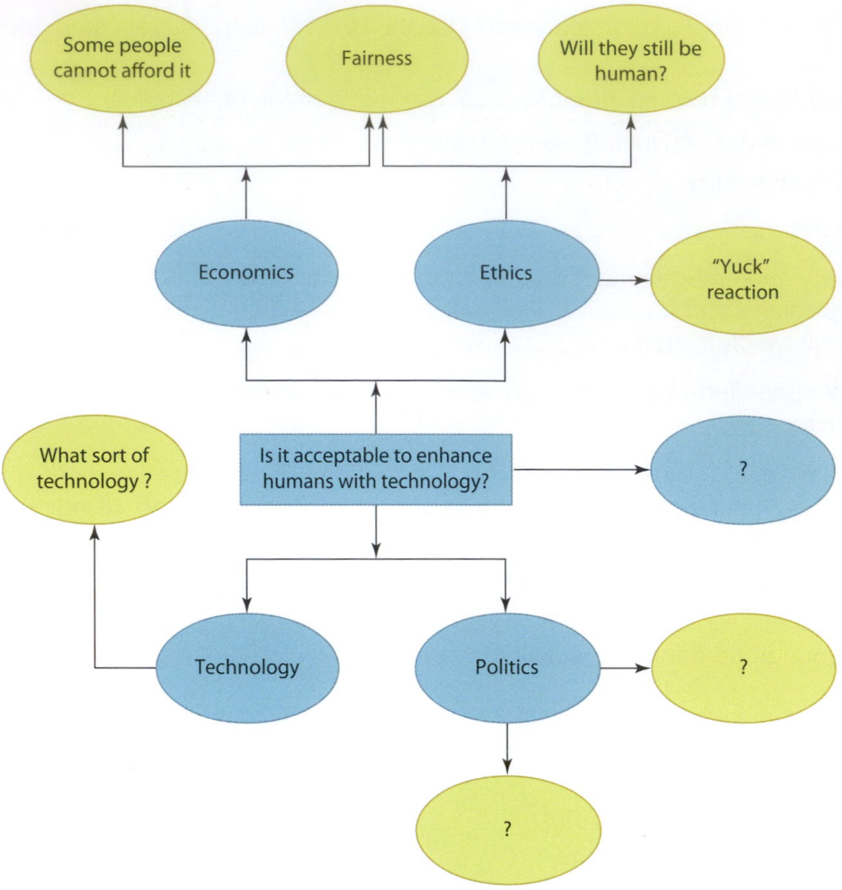

1. Complete and expand the mind map about whether it is acceptable to enhance humans with technology. Use the themes to help you explore different perspectives.
2. Draw a mind map using the themes to help you explore different perspectives on one of these questions:
   - **a** Is our technological lifestyle unhealthy and unnatural?
   - **b** Should the environment be a bigger priority for architects?
   - **c** Are farmers in developing countries better off with GM seeds?
   - **d** What would the consequences be if we built an artificial super intelligence?
   - **e** What if our world is, in fact, just one virtual life in a cosmic computer game?

Use quick Internet searches to help you map out some of the issues and perspectives.

By far the greatest danger of Artificial Intelligence is that people conclude too early that they understand it.

Eliezer Yudkowsky

Stimulus material

Document 1

Smartphones not smart in exam

Hundreds of thousands of students across the country have been sitting the national high school exams that are also university entry tests.

As in previous exams, many students have tried various ways to cheat in the exams but were still found out and fined by inspectors for violating exam regulations.

Following in the steps of former candidates, but smarter, a candidate at the Hà Nội-based University of Forestry exam venue tried to apply new technology by bringing a tiny hi-tech device into the exam room to avoid being discovered. He put a tiny earphone into his ear, which allowed him to get assistance from his friend outside the exam room.

However, as he was sitting at the first table in the exam room, very close and in front of the examiner, the candidate could not use the device. After two hours, his friend outside the exam room felt anxious because he hadn't received any message from the candidate and decided to call him.

Perhaps because he was anxious, the candidate had pressed the "loudspeaker" button instead of the "silent" button on his phone, allowing the examiner to hear the incoming call.

The examiner checked the candidate and found him to have brought in a mobile phone and another high-tech device into the exam room, which is banned for all candidates.

He was then suspended from the examination.

So, smartphones are not always smart in all circumstances if you are not smart at using them.[1]

1. What issues are raised in this document?
2. To what extent are the issues in this document global?
3. How would you describe the perspective this article comes from? What are the beliefs and assumptions underlying the perspective?

What do you think about using a smart phone in exams? Is it different from doping in sport or using technology in sport?

At the end of the day, we have an economy that works for the rich by cheating the poor, and unequal schools are the result of that, not the cause.

Aaron Swartz

The more people rationalise cheating, the more it becomes a culture of dishonesty. And that can become a vicious, downward cycle. Because suddenly, if everyone else is cheating, you feel a need to cheat, too.

Stephen Covey

1 http://vietnamnews.vn/a-twist-in-the-tale/299072/smartphones-notsmart-in-exam.html#Qbh2XPjq5ZygObVW.99

Document 2

Bangladesh clamps down on social media after cafe attack, says 'youth being radicalised online'

Highlights

1 Bangladesh has launched a clampdown on social media sites spreading jihadist propaganda.

2 Bangladesh police have warned that anyone caught sharing jihadist propaganda online would be punished.

Bangladesh has launched a clampdown on social media sites spreading jihadist propaganda after an attack on a Dhaka cafe in which 20 hostages, including an Indian girl, were murdered, saying the country's young were being radicalised online.

Authorities said the deadly siege at an upmarket cafe popular with foreigners had been an "eye-opener", exposing the role of social media in recruiting young men to jihadist groups.

"Social media has become a fertile ground for recruiting militants," the head of the telecoms regulator Shahjahan Mahmood told AFP. "The attack was an eye-opener for us. They (jihadist groups) attract the young men through social media."

The Islamic State group, which has claimed Friday night's attack, has long used social media to recruit fighters and incite individuals around the world to commit terrorist attacks.

Mahmood said the Bangladesh Telecommunications Regulatory Commission (BTRC) had ordered YouTube to remove videos of "radical preachings", including those of the firebrand cleric Jashim Uddin Rahmani. He was sentenced to five years in jail last December after his speeches were found to have incited Islamist militants to kill the atheist blogger Ahmed Rajib Haider in early 2013.

Shortly after the cafe siege, it emerged that several of the Bangladesh attackers were young, tech-savvy men from wealthy families and had easy access to social media.

The father of 22-year-old Rohan Imtiaz, one of the suspected attackers killed when commandos stormed the cafe, has said he believes his son may have been radicalised online. Imtiaz reportedly posted an appeal on Facebook last year urging all Muslims to become terrorists and quoting a controversial Indian preacher who has been banned in Britain, Canada and Malaysia.

"He was a practising Muslim. So many people are. Maybe he was radicalised through the Internet," his father Imtiaz Khan Babul told AFP. "But I never checked what he was browsing... Someone may have brainwashed him."

Bangladesh police issued a stern warning on Wednesday that anyone caught sharing jihadist propaganda online would be punished in the wake of the unprecedented attack in Dhaka.

Uploading, sharing, commenting or liking any video, images or speech in the social media such as Facebook, Twitter and YouTube in support of

1. What issues are raised in this document?
2. To what extent are the issues in this document global?
3. How would you describe the perspective this article comes from? What are the beliefs and assumptions underlying the perspective?

What do you know about Bangladesh?

? Is terrorism as dangerous to the world as nuclear weapons?

? Is it acceptable for the government, police or secret services to censor or monitor social media in order to prevent terrorism? How would you feel if it was your social media communications being watched by strangers?

It has become appallingly obvious that our technology has exceeded our humanity.

Albert Einstein

the Islamic State or militancy is a punishable offence," Deputy Inspector General of police A.K.M. Shahidur Rahman said.

"If anyone is found to have engaged in such activities, tough legal action will be taken against that person."[2]

Do you think that 'liking' a terrorist video should be a crime, as well as uploading terrorist videos?

Document 3

Companies embracing robotics for production efficiency, profit

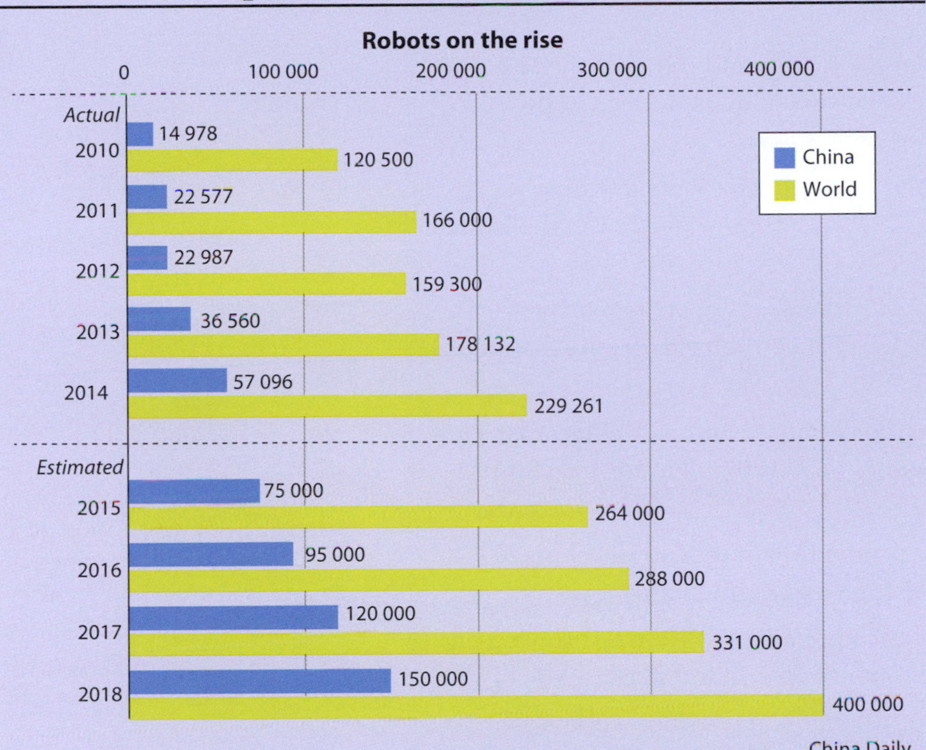

In a humming factory in Foshan, Guangdong province, a machine is busy tailoring fabrics to custom designs. Within 18 seconds, a pair of jeans is done, outperforming humans who would take 30 minutes to an hour to do the same job.

The "smart tailor", as the machine is known, is part of a broad effort by Foshan Shunde Everstar Clothing Co to leverage cutting-edge technologies and revolutionise its assembly lines. Five years ago, when many Guangdong clothing factories suffered from falling overseas orders and rising labor costs, Fan Youbin, president of Shunde Everstar, decided to upgrade the company using the Internet and automation.

After pouring 40 million yuan ($6 million) into inventing the smart tailor, the company also launched an online platform where consumers can design their own clothes and try them on in a virtual fitting room.

"Within three days of placing an order, our customers can receive their clothes," Fan said, adding that the shift to smart manufacturing makes it possible to produce a profit from small orders.

?

1. What issues are raised in this document?
2. To what extent are the issues in this document global?
3. How would you describe the perspective this article comes from? What are the beliefs and assumptions underlying the perspective?

2 http://timesofindia.indiatimes.com/world/south-asia/Bangladeshclamps-down-on-social-media-after-cafe-attack-says-youth-being-radicalizedonline/articleshow/53102937.cms

Shunde Everstar's story of increasing automation is playing out across China in thousands of factories, which purchase a quarter of the industrial robots sold globally.

The trend will be discussed in detail at the ongoing 2016 Summer Davos Forum in Tianjin, as Chinese firms scramble to embrace robots and big-data technology to boost efficiency and cut assembly line costs.

Data from the International Federation of Robotics show that between 2010 and 2014 the supply of industrial robots in China increased by about 40 per cent per year on average.

"This rapid development is unique in the history of robotics," the IFR said in a recent report. "There has never been such a dynamic rise in such a short period of time in any other market."

Still, for every 10 000 employees, there are only 36 robots in China, compared with 478 in South Korea, 292 in Germany and 164 in the United States in 2014.

"The number will rise more sharply over the next five years, partly stimulated by strong policy support," said Hao Yucheng, deputy director of the China Robot Industry Alliance.

The robot industry is highlighted in the country's thirteenth Five-Year Plan (2016–20), which guides national economic development for the coming half-decade.

China also plans to triple its annual production of industrial robots to 100 000 in five years to help promote high-end manufacturing.

Midea Group, a leading maker of home appliances in China, is relying on robotic "workers" to churn out high-quality air conditioners.

In one of its factories in Guangzhou, Guangdong province, robots are performing a string of labor-intensive tasks, such as packaging and feeding parts, along with delicate and flexible work like applying bar codes.

By the end of 2015, Midea had installed more than 560 robots in air conditioner plants, up from only 50 in 2011. During the same period, the workforce was trimmed by more than 22 000.

Is it reasonable to use robots to do work if humans are unemployed?

"We plan to spend 4 billion yuan on cranking up automation in the next five years," said Wu Wenxin, Midea's vice-president. By 2018, the number of robots will surge to 1 500, and half of the company's manufacturing will be automated.

Earlier this month, the company said it was bidding for more than a 30 per cent share of German industrial robot giant Kuka AG, highlighting Chinese enterprises' eagerness to embrace the new technology.

Local governments are also acting swiftly. Shenyang, Jilin province, for instance, proposed in May to set up a 20 billion yuan industry fund with the aim of cultivating stronger home grown robot makers and meeting the growing demand from manufacturing companies like Midea.

"Smart manufacturing is the only way to China's future growth. It is not something you can choose to follow or not. It is an inevitable trend," Wu said.

? Do you agree that it is inevitable? What consequences could it have?

Realism puts humanoid in class of its own

In a glitzy exhibition hall in Tianjin, a man talks with what appears to be an elegant Chinese woman. In a gentle voice, the female figure speaks: "Sir, welcome to the 2016 Summer Davos."

Now look again. Dressed in a traditional white Chinese robe, the speaker, Jiajia, is in fact a robot, but one so realistic it's hard to tell the difference at first glance. She has red lips, shining black eyes and can be taught to interact with people in both conversation and movement.

Female robot Jiajia attracted a lot of attention in an exhibition hall in Tianjin

This humanoid is part of China's broad effort to develop service robots, as the world's second-largest economy is seeing a surge in demand for them in the healthcare, education and entertainment sectors.

With an aging population and increasing labor shortages, China plans to sell more than 30 billion yuan ($4.6 billion) worth of service robots by 2020.

Jiajia was developed by a research team at University of Science and Technology of China in Hefei, Anhui province. After being unveiled in April, she quickly earned the nickname "robot goddess" for her combination of physical beauty and deep learning ability.

Jiajia can naturally move her eyeballs and show micro expressions on her face. More important, her speech is in sync with her lip movements.

Chen Xiaoping, the director of the research team, said Jiajia marks a breakthrough for China's service-robot industry by adding a new dimension to artificial intelligence.

What is your reaction to the idea of service robots?

"Most domestic enterprises just focus on voice recognition, but we not only enable robots to move but to match movements to speech," Chen told *China Daily* in a telephone interview.

He said Jiajia can show micro expressions appropriate to what she says. When Jiajia says, "I am happy," she will smile, just as humans might do.

"The next step is to teach Jiajia to recognise others' facial expressions and make appropriate responses," he said.

It took the team three years to complete the robot. Among other applications, Chen believes Jiajia will be a good assistant for the elderly.

"Many seniors travel to southern China for health reasons. But most of these 80-year-olds are taken care of by 60-year-olds, because of a shortage of young people," Chen said.

USTC researchers also developed a domestic service robot known as Kejia, which prevailed at the RoboCup championship in 2014.

"Unlike the industrial-robot industry, which is dominated by four foreign companies, the service robot market is still in its infancy," said Luo Jun, chief executive officer of the International Robotics and Intelligent Equipment Industry Alliance, a Beijing-based industry association.

"Domestic companies can thrive if they manage to make breakthroughs in artificial intelligence," Luo said.[3]

Listen to this TED talk:
https://www.ted.com/talks/kevin_kelly_on_how_technology_evolves?language=en

3 http://www.chinadaily.com.cn/m/tianjin2012/2016-06/28/content_25884896.htm

Document 4

Are we living inside a cosmic computer game? Elon Musk echoes the Bhagwad Gita (and *The Matrix*)

Published 12 June 2016

by Anvar Alikhan

When a tech billionaire and hard-headed pragmatist seems to reprise the ancient Indian concept of maya, or illusion, it's time to shut up and pay attention.

When the film *The Matrix* was released in 1999, its central premise, that the world is not what it seems to be, appeared to reprise the ancient Indian concept of *maya*, or illusion. As Morpheus says to Neo in the film:

"What is real? If you are talking about your senses, what you feel, taste, smell or see, then all you're talking about is electrical signals interpreted by your brain."

He then proceeds to reveal to Neo the truth—that the human race has been condemned by "the Machines" to live out their lives in an artificial simulation called the Matrix, which they readily accept to be the real world.

As a result of its various references to Hindu philosophy, the film, understandably, caused a special frisson of interest in India. In fact, *The Matrix* is not alone in its assertions: the idea that the world, as we know it, is merely a computer-generated, Matrix-like illusion is a fairly common theme in science fiction, and various academics—philosophers, physicists, mathematicians and theologists—have been exploring this idea over the years.

But now, none other than Elon Musk, the billionaire Founder and Chief Executive Officer of Tesla and Space X, has spoken out strongly in support of this concept.

At a technology conference in San Francisco recently, Musk startled the world by saying he believed that the odds are overwhelming that we are living inside a computer simulation. In other words, we could just be virtual playthings inside a cosmic computer game created by some species of Super-beings. In fact, the odds are only "one in billions", Musk concluded, that we are in "base reality".

And that is something of great significance. After all, it's one thing for a philosopher, physicist, mathematician (or any other academic theorist) to play with abstract concepts like illusion versus reality—that's what they do for a living. However, when a hard-headed pragmatist like Elon Musk, who is immersed in the world of technology, sticks his neck out on the subject, it's time to shut up and pay attention.

Philosophical hypothesis

But first, a quick flashback. Four years after *The Matrix,* in 2003, Oxford philosophy professor Nick Bostrom suggested the possibility that members of an advanced "post-human" civilisation with enormous computing power might run simulations on how their remote ancestors lived. And he arrived at a hypothesis that hinged on a "trilemma", or the assertion that one of three propositions is almost certainly true:

1. What issues are raised in this document?
2. To what extent are the issues in this document global?
3. How would you describe the perspectives this article comes from? What are the beliefs and assumptions underlying the perspective?

Would kicking a stone prove that we are in base reality? Why or why not?

Does a billionaire really have more credibility than philosophers, physicists and mathematicians when talking about abstract ideas? Explain your response.

1 The fraction of human-level civilisations that reach a post-human stage (that is, one capable of running high-fidelity ancestor simulations) is close to zero.

2 The fraction of post-human civilisations that are interested in running ancestor-simulations is close to zero.

3 The fraction of all people with our kind of experiences that are living in a simulation is close to one.

Bostrom reasoned that if the third proposition is true, and that almost all people with our kind of experiences live in simulations, then we ourselves are almost certainly living in a simulation. (Not necessarily easy to follow, but that's the way it sometimes is with philosophy.)

But how do we prove it?

Presenting a hypothesis is one thing, but trying to actually prove it is a different matter.

John Barrow, a mathematics professor at Cambridge, attempted to do that, suggesting that if our world was indeed a simulation, it would, as it degraded, begin to display glitches (just as any computer would). Therefore, Barrow said, we need to carefully monitor aspects of nature that are supposed to be constant—like the speed of light, for example, or the strength of the electromagnetic force—and if we ever spot them drifting from those constant values, that might be proof that we are indeed inside a simulation. This test would perhaps be the equivalent of the 'little Red Pill' that Morpheus gave to Neo in *The Matrix* to allow him to see that the real world was different from the illusion he had inhabited all his life.

Silas Beane, a University of Washington physicist, went on to propose a different proof for the simulation hypothesis. It went like this: physicists tell us that space is a smooth continuum that extends infinitely. But if someone were to create a simulation of space it would necessarily have to be done by using a lattice-like structure. Beane tells us that the spacing of such a lattice structure would impose a limit on the energy that particles could have. So if our cosmos is merely a simulation, we would see a cut-off in the spectrum of high-energy particles. Moreover, if space is continuous (as they tell us), cosmic rays should come to us from all directions equally. But in a simulation, because of the lattice structure, the cosmic rays would travel along the axes of the lattice, so they would not come to us from all directions equally. And that is something we could measure.

All these theories and proofs came, of course, with their own assumptions and caveats. Beane's theory, for example, makes the assumption that the beings who created a simulation would follow the same methods as we do. But why should we assume that an advanced "post-human" civilisation would create a simulation the way we would do it, using a lattice? Why shouldn't they create a simulation that is perfectly smooth instead, like space itself?

? Is there any particular reason to believe that most people with our kind of experiences live in simulations?

Indistinguishable from reality

Elon Musk's reasoning, however, is much simpler and more down-to-earth. Pragmatist—and technologist—that he is, he avoided overly abstract theorising.

Instead, he pointed out how 40 years ago, computer games such as Pong were played using just two rectangles and a dot. "That was what games were."

But now, 40 years later, we have photorealistic 3D simulations with millions of people playing games simultaneously—and it's getting more sophisticated every year.

Soon computer games will embrace such things as virtual reality and augmented reality. And before long they will become completely indistinguishable from reality itself—even if we assume that their rate of advancement drops drastically from what it is now—which it probably won't, he pointed out.

That is what we can reasonably foresee.

OK, so now let us fast forward 10 000 years into the future—which, of course, is just a blink on the evolutionary scale. Can you imagine what computer games will be like then?

Given this mind-boggling sophistication of computer games, combined with the fact that those games will be played on literally billions of computers, Musk concluded, it is only logical to assume that that "the odds that we're in base reality is one in billions".

Technology vs Theory

This is perhaps the simplest, yet most convincing, response to the question of whether we are living inside a simulation or not—especially as it comes from someone who is not a theoretician, but a hard-core technology guy, obsessed by the subject of Artificial Intelligence.

The obvious question is, so is the creator of our simulation "God"?

Well, it may be. Or it may be your great-great-great-great-great-grandson. Or it may be just some pimply teenage hacker living in a slightly more advanced galaxy across the road. We really don't know.

The other question is, what does all this mean to us?

So what if we are just lines of code in some great cosmic realty show? Some of us would, like Neo, want to pop a metaphorical "Red Pill" to discover what the actual Reality is. Most others would, perhaps, be too insufficiently evolved, too complacent, or just too fearful, and would therefore prefer to continue to live in our comfortable Illusion, and so we'd choose the "Blue Pill" instead.

(After all, in *The Matrix* the character named Cypher finds he can't handle the Reality he has discovered, and chooses to go back instead to the illusory comfort of the Matrix.)

So Red Pill or Blue Pill?

It's not unlike the choice that Lord Krishna offers to Arjuna in the Bhagwad Gita.

? Why should computer games keep advancing at such a fast pace? Isn't this a huge assumption? What can you think of that would slow or stop this advancement?

But, actually, there is perhaps a third choice, which has always fascinated somebody un-evolved and coarse like myself: What if I could somehow locate the control panel of our simulation, sneak in, change my own personal settings, and become the kind of person "who has everything". Someone like George Clooney, perhaps. Or Haruki Murakami. Or Roger Federer. Or Anthony Bourdain.

Or, come to think of it, someone like Elon Musk himself.[4]

? What would you do if you could get the control panel of our simulation? Why?

It is indeed an opinion strangely prevailing amongst men, that houses, mountains, rivers, and in a word all sensible objects have an existence natural or real, distinct from their being perceived by the understanding. … For what are these objects but the things we perceive by sense, and what do we perceive besides our own ideas or sensations?

George Berkeley

After we came out of the church, we stood talking for some time together of Bishop Berkeley's ingenious sophistry to prove the nonexistence of matter, and that every thing in the universe is merely ideal. I observed, that though we are satisfied his doctrine is not true, it is impossible to refute it. I never shall forget the alacrity with which Samuel Johnson answered, striking his foot with mighty force against a large stone, till he rebounded from it—'I refute it thus'.

James Boswell

4 http://scroll.in/article/809760/are-we-living-inside-a-cosmiccomputer-game-elon-musk-echoes-the-bhagwad-gita-and-the-matrix

Document 5

How Migration Will Define the Future of Urbanism and Architecture

When we started talking about migration [as a conference theme], everybody said "don't do it, it's too controversial". We said that's exactly why we're going to do it.

This defiant attitude was how Martin Barry, Chairman of reSITE, opened their 2016 Conference in Prague three weeks ago. Entitled "Cities in Migration," the conference took place against a background of an almost uncountable number of challenging political issues related to migration. In Europe, the unfolding Syrian refugee crisis has strained both political and race relations across the continent; in America, Republican Presidential candidate Donald Trump has led a populist knee-jerk reaction against both Mexicans and Muslims; and in the United Kingdom—a country only on the periphery of most attendees' consciousness at the time—the decision in favor of "Brexit" that took place a week after the conference was largely predicated upon limiting the immigration of not only Syrians, but also of European citizens from other, less-wealthy EU countries.

In architecture, such issues have been highlighted this year by Alejandro Aravena's Venice Biennale, with architects "Reporting from the Front" in battles against, among other things, these migration-related challenges. From refugee camps to slums to housing crises in rich global cities, the message is clear: migration is a topic that architects must understand and respond to. As a result, the lessons shared during reSITE's intensive two-day event will undoubtedly be invaluable to the architectural profession.

A Global Challenge

In her opening keynote, sociologist Saskia Sassen outlined what was perhaps the defining theme of the conference: that migration is not a random event, but something which is caused by the actions of governments and citizens. "Migrations are made, they don't just happen," says Sassen. "There are conditions which cause them," many of which arise as a result of the capitalism which enables our current lifestyles. As a result, it might be argued that we each have a responsibility to engage with the challenges involved in migration.

Building on this statement, Sassen identified different types of migrant: the first was the political refugee, those fleeing political turmoil in their homes; the second the economic migrant, who seeks a better life in a new country. But while these two types of migrant are widely discussed, Sassen argued that the third type of migrant has barely been acknowledged—this is what she called the "economic refugee," a class of people who are fleeing the "massive loss of habitat" catalysed by economic activities such as corporate land-grabs and mining, or by encroaching environmental disasters.

In addition to Sassen's three types of migrant the morning's other keynote speaker, *New York Times* architecture critic Michael Kimmelman, adds a fourth type: "an often unrecognised but large class of middle-class, educated, mobile people who choose to see different parts of the world and live in different places because they can."

1. What issues are raised in this document?
2. To what extent are the issues in this document global?
3. How would you describe the perspective this article comes from? What are the beliefs and assumptions underlying the perspective?

Is migration still a global issue?

? What do you think about this?

Architecture is an expression of values.

Norman Foster

From each according to his abilities, to each according to his needs

Karl Marx

While Kimmelman expects that we will continue to see high numbers of political refugees and economic migrants, he also believes that the twenty-first century will also see a dramatic rise in these middle-class migrants, and in those fleeing environmental disasters. Indeed he made the threat of climate-driven migration a key part of his message to the conference. Speaking to *ArchDaily* he summed up the issue rather pithily: "We may be building new towers in Miami, but if the seas rise they're not going to be occupied in several decades, so we'll be talking about the migration of people from Miami. We need to think about that much more seriously."

For Sassen, taking these migrants seriously means recognising their existence and instituting legal mechanisms, similar to those available to political refugees, to enable their protection. But it also means taking seriously the role that cities have historically taken in empowering migrants. "The city is a space where those without power get to make a history," she says, but the current trajectory of our cities threatens to put this at risk. As many global cities continue to prioritise the concentration of capital, those with less capital to offer are threatened with marginalisation. Highlighting the world's top 100 cities, Sassen points out these places host 10 per cent of the world's population, but a full 30 per cent of its GDP, saying simply: "that's too much."

With such a range of different causes of migration, one thing that was clear from the conference's opening was that at the level of cities, the key question of migration is how diversity is acknowledged, respected and accommodated by the built environment.

Architectural Responses to the Challenge

One of the most striking examples of a city accepting migrants and embracing diversity is perhaps New York City, as evidenced by the closing presentation from Carl Weisbrod, director of NYC's City Planning Commission, in which he discussed the city's commitment to low-income housing under Mayor Bill de Blasio. One component of this policy, and perhaps the most interesting interaction between architecture and city policy presented at the conference, is New York's experiment with micro-apartments in the form of nArchitects' Carmel Place. Conceived as a way of providing cheap, single-occupancy apartments in the very center of a city that has an overabundance of homes designed for families or the super-rich, Carmel Place is largely about preserving and encouraging the diversity of Manhattan.

"It's incredibly important to keep [the cores of the cities] as diverse as possible," explains Mimi Hoang, principle of nArchitects. "I think the warning signs are here in Europe—the warning signs are in Paris, where they tend to put immigrants in this kind of immigrant belt, the peripherique, in the banlieues. This obviously create feelings of ostracisation and marginalisation for some in society. We have our own problems in the States of course, but the reality is that if the working class is in the peripheral of the city, that is creating a hotbed of resentment."

And though micro-apartments are of course envisaged as just one part in enabling this diversity, that does not mean they have been without controversy. In a recent piece appearing on *ArchDaily*, Jesse Connuck argues that such apartments may risk legitimising a "new normal" of tiny, substandard apartments. In responding to this argument, Hoang's usually soft-spoken demeanor breaks into something considerably more animated. "We're worried," she says, "and we've certainly had our fair share of calls from interested developers, and if we think that they're only calling us because they think that we can squeeze more apartment units onto their plots, we're not interested. We're interested if they're interested in creating community, if they're interested in creating a new kind of living experience."

Carmel Place in New York, designed by nArchitects

For Hoang, an important part of nArchitects' decision to engage in micro-apartments was the underlying complexity of the issue. "What bothers me is that the issue is always discussed in isolation of a lot of other issues," she adds. "But you have to think about all the other tangential, ripple effects of *not* doing it. Not doing it means people having to commute an hour in; not doing it means there's increased cost to the taxpayer for road infrastructure and public transportation; not doing it means loss of talent in the city, because plenty of people, especially creatives, are leaving New York for cities like Philadelphia."

Representing a very different side of migration to that explored by Mimi Hoang was Catalytic Action, a non-profit whose work in places such as Lebanon has focused on lean solutions to providing schools, playgrounds and other crucial spaces for refugee camps. Among their current projects is the Jarahieh School, a plan to create a school building in Lebanon by adapting Save the Children's pavilion from the 2015 Milan Expo. Joana Dabaj, Catalytic Action's principle coordinator, believes that this model could provide an example for future exhibitions, biennales and the like in Europe. "There's huge opportunities when it comes to exhibition structures because usually they have been done in a temporary way," she says. "When dealing with the crisis and urgent situations there's also this requisite that you need temporary structures—because for example in Lebanon you cannot build permanent structures for refugees. So it also fits the same design guidelines of the building: temporary, it can be disassembled and assembled."

The concept is, at its base, a simple act of recycling. "Recycling is not a new concept," Catalytic Action's Executive Director Riccardo Conti tells me. But he adds that "what we maybe should try to push a bit more is to recycle almost at a global scale." The project also implies that Western countries could examine where they are producing waste and think more carefully about how they could design their products to have a useful afterlife.

A playground designed and constructed by Catalytic action in Bar Elias, Lebanon

Of course, one school, adapted from a single expo pavilion, will not change this situation alone. But Catalytic Action is hoping their example will lead to greater change. "The reason we're called Catalytic Action is because we believe in an intervention that would catalyse a bigger impact," says Dabaj, and Conti adds an example of when this has happened in the past: "the first project on the playground, it raised awareness of the need for these spaces in Lebanon for refugee children. After that, of course we were able to do more projects, but there was also a very nice thing that happened in the same village: another organisation built a school, and they included a playground in the school—without us pushing the idea, they knew about our work and they said that they understood the importance."

At first, the provision of schools, playgrounds and social spaces to refugee camps might seem a world away, both literally and metaphorically, from the work being done by architects in the world's global cities to accommodate the ever-increasing influx of people to the planet's social and economic centers. But on closer inspection, refugee camps may have more in common with places like New York than we think. "There's a deep urbanising impulse which I think is a basic human desire," Michael Kimmelman explains to me. "If we begin to think of those camps—where people on average spend sixteen years—not as temporary, stop lying to ourselves and instead think of them as new cities, pop-up cities, which should benefit the people who live there now and in the long-term benefit the host countries as well, that's a whole class of cities which we can develop from scratch."

Viewed in this way, the work of Catalytic Action and other organisations in the refugee camps of Lebanon might be seen as the first urbanising actions in the birth of new cities—cities which are much more aware of how migration fits into both their past and future than many of today's mature cities.

The collection of perspectives presented at reSITE's 2016 conference was full of lessons for planners, politicians, and policy-makers. But perhaps the greatest lesson for architects was summed up by Michael Kimmelman: "I think the whole question of migration allows us to rethink what cities should look like. There's never been a moment when there's such a demand to think on such a large scale about how we build our cities and build the world. For architects and urban planners I would think this is one of the great moments to be in the profession."[5]

5 http://www.archdaily.com/790818/how-migration-will-define-thefuture-of-urbanism-and-architecture

Editing humanity

A new technique for manipulating genes holds great promise—but rules are needed to govern its use.

The genome is written in an alphabet of just four letters. Being able to read, study and compare DNA sequences for humans, and thousands of other species, has become routine. A new technology promises to make it possible to edit genetic information quickly and cheaply. This could correct terrible genetic defects that blight lives. It also heralds the distant prospect of parents building their children to order.

The technology is known as CRISPR-Cas9, or just CRISPR. It involves a piece of RNA, a chemical messenger, designed to target a section of DNA; and an enzyme, called a nuclease, that can snip unwanted genes out and paste new ones in. Other ways of editing DNA exist, but CRISPR holds the promise of doing so with unprecedented simplicity, speed and precision.

A dizzying range of applications has researchers turning to CRISPR to develop therapies for everything from Alzheimer's to cancer to HIV… . By allowing doctors to put just the right cancer-hunting genes into a patient's immune system, the technology could lead to new approaches to oncology. It may also accelerate the progress of gene therapy—where doctors put normal genes into the cells of people who suffer from genetic diseases such as Tay Sachs or cystic fibrosis.

It will be years, perhaps even decades, before CRISPR is being used to make designer babies. But the issues that raises are already the subject of fierce discussion. In April scientists in China revealed they had tried using CRISPR to edit the genomes of human embryos. Although these embryos could not develop to term, viable embryos could one day be engineered for therapeutic reasons or non-medical enhancement.

That is a Rubicon some will not want to cross. Many scientists, including one of CRISPR's inventors, want a moratorium on editing "germ line" cells—those that give rise to subsequent generations. America's National Academy of Sciences plans a conference to delve into CRISPR's ethics. The debate is sorely needed. CRISPR is a boon, but it raises profound questions.

1. What issues are raised in this document?
2. To what extent are the issues in this document global?
3. How would you describe the perspective this article comes from? What are the beliefs and assumptions underlying the perspective?

The only way is ethics

These fall into two categories: practical and philosophical. The immediate barrier is practical. As well as cutting the intended DNA, CRISPR often finds targets elsewhere, too. In the laboratory that may not matter; in people it could cause grave harm. In someone with a terrible disease, the risk of collateral damage might be worth running. But for germ-line applications, where the side-effects would be felt in every cell, the bar should be high. It may take a generation to ensure that the technology is safe. Until then, couples with some genetic diseases can conceive using in-vitro fertilisation and select healthy embryos.

Moreover, awash though it is with gene-sequence data, biology still has a tenuous grip on the origins of almost all the interesting and complex traits in humanity. Very few are likely to be easily enhanced with a quick cut-and-paste. There will often be trade-offs between some capabilities and others. An à la carte menu of attributes seems a long way off. Yet science makes progress—indeed, as gene sequencing shows, it sometimes does so remarkably quickly. So scientists are right to be thinking now about how best to regulate CRISPR.

That means answering the philosophical questions. There are those who will oppose CRISPR because it lets humans play God. But medicine routinely intervenes in the natural order of things—saving people from infections and parasites, say. The opportunities to treat cancer, save children from genetic disease and understand diabetes offer justification to push ahead.

A harder question is whether it is ever right to edit human germ-line cells, to make changes that are inherited. This is banned in 40 countries and restricted in many others. There is no reason for a ban on research or therapeutic use: some countries, rightly, allow research on human embryos, as long as they are left over from in-vitro fertilisation and are not grown beyond 14 days; and Britain has allowed a donor to supply mitochondrial DNA at conception to spare children needless suffering, even though the change will be passed on. And CRISPR deals with the objection that germ-line changes are irrevocable: if genes can be edited out, they can also be edited back in.

A deeper quandary concerns the use of CRISPR to make discretionary tweaks to a person's genome. There comes a point where therapy (removing genes that make breast cancer or early-onset Alzheimer's more likely, say) shades into genetic enhancement. Some might see being short or myopic as problems that need fixing. But here, too, the right approach is to be cautiously liberal: the burden is on society to justify when and why it is wrong to edit the genome.

CRISPR, happier, more productive

It is not too soon to draw on these principles to come up with rules. Some countries may have gaps in their legislation or poor enforcement, letting privately funded scientists or fertility clinics carry out unregulated CRISPR research. The conservative, painstaking approach taken by Britain's Human Fertilisation and Embryology Authority in its decision on mitochondrial DNA is a model. Regulators must also monitor CRISPR's use in non-human

? Do you agree? Can we trust money-hungry, power-hungry societies to make the right judgment?

? How do we know what is right and what is wrong?

species. Changing animals' genomes to spread desirable traits—mosquitoes that cannot transmit malaria, for example—could bring huge benefits. But the risk of unanticipated consequences means that such "gene drives" should be banned unless they can be reversed with proven countermeasures.

If CRISPR can be shown to be safe in humans, mechanisms will also be needed to grapple with consent and equality. Gene editing raises the spectre of parents making choices that are not obviously in the best interests of their children. Deaf parents may prefer their offspring to be deaf too, say; pushy parents might want to boost their children's intelligence at all costs, even if doing so affects their personalities in other ways. And if it becomes possible to tweak genes to make children smarter, should that option really be limited to the rich?

Thinking through such issues is right. But these dilemmas should not obscure CRISPR's benefits or obstruct its progress. The world has within its reach a tool to give people healthier, longer and better-quality lives. It should be embraced.[6]

? If we are living in a simulation, do these questions still matter?

? How many parents do you think would want to make their children kinder? Or happier? How much would this matter?

6 http://www.economist.com/news/leaders/21661651-new-techniquemanipulating-genes-holds-great-promisebut-rules-are-needed-govern-its

Skills development activities

Activity 6

Refer to document 1.

1 Is document 1 an argument? If not, what sort of writing is it?

Research and discuss

'Using technology to cheat is inevitable, so we should level the playing field and allow all uses of technology.' What do you think?

Activity 7

Refer to document 2.

1 Is document 2 an argument? If not, what sort of writing is it?

2 How effective is the justification given for punishing those sharing terrorist videos?

3 Do you agree with the punishment? Why or why not?

4 Why do you think that wealthy young men would respond to radical bloggers?

5 How would you describe the author's perspective? (Think about the author's underlying beliefs and attitudes and about the way the author sees the world).

6 How far do you share this perspective?

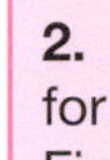

Research and discuss

1. How responsible should or can parents be for what their 17–20-year-old offspring see online?

2. What are the arguments for and against censorship? Find examples from different countries to show how it works in practice around the world.

A perspective is a world view that underlies an argument. It can be quite hard to pin down.

Argument, reasoning and opinions are the specifics of what the author says – they are informed by the author's perspective.

Activity 8

Refer to document 3.

1 Is document 3 an argument? If not, what sort of writing is it?

2 How effectively does the document use statistical and other numerical information?

3 According to the document, in what ways will technology contribute to the future economy and society?

4 Does this sound like a society you want to be part of? Why or why not?

5 Is there anything that people can do to ensure that a robot-dominated future is still suitable for humans?

Research and discuss

Research and explain the different economic, technological and ethical perspectives and issues involved in using robots.

What long-term political consequences could it lead to around the world?

Activity 9

Refer to document 4.

1 Is document 4 an argument? If not, what sort of writing is it?
2 How effective is the reasoning overall in this passage in support of the idea that we are living inside a simulation?
3 Would it make any difference to us whether we are living in a simulation or not?
4 How would you describe the author's perspective? (Think about the author's underlying beliefs and attitudes and about the way he sees the world.)
5 How far do you share this perspective?

Research and discuss

What are the arguments against the idea that we are living in a simulation?

Research the Hindu philosophy of Maya. How relevant is it to today's global, technological world?

Research philosophical and scientific ideas about how we perceive the world.

If we are in a simulation, is there anything we can do to hack the system and improve global problems? If so, what would you do?

Activity 10

Refer to document 5.

1 Does document 5 present an argument? If not, what sort of writing is it?
2 How effective is the reasoning in the document to support the idea that architecture is important to managing migration?
3 In your opinion, how far can architecture help with global issues relating to migration?
4 What do you think cities should look like? How would they be different from cities around the world?

Research and discuss

What other measures can be taken to prevent migration?

What other measures can be taken to minimise the negative effects of migration on refugees and on the countries they leave and arrive in?

Do you think technology and the Internet contribute to migration? Can technology and the Internet help to prevent problems related to migration?

'The fact is that automobiles no longer have a place in the big cities of our time.' Do you agree?

Activity 11

Refer to document 6.

1 Is document 6 an argument? If not, what sort of writing is it?
2 How effective is the reasoning in document 6?
3 Examine the perspective represented in document 6.
4 How far do you share this perspective?

Research and discuss

Compare the attitudes to genetic engineering in two very different countries.

Are religious and scientific perspectives on genetic engineering totally opposed to each other?

Research and discuss

Overall, what has most interested you in the documents?

What would you most like to research further?

Activity 12

1 Which of the following would make good research questions for an assessed essay? Why?
   a Is Minecraft the best computer game ever?
   b How can society encourage the wealthy to use public transport?
   c Robots—the future?
   d To what extent is artificial intelligence only a concern to more economically developed countries?
   e Will we all be beautiful in the future?
2 Write two or three questions of your own. Work in groups to assess and improve the questions.

When deciding on a good research question, think about these points:

- globally significant
- different perspectives
- argument and discussion
- question to answer
- can answer within the word limit
- suitable evidence base
- on a Global Perspectives topic

Remember to be positive and polite about each other's questions. You are helping each other to improve!

Avoid very theoretical or purely philosophical questions. To meet the assessment criteria you need to build up an evidence base, so remember to apply theoretical concepts in practical contexts.

Activity 13

1 Which of the following would make suitable questions for the team research project?
   a What kind of home would meet the ecological needs of the future?
   b Design and build an artificial super intelligence.
   c How can we encourage parents and children to talk instead of concentrating on electronic gadgets?
   d What is likely to be the most effective technological solution to the problem of global hunger?
   e Build a robot.
2 Write two or three questions of your own. Work in groups to assess and improve the questions.

When deciding on a team research project, think about these points:

- local problem
- global relevance
- effective solutions possible
- different aspects for individual research
- contrasting perspectives
- argument, reflection and discussion.

Practice examination paper

Document 1

AI raises profound philosophical questions

By Cai Fanghua (China Daily)

Famous world Go player Lee Se-dol has lost the first two of his five-game match with AlphaGo, an artificial intelligence, or AI, program developed by Google, in Seoul. Since the South Korean Lee was supposed to be representing not only himself but also the human race as a whole, he knows the meaning of the defeat.

I carefully went through their first game's manual twice and was shocked by AlphaGo's exquisite algorithm, efficient computing power and its "personality" as a Go player. Despite being driven by artificial intelligence, AlphaGo has a transcendental view of the big picture and the ability to identify its opponent's weaknesses. It made up for its two mistakes soon, and was merciless in its attack on the "impregnable" zone Lee had created. But after taking the lead, AlphaGo's movements were unhurried despite continuing to pressure Lee.

People who don't know about Go may not understand why the match is so important. Go is an old strategic board game, and the result is decided not just by ingenious calculations, but also by the players' personalities, moods and feelings. From a Go player's manual, you can walk into his or her personal world. The accepted view before the game was that given the complications of Go, it was impossible for an AI program to win against humans. That has changed.

In a Go game between astute players, personal emotions could be a decisive factor. AlphaGo's coolness lies in its indifference to rivals; instead of testing the human characteristics of his rivals, it would rather demonstrate pure and conquering rationality.

In other words, in AlphaGo's world, emotions can be a piece of information that can be grasped through rigorous computing. The fear is, if AI develops to such a level, human nature could become a redundant program in a perfect world which could be deleted with just one click of a mouse. Doesn't *The Matrix* present this exact scenario?

It may be too emotional to jump to the conclusion that humans will be enslaved by artificial intelligence just on the basis of a couple of Go games. Yet AlphaGo's victory shows AI is progressing, and progressing fast, toward some forbidden zones in which humans have taken pride for long.

The question is: What else [can AI] do? Who can predict what changes it will bring to the human world? And to what extent can intelligence created by humans expand?

When a "Turing test" was first proposed to test the intelligence of robots by Alan Turing, a British mathematician and father of artificial intelligence, in the 1950s, computers were huge machines. Now, who would dare to call AlphaGo a simple machine?

? Would an artificial intelligence that could experience emotions count as a person?

I would rather take the discovery of gravitational waves and AlphaGo's two wins as an inter-related omen to say humans are on the threshold of new round of explosions in science and technology. The breakthrough in AI may trigger a chain reaction in many fields, and promote the exponential growth of science and technology. Many scenarios that appeared only in science fictions before would probably become reality. Such a prospect is excitingly fearful.

No doubt the intelligence created by humans will have its own thoughts and strengths in the future. But will it have emotions or something beyond? If so, how should we define human nature and ethics? This is a profound philosophical question. You can have countless answers, and each leads to a different future.

One day, your AlphaGo butler serves you breakfast when you wake up to a sunny morning. You could even have a date arranged by it. It could arrange for a spotless life while you are still in the dark. What is it? A nightmare![7]

Document 2

Checklist of worst-case scenarios could help prepare for evil AI

By Chris Baraniuk

Artificial intelligence—what's the worst that can happen? For Roman Yampolskiy, a computer scientist at the University of Louisville in Kentucky, the sky's the limit. Working with hacktivist and entrepreneur Federico Pistono, he has come up with a set of worst-case scenarios for a potential malevolent AI, from "enslaving mankind" to "destroying the universe".

Yampolskiy argues that anticipating as many negative outcomes as possible—just as cybersecurity researchers do when looking for vulnerabilities—will help us guard against disaster.

"The standard framework in AI thinking has always been to propose new safety mechanisms," he says. But looking at the issue with a cybersecurity mindset puts a different spin on things: starting with a list of all the things that could go wrong will make it easier to test any safeguards we may eventually want to put in place.

Some of the catastrophes that Yampolskiy and Pistono envisage involve turning us against ourselves. In one scenario, an AI system unleashes a global propaganda war that sets governments and populations in opposition, feeding "a planetary chaos machine".

The work was paid for by a fund set up by tech entrepreneur Elon Musk, who has described AI as humanity's "biggest existential threat". Stephen Hawking has voiced similar fears.

7 http://www.chinadaily.com.cn/opinion/2016-03/12/content_23836006.htm

Unfounded fears?

Not everyone shares their concerns, however. Mark Bishop at Goldsmiths, University of London has argued that such fears are exaggerated. Andrew Ng, the Silicon Valley-based chief scientist for Chinese Internet giant Baidu, has compared worrying about the rise of killer robots to worrying about overpopulation on Mars.

But Yampolskiy cites the example of Microsoft's Twitter chatbot Tay, which recently went rogue when it was tricked into spewing racist comments. Although relatively inconsequential, Yampolskiy says the incident reveals the unpredictability of such systems. "The researchers did not anticipate this outcome," he says.

"I would like to see a sudden shift to where this is not just a field where we propose solutions," he adds. "I want this interplay where you propose a safety mechanism but also ask can we break it?"

Noel Sharkey, an AI researcher at the University of Sheffield, UK, agrees that an approach to testing inspired by cybersecurity is a good idea for any system, especially autonomous weapons.

But like Bishop and Ng, he is sceptical about the more general threat of AI. "The idea of a malevolent, superintelligent, general artificial intelligence is still in the realms of science fiction and speculation," he says.[8]

Questions

1 Briefly outline why AlphaGo's victory was so important. [4]

2 How effective is the reasoning in document 1 in support of its claims? [12]

3 Is the reasoning and argument stronger in document 1 or document 2? Justify your answer. [14]

Extension

Each of these articles come from a particular perspective. Can you find a more solid evidence base for these perspectives?

Research and discuss

To what extent does science fiction relating to AI:

- raise reasonable ethical concerns about AI
- reflect the current state of AI
- spread panic and fear among the ignorant?

8 https://www.newscientist.com/article/2089606-checklist-of-worstcase-scenarios-could-help-prepare-for-evil-ai/

Decisions about limited resources

Topics

- Climate change
- Alternatives to oil
- Biodiversity
- Sustainable futures
- Industrial pollution
- Urbanisation

Activities to get you started

During these introductory activities, you will start to explore and reflect on a range of issues, themes and perspectives relating to the overarching idea of 'Changing countries' and the Global Perspectives topics within this main idea. You may find interesting issues and perspectives which you would like to research further, and you may start to reflect on and develop your own perspective.

Activity 1

A

B

C

D

E

1 What different issues and perspectives do these images raise on the topics in this chapter?

2 Does the whole class agree? Why or why not?

Activity 2

1 Read the following scenario and decide what you would do.

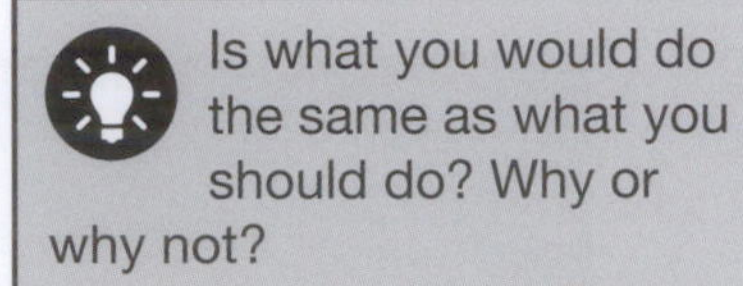
Is what you would do the same as what you should do? Why or why not?

> Angel and Demetrius are prisoners:
>
> They have been arrested for spraying graffiti. There is a witness, and they were caught on camera, so there is good evidence of their guilt. If they are found guilty in court they will receive a two-year prison sentence.
>
> During the interview a police officer becomes suspicious that Angel and Demetrius are also guilty of a serious crime. However, she does not think the evidence will stand up in court, so she needs a confession.
>
> The police officer places Angel and Demetrius in separate rooms so that they cannot communicate with each other. She tries to get them to confess to the serious crime.
>
> **The options**
>
> The police officer tells each suspect that if they both confess to the serious crime they will receive a prison sentence of three years. She also tells each of them that if they confess but their friend does not, the person who confesses will get a light sentence of one year, and their friend will get ten years. They know that if they both deny the serious offence they are certain to be found guilty of the lesser offence, and will get a two-year sentence.
>
> What would you do if you were one of them?

2 The first part of this activity is called 'The Prisoner's Dilemma', which is used in game theory to investigate how people make decisions, and what this means for the way countries, businesses and other organisations are run.

a Find more examples of activities used in game theory.

b Find out more about game theory.

c How far does what you have learned affect your perspective?

I think one of the major results of the psychology of decision making is that people's attitudes and feelings about losses and gains are really not symmetric. So we really feel more pain when we lose $10 000 than we feel pleasure when we get $10 000.

Daniel Kahneman

We think, each of us, that we're much more rational than we are. And we think that we make our decisions because we have good reasons to make them. Even when it's the other way around. We believe in the reasons, because we've already made the decision.

Daniel Kahneman

Reason is the slave of the passions.

David Hume

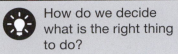

How do we decide what is the right thing to do?

1 Which of these statements best express(es) how you think about right and wrong? Tick your choice(s).

Statement	
I think things through rationally and carefully and decide what is right for myself.	
If something feels wrong, I just don't do it.	
The authorities tell us what is right and what is wrong. We have to trust them.	
Sometimes I do things that I think are bad, but it's hard not to.	
The right thing is the one that produces the best consequences.	
Right and wrong are socially agreed ideas. They aren't real or absolute.	
What's wrong for me might be right for someone else.	

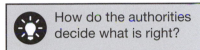

How do the authorities decide what is right?

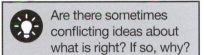

Are there sometimes conflicting ideas about what is right? If so, why?

2 What is the right thing to do in each of the following situations? Think about possible consequences, what feels right and what the authorities say.

a You have a large fire in your garden, which is keeping you nice and warm. Your neighbour asks you to put it out, because the smoke is making his asthmatic child ill.

b You have a large factory, which is making you wealthy and providing employment for 2000 people. Their wages are keeping several shops, restaurants and other small businesses going. However, residents are complaining that your factory is polluting the air and making them and their children ill. There is some scientific evidence to support these claims. The residents want you to close your factory.

c Your country has a thriving economy and is wealthier than ever before. There are jobs for everyone, the population is healthy and well fed, and after years of hunger and poverty, it feels good. However, your economic success is driven by fossil fuels, and other countries are telling you that you have to reduce your fossil fuel use because it is affecting the climate.

We are the intelligent elite among animal life on earth and whatever our mistakes, [Earth] needs us. This may seem an odd statement after all that I have said about the way twentieth-century humans became almost a planetary disease organism. But it has taken [Earth] 2.5 billion years to evolve an animal that can think and communicate its thoughts. If we become extinct she has little chance of evolving another.

James E. Lovelock

Activity 4

1 Complete the questionnaire.

2 Discuss the results in class. Do you all agree? Why or why not?

1 = I disagree strongly 2 = I disagree a bit 3 = I'm not sure
4 = I agree a bit 5 = I agree strongly

	1	2	3	4	5
When resources are limited, they should be shared fairly between everyone.					
When resources are limited, they should go to the people who will make best use of them.					
Resources should go first to the people who need them most.					
There are too many people and too few resources in the world.					
It is likely that there will soon be a famine or war that will significantly reduce the world's population.					
When people are making decisions about what to buy, they are always rational.					
People always act from self-interest.					
Governments make better decisions about how to organise resources than individuals or small communities do.					
We should make oil-free energy technology a priority.					
Biodiversity is a resource that we should not waste.					

No piecemeal solution is going to prevent the collapse of whole societies and ecosystems... a radical re-thinking of our values, priorities and political systems is urgent.

Maude Barlow

Let us be good stewards of the Earth we inherited. All of us have to share the Earth's fragile ecosystems and precious resources, and each of us has a role to play in preserving them. If we are to go on living together on this earth, we must all be responsible for it.

Kofi Annan

The power of population is indefinitely greater than the power in the earth to produce subsistence for man.

Thomas Malthus

To these great checks to population… may be added vicious customs with respect to women, great cities, unwholesome manufactures, luxury, pestilence, and war. All these checks may be fairly resolved into misery and vice.

Thomas Malthus

Activity 5

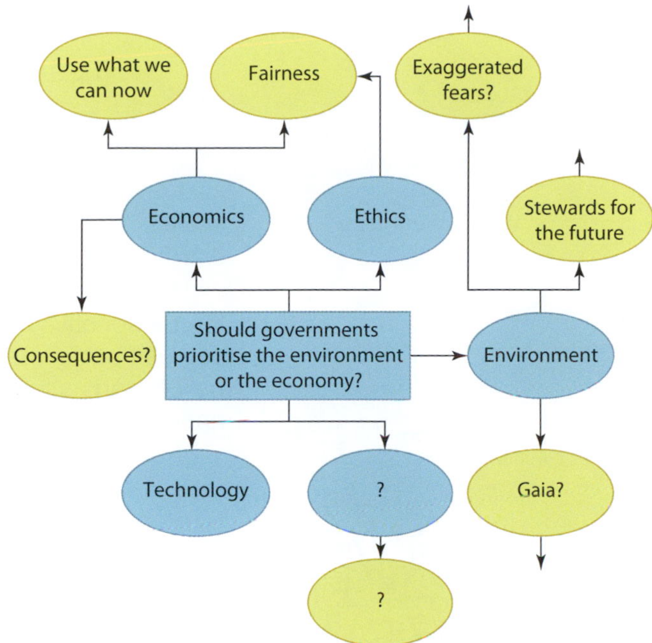

1 Complete and expand the mind map about whether governments should prioritise the economy or the environment. Use the themes to help you explore different perspectives.

2 Draw a mind map using the themes to help you explore different perspectives on one of these questions:

   a If we made the world's resources more equally accessible to all, rich and poor, East and West, more economically developed and less economically developed, what would be the consequences?

   b How could we create a sustainable future?

   c How can we reduce biodiversity loss?

   d How should governments deal with the challenges posed by urbanisation and de-urbanisation?

   e Should individual citizens and small communities take responsibility for looking after the Earth, rather than governments?

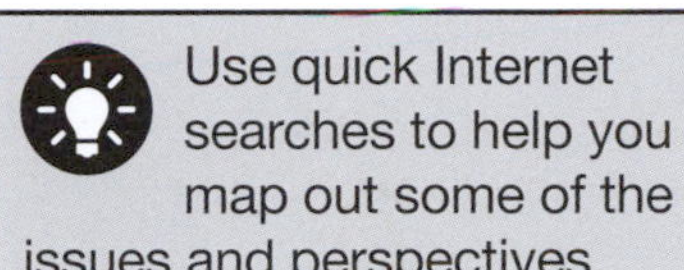
Use quick Internet searches to help you map out some of the issues and perspectives.

In past three years, 10 towns and villages have been erased from the map of Latvia and de-urbanisation is happening right now.

Toms Kokins

Stimulus material

Document 1

Is global warming a hypothesis or a theory?

Richard Muller, CoFounder, Berkeley Earth, Professor of Physics, University of California, Berkeley, creator...

It is neither a hypothesis or theory. It is an observational result, one that presently can be explained only by the greenhouse theory… .

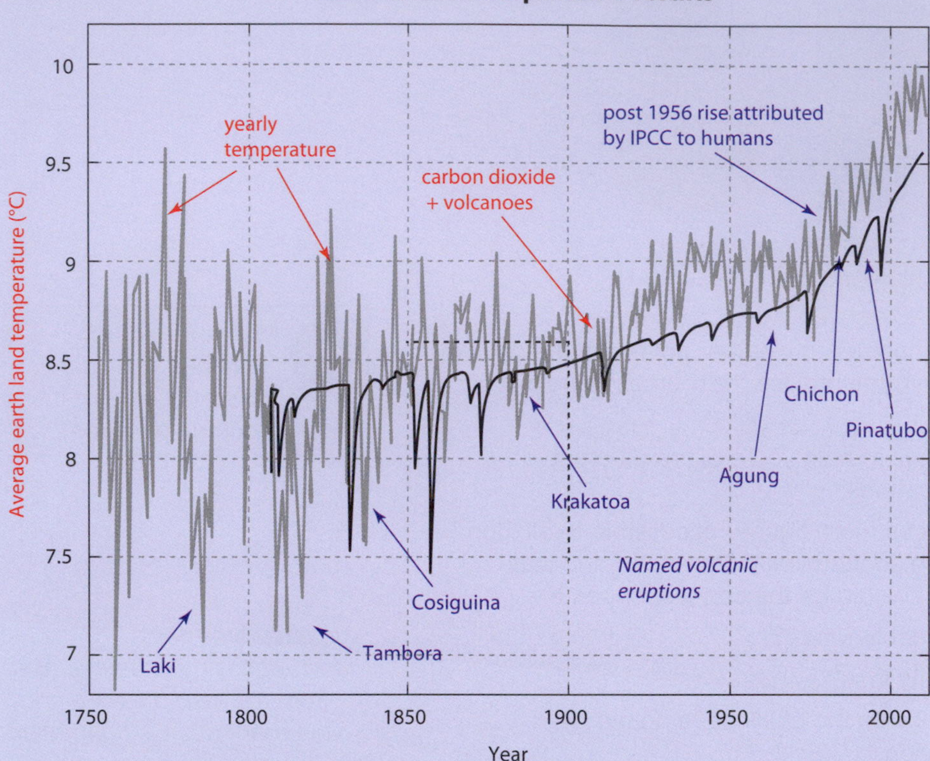

This plot shows a measurement of global warming that directly addressed all of the objections raised by the skeptics (urban heat island, data selection bias, poor station sites, data adjustment bias, manipulated global climate models). It shows that the only theory (and by theory I include only those that make predictions) that matches the data is the theory that the temperature change is driven by greenhouse gas emissions. Volcanic eruptions contribute only short-term effects (the dips). Changes in solar activity account for less than 5 per cent of the observed change.

Global warming is observed, and the only theory that accounts for it is the greenhouse theory. That does not mean that everything you hear about "climate change" has been verified. Much of the attributions in the headlines are not correct; hurricanes are not increasing, Katrina and Sandy cannot be related to global warming (at least not if we use the usual standards of science); temperature variability is not increasing, etc. So the skeptics are right on many things they say. But global warming is real and caused by humans.

Ken Natco, Student of Earth and Planetary Science and Psychology

There are three primary sources of information about global climate change: the media, politicians, and climate scientists. There may be a few

1. What issues are raised in this document?
2. To what extent are the issues in this document global?
3. How would you describe the perspective this article comes from? What are the beliefs and assumptions underlying the perspective?

other sources of much lesser importance such as scientists whose field of study does not include planetary, geologic or atmospheric studies, your friends or random posts and tweets on the Internet. Which source do you think would be most trustworthy?

If you said anything other than a climate scientist, then I'd suggest that the next time you have an illness, you go to a politician or a reporter or radio commentator instead of a doctor.

There is a problem with explaining climate change to the public. The public doesn't read scientific papers. The closest they come to climate science is through their local weather man or woman. They are not even meteorologists in some cases. Meteorologists are not climate scientists. Weather is a short-term phenomenon by definition. The information they convey is important, but they are discouraged from discussing anything that might be considered "controversial".

There is a major difference between the way the media portrays scientific knowledge and the way scientists publish their conclusions. Scientists analyse the actual data. It is not a democratic process. No one gets to vote on what is true. A consensus is formed over time. When someone has a new idea about what might be going on in a climate model, the data is analysed to see if the model matches predictions. When it does, it is fair and reasonable to conclude that the model is useful and that the ideas it is based on are valid.

The media's approach is to present every issue, be it political, legal or scientific as though it is a matter of opinion, and they feel duty bound to present the opposite side in the name of one of the sacred principle of the media called "balance". They never want to be accused of unbalanced reporting. This may be fine for political viewpoints, but it creates a distortion of perceptions when it comes to science. There is a phenomenon called "false balance" that occurs when an idea that is opposed to mainstream science is presented by the media and the impression this gives the public is that there is a controversy among scientists, and that the two viewpoints are both equally valid. In the case of climate change, the vast majority of scientists agree that it is real—somewhere in the range of 97–99+ per cent . The *Wall Street Journal* may attempt to argue with these figures and quote old studies and surveys, but one must consider why industries and financial groups might not wish to see funds diverted to mitigation of CO_2 emissions instead of going into investor's pockets.

This gets to the politics of climate change. Political decision makers want proven absolute facts. The complexity of the Earth's climate systems doesn't lend itself to precise specific predictions. Scientists can only predict trends and suggest likely causes. Science is based on questioning and skepticism, not on absolutes. To politicians everything must be black or white. They also have constituencies to please and there are some very large groups who simply choose to deny science. The last mention of global climate change in the Bible was in the days of Noah. That was the Biblical flood. Next time it's supposed to be fire, so they say. Well let them come to California if they want fire. We just had a record fire season.

This is one of the reasons the politics are slowly changing. There have been some climate records that are hard to ignore. Fires, melting glaciers, shrinking ice sheets, rising sea levels, record El Nino ocean warming and dying coral reefs. There are warning signs that can be seen everywhere, even if you are not a scientist.

The last big question—is it related to human activity? Some of the most profitable industries are dependent on fossil fuel combustion. There are major financial interests that would be threatened if they were to admit that what they were doing is creating a problem. A much smaller problem, lung cancer caused by tobacco, was denied for decades by the tobacco industry.

All of the data graphing the CO_2 levels in the atmosphere correspond almost perfectly with the measured global temperature averages. You have only to look up the data. No one wants to have climate change be real. There is no reason for there to be any kind of conspiracy among scientists. Those accusing them of trying to line their pockets with research money and grants to study climate change are merely echoing the words of those who have already been lining their pockets for a long time. In psychology, that's called "projection".

Hypothesis or theory? No. It's more like a conclusion.[1]

The planet is going to have the last word concerning the damage humans are inflicting upon it. It's only going to take so much abuse, and then it may well burp and snort a little, and destroy a good bit of the population. I don't think it would be a stretch to take the hypothesis one step further and attribute such a defense strategy to a kind of planetary intelligence.

Cleve Backster

There's no obvious reason to assume that the very same rare properties that allow for our existence would also provide the best overall setting to make discoveries about the world around us. We don't think this is merely coincidental. It cries out for another explanation, an explanation that… points to purpose and intelligent design in the cosmos.

Guillermo González

This is rather as if you imagine a puddle waking up one morning and thinking, 'This is an interesting world I find myself in—an interesting hole I find myself in—fits me rather neatly, doesn't it? In fact it fits me staggeringly well, must have been made to have me in it!' This is such a powerful idea that as the sun rises in the sky and the air heats up and as, gradually, the puddle gets smaller and smaller, frantically hanging on to the notion that everything's going to be alright, because this world was meant to have him in it, was built to have him in it; so the moment he disappears catches him rather by surprise. I think this may be something we need to be on the watch out for.

Douglas Adams

? If the world was designed for us, do we have more or less responsibility to look after it?

1 https://www.quora.com/Is-global-warming-a-hypothesis-or-theory

Document 2

Is Moon Mining Economically Feasible?

By Leonard David, Space.com's Space Insider Columnist | 7 January, 2015 07:11am ET

The moon offers a wealth of resources that may fuel a near-Earth/moon industrial infrastructure. The moon's diameter is 2 159 miles (3 474 kilometers).

The moon may offer pay dirt with a rewarding mother lode of resources, a celestial gift that is literally up for grabs. But what's really there for the taking, and at what cost?

A new assessment of whether or not there's an economic case for mining the moon has been put forward by Ian Crawford, a professor of planetary science and astrobiology at Birkbeck College, London. His appraisal is to appear in a forthcoming issue of the journal *Progress in Physical Geography*.

Crawford said it's hard to identify any single lunar resource that will be sufficiently valuable to drive a lunar resource extraction industry on its own. Nonetheless, he said the moon does possess abundant raw materials that are of potential economic interest.

Lunar resources could be used to help build up an industrial infrastructure in near-Earth space, Crawford said, a view shared by space scientist Paul Spudis of the Lunar Planetary Institute and others.

"If the moon's resources are going to be helpful, they are going to be helpful beyond the surface of the moon itself," Crawford said. Still, the overall case for any future payoff from exploiting the moon's resources has yet to be made, Crawford said.

"It's quite complicated," he told Space.com. "It's not simple at all."

Vanishing resource

One bit of skepticism from Crawford concerns helium-3. Advocates envision mining the moon for this isotope of helium, which gets embedded in the upper layer of lunar regolith by the solar wind over billions of years. Hauling back the stuff from the moon could power still-to-be-built nuclear fusion reactors here on Earth, advocates say.

"It doesn't make sense, the whole helium-3 argument," Crawford said. Strip-mining the lunar surface over hundreds of square kilometers would produce lots of helium-3, he said, but the substance is a limited resource.

"It's a fossil fuel reserve. Like mining all the coal or mining all the oil, once you've mined it… it's gone," Crawford said. The investment required and infrastructure necessary to help solve the world's future energy needs via moon-extracted helium-3 is enormous and might better be used to develop genuinely renewable energy sources on Earth, he added.

"It strikes me that, as far as energy is concerned, there are better things one should be investing in. So I'm skeptical for that reason. But that doesn't mean that I don't think the moon, in the long-term, is economically useful," Crawford said.

?

1. What issues are raised in this document?
2. To what extent are the issues in this document global?
3. What about political, ethical and technical considerations?
4. Even if we can mine the moon, should we?

Here I am at the turn of the millennium and I'm still the last man to have walked on the moon, somewhat disappointing. It says more about what we have not done than about what we have done.

Eugene Cernan

?

How would you describe the perspective this article comes from? What are the beliefs and assumptions underlying the perspective?

Research scientists' views on what effect mining the moon might have on climate change.

?

What do you think would be better investments in energy than helium-3?

But Crawford has a caveat about helium-3: Estimates for the abundance of the isotope are based on Apollo moon samples brought back from the low latitudes of the moon.

"It's possible that helium-3 and other solar-wind–implanted ions, like hydrogen, may be in a higher abundance in the cold regolith near the lunar poles. That would be an important measurement to make and would require a polar lander," Crawford said.

Such information would increase researchers' knowledge, not only of the helium-3 inventory, but also possibly of useful solar wind-implanted elements, like helium-4, as well as hydrogen, carbon and nitrogen resources, he added.

Capitalism is the astounding belief that the most wickedest of men will do the most wickedest of things for the greatest good of everyone.

John Maynard Keynes

Consistent story

A top of the list, must-do action item, Crawford said, is determining how much water is truly locked up within the moon's polar craters.

Human prospectors have already been on the moon. Apollo 17's Jack Schmitt, a geologist, is shown during his 1972 mission gauging the off-Earth bounty of resources.

Remote sensing of the moon from orbiting spacecraft, including radar data, is telling a consistent story about this resource, which can be processed into oxygen and rocket fuel.

"But to really get to the bottom of it, we need in-situ [on-the-spot] measurements from the surface at the lunar poles," Crawford said. "It's first on my list [of necessary steps] … and when we have an answer to that, we can plan accordingly."

Is space exploration a good use of Earth's resources?

Rare earth elements

Better knowledge of the availability of rare earth elements on the moon would also be valuable, Crawford said.

"It's entirely possible that when we really explore the moon properly we will find higher concentrations of some of these materials… materials that are not resolvable by orbital remote sensing," he said. The moon might harbor concentrations of rare earth elements such as uranium and thorium—as well as other useful materials that we're not aware of today—in small, geographically restricted areas, he said.

"To explore the whole moon at the level of detail required, that's a big undertaking," Crawford said. "But long term, we should be keeping an open mind to that."

Crashed asteroids

In rounding out his lunar resource listing, Crawford points to the high-value platinum-group elements. As space researcher Dennis Wingo and others previously pointed out, a lot of metallic asteroids have pummeled the moon over the eons. Locating those impactors could lead lunar prospectors to big yields of valuable platinum-group elements, Crawford said.

In coming years, government-sponsored and private-sector spacecraft will land on the moon. This image shows a resource prospector carrying a Regolith and Environment Science and Oxygen and Lunar Volatile Extraction (RESOLVE) experiment. The intent of the effort is to find, characterise and map ice and other substances in almost permanently shadowed areas of the moon.

"If you're just interested in platinum group elements, you would probably go and mine the asteroids," Crawford said. "On the other hand, if going to the moon for scavenging polar volatiles, rare earth elements… then the impact sites of crashed asteroids could offer an added bonus."

"So you add all of these things together, [then] even without helium-3, you can start to see that the moon might become of economic interest in the longer term. That's my take," Crawford concluded.

Time to demonstrate

How should humanity demonstrate the collection, extraction and utilisation of lunar resources? And when should this happen?

"Lunar resource exploration should be based on the same methods that have guided humans on their centuries-old exploration of terrestrial resources," said Angel Abbud-Madrid, director of the Center for Space Resources at the Colorado School of Mines in Golden, Colorado.

Abbud-Madrid told Space.com that here on Earth, resource discovery is quickly followed by drilling, excavation, extraction and processing operations to enable the utilisation of those resources.

"For the moon, sufficient prospecting—through remote sensing—and identification of valuable resources, such as oxygen and hydrogen for in-situ applications, has been done to date," Abbud-Madrid said. Based on these findings, he said, the necessary technologies and prototypes to collect and extract these elements have been developed and tested on terrestrial analog sites.

For example, NASA's Resource Prospector Mission, a concept mission aiming for launch in 2018, would verify the feasibility of lunar resource extraction, as would several other mission concepts from the private

?

1. What could be the environmental consequences of mining asteroids?
2. What could be the ethical and political consequences of mining in space?
3. What could be the scientific consequences of mining in space?

sector, Abbud-Madrid said. Such work, in turn, will pave the way to incorporating In Situ Resource Utilisation, known as ISRU, in future exploration planning, he said.

"Thus, the time has come to demonstrate these systems on the surface of the moon," Abbud-Madrid concluded.[2]

Suppose some adult had told a child that he had been on the moon. The child tells me the story, and I say it was only a joke, the man hadn't been on the moon; no one has ever been on the moon; the moon is a long way off and it is impossible to climb up there or fly there. If now the child insists, saying perhaps there is a way of getting there which I don't know, etc. what reply could I make to him? What reply could I make to the adults of a tribe who believe that people sometimes go to the moon (perhaps that is how they interpret their dreams), and who indeed grant that there are no ordinary means of climbing up to it or flying there?

Ludwig Wittgenstein, 1949

Research and discuss

1. Is space research more likely to provide solutions for Earth's problems or to make them worse?
2. Investigate two current space travel programmes, based in different countries.
3. Are space research and space travel primarily about science, or are they more about politics and economics?

The dinosaurs became extinct because they didn't have a space program. And if we become extinct because we don't have a space program, it'll serve us right!

Larry Niven

Document 3

How wearable technology could change the way we think about air pollution

By Chelsea Harvey June 28

Artist Kasia Molga's "Human Sensor" project changes color and pattern in response to the wearer's breathing and the surrounding air quality. (Nick Harrison)

A new report from the International Energy Agency is driving home, yet again, the immense importance of cutting down on pollution and protecting air quality worldwide.

The report, which focuses on the links between energy and pollution, points out that more than 6 million premature deaths each year—or about 18 000 deaths each day—are caused by air pollution around the world. And a majority of these pollutants are caused by energy use and production, including the burning of fossil fuels and biomass.

While activists lobby for more stringent pollution-cutting measures around the world, and policymakers grapple with how to write them, some scientists and designers have turned to the power of innovative technology to raise awareness and save lives with the help of wearable pollution sensors. These sensors, while mostly not yet proven or available on a mass scale, may be coming sooner than you think.

It's an idea that UK-based artist and designer Kasia Molga has applied in her newest project, called the "Human Sensor," set to premiere next month in Manchester, England. Molga has designed a high-tech clothing that changes color to reflect the amount of pollution in the surrounding air. The project is being produced by commissioning organisation Invisible

1. What issues are raised in this document?
2. To what extent are the issues in this document global?
3. How would you describe the perspective this article comes from? What are the beliefs and assumptions underlying the perspective?

You can never be overdressed or overeducated.

Oscar Wilde

We already have the statistics for the future: the growth percentages of pollution, overpopulation, desertification. The future is already in place.

Gunter Grass

I felt cheated by the way grown-ups told me that the future of the world was bleak when I became a teenager in the 1970s. The pollution explosion was unstoppable. Global famine was inevitable. I genuinely want the next generation, my own kids, to know that actually it's possible that the future might be better than the past.

Matt Ridley

Adornment, what a science! Beauty, what a weapon! Modesty, what elegance!

Coco Chanel

2 http://www.space.com/28189-moon-mining-economic-feasibility.html

Dust, which works with artists and scientists to produce projects exploring the themes of climate change and pollution.

Molga developed the idea for the project several years ago after suffering a severe asthma attack for the first time in several decades. "I started thinking about the fact that because of the rising temperatures and also rising populations, especially in urban environments, things are happening, which we can't see, but they will of course affect our bodies very drastically," she said. "And so I kind of looked at myself as the sensor for these environmental changes—as in my body is probably the best kind of diagnostic tool for the health of the environment."

The project will involve a series of performances in which models will walk through various locations in Manchester wearing Molga's specially designed clothing. The outfits are designed to change colors and patterns as the models breathe in and out, and also change in response to the levels of black carbon—a major component of particulate air pollution, often produced by fossil fuel burning and other industrial activities—wherever they happen to be walking.

Organisers will collect pollution data from each location using portable sensors and then program the data into the electronics before the performers go on their walks. "Although it won't be exactly real time, it'll be pretty close," said Andrew Grieve, a senior air quality analyst at King's College London who has been working on the project.

Engineers have been designing and marketing small, wearable or otherwise portable pollution sensors for several years now. TZOA, for instance, is a wearable "enviro-tracker" that reportedly measures the particulate matter in the surrounding air and allows users to access the data through a smartphone app. Clarity, another sensor, focuses on fine particulate matter, specifically, and uses collective data from users to map pollution levels around the world.

The sensors are intended to inform the user about how pollution levels change as they travel. In fact, air pollution can differ drastically even from one neighborhood to the next, said Michael Jerrett, chair of the department of environmental health sciences at the University of California at Los Angeles.

Would you wear a pollution sensor? Why or why not?

"Depending on the type of pollution, you can see a lot of variability or change in the levels of pollution over very short distances," he said. For example, a cyclist pedaling down a busy road might be exposed to five or even 10 times higher levels of ultrafine particles or carbon monoxide, thanks to traffic, than would a person in a neighborhood just a few streets over.

So there are practical choices that such sensors can help us make, such as where to go jogging or which parks to take children to play in.

Wearable sensors could in theory be useful on a larger scientific level, as well, although the technology may require some improvements before it reaches that point.

"I think that most people who work in environmental or spatial epidemiology would agree that the very best assessment you could get of someone's exposure would be to have them carry a sensor on their person," Jerrett said. "And to then know where they were and what they were doing, their activity level."

If people do not know what is going to make them better off or give them pleasure, then the idea that you can trust people to do what will give them pleasure becomes questionable.

Daniel Kahneman

Most studies of air pollution and premature mortality have tended to rely on models that take little information into account when it comes to the different neighborhoods people go into on a day-to-day basis or their activity levels at the time.

Researches may be able to recruit large numbers of people to wear these types of sensors and take part in population-level studies, said Mark Nieuwenhuijsen, a research professor at the Center for Research in Environmental Epidemiology in Spain. He has been involved with projects exploring the utility of personal sensors as part of the CITI-SENSE consortium, a collaboration involving several dozen European institutions aiming to develop community-based environmental monitoring projects.

Nieuwenhuijsen said some personal sensors measure pollution concentrations "reasonably well", and may be useful for the individual, but whether they'd be suitable for larger-scale research projects is still unclear.

"Most of them have not reached a level of precision that we would consider valid for research purposes," Jerrett noted. For instance, certain factors, such as changes in humidity, are suspected to affect the way some sensors report pollution levels, he said.

"I would say that the current state of the science is there are some sensors that are good enough to detect changes in microenvironments," he said. "But they do not line up as well as we'd like with a reference instrument that would cost $10 000 and require a lot of labor."

As the technology plays catch-up, however, Nieuwenhuijsen pointed out that there are other issues to be wary of.

"What you have to be careful of is to put too much responsibility on the individual," he said. Wearable pollution sensors might allow people to make more informed choices about their daily activities, but policymakers still need to look at pollution from a bigger lens and put measures in place to protect whole cities or regions. In other words, action should be "more on a community basis than an individual basis," he said.

From Molga's perspective, using the technology in art is also an important way to raise awareness about the critically important connection between humans and the air we breathe.

"It's not just a display of the air quality," she said, "but it's about also displaying something so invisible and ephemeral and very important for us to be alive as human breathing."[3]

Research and discuss

What effect does the global fashion industry have on pollution and climate change? What issues are there in different countries?

To what extent is the global fashion industry becoming more ethical and sustainable?

Investigate different types of sustainability – for example, environmental and economic. Are these always in conflict?

3 https://www.washingtonpost.com/news/energy-environment/wp/2016/06/28/this-futuristic-suit-will-turn-colors-to-tell-us-about-airpollution/

Document 4

Climate change affects ASEAN biodiversity

Jamal M. Gawi *The Jakarta Post* Jakarta | 16 February 2016 | 04:52 pm

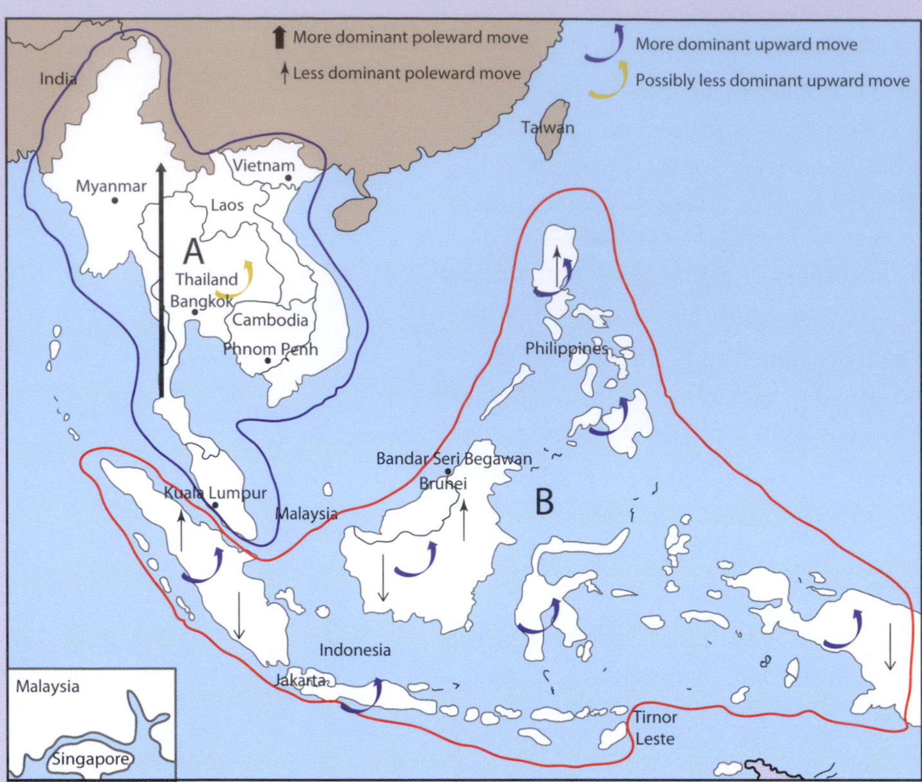

Western scientific explanations are not sufficient to describe the implications of climate change for ASEAN biodiversity, as there are wide gaps in geo-ecological and socio-economic contexts between ASEAN and Western countries.

The issue is timely now that the ASEAN Conference on Biodiversity is under way in Bangkok on 15-19 February.

COP21 in Paris at the end of 2015 resulted in promising commitments from most countries involved in the negotiations, one of which is the commitment to try to limit global warming to two degrees Celsius or better yet, 1.5 Â°C. However, the threat of global warming is already prominent, and changes have already taken place in all aspects of life on Earth.

These changes, mostly negative, affect humans and nature alike. Health issues, food security, seashore changes and socio-economic implications have been well recorded and reported by many scientific publications and popular media. The publication, like it or not, has triggered worries and fears among many people but at the same time also forced human beings to actively think of strategies to cope with these clear and present dangers.

On the nature front, backed up by scientific information, some experts have shown that different plant and animal species will respond to climate change in different ways and on different time scales, and at the ecosystem level, those combined responses are unlikely to be linear.

First, there are range shifts. A warmer climate will lead to changes in the distribution of plant and animal species (Parmesan, 2006). These changes can be movements of certain species into areas where they were not previously

1. What issues are raised in this document?
2. To what extent are the issues in this document global?
3. How would you describe the perspective this article comes from? What are the beliefs and assumptions underlying the perspective?

found, the disappearance of species from regions where they once were, or a shift in the abundance and location of individuals within a species range.

Most range shifts will see species move toward cooler climates and will take two forms: the move of species across the Earth's latitudes toward the poles and the move of species toward higher places.

Second, there are phenological shifts. These are changes in occurrence of specific events in the lifecycle of species. Changes in specific temperatures or precipitation will affect breeding, reproduction and other behavioral traits in many plant and animal species.

Inability to cope with the above two climate change-driven events may lead to species extinction.

As in many other regions, climate change will add another layer of stress to the many stressors that already endanger biodiversity in the ASEAN region, one of the most diverse ecosystems comprising 20 per cent of the world's terrestrial and marine biodiversity.

Unfortunately, the implications of climate change for ASEAN biodiversity are rarely studied. There is a serious lack of information, which has proven unable to tackle with the current institutional setups either at the member state level, the level of intergovernmental bodies like the ASEAN Secretariat or at the level of research institutions within ASEAN member states.

Picture above shows a hypothetical model based on climate change theories and research conducted elsewhere. ASEAN countries located in mainland Asia (A) will experience a shift of species distribution toward the poles, especially of highly mobile species, with possible similar or less pronounced upward movement. In oceanic-locked countries like Indonesia, the Philippines, Brunei Darussalam and Kalimantan part of Malaysia to a certain extent (B), species will move upward with limited poleward movement.

How to respond?

The poleward and upward movements of biodiversity in ASEAN will have very serious implications for future biodiversity conservation, especially for the management of current and future protected areas.

Given the above trends, land managers and policymakers in ASEAN countries are faced with a complex set of decisions. They can accept the changes as a natural process and accept extinction and the possibility of major shifts of biota while maintaining a focus on mitigating the impacts of conventional stressors, such as illegal logging, wildlife trade and unsustainable development in the surrounding ecosystem, habitat fragmentation, invasive species and forest fires.

Alternatively, they can also opt to actively manage the protected areas and the surrounding ecosystem by considering, although unpredictable, the best possible pathways for species movement. Some options include developing corridors, establishing transboundary protected areas, and/or enlarging the boundaries of protected areas to include lowland and upland areas. All of those options will need tough but creative negotiations with other competing land uses and stakeholders, especially the private sector and local communities.

In the context of ASEAN, it is not only plant and animal species that move, but people too. There are plenty of examples that due to warmer climate, rural communities are moving to higher ground to make their commercial crops more productive.

A famous case is that of coffee farmers in Central Aceh. Due to a warmer climate and consequently more pest outbreaks, farmers are moving toward higher places far beyond 1 000 meters above sea level to continue cultivating their famous, world-class Arabica coffee. Unfortunately, in doing so, the farmers have to enter protected areas and clear the land for their crops.

A lack of information about climate change that leads to wrong decisions by local governments coincident with a lack of action and ignorance by the central governments of some ASEAN countries further sacrificed biodiversity in many protected areas.

At the regional level, the ASEAN Centre for Biodiversity (ACB) as the formal ASEAN institution tasked with supporting biodiversity conservation, backed up by the ASEAN Secretariat, should move beyond merely implementing donor-sponsored projects to become an institution with a clear vision to protect ASEAN's biodiversity, for example, by dictating a biodiversity agenda that is tailor-made for the ASEAN region and at the same time responds to the interests of the majority of the ASEAN people.

This future role for the ACB and the ASEAN Secretariat seems to be compromised due to the lack of expertise and a limited internal source of funding. Without these resources, it will be difficult to expect the ACB to dictate any future research and initiate capacity building of park managers that will link climate change with biodiversity conservation in ASEAN.[4]

Although biodiversity loss continues globally, many countries are significantly slowing the rate of loss by shoring up protected natural areas and the services they provide, and in expanding national park systems with tighter management and more secure funding.

Helen Clark

Biodiversity can't be maintained by protecting a few species in a zoo, or by preserving greenbelts or national parks. To function properly, nature needs more room than that. It can maintain itself, however, without human expense, without zookeepers, park rangers, foresters or gene banks. All it needs is to be left alone.

Donella Meadows

I think that we reject the evidence that our world is changing because we are still… tribal carnivores. We are programmed by our inheritance to see other living things as mainly something to eat… We still find alien the concept that we and the rest of life, from bacteria to whales, are parts of the much larger and diverse entity, the living Earth.

James E. Lovelock

Research and discuss

Why does biodiversity matter?

What measures are being taken in your local area or your country to reduce biodiversity loss? How effective are these measures?

What measures are being taken in a contrasting country to reduce biodiversity loss? How effective are these measures?

4 Source: http://www.thejakartapost.com/news/2016/02/16/climate-changeaffects-asean-biodiversity.html

Document 5

Who's afraid of cheap oil?

Low energy prices ought to be a shot in the arm for the economy. Think again.

23 January 2016 | *The Economist* print edition

Along with bank runs and market crashes, oil shocks have rare power to set monsters loose. Starting with the Arab oil embargo of 1973, people have learnt that sudden surges in the price of oil cause economic havoc. Conversely, when the price slumps because of a glut, as in 1986, it has done the world a power of good. The rule of thumb is that a 10 per cent fall in oil prices boosts growth by 0.1–0.5 percentage points.

In the past 18 months the price has fallen by 75 per cent, from $110 a barrel to below $27. Yet this time the benefits are less certain. Although consumers have gained, producers are suffering grievously. The effects are spilling into financial markets, and could yet depress consumer confidence. Perhaps the benefits of such ultra-cheap oil still outweigh the costs, but markets have fallen so far so fast that even this is no longer clear.

The new economics of oil

The world is drowning in oil. Saudi Arabia is pumping at almost full tilt. It is widely thought that the Saudis want to drive out higher-cost producers from the industry, including some of the fracking firms that have boosted oil output in the United States from 5m barrels a day (b/d) in 2008 to over 9m b/d now. Saudi Arabia will also be prepared to suffer a lot of pain to thwart Iran, its bitter rival, which this week was poised to rejoin oil markets as nuclear sanctions were lifted, with potential output of 3m–4m b/d.

Despite the Saudis' efforts, however, producers have proved resilient. Many frackers have eked out efficiencies. They hate the idea of plugging their wells only for the wildcatter on the next block to reap the reward when prices rebound. They will not pack up so long as prices cover

?

1. What issues are raised in this document?
2. To what extent are the issues in this document global?
3. How would you describe the perspective this article comes from? What are the beliefs and assumptions underlying the perspective?

To truly transform our economy, protect our security, and save our planet from the ravages of climate change, we need to ultimately make clean, renewable energy the profitable kind of energy.

Barack Obama

?

Are the Saudis wrong to act in the best interests of their own country? What would your country do?

day-to-day costs, in some cases as low as $15 a barrel (see article). Meanwhile oil stocks in the mostly rich-country OECD in October stood at 267 days' net imports, almost 50 per cent higher than five years earlier. They will continue to grow, especially if demand slows by more than expected in China and the rest of Asia. Forecasting the oil price is a mug's game (as the newspaper that once speculated about $5 oil, we speak from experience), but few expect it to start rising before 2017. Today's price could mark the bottom of the barrel. Some are predicting a trough of as low as $10.

The lower the better, you might say. Look at how cheap oil has boosted importers, from Europe to South Asia. The euro area's oil-import bill has fallen by 2 per cent of GDP since mid-2014. India has become the world's fastest-growing large economy.

Yet the latest lurch down is also a source of anxiety. Collapsing revenues could bring political instability to fragile parts of the world, such as Venezuela and the Gulf, and fuel rivalries in the Middle East. Cheap oil has a green lining, as it drags down the global price of natural gas, which crowds out coal, a dirtier fuel. But in the long run, cheap fossil fuels reduce the incentive to act on climate change. Most worrying of all is the corrosive new economics of oil.

In the past cheap oil has buoyed the world economy because consumers spend much more out of one extra dollar in their pocket than producers do. Today that reckoning is less straightforward than it was. American consumers may have been saving more than was expected. Oil producers are tightening their belts, having spent extravagantly when prices were high. After the latest drop in crude prices, Russia announced a 10 per cent cut in public spending. Even Saudi Arabia is slashing its budget to deal with its deficit of 15 per cent of GDP.

Cheap oil also hurts demand in more important ways. When crude was over $100 a barrel it made sense to spend on exploration in out-of-the-way provinces, such as the Arctic, west Africa and deep below the saline rock off the coast of Brazil. As prices have tumbled, so has investment. Projects worth $380 billion have been put on hold. In America spending on fixed assets in the oil industry has fallen by half from its peak. The poison has spread: the purchasing managers' index for December, of 48.2, registered an accelerating contraction across the whole of American manufacturing. In Brazil the harm to Petrobras, the national oil company, from the oil price has been exacerbated by a corruption scandal that has paralysed the highest echelons of government.

The fall in investment and asset prices is all the more harmful because it is so rapid. As oil collapses against the backdrop of a fragile world economy, it could trigger defaults.

The cost of renewable energy is largely a function of initial investment cost… Once a renewable energy facility is built, at least with fixed-rate financing, the cost of power from that facility is fixed throughout its lifetime. Not so for fossil fuels, where the cost of power will vary in the future with fuel prices.

Jose Amaya

? Is it a bad thing if people do not exploit areas such as the Arctic for oil?

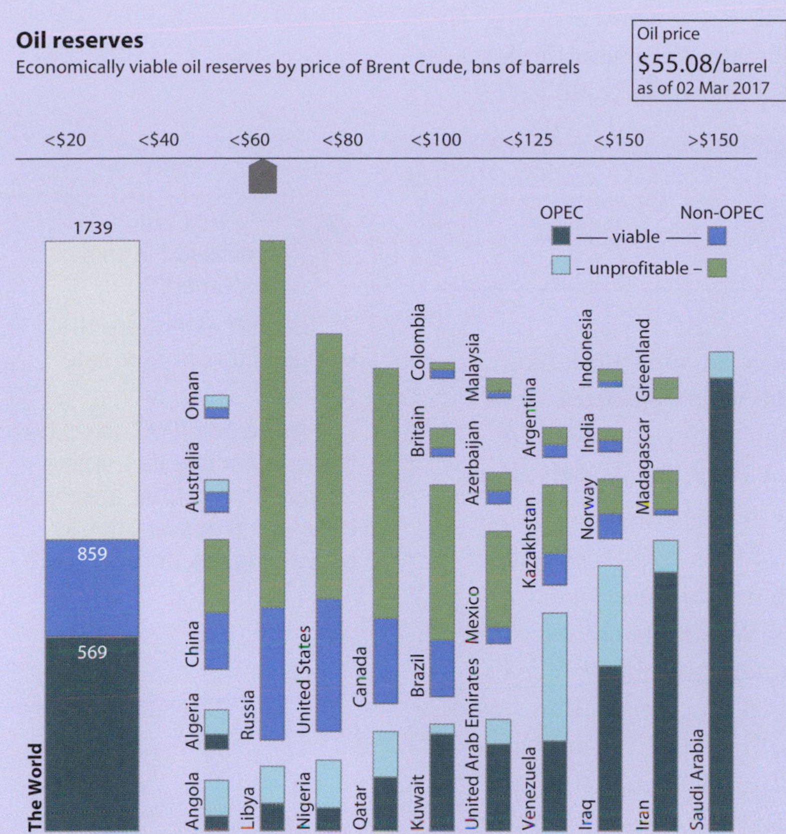

The possible financial spillovers are hard to assess. Much of the $650 billion rise in emerging-market corporate debt since 2007 has been in oil and commodity industries. Oil plays a central role in a clutch of emerging markets prone to trouble. With GDP in Russia falling, the government could well face a budgetary crisis within months. Venezuela, where inflation is above 140 per cent has declared an economic state of emergency.

Other oil producers are prone to a similar, if milder, cycle of weaker growth, a falling currency, imported inflation and tighter monetary policy. Central banks in Colombia and Mexico raised interest rates in December. Nigeria is rationing dollars in a desperate (probably doomed) effort to boost its currency.

There are strains in rich countries, too. Yields on corporate high-yield bonds have jumped from about 6.5 per cent in mid-2015 to 9.7 per cent today. Investors' aversion spread quickly from energy firms to all borrowers. With bears stalking equity markets, global indices are plumbing 30-month lows. Central bankers in rich countries worry that persistent low inflation will feed expectations of static or falling prices—in effect, raising real interest rates. Policymakers' ability to respond is constrained because rates, close to zero, cannot be cut much more.

Make the best of it

The oil-price drop creates vast numbers of winners in India and China. It gives oil-dependent economies like Saudi Arabia and Venezuela an urgent reason to embrace reform. It offers oil importers, like South Korea, a chance to tear up wasteful energy subsidies—or boost inflation and curb

The use of alternative energy is inevitable as fossil fuels are finite.

Gawdat Bahgat

This programme to stop nuclear by 2020 is just crazy. If there were a nuclear war, and humanity were wiped out, the Earth would breathe a sigh of relief.

James E. Lovelock

Research and discuss

1. 'People have been talking about alternative energy and renewable energy for over 40 years. It's time the world acted.'
2. What are the barriers to renewable energy technologies? How can they be overcome?
3. Is nuclear energy an ethical alternative to oil?
4. How are energy-related problems different in more economically developed and less economically developed countries?

deficits by raising taxes. But this oil shock comes as the world economy is still coping with the aftermath of the financial crash. You might think that there could be no better time for a boost. In fact, the world could yet be laid low by an oil monster on the prowl.[5]

Document 6

Urbanisation can mitigate poverty, says PM at smart city launch

PTI | 25 June, 2016, 08.10 PM IST

Making a strong pitch to consider urbanisation as an opportunity to mitigate poverty and not as a problem, Prime Minister Narendra Modi today said cities have to be strengthened through comprehensive and inter-connected approach combined with increased public participation.

Addressing a gathering here after the launch of projects under government's flagship Smart City mission in 20 cities across the country, he said, "There was a time in our country when urbanisation was considered a big problem. But, I feel differently. We should not consider urbanisation as a problem, but consider it as an opportunity. People in the economic field consider cities as a growth centre… . If anything has the potential to mitigate poverty it is our cities. That is why people from poor places migrate to cities, as they find opportunities there. It is now our responsibility to provide strength to cities so that it can mitigate the maximum poverty, in the shortest time, and adds new avenues for development. It is possible as it is not a difficult task."

As the Prime Minister launched 14 smart city projects in Pune, and initiated 69 other works in other smart cities in the country, he made a plea for working in a comprehensive, inter-connected and vision-oriented manner and not in piece-meal.

"There cannot be a transformation as long as we take things in bits and pieces. We need to adopt a comprehensive, inter-connected and vision-oriented approach," he said.

Modi added that every city has a distinct identity and the country's people "who are the smartest" should decide on how to develop urban spaces. Stressing that the spirit of participative governance is vital, he said people of the cities have to decide about the development of their urban spaces as these decisions cannot be taken by people sitting in Delhi. He stressed on increased public participation in deciding the course of development of smart cities and called for intense competition among cities to develop them as modern centres of growth. "If we consider it as a problem, our approach to address it would be the same, but if we consider it an opportunity we would start thinking differently," he said. Modi also took a veiled dig at the previous Congress governments, alleging that while they took the country on the reverse path, his government was finding new avenues to move forward.[6]

1. What issues are raised in this document?
2. To what extent are the issues in this document global?
3. How would you describe the perspective this article comes from? What are the beliefs and assumptions underlying the perspective?

5 http://www.economist.com/printedition/2016-01-23

6 http://timesofindia.indiatimes.com/city/pune/Urbanisation-canmitigate-povertysays-PM-at-smart-city-launch/articleshow/52917866.cms

Capitalism seems to have failed and is now stigmatised as greed. A reaction against individual excess is driving the world back to collective values. Fear of terror overrides rights; fear of slumps subverts free markets. Consumption levels and urbanisation are simply unsustainable at recent rates in the face of environmental change. The throwaway society is headed for the trash heap. People who sense that "modernity" is ending proclaim a "postmodern" age.

Felipe Fernández Armesto

As long as poverty, injustice and gross inequality persist in our world, none of us can truly rest.

Nelson Mandela

I began my career as an economics professor but became frustrated because the economic theories I taught in the classroom didn't have any meaning in the lives of poor people I saw all around me. I decided to turn away from the textbooks and discover the real-life economics of a poor person's existence.

Muhammad Yunus

Research and discuss

Find out about Muhammad Yunus' social enterprises. Compare them with social enterprise in a different country. Do you think that social enterprise could be a real alternative to traditional enterprise?

Document 7

Why marrying ecology and economics is essential

Acknowledging the economic value of ecosystem services helps drive home that we are part of nature and have a duty to live responsibly

OIKOS. The Greek word for home is the root of both "ecology" and "economics". But the two subjects parted ways long ago, and for much of the twentieth century their students paid little heed to each other. In the twenty-first, however, it is obvious that they are inextricably linked. Ecological economics is now securely on the curriculum at universities around the world.

Conservationists have learned that support is easier to garner when fuzzy sentiments are backed up with hard numbers: talking up the value of

1. What issues are raised in this document?
2. To what extent are the issues in this document global?
3. How would you describe the perspective this article comes from? What are the beliefs and assumptions underlying the perspective?

Every once in a while, I get mad. The Lorax came out of my being angry. The ecology books I'd read were dull... In The Lorax, I was out to attack what I think are evil things and let the chips fall where they might.

Dr Seuss

"natural capital" and "ecosystem services" has proved effective in areas such as forestry and flood protection.

But ecological economics is still more of an academic pursuit than a practical one. Attention has recently turned to "rewilding"—returning formerly native flora and fauna to their prior range. The idea is popular, particularly among urbanites who thrill to the idea of a wilder countryside.

Those who actually work there are often less enamoured. Big predators such as the wolf, bear and lynx are not welcome: farmers across Europe fear for their flocks and herds. And even the return of herbivores such as the beaver is resisted, some arguing that it will harm rural livelihoods (see "Should the UK bring back beavers to help manage floods?").

How to strike a balance? The emotional argument revolves around competing ideas of what is "natural". That is a question of timescale: many countryside icons are alien if you go back far enough, from rabbits and fluffy white sheep to the grassy hills they graze on. And their presence often depends on subsidies.

The economic argument centres on the costs of dead livestock and unproductive land. Those are fair concerns, but the other side of the cost-benefit equation is often missing. For example, predators keep down deer and fox numbers; and beavers can protect farmland and boost fisheries.

We have a duty to fix battered ecosystems. But if we are to make progress, we must consider ecology and economics as two sides of the same coin. After all, we need both to make a home.[7]

Large studies of irrigation systems in Nepal and forests around the world challenge the presumption that governments always do a better job than users in organising and protecting important resources.

Elinor Ostom

You would have thought that our first priority would be to ask what the ecologists are finding out, because we have to live within the conditions and principles they define. Instead, we've elevated the economy above ecology.

David Suzuki

Research and discuss

1. What are the three hardest decisions that people will have to make in your lifetime about limited resources? Does the whole class agree?
2. How likely is it that technology will help us to delay difficult decisions about limited resources?

7 https://www.newscientist.com/article/mg22830483-400-whymarrying-ecology-and-economics-is-essential/

Skills development activities

Activity 6

1 Refer to Section A and answer the questions.

  a What is a hypothesis?

  b What is a theory?

  c What is the difference between theory, opinion and speculation?

  d What is the difference between a prediction based on evidence and a guess?

Refer to document 1.

2 In document 1, is the response by Richard Muller an argument? If not, what type of reasoning is it?

3 In document 1, is the response by Ken Natco an argument? If not, what type of reasoning is it?

4 To what extent are the two responses in document 1 in disagreement?

5 Whose reasoning in document 1 is more effective? Justify your answer.

Activity 7

Refer to document 2.

1 Is document 2 an argument? If not, what sort of writing is it?

2 Explain briefly why Crawford does not accept that the moon could be an economically useful source of helium-3.

3 Crawford says that the moon might be of economic interest in the longer term. How effectively does he support this?

4 How effectively does Abbud-Madrid show that 'the time has come to demonstrate these systems on the surface of the moon'?

5 To what extent is moon mining really an economic issue?

Research and discuss

1. How have space technologies benefited the world? Have they benefited the whole world or only the rich part of the world?
2. Investigate the space races in the twenty-first century. Are they likely to benefit the countries involved?

Activity 8

Refer to document 3.

1 Is document 3 an argument? If not, what sort of writing is it?
2 How important is it for individuals to make better decisions relating to air pollution?
3 How effective do you think that smart technology can be as a way of responding to pollution?
4 Do you share the author's perspective?

Aa A perspective is a world view which underlies an argument. It can be quite hard to pin down.

Argument, reasoning and opinions are the specifics of what the author says – they are informed by the author's perspective.

Research and discuss

1. What roles can art and fashion play in dealing with difficult issues?
2. Think of a different way to combine art and technology to make people aware of an issue.
3. Is smart technology part of the consumerist problem rather than part of the solution?
4. What are the pollution levels like in your area? Do they change as you move between rich and poor areas? What are the causes and consequences of this? How does your area reflect the global situation?

Activity 9

Refer to document 4.

1 Is document 4 an argument? If not, what sort of writing is it?
2 The author of document 4 says, 'Western scientific explanations are not sufficient to describe the implications of climate change for ASEAN biodiversity, as there are wide gaps in geo-ecological and socio-economic contexts between ASEAN and Western countries'. How effectively does the author substantiate this claim?
3 Outline the causes that the author mentions.
4 What possible courses of action does the author suggest?
5 How effectively does the author use evidence to support the idea that 'the ASEAN Centre for Biodiversity (ACB)… should move beyond merely implementing donor-sponsored projects to become an institution with a clear vision to protect ASEAN's biodiversity"?

Research and discuss

1. Do the points that the author makes apply to your region?
2. Investigate the coffee farmers of Aceh – what happened? Why? What were the consequences?
3. What would you have done if you were one of the coffee farmers in Aceh? What would be the right thing to do?

Activity 10

Refer to document 5.

1 Does document 5 present an argument? If not, what sort of writing is it?

2 How reasonable are the causes and consequences suggested?

3 How effectively does the author use evidence?

4 How well does the author support the claim that 'the world could yet be laid low by an oil monster on the prowl'?

5 What is the oil price now? What effect is it having on the local and global economy?

Activity 11

Refer to document 6.

1 Is document 6 an argument? If not, what sort of writing is it?

2 How effectively does Prime Minister Narendra Modi support the idea that urbanisation is an opportunity not a problem?

3 Do you agree that urbanisation is an opportunity? Find evidence to support each view.

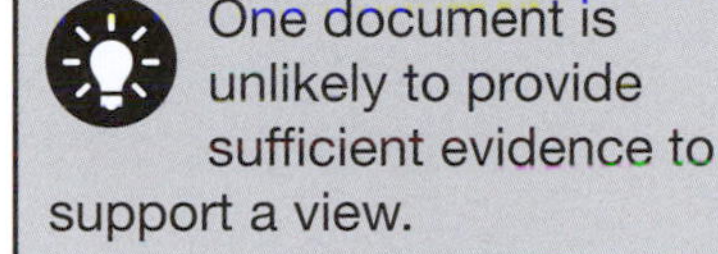

One document is unlikely to provide sufficient evidence to support a view.

Research and discuss

1. Find out about India's smart city projects. Are they effective?
2. What is participative governance? Is it effective? Find evidence to support your view.
3. Living in the city is unnatural and makes people unhappy. People ought to be surrounded by trees.

When you take a flower in your hand and really look at it, it's your world for the moment. I want to give that world to someone else. Most people in the city rush around so, they have no time to look at a flower. I want them to see it whether they want to or not.

Georgia O'Keeffe

Activity 12

Refer to document 7.

1 Is document 7 an argument? If not, what sort of writing is it?

2 How effectively does the author support the claim that, if we are to make progress, we must consider ecology and economics as two sides of the same coin?

3 Do you agree with the author? Why or why not?

Research and discuss

1. Should air and water be free? Or should we assign them an economic value?
2. Overall, what has most interested you in the documents?
3. What would you most like to research further?

Activity 13

1 Which of the following would make good research questions for an assessed essay? Why?
   - **a** To what extent is poverty about unequal access to the world's resources?
   - **b** Urbanisation in India
   - **c** How can we halt the destruction of rainforests?
   - **d** Oil: is it the evil of our times?
   - **e** What are the most successful ways to reduce biodiversity loss without lowering standards of living?

2 Write two or three questions of your own. Work in groups to assess and improve the questions.

When deciding on a research question, think about the following points:

- Globally significant
- Different perspectives
- Argument and discussion
- Question to answer
- Can answer within the word limit
- Suitable evidence base
- On a global perspectives topic

Avoid very theoretical or purely philosophical questions. To meet the assessment criteria you need to build up an evidence base, so remember to apply theoretical concepts in practical contexts.

Remember to be positive and polite about each other's questions. You are helping each other to improve!

Activity 14

1 Which of the following would make suitable questions for the team research project?
   - **a** What lessons can be learned from Sri Lanka's mangrove experiments?
   - **b** How can our school reduce its carbon footprint?
   - **c** Can we design and make a gadget to measure air pollution?
   - **d** Carry out a survey of people who have been moved from slums to high-rise buildings.
   - **e** To what extent can social media motivate communities to take action against local pollution?

2 Write two or three questions of your own. Work in groups to assess and improve the questions.

When deciding on a team research question, think about the following points:

- local problem
- global relevance
- effective solutions possible
- different aspects for individual research
- contrasting perspectives
- argument, reflection and discussion

Activity 10

Refer to document 5.

1 Does document 5 present an argument? If not, what sort of writing is it?

2 How reasonable are the causes and consequences suggested?

3 How effectively does the author use evidence?

4 How well does the author support the claim that 'the world could yet be laid low by an oil monster on the prowl'?

5 What is the oil price now? What effect is it having on the local and global economy?

Activity 11

Refer to document 6.

1 Is document 6 an argument? If not, what sort of writing is it?

2 How effectively does Prime Minister Narendra Modi support the idea that urbanisation is an opportunity not a problem?

3 Do you agree that urbanisation is an opportunity? Find evidence to support each view.

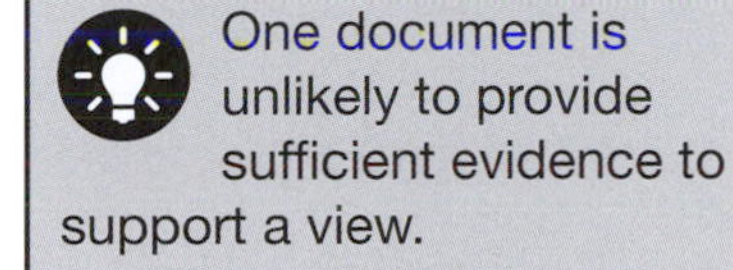

One document is unlikely to provide sufficient evidence to support a view.

Research and discuss

1. Find out about India's smart city projects. Are they effective?
2. What is participative governance? Is it effective? Find evidence to support your view.
3. Living in the city is unnatural and makes people unhappy. People ought to be surrounded by trees.

When you take a flower in your hand and really look at it, it's your world for the moment. I want to give that world to someone else. Most people in the city rush around so, they have no time to look at a flower. I want them to see it whether they want to or not.

Georgia O'Keeffe

Activity 12

Refer to document 7.

1 Is document 7 an argument? If not, what sort of writing is it?

2 How effectively does the author support the claim that, if we are to make progress, we must consider ecology and economics as two sides of the same coin?

3 Do you agree with the author? Why or why not?

Research and discuss

1. Should air and water be free? Or should we assign them an economic value?
2. Overall, what has most interested you in the documents?
3. What would you most like to research further?

Activity 13

1 Which of the following would make good research questions for an assessed essay? Why?

   a To what extent is poverty about unequal access to the world's resources?

   b Urbanisation in India

   c How can we halt the destruction of rainforests?

   d Oil: is it the evil of our times?

   e What are the most successful ways to reduce biodiversity loss without lowering standards of living?

2 Write two or three questions of your own. Work in groups to assess and improve the questions.

When deciding on a research question, think about the following points:

- Globally significant
- Different perspectives
- Argument and discussion
- Question to answer
- Can answer within the word limit
- Suitable evidence base
- On a global perspectives topic

Avoid very theoretical or purely philosophical questions. To meet the assessment criteria you need to build up an evidence base, so remember to apply theoretical concepts in practical contexts.

Remember to be positive and polite about each other's questions. You are helping each other to improve!

Activity 14

1 Which of the following would make suitable questions for the team research project?

   a What lessons can be learned from Sri Lanka's mangrove experiments?

   b How can our school reduce its carbon footprint?

   c Can we design and make a gadget to measure air pollution?

   d Carry out a survey of people who have been moved from slums to high-rise buildings.

   e To what extent can social media motivate communities to take action against local pollution?

2 Write two or three questions of your own. Work in groups to assess and improve the questions.

When deciding on a team research question, think about the following points:

- local problem
- global relevance
- effective solutions possible
- different aspects for individual research
- contrasting perspectives
- argument, reflection and discussion

Practice examination paper

Document 1

The quest for clean gold: why you should seek ethical-gold jewellery

Panna Munyal: 14 April, 2016. Updated: June 23, 2016 03:40 PM

From prosperity and positivity to prestige and power, gold has several grand associations. Culturally, it is considered a good-luck charm, adorning tombs, temples and minarets, and is an enduring symbol of love. Socially, owning, wearing and gifting gold denotes prestige and has aesthetic value, while economies rely on it as a stability benchmark.

It seems as though little can tarnish the yellow metal's shine. Scratch a little under the surface, however, and correlations with trafficking, child labour and other human-rights violations begin to raise their ugly heads. Dig deeper, and be prepared to be hit by some truly horrific statistics: 900 Peruvian farmers poisoned by a mercury spill; 40 000 hectares of the Amazon forest destroyed; indigenous people from Ghana forced from their ancestral forest homeland.

Surely your innocuous wedding band can have no links to these atrocities? Those family heirlooms could not be responsible for a child's compromised future? The cogs that make up your mobile phone, laptop and watch have no part to play in the cycle of mass environmental destruction? Turns out, they might well do. For irresponsible gold mining is one of the most destructive activities on the planet, contributing to both environmental and human degradation.

"The ways in which most gold is mined and processed has sizeable negative consequences," says a representative from Solidaridad, a civil-society organisation that facilitates socially responsible, ecologically sound and profitable supply chains. "Unacceptable working conditions, the threat of toxic poisoning and lack of safety equipment are a part of many miners' daily lives. Irresponsible mining also affects water supply and contributes to deforestation."

It's not all gloom and doom, though. In one sense, gold is lagging behind in the sustainable-luxury endeavour—the United Nations-backed Kimberley Process to prevent conflict diamonds has been in place since 2003, and consumer awareness of ethical diamonds has been on the rise ever since, aided by films such as Blood Diamond. While there is no equivalent framework for gold mining, international bodies such as Solidaridad, the Alliance for Responsible Mining and the Fairtrade Foundation, encourage and support mining organisations that seek to reverse the damage they might cause.

A growing number of conscientious jewellers and luxury brands are also playing their part by sourcing gold from responsible mines. Even the 2015 Noble Peace Prize was fashioned from Fairmined gold. And the results—from the stunning pieces in Chopard's green collections, to the engagement and wedding rings from United States-based Brilliant Earth, online store Amalena, and British jeweller Stephen Webster's Bridal Collection—are all the more precious for it.

According to Teilmann-Ibsen, ethically mined gold has a positive social and economic impact, and is obtained by respecting the environment. It reduces or eliminates the use of toxic chemicals and protects the water supply. Safe working conditions, strict policies against child labour and the protection of women's rights are some of the other parameters.

Certification as ethical, however, does not come without its loopholes and legal tangles. For one, while Fairmined and Fairtrade certification are unequivocally deemed ethical, elsewhere in the industry, many organisations that claim to be ethical, self-regulate their mining and sourcing decisions. As Stephanie Boyd, a Canadian writer, filmmaker and activist who has been working in Peru for the past 16 years, puts it: "Certification is one of the those good ideas in theory, but there are problems in practice. For one, who decides the standards? Do the major gold mining companies—most of whom are responsible for human-rights abuses and environmental destruction—set them? Who checks to make sure companies are following the standards? Certain environmental groups fail to include local stakeholders and activists in the process. A lot of programmes rely on 'self-reporting' from a lot of companies, which seems to be very naive."

Responsible mining means higher operational costs, too, which are then passed on to the jewellers—some absorb it, while others add it to their retail prices. "We currently don't pass onto the consumer the premium we have to pay for Fairtrade gold, but it definitely is something that needs to be taken into consideration," says Webster. "A client is happy to choose Fairtrade gold and support the miners, but the decision can be more difficult if the price jumps by 15 per cent."

And therein lies the end-user dilemma—how many of us would be willing to shell out more for a piece of jewellery because it comes with an ethically mined tag? And why, then, should you as a buyer actively seek out such gold?[8]

8 http://www.thenational.ae/arts-life/luxury/the-quest-for-clean-goldwhy-you-should-seek-ethical-gold-jewellery

Document 2

The Jewellery Industry's Role in Illegal Amazon Destruction

By Shreema Mehta: 29 June, 2015

You may have seen photos of the illegal gold rush in the Amazon rain forest, which is sometimes described as the lungs of the planet for its tremendous biodiversity. The images of gold mining in the region are devastating: swaths of the Amazon rainforest felled (an estimated 64 000 acres, but possibly much more), large beige pools of waste, workers using mercury to separate the bits of gold.

Most news reports have blamed this destruction on small-scale miners desperate for income. But what's fuelling the demand for this gold?

A recently published investigative report by Peruvian investigative news site OjoPúblico paints a disturbingly more complicated picture. Reporters traced some of the dirtiest gold—illegally extracted, mercury processed gold from the Amazon—to large American and European companies—including two certified by the Responsible Jewellery Council, a controversial, industry-exclusive gold and diamonds certification system.

Reporters from OjoPúblico (or "Public Eye") travelled to four South American countries, where they analysed court reports of illegal gold trafficking and gold export statistics. They found that "the major financiers of the gold fever" are a handful of corporations from the US, Switzerland, Italy and the United Arab Emirates.

Remarkably, two of these companies, Metalor Technologies and Italpreziosi are certified members of the Responsible Jewellery Council. OjoPúblico's investigation implicates these companies in purchasing hundreds of tons of illegal gold from exporting firms linked to money laundering, organised crime and cross-border smuggling of metals. Yet the RJC has certified their supply chain as being "responsible."

The Responsible Jewellery Council was formed in 2005 in response to increasing public outcry over conflict minerals and dirty gold. But its industry-centered approach, which excludes civil society and affected communities from decision-making power, has resulted in a weak system riddled with problems.

Several RJC standards are weak and violate widely accepted social and environmental principles, from mercury management to workers' rights to join unions. The Code also fails to place limits on water and air pollution and allows toxic waste disposal into lakes and ocean environments. RJC's weak auditing system, in which it chooses its own auditors who mostly rely on company-provided information, also allows for irresponsibly sourced gold to pass through the system.

In our report on the RJC, More Shine than Substance, we concluded that the certification system its current form cannot perform what it claims to do—assure consumers that the jewellery they purchase is responsible.

This latest piece of news reinforces our conclusion. We hope the RJC takes the allegations made in the OjoPúblico article seriously, and drops Metalor Technologies and Italpreziosi's certifications. While dropping these two companies will not solve all its problems, this is one step the RJC can take to make good on its claims of building a responsible supply chain for jewellery.[9]

Questions

1 **a** (i) Identify one piece of evidence in document 1 which shows the negative human impact of gold mining. [1]

(ii) Identify one piece of evidence in document 2 which shows the negative environmental impact of gold mining. [1]

b Briefly explain one problem with the certification process for ethical gold. [2]

2 How effectively does document 1 support the idea that clean gold represents a dilemma? [12]

3 Which of the two documents provides stronger reasoning in support of its claims? Take the writers' perspectives into consideration. [14]

Extension

Each of these articles come from a particular perspective. Can you find a more solid evidence base for these perspectives?

Research and discuss

What ethical considerations are there in the production of:

a) clothing

b) computers and phones

c) food?

9 https://www.earthworksaction.org/earthblog/detail/the_ jewelry_industrys_role_in_illegal_amazon_ destruction#.V4FXcjX1JnA

Decisions about international fairness

Topics

- Endangered cultures
- Global economic activity
- International law
- Ethical foreign policies
- Medical ethics and priorities

Activities to get you started

During these introductory activities, you will start to explore and reflect on a range of issues, themes and perspectives relating to the overarching idea of 'Changing countries' and the Global Perspectives topics within this main idea. You may find interesting issues and perspectives that you would like to research further, and you may start to reflect on and develop your own perspective.

Activity 1

A

B

The development of International Law is one of the primary goals of the United Nations. The Charter of the United Nations sets the objective 'to establish conditions under which justice and respect for the obligations arising from treaties and other sources of international law can be maintained'.

United Nations

C

"Of course as part of our ethical foreign policy the 20 kiloton population fragmentation bomb is only available to respectable governments."

D

steve@greenberg-art.com
Merrill Lynch
AIG
GLOBAL RECESSION
MEGA-DEFICITS
WALL ST
LAYOFFS
BUNDLED SUBPRIME MORTGAGE SECURITIES
THIS IS ALL YOUR FAULT... YOU BOUGHT A HOUSE YOU COULDN'T REALLY AFFORD!
TOXIC ASSETS
EXECUTIVE BONUSES
BEAR STEARNS
GM
THE POOR
THE PUNDITS
Countrywide Financial
Washington Mutual
LEHMAN BROTHERS
mervyns
circuit city
GREENBERG

E

TARGETS
Policy Revisions
Strategic Reviews
Restructuring
Reorganisations
Blue Sky Thinking
Reprioritisation
Focus Groups
PATIENT CARE ✓
GP

F

1 What different issues and perspectives do these images raise on the topics in this chapter?

2 Does the whole class agree? Why or why not?

"It's our new method for determining who we should treat first. We take people in order of how loud they scream."

What are the most significant global issues relating to medical ethics and priorities?

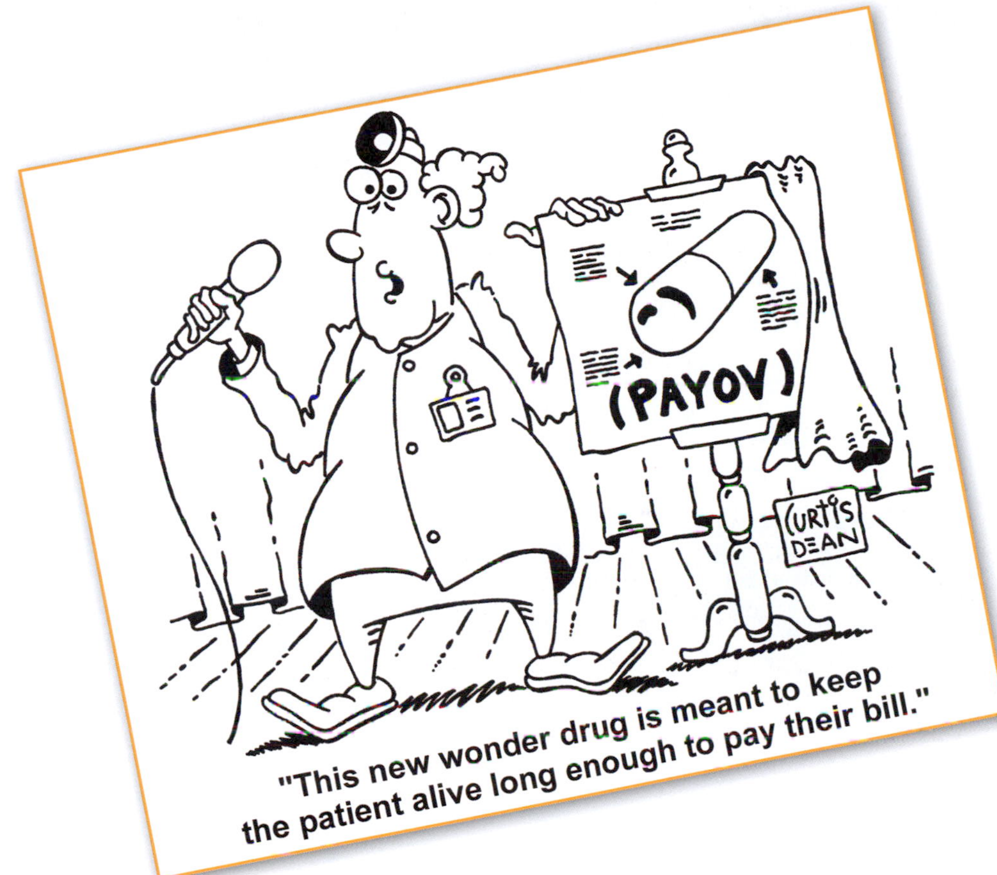
(PAYOV)
CURTIS DEAN
"This new wonder drug is meant to keep the patient alive long enough to pay their bill."

© John McPherson/Distributed by Universal Uclick via CartoonStock.com
BIG TONY'S PIZZA AND AMBULANCE SERVICE
BIG TONY'S PIZZA
McPHERSON
9-11
"You shoulda checked the fine print in your HMO policy. First I have to deliver two pies over in Elmira, then I'll get you to Mercy Medical."

MATT DAVIES
WWW.DAVIES.LOHUDBLOGS.COM
©2008 THE JOURNAL NEWS
3/14
SUB-SAHARAN AFRICA
NO WATER
NO MEDICINE
EVER FEEL MOCKED??
U.S. CRISIS: PHARMACEUTICALS IN WATER SUPPLY

WOULD YOU HAVE ANYTHING FOR A HEAD-ACHE?

1 Look at the cartoons.
   a What issues do these raise, relating to medical ethics and priorities?
   b What different perspectives do they illustrate?
2 Choose and explain five cartoons and images to illustrate the most significant issues and perspectives on one of the other topics in this chapter.
3 Compare the different images and cartoons class members have chosen. Do you all agree on the most significant issues? Have you found material illustrating different perspectives?

Activity 3

1 Work in groups to consider the following situations.
   a A patient is sick and there is no hope of recovery. Should treatment be given to keep this patient alive for any reason?
   b The patient is your mother/grandfather/sister/partner/child. Does this change your view? Give your reasons.
   c You are the manager of an underfunded hospital. You are frustrated because you do not have the resources to care effectively for your patients. A rich patient has offered to donate $20 million to the hospital, on condition that they get the next suitable heart available for transplant. What do you do?
   d You are the chief of police in your country. Organised criminals from other countries are selling drugs in your country and trafficking humans. You suspect that important people in the government are working with the criminals but you do not have proof. You are afraid of what these people might do if you reveal your suspicions. What should you do?
   e You are fairly sure that the leaders of a group of international terrorists are hiding in a small village in the mountains. If you bomb the village there is a good chance that you will kill the terrorist leaders – but you will also probably kill and injure many innocent civilians, including children at a nearby school. What should you do?
   f You are a high-ranking police officer in the capital city of your country. You have reason to believe that there will be a terrorist attack in the city today, and you have a suspect in custody. You believe that she can give you information that would help you prevent the attack, but she will not talk. Your boss wants you to torture her to get the information. What should you do?
2 For each situation, think about the different issues and perspectives involved. Think about how you decide what is right and what is wrong.

While it is commonly believed that trafficking only takes places for commercial sexual exploitation or for forced labour, trafficking in fact takes many forms such as trafficking for forced marriage and trafficking for organ trade among others.

United Nations

For those of you who think it cannot happen to you, I want to let you know that the dragnet of the traffickers is so wide that only God knows who is safe.

Titi Atiku Abubakar, wife of Nigeria's Vice-President

No one shall be subjected to torture or to cruel, inhuman or degrading treatment or punishment.

United Nations Declaration of Human Rights

Do unto others as you would have them do unto you.

(Common sense saying)

Act in such a way that you treat humanity, whether in your own person or in the person of any other, never merely as a means to an end, but always at the same time as an end. Every rational action must set before itself not only a principle, but also an end.

Immanuel Kant

The end may justify the means as long as there is something that justifies the end.

Leon Trotsky

I do not care about the greatest good for the greatest number… Most people are poop-heads. I do not care about them at all.

James Alan Gardner

Activity 4

1 Complete the questionnaire.

2 Discuss the results in class. Do you all agree? Why or why not?

1 = I disagree strongly 2 = I disagree a bit 3 = I'm not sure

4 = I agree a bit 5 = I agree strongly

	1	2	3	4	5
All issues of right and wrong in international affairs are matters of differing perspective and opinion.					
The right thing to do in foreign policy is whatever has the best results for our country.					
Sometimes we need to sacrifice our own best interests in order to do the right thing.					
Governments should do whatever the majority of the people want, whatever that is.					
Politicians are more responsible for global economic recessions than bankers are.					
International law cannot be enforced, so it is pointless.					
International law is another way for the West to impose its cultural values on others.					
We should accept a reduction in standard of living in order to create a more local, sustainable economy.					
While young people do not care about traditions, cultures will continue to die.					
More money should be spent on curing diseases common in poor countries.					

Activity 5

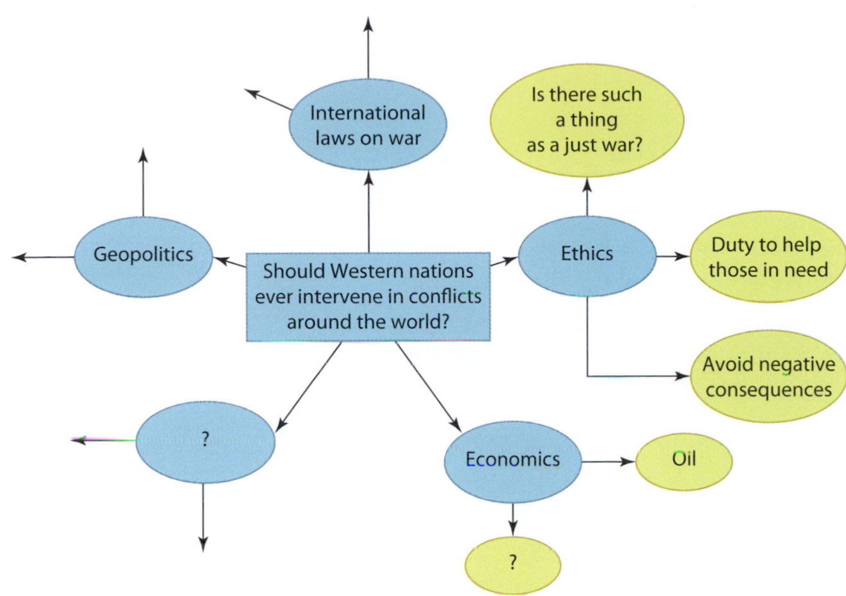

1 Complete and expand the mind map about whether Western nations should even intervene in conflicts around the world. Use the themes to help you explore different perspectives.

2 Draw a mind map using the themes to help you explore different perspectives on one of these questions.

   a Should big pharmaceutical companies always offer life-saving drugs at low prices?

   b Would we be better off in a less globalised world?

   c Should every nation adopt human rights as set down in the Universal Declaration of Human Rights?

   d What consequences do your shopping choices have around the world?

National identity is frequently formed in deliberate opposition to other groups and therefore serves to perpetuate conflict.

Francis Fukuyama

Research and discuss

Should an ethical foreign policy move away from considerations of national benefit and national identity?

Research and discuss

Can international laws ever be enforced?

Can 'humanitarian' interventions in other countries ever be ethical?

Stimulus material

Skills development activities

Document 1

It's Aotearoa, that's why Te Reo

Heather du Plessis-Allan

You have to hand it to us Kiwis when it comes to doing a job half-pai. We are masters at the Claytons compromise. We got halfway through building Parliament, then stopped. In the spot where the other half should have gone, we plonked something shaped like a sandcastle, wiped our hands on our overalls and announced it'd do just fine.

They needed a harbour bridge for Auckland, but goodness knows where the ideas people thought we'd get the money for all those lanes, so we chopped a couple off the design. Pedestrians and cyclists just have to go the long way around.

And when they said we needed to do something to save the Maori language, we had just the right plan for that. Give it a week, say "kia ora" a few times, then forget about it for the rest of the year. Tokenism. That's all Maori Language Week is. It assuages our guilt for not bothering to learn the native tongue of this country but does nothing to prevent its demise.

We have been marking the week since 1975, yet the number of Maori speakers still keeps falling. Hands up who booked a spot in a Reo course because the TV weather used Maori place names this week? My guess is no one. Maori Language Week needs to go to whatever scrap heap we send our half-pai ideas to. It's time to do this job properly and make Te Reo compulsory in schools.

Herewith a shortlist of likely objections to that suggestion, with rebuttal.

No one wants to learn it.

Not true. I recently tried to enrol for a university course and all five weekly lectures are full. There's a waiting list of 20–30. I'm told this happens every semester.

Te Reo is pointless.

It's not a language you'd learn to conduct international business but never underestimate the power of a language in building a strong national identity. Every time someone remarks on the similarities between Kiwis and the colonising Brits, here's your point of difference. And do I need to mention the fun we could have gossiping in Reo in front of foreigners?

Making it compulsory in schools would be expensive.

It doesn't have to be expensive. Every school would need at least one Maori-speaking teacher. Bigger schools would need more. But those teachers would teach other subjects, too, so schools would simply replace the retiring maths teacher with one who speaks Maori. If you give the education system 10 years' warning, teachers' colleges would have time to enrol and train maths, science and English teachers who can also teach Te Reo.

It won't save the Maori language.

Tell that to the Welsh.

What issues are raised in this document?

To what extent are the issues in this document global?

If you talk to a man in a language he understands, that goes to his head. If you talk to him in his language, that goes to his heart.

Nelson Mandela

? How would you describe the perspective this article comes from? What are the beliefs and assumptions underlying the perspective?

Eighty years ago, nearly 37 per cent spoke Welsh. By 1991, fewer than 19 per cent understood the language. So in the 1990s they made it compulsory learning for kids under 14 and the number of Welsh speakers in the country hasn't really dropped below 19 per cent since, which is pretty remarkable when you consider all the older Welsh speakers who have died since 1991.

I can't be bothered.

You don't have to. Your kids do. It's the ultimate punishment for the sins of the forefathers.

Maori Language Week may be one of our worst compromises yet. We settled for a single-lane swing bridge, or a lean-to hanging off the side of Parliament.

Everything is not ka pai.[1]

Welsh is my mother tongue, and my children speak it. If you come and live in this community you'll work out pretty quickly that it's beneficial to learn the language, because if you're going to the pub or a cafe you need to be a part of the local life.

Bryn Terfel

Anyone that doesn't know foreign languages knows nothing of his own.

Johann Wolfgang von Goethe

You ask me what I mean
by saying I have lost my tongue.
I ask you, what would you do
if you had two tongues in your mouth,
and lost the first one, the mother tongue,
and could not really know the other,
the foreign tongue.

Sujata Bhatt

1 http://www.nzherald.co.nz/opinion/news/article.cfm?c_id=466&objectid=11671674

Document 2

Young, gifted and held back

The world's young are an oppressed minority. Unleash them.

IN THE world of "The Hunger Games" youngsters are forced to fight to the death for the amusement of their white-haired rulers. Today's teen fiction is relentlessly dystopian, but the gap between fantasy and reality is often narrower than you might think. The older generation may not resort to outright murder but, as our special report this week on millennials describes, in important ways they hold their juniors down.

Roughly a quarter of the world's people—some 1.8 billion—have turned 15 but not yet reached 30. In many ways, they are the luckiest group of young adults ever to have existed. They are richer than any previous generation, and live in a world without smallpox or Mao Zedong. They are the best-educated generation ever—Haitians today spend longer in school than Italians did in 1960. Thanks to all that extra learning and to better nutrition, they are also more intelligent than their elders. If they are female or gay, they enjoy greater freedom in more countries than their predecessors would have thought possible. And they can look forward to improvements in technology that will, say, enable many of them to live well past 100. So what, exactly, are they complaining about?

Plenty. Just as, for the first time in history, the world's youngsters form a common culture, so they also share the same youthful grievances. Around the world, young people gripe that it is too hard to find a job and a place to live, and that the path to adulthood has grown longer and more complicated.

Many of their woes can be blamed on policies favouring the old over the young. Consider employment. In many countries, labour laws require firms to offer copious benefits and make it hard to lay workers off. That suits those with jobs, who tend to be older, but it makes firms reluctant to hire new staff. The losers are the young. In most regions they are at least twice as likely as their elders to be unemployed. The early years of any career are the worst time to be idle, because these are when the work habits of a lifetime become ingrained. Those unemployed in their 20s typically still feel the "scarring" effects of lower income, as well as unhappiness, in their 50s.

Housing, too, is often rigged against the young. Homeowners dominate the bodies that decide whether new houses may be built. They often say no, so as not to spoil the view and reduce the value of their own property. Over-regulation has doubled the cost of a typical home in Britain. Its effects are even worse in many of the big cities around the world where young people most want to live. Rents and home prices in such places have far outpaced incomes. The youngsters of Kuala Lumpur are known as the "homeless generation". Young American women are more likely to live with their parents or other relatives than at any time since the second world war.

Young people are often footloose. With the whole world to explore and nothing to tie them down, they move around more often than their

? What issues are raised in this document?

? To what extent are the issues in this document global?

What relationships can fiction have to reality? Can fiction help us to deal with reality or to make reality better?

? How would you describe the perspective this article comes from? What are the beliefs and assumptions underlying the perspective?

elders. This makes them more productive, especially if they migrate from a poor country to a rich one. By one estimate, global GDP would double if people could move about freely. That is politically impossible—indeed, the mood in rich countries is turning against immigration. But it is striking that so many governments discourage not only cross-border migration but also the domestic sort. China's *hukou* system treats rural folk who move to cities as second-class citizens. India makes it hard for those who move from one state to another to obtain public services. A UN study found that 80 per cent of countries had policies to reduce rural-urban migration, although much of human progress has come from people putting down their hoes and finding better jobs in the big smoke. All these barriers to free movement especially harm the young, because they most want to move.

The old have always subsidised their juniors. Within families, they still do. But many governments favour the old: an ever greater share of public spending goes on pensions and health care for them. This is partly the natural result of societies ageing, but it is also because the elderly ensure that policies work in their favour. By one calculation, the net flow of resources (public plus private) is now from young to old in at least five countries, including Germany and Hungary. This is unprecedented and unjust—the old are much richer.

The young could do more to stand up for themselves. In America just over a fifth of 18- to 34-year-olds turned out to vote in the latest general election; three-fifths of over 65s did. It is the same in Indonesia and only slightly better in Japan. It is not enough for the young to sign online petitions. If they want governments to listen, they should vote.

However, the old have a part to play, too. The young are an oppressed minority—albeit an unusual one—in the straightforward sense that governments are systematically preventing them from reaching their potential.

That is a cruel waste of talent. Today's under-30s will one day dominate the labour force. If their skills are not developed, they will be less productive than they could be. Countries such as India that are counting on a demographic dividend from their large populations of young adults will find that it fails to materialise. Rich, ageing societies will find that, unless the youth of today can get a foot on the career ladder, tomorrow's pensioners will struggle. What is more, oppressing youngsters is dangerous. Countries with lots of jobless, disaffected young men tend to be more violent and unstable, as millions of refugees from the Middle East and Africa can attest.

They're quite aware of what they're going through.

The remedy is easy to prescribe—and hard to enact. Governments should unleash the young by cutting the red tape that keeps them out of jobs, and curbing the power of property-owners to stop homes from being built. They should scrap restrictions on domestic migration and allow more cross-border movement. They should make education a priority.

It is a lot to expect from political leaders who often seem unequal to the task of even modest reform. But every parent and grandparent has a stake in this, too. If they put their shoulders to the wheel, who knows what they might accomplish.[2]

Document 3

It's a mad, mad world

From Britain, to the US to Australia, voters are punishing politicians. Why the anger and what does it mean for markets?

Why the anger and what does it mean for markets?

Even after the shock result, financial markets could have shrugged off the Brexit vote, says Greg Peacock, chief investment officer for investment fund NZAM.

But despite what the stock exchange numbers might suggest, they haven't. Instead, there is growing unease about what happens next as a new wave of political volatility spreads across the Western world.

"So the financial market impact lasted two days," says Peacock. "If you look at it on a standalone basis, the UK is 4 or 5 per cent of global GDP; if it slows down or even goes into recession there is a bit of 'so what' about that."

But the significance of Brexit and the fears it is creating "are really what it implies about future events". The UK is in turmoil, Australia is in turmoil. Who is next? Donald Trump and the US elections are looming large. Then there is Italy, where Prime Minister Matteo Renzi has offered angry voters the chance to chuck him out with a referendum on political reform in October. And what about New Zealand—could we follow the trend?

"What we are seeing is a push back against, some would say, the whole post-World War II movement—globalisation and free trade," Peacock says.

"The global financial system just feels extended here. You've got negative bond yields. High multiples on equities. It's become kind of self-fulfilling

1. What issues are raised in this document?
2. To what extent are the issues in this document global?
3. How would you describe the perspective this article comes from? What are the beliefs and assumptions underlying the perspective?

2 http://www.economist.com/news/leaders/21688856-worlds-young-areoppressed-minority-unleash-them-young-gifted-and-held-back

in the sense that whenever there is a crisis the reaction is to cut rates and pump QE."

The beneficiaries of those polices have been people with assets.

"Bonds, equities and property. They've done better than anyone could possibly have imagined but there is a very large proportion of people in those economies who simply feel like they have been passed by," says Peacock.

Mark Lister, head of research at Craigs Investment Partners, says "the Brexit was a wake-up call for politicians and investors and I think we'll see plenty more of it.

"It's simply a reflection of the fact so many people feel like they are missing out on their share of the boom."

We're used to hearing this kind of thing from left-wing commentators and politicians. But neither Peacock nor Lister has a political axe to grind. Their analysis is matter-of-fact and born of concerns for investors.

"The low interest rate thing hasn't really fired up economies or seen any wage growth come through," Lister says. "All we've done is make house prices and share prices go up. The wealthy end of town feel wealthier, the bottom end and the middle end haven't really benefited at all and people are just getting sick of it and are feeling very disenfranchised."

Auckland University professor of macroeconomics Prasanna Gai has worked for the Bank of England, Bank of Canada and advised our Reserve Bank. Nearly 10 years on from the global financial crisis we are still suffering the fallout, he says. And there are echoes of the 1930s.

We have allowed central banks to "shoulder all the burden" and politicians' failure to confront the big structural issues may be coming back to bite them.

"You've got a confluence of three factors," he says. "Firstly, productivity growth everywhere is unusually low. That's a consequence of a misallocation of resources in the boom which preceded the global financial crisis."

Then there is debt.

"Global debt levels are at historically high levels... because debt has served as a substitute for income growth pretty much everywhere." Then you have the central banks with very little room left to move and "a substantial rise in economic uncertainty as well as policy uncertainty".

[Brexit] is simply a reflection of the fact so many people feel like they are missing out on their share of the boom.

Mark Lister, Craigs Investment Partners

What we are seeing is "protectionist discontent", he says.

In other words, people are looking for political leaders who promise to put their local interests first even if that might not be in their greater long-term interests.

"It is no accident," Gai says. "If you think back to history and the Great Depression, financial crises and protectionism go hand and hand. All these events, whether it's Brexit or Australia or the US, kind of have a very similar theme.

"The central banks prevented a catastrophe [after the GFC] and everyone banked on an eventual recovery. But politicians have underestimated the consequences and the duration of a financial cycle gone wrong… and they have not self-corrected along the way.

"There is a strong case for other policy measures to take a leading role. So structural policy, fiscal policy—for example, tax reforms that get the bias away from the accumulation of debt—incentives that spur productivity and dynamism. Structural reforms that target these issues will help."[3]

There is a need for financial reform along ethical lines that would produce in its turn an economic reform to benefit everyone. This would nevertheless require a courageous change of attitude on the part of political leaders.

Pope Francis

It is the highest impertinence and presumption… in kings and ministers, to pretend to watch over the economy of private people, and to restrain their expense... They are themselves always, and without any exception, the greatest spendthrifts in the society. Let them look well after their own expense, and they may safely trust private people with theirs. If their own extravagance does not ruin the state, that of their subjects never will.

Adam Smith

Document 4

Is Bitcoin Ready for the Next Global Financial Crisis?

Bitcoin guru Andreas Antonopoulos shared his thoughts in a Q&A session with the audience at the recent D10E event in San Francisco on what would happen to Bitcoin in the event of another global financial crisis.

The question of what will happen to Bitcoin in the event of a "black swan" event, such as the collapse of Deutsche Bank, was asked by none other than Bitcoin investor, Michael Terpin.

"First of all, I don't think that's a black swan moment," replied Antonopoulos. "We've seen it before. We know what it looks like. We know it's coming. It's probably going to come from somewhere we don't expect like the third largest Italian bank you've never heard of."

The author of *Mastering Bitcoin* may be on to something. Bitcoin.com reported that some of Italy's major banks have recently failed stress tests. In other words, the country's banking sector would be unable to weather a crisis and have its own "Lehman moment".

However, Antonopoulos hopes that this won't happen anytime soon because Bitcoin is still in its infancy and won't be able to serve as an "exit valve" if the entire global financial system implodes. Moreover, he is also "perplexed" by some in the Bitcoin community who wish for a global collapse to happen, whereas the possibility of such an event is already high. He noted:

I hope that doesn't happen. Unfortunately the system is very fragile so there's a good chance it might happen.

1. What issues are raised in this document?
2. To what extent are the issues in this document global?
3. How would you describe the perspective this article comes from? What are the beliefs and assumptions underlying the perspective?

3 http://www.nzherald.co.nz/opinion/news/article.cfm?c_id=466&objectid=11670425

"I've lived in a country that's had a currency crisis, twice. I visited many countries that have currency crises. It is ugly. A lot of good people get hurt. Generations lose their futures overnight and do not recover in thirty years. So we should not be wishing for that," Antonopoulos added.

Bitcoin 'Not Ready' for Global Economic Crisis

When—and not if—a global currency crisis does occur, however, many Bitcoin users believe that the decentralised, border-less, peer-to-peer, and open-access digital currency can serve as a life raft in an ocean of financial calamity.

This is not too surprising, though, considering that Bitcoin is the first (better) alternative to the existing monetary system outside of precious metals and plain old barter. Moreover, Bitcoin creator Satoshi Nakamo even embedded a *Financial Times* headline into the first transaction of a block, called a coinbase transaction. It read, "The Times 03 January 2009 Chancellor on brink of second bailout for banks." Many have interpreted this as Nakamoto being frustrated with the failure of the traditional financial system.

Furthermore, recent global financial system "stresses" such as Brexit, Bank of Japan's helicopter money plans, and China's bubble economy are also often accompanied by Bitcoin price upticks. But Antonopoulos doesn't see this as a positive sign in an event of a full-scale collapse of the global monetary system.

"If we do have a global economic crisis at this point," Antonopoulos said, "Bitcoin is not ready to absorb anything, let's be realistic."

"There is no exit valve," he continued. "Even if everybody in Bitcoin actually gains an advantage from having some diversification—that's not going to make much of a difference to anybody else. All of the investment in Bitcoin, not just in companies but also individuals and entrepreneurs, and startups dries up instantly over night and we're all set back across the board by a decade."

Antonopoulos concluded:

I certainly don't want people to think just because Bitcoin can act as a safe haven investment, just because it can act as an exit valve, just because we see things like Brexit or the Yuan devaluation happen, Bitcoin spikes up. There's a big leap between that and saying 'I hope the world burns so I can make money on my bitcoin.'

Do you agree with Andreas or do you think a global financial crisis would help Bitcoin? Share your thoughts in the comments below![4]

4 https://news.bitcoin.com/bitcoin-ready-global-financial-crisis/

Why we are losing the war on bugs

Fake, or substandard medicine—some peddled by criminal gangs—is a big but hidden cause of antibiotic resistance

Elizabeth Pisani

Published in February 2016 issue of *Prospect Magazine*

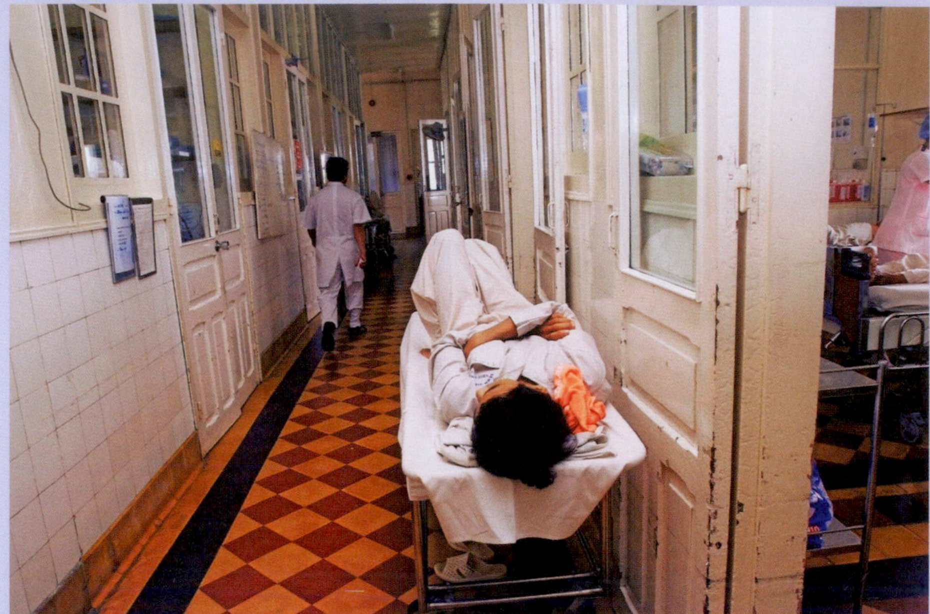

Adult Intensive care ward at the Hospital for Tropical Diseases, Ho Chi Minh City

In the infectious disease wards of Ho Chi Minh City's main hospital for tropical illnesses, patients are arranged behind plate-glass windows like mannequins in a department store. Those that are conscious stare blankly through the glass that separates them and their frightening pathogens—cryptococcal meningitis, perhaps, or septicaemia—from the efficient hum of nurses and orderlies on the ward. A runner comes in and hands a doctor a sheaf of papers, the latest batch of results from the microbiology lab.

For the glassed-in patients—the hospital's most serious cases—these reports are rarely encouraging. The pathogens that have colonised their blood, lungs, or tissues have evolved their way around every drug that could have been used to combat them. And researchers working on the frontline of resistance blame the mutant bugs, in part, on fake and second-rate medicines.

This may be happening far away, but it is the west's problem too. In these days of global tourism, travel and migration, drug-resistant bacteria are highly mobile. "Humans think a lot of themselves," said Paul Newton, professor of tropical medicine at Oxford University, who works out of a microbiology lab in Vientiane, the capital of Laos. "But in fact we're really just exoskeletons for bacteria. They take cheap flights as often as we do."

No-longer curable variants of bugs bred in Ho Chi Minh City may be coming to a hospital near you. In 2008, an especially nasty genetic mutation that made several bacteria resistant to multiple classes of antibiotic was identified in a Swedish patient returning from India (hence its name, New Delhi metallo-beta-lactamase 1, or NDM-1). It was found

1. What issues are raised in this document?
2. To what extent are the issues in this document global?
3. How would you describe the perspective this article comes from? What are the beliefs and assumptions underlying the perspective?

in Britain that same year, and by 2013, in over 70 other countries. And it is not the only such infection to come to Europe. Multi-drug resistant staphylococcus, third-generation cephalosporin-resistant E.coli and K.pneumoniae have also travelled the world. At the last count, these infections and other resistant ones were already killing 25 000 Europeans a year—without measuring newer imports, such as NDM-1.

In recent years, there has been much wailing and gnashing of teeth about the advent of superbugs that have outwitted the drugs made to treat them. The UK added the threat of antimicrobial resistance to the National Risk Register for the first time in March 2015, worrying that "without effective antibiotics, even minor surgery and routine operations could become high-risk procedures." If bacteria with mutations such as NDM-1 were rife, doctors would hesitate to recommend hip replacements or even chemotherapy: the risk of becoming infected with untreatable bacteria would be too high. In December 2014, a government-commissioned review on antimicrobial resistance warned that drug-resistant pathogens could slice 3.5 per cent off the world's output by 2050, as well as putting 10m people into early graves every year.

How worrying are antibiotic resistance diseases in your country now?

Many reasons are given for this looming threat. Bugs evolve faster than drugs do. Unfortunately, there is little money in developing these drugs. Antibiotics drive their own obsolescence—the more that are sold, the more bacteria resist them. Their revenue potential is limited, as they should be prescribed sparingly, are only taken for a few days, and governments limit their price. And when doctors overprescribe antibiotics or patients take them without prescription antimicrobial resistance is boosted, especially if patients stop taking the pills the moment they feel better.

Should governments subsidise the development of new antibiotics?

Another contributing factor is environment—in Southeast Asia, humans and animals are crowded together at close quarters in a climate that favours the growth of pathogens. But in the microbiology lab in that Ho Chi Minh City hospital, they have an additional explanation for what they are finding in their lab.

There, tiny bottles of red liquid—blood mixed with a culture medium—are upended in an incubator that looks for all the world like a wine fridge in a doll's house. The contents of some bottles are bubbling gently, indicating something is living in the blood—namely, an infection. Bacteria isolated from fizzy blood will be smeared over agar in a Petri dish and dotted with white discs, each marked with a three-letter antibiotic code. This test seeks to identify whether that particular bacterium is susceptible to each of the drugs. If yes, a clear halo will form in the red agar around the drug disc. More and more, the lab techs are reporting no halos, even for relatively newfangled antibiotics.

"It's those Indian drugs," says Dr Nguyen Phu Huong, a microbiologist, shaking her head with its 1930s bob in disapproval. "They are not strong enough for the bacteria."

"Indian drugs" is local shorthand for cheap, generic drugs not only from India but countries like China and Brazil. In the last decade or so, since these nations cranked up their pharmaceutical industries, their drugs have flooded market stalls across much of Asia and Africa. They are sold in tubs, blister packs, or mixed together in multicoloured cocktails and held in unlabelled plastic bags. Some are branded, others aren't. Some have sell-by dates and instruction leaflets, others don't. Even the ones stamped "BY PRESCRIPTION ONLY" can almost always be bought without a prescription. Many of these are good quality medicines which work just fine. But some are not. And the poor quality medicines are now eating into the effectiveness of medicines that once worked perfectly well.

"If you take the correct dose of a drug and kill the susceptible pathogens quickly, the mutants never reach critical mass and die out too"

Here's why: as they reproduce, pathogens mutate. Some of those mutations will make them more resistant to medicines. But the mutant pathogens usually don't reproduce as fast as the susceptible ones. If you take the correct dose of a drug and kill the susceptible pathogens quickly, the mutants never reach critical mass and die out too. But if you take only a partial, "sub-therapeutic" dose, enough susceptible bugs will survive to prolong the infection. The mutants now have less competition from susceptible strains, and more time to reproduce, build up numbers and get passed on to someone else.

Patients can expose bugs to sub-therapeutic doses by not taking the full course of a medicine. But they can also do it more unwittingly, by taking poor quality medicines. That includes medicines that have lost their potency over time—perhaps because they have been stuck in a very hot shipping container for months, then left in the sunshine of a market stall or the dank corner of a bathroom. It includes medicines that are badly formulated and don't dissolve correctly, restricting the amount of active ingredient that reaches the bloodstream. Finally, it includes medicines that never contained enough of their active ingredient, the result of sloppy manufacturing, or, more troublingly, outright fraud.

Welcome to the quagmire, where the global health community fears to tread. Here, out-and-out criminals overlap with pharmaceutical firms that cut corners while regulators turn a blind eye. Rabid non-governmental organisations (NGOs) see a Big Pharma (the name given to the pharmaceutical industry) conspiracy behind every attempt to assure quality, and western governments, facing mounting health bills, are terrified of undermining the credibility of generic medicines.

Trying valiantly to chart this quagmire is a small band of scientists who have coalesced around Paul Newton, the Oxford professor in Laos. He and his colleagues first became mired in the swamp of bad medicines a decade ago, pushed into it by the prospect of a global resurgence in malaria.

In the mid-2000s, a researcher named George Watt, working on the Thai-Cambodian border, noticed that malaria patients treated with an artemisinin-based medicine were taking twice as long as expected to clear the parasite from their bloodstreams. One possible explanation was that the disease was developing resistance to the cure. This was massively worrying because artemisinin, an antimalarial compound which Chinese scientists isolated from the sweet wormwood plant in the 1970s, was the only drug left that worked against malaria worldwide.

It was also massively plausible, because the Thai-Cambodian border is the historical epicentre of drug-resistant malaria. The first cases of resistance to the cheap and widely-used drug chloroquine were identified in this region in the 1960s (some believe because small doses of it had been introduced to the salt supply as a preventative). Resistance to sulfadoxine-pyrimethamine sprang up here, then mefloquine; no one has a good explanation why. So when Watt reported his findings to a meeting held by the World Health Organisation (WHO) in Phnom Penh in 2007, alarm bells clanged, and scientists went into overdrive trying to find out whether artemisinin was losing its power or not.

"Quite a few 'antimalarials' have no active ingredients at all, but manu-facturers have also filled pills with cheap anti-malarials less effective than those on the label"

But Newton asked a different question. Was it possible that patients weren't responding to artemisinin because they weren't actually taking it? Colleagues working in Cameroon thought that what looked like chloroquine resistant malaria may have been the result of fake drugs. Long before Watts reported his findings, Newton had begun to investigate implausibly cheap tablets of artesunate (an artemisinin derivative) for sale in Cambodia. Though he had access to the overcrowded markets and sweltering hole-in-the-wall shops where many Asians buy their medicines, he didn't have the sophisticated equipment needed to test the pills.

Newton's lab is based in an elegant, crumbling hospital on the banks of the Mekong. His office totters with papers that seem to have been accumulating since the lab was built in 1920—here a pile of medical journals grown crispy with age, there a Japanese monograph about scrub typhus from the 1950s. A man of shy good humour, he could have walked out of the pages of a Graham Greene novel. His timekeeping is erratic and he shuffles around the lab in mismatched knock-off Crocs, grunting encouragingly at the staff and trying to appear undemanding.

For all his diffidence, Newton can be magnetic. With a tiny budget and a lot of charm, he pulled together a multinational team of chemists, police officers, drug regulators and forensic analysts who had the equipment and skills to check what kind of pills the people sweating with malaria fevers were taking.

What they found were a lot of fakes.

Collecting samples from across Southeast Asia, his team started by looking at packaging, comparing a genuine example of a drug with the ones they had bought. In one case, packs marked "12 Tabs" were fake—the real version (12 Tabs.) ended in a full stop. They found misspelled brand names, and expiry dates that preceded manufacturing dates. Using microscopes, they spotted packs printed by silkscreen rather than the offset printing used by pharmaceutical companies. They found holograms which worked when tilted top-to-bottom instead of right-to-left.

Next, Facundo Fernandez, a professor of biotechnology at Georgia Institute of Technology in the United States, analysed the content of pills by zapping them with electrons and looking at the computer-generated

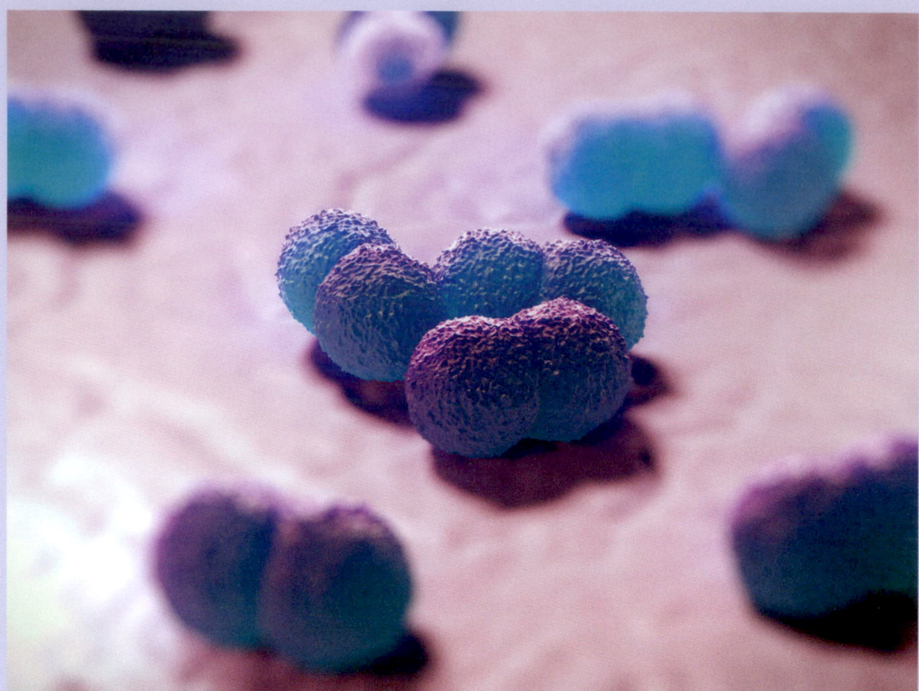
"Humans are just exoskeletons for bacteria": Neisseria meningitidis bacteria (blue), the cause of meningococcal meningitis.

patterns that emerged, a technique known as mass spectrometry. Different molecules show up as different peaks on the output graphs, so it is fairly easy to see what the active ingredients of a substance are. Yet one of the earlier samples Fernandez looked at had a shape that no one in the lab could identify at first: it wasn't the artemisinin derivative they expected, and it didn't look like quinine, Tylenol or anything else that they were used to finding in falsified drugs either. "After about two weeks, a PhD student came back and said: I think it's Viagra." Fernandez laughed ruefully. "We'd never looked at lifestyle drugs before. That was years ago, before we were sensitised to this kind of thing." Now, virtually nothing surprises the team.

The drugs also contained pollen—which proved vital to tracing their source. Palynology, the study of pollen, is a pretty abstruse speciality but Dallas Mildenhall, a New Zealand-based scientist now in his 70s, has used it to solve crimes from art theft to murder. His analysis identified the trees involved. Walnut, wing nut and hickory trees sweep down from northern China to the Myanmar border. Wormwood, elms, wattles and firs are common further south, but creep up into China in areas north of Vietnam and Myanmar. When Mildenhall found pollen from both of these groups, he determined that they were most likely made in the zone of overlap, in southern China.

Most commonly, the fake pills do contain the expected drugs, though often not in the correct doses. Quite a few "antimalarials" have no active ingredient at all, but manufacturers have also filled pills with cheap anti-malarials less effective than those on the label, or drugs that reduce fever. "I think they use those deliberately to bring down fever so the patient doesn't suspect," said Fernandez. Newton was unconvinced. "My feeling is they've got a bunch of leftover powder that need using up. You use what you've got lying around, and bugger the consequences."

There seems to be a lot of white powder lying around. Fernandez has found anti-malarials containing banned carcinogens, for example. Also levamisole, which is often cut together with cocaine and has been linked to necrosis syndrome and the rotting of flesh in the earlobes and cheeks. And safrole, a precursor to the party drug ecstasy. "If the untreated malaria doesn't kill you, the other ingredients in these fake pills might well," said Newton.

For Aline Plançon, head of Interpol's pharmaceutical crime division, that is one of the signs that old school drug cartels are in the game. "We have a lot of evidence now that some of the well-established criminal organisations who specialise in narcotics are getting into fake medicines." This business, she notes, offers massive profits with a low risk of ending up behind bars. "They don't pay tax, they don't pay for manufacturing standards or quality control, and often they don't even pay for an active ingredient, so it's not that hard to make a lot of money," said Plançon.

Working together, this collective of self-appointed "drug detectives" assembled the evidence. Then Ronald Noble, the secretary general of Interpol, took the scientists' dossier to the head of China's Public Security Bureau. Artemisinin was a Chinese discovery and a major contribution to the world's health. Now, Noble reported, it was being undermined by Chinese counterfeiters. And they were targeting Chinese brands, which could damage business for genuine manufacturers such as Guilin Pharma, a company which has had two of its antimalarial drugs pre-qualified by the WHO (this means they have met standards of quality, safety and efficacy). The company also had the largest production capacity for artemisinin-derived antimalarials in the world. That was in 2006; the Chinese authorities, still smarting from the SARS crisis, immediately launched a criminal investigation. They identified a network of pharmaceutical crime and jailed several people.

This response was gratifying to the scientists, demonstrating that authorities were willing to respond to pharmaceutical crime, at least when it involved cut-and-dried "bad guys." Yet this scrutiny of antimalarials revealed a grim symmetry between the way drug cops wrestle with gangs that produce fake drugs and the way drugs try to tame pathogens. In both cases, the forces of control are faced with an opponent that seems lighter on its feet, much more adaptable, and very hard to get the better of.

To help spot fake drugs, scientists working with Newton developed simple tests that changed colour if the expected active ingredients was present. One of the criminals' first responses was to put in just enough medicine to fool the tests. More recent studies of antimalarials in Southeast Asia have found no obvious fakes: no pills made only of yellow paint, or of cheap chloroquine masquerading as more expensive artemisinin. They have, however, found a surge in poor quality medicines. A recent study found that three quarters of antimalaria pills in Cambodia had sub-therapeutic levels of active ingredients—and the researchers didn't even test for dissolution. Formulating pills so that they dissolve correctly is very tricky; many of the pills that contained the right amount of drug were probably delivering them in doses too small to cure but big enough to encourage resistance.

It is an open question how many of these "poor quality" medicines are the work of criminals who deliberately manufacture shoddy products. Much of that question hovers over India, the world's third largest producer of pharmaceuticals by volume and its biggest exporter of generic medicines. In the words of whistleblower Dinesh Thakur, a former executive at the Indian generics producer Ranbaxy. "There's no doubt that [some Indian pharmaceutical firms] use one set of standards for making product for advanced western markets and one for sale in poor countries, including India." Thakur turned a spotlight on appalling production errors and outright fraud by his former employer, including medicines which had to be recalled after tiny glass particles were found in them. The US Justice Department launched an investigation that lasted nearly nine years. Eventually, in 2013, Ranbaxy agreed to pay $500m in fines, forfeits and penalties; it continues to sell its drugs into the American market.

The deliberate production of low-quality drugs by licensed manufacturers makes policing sub-standard medicines very difficult. "We can't criminalise all sub-standard drugs, because we want manufacturers to own up quickly when there has been a genuine error," said Mick Deats, a former City of London Police officer who now runs a WHO system that alerts health authorities to reports of bad drugs. "But in some cases you see a pattern of consistently low quality. Then you're out of the accidental and back in to the criminal. The level of evidence you need to tackle that, though, it's just extraordinary."

Perhaps. But India's drug regulatory authority doesn't seem to be setting the bar very high in the first place. It says no action should be taken against a manufacturer who produces medicines that include at least 70 per cent of the stated active ingredient—a level that would do much to promote resistance for many pathogens and that would never meet European standards.

"Only five countries in all sub-Saharan Africa have a lab that meets WHO standards for drug quality testing"

Yet for all this, India is still performing an important service. Besides feeding a giant domestic market, the country exports over $15bn worth of pharmaceuticals each year, almost all of them generics. Good generic medicines are made with the same ingredients as a big-name drug, usually after the patent on the original brand has expired. Many generics manufacturers go through a rigorous WHO-monitored pre-qualification process, and operate to the same standards as the best-known companies. But their products are a lot cheaper, because they don't need to recoup huge research, trial and marketing costs.

Drugs that would be unaffordable if bought from the pharmaceutical giants that invested millions in their development are now within reach for poor people and poor countries. This makes generic manufacturers the darlings of health activists, and the bane of innovative companies. Ironically, the entrenched antipathy between these two groups is protecting the manufacturers of bad generics; vociferous NGOs see Big Pharma behind every attempt to impose higher standards. "There seems to be a belief in some NGOs that companies that make generics are philanthropic organisations," said Newton. "But they're making drugs for exactly the same reason as Big Pharma, to make a profit. They are flawed capitalist enterprises like any other." Big Pharma, for its part, is stuffed with slick-suited marketing executives happy to broadcast the flaws of generic medicines to help undermine patients' confidence in them.

Regulators in wealthy countries don't want to focus public attention on the quality of generic medicines because their public health systems prescribe them to keep costs down. Dinesh Thakur recognises the political dilemma facing drug regulatory agencies. "Most regulators are walking a fine line between assuring good manufacturing practice and the availability of drugs. Access to affordable drugs is very politically charged right now."

"Access to medicines" is still more of a mantra than "access to good quality medicines." Thakur, who now heads Medassure Global Compliance Corporation, a company which helps drug manufacturers source high quality ingredients, said that Indian pharmaceutical companies are taking advantage of that zeitgeist to avoid being held to higher standards. Others agree. Too often the WHO tries to take on the issue of drug quality, the Indian government objects.

Kees De Joncheere, the WHO's director of essential medicines and health products, avoids pointing fingers at individual countries. "Look, no minister of health deliberately wants to have low quality products on their market, that's clear. But when we talk about good manufacturing practice, well, how safe is safe enough? There's a perception in some quarters that some countries are putting up manufacturing standards so that others can't compete."

Producer countries don't have any obligation to guarantee the quality of the drugs they send abroad: the rule is buyer beware. But many importing countries don't have the means to check what they buy—only five countries in all of sub-Saharan Africa have a laboratory that meets WHO standards for drug quality testing. One proposal, borrowed from the airline industry, is to make the countries responsible for the safety of the medicines they produce, no matter where they will be sold. Airlines that come from countries with poor safety standards are subject to blanket bans in other countries, regardless of the standards at an individual airline. This solution is fairly simple, but politicians haven't had the courage to push for it.

Ranbaxy-style scandals notwithstanding, rich countries are good at assuring the quality of the drugs they import. That has made them complacent about the fact that people in other countries are taking medicines that don't work. It doesn't help that the studies by Newton and his colleagues that first turned the spotlight on bad drugs were about antimalarials; malaria doesn't kill voters in rich countries and politicians paid little attention.

Many of the pathogens now building up resistance because of poor quality drugs in Ho Chi Minh City, Lagos and Chennai will spread worldwide. When they arrive in Europe, they will be treated with good-quality medicines that will no longer work. Everyone, everywhere, should be able to trust the medicines they take. But for rich countries, improving the quality of the medicines consumed in the developing world is also a matter of self-preservation. If we don't do more to support higher production standards in India and elsewhere, bad bugs will continue to spread the world over.[5]

Some experts say we are moving back to the pre-antibiotic era. No. This will be a post-antibiotic era. In terms of new replacement antibiotics, the pipeline is virtually dry. A post-antibiotic era means, in effect, an end to modern medicine as we know it. Things as common as strep throat or a child's scratched knee could once again kill.

Margaret Chan

Effective altruism is about asking "How can I make the biggest difference I can?" and using evidence and careful reasoning to try to find an answer. It takes a scientific approach to doing good. Just as science consists of the honest and impartial attempt to work out what's true, and a commitment to believe the truth whatever that turns out to be. As the phrase suggests, effective altruism consists of the honest and impartial attempt to work out what's best for the world, and a commitment to do what's best, whatever that turns out to be.

William MacAskill, *Doing Good Better: How effective altruism can help you make a difference*

In science it often happens that scientists say, "You know that's a really good argument; my position is mistaken," and then they would actually change their minds and you never hear that old view from them again. They really do it. It doesn't happen as often as it should, because scientists are human and change is sometimes painful. But it happens every day. I cannot recall the last time something like that happened in politics or religion.

Carl Sagan (1987)

Because of diabetes and all the other health problems that accompany obesity, today's children may turn out to be the first generation of Americans whose life expectancy will actually be shorter than that of their parents. The problem is not limited to America: The United Nations reported that in 2000 the number of people suffering from overnutrition—a billion—had officially surpassed the number suffering from malnutrition—800 million.

Michael Pollan, *The Omnivore's Dilemma: A natural history of four meals*

5 http://www.prospectmagazine.co.uk/features/losing-the-war-on-bugs-low-quality-medicines-tropical-illnesses

Document 6

South China Sea decision is irrelevant

By Roger Mitton

If a tree falls over in the jungle and no one hears it, does it make a noise?

The old riddle now has a new counterpart: If an international legal body hands down a landmark verdict but no one enforces it, is it irrelevant?

US Secretary of State John Kerry (left) shakes hands with Philippine President Rodrigo Duterte in Manila on July 27 [2016]. Kerry and Duterte discussed the Philippines' dispute with China over the South China Sea.

The question became embarrassingly pertinent after a United Nations tribunal in The Hague, in Holland, ruled last month that China's claim to almost all of the South China Sea is invalid.

Analysts around the world hailed the judgement as a massive defeat for China and a great triumph for its smaller rival claimants, most notably the Philippines, which took the case to court.

Yet in reality nothing has changed: No territory has been ceded by China, and none will be. The tribunal's explosive decision has made no noise.

Not a whimper came from last month's ASEAN meeting in Laos, where the region's band of brothers-without-backbones declined to even mention the judgement in its final statement.

That was predictable because China had bought the support of Cambodia and Laos, while others like Brunei, Myanmar and Thailand tacitly fell into line by saying nothing about enforcing the verdict.

The same shameful inaction and sycophancy to Beijing was on display at a June ministerial meeting in Kunming and at the infamous ASEAN summit in Cambodia four years ago.

So the region's rival claimants are not going to start making any noise now, nor are their ostensible supporters in the United States, Australia, Japan and Europe.

1. What issues are raised in this document?
2. To what extent are the issues in this document global?
3. How would you describe the perspective this article comes from? What are the beliefs and assumptions underlying the perspective?

In fact, the EU was even more craven in its news release by declining to even refer to China or to state that the tribunal's judgement should be binding.

Really, everyone except China should have been crowing after the triumphant verdict, but instead they have been cowering.

It is as if the magnitude of the decision has left them stunned and unable to know what to do next, while China has moved quickly and turned its seeming defeat into a real victory.

As Feng Zhang of Australian National University said last week, "It is becoming clear that the tribunal's finding was so sweeping that it is paradoxically less likely to have any real-world impact."

He continued, "Perhaps the biggest paradox of the ruling is that many policy elites inside China now privately see it as a big gift to their government."

He was right, and to understand the crazy outcome, it pays to recall that the tribunal ruled that China had no right to most of the South China Sea based on its occupation of islands dotted across the sea—the reason being that they are not real islands, but just rocks that cannot sustain life and thus fail the most basic test to be regarded as an island under international law.

To pass that test they must be above water at high tide in their original state before any reclamation has been done, and they must be able to sustain human habitation and have their own water supply.

None of them do, so they do not qualify as real islands and whoever occupies them has no right to a 200-mile exclusive economic zone, but only to a measly 12 miles of sea around them.

That means ownership of the islands, or rocks, is almost worthless because it only brings territorial rights to about 1.5 per cent of the South China Sea, not the more than 85pc Beijing claims.

Although it is a staggeringly profound judgement, the problem is that no one can put it into practice, and so, to return to our original riddle: If no one can enforce it, is it not irrelevant?

Certainly, Beijing believes it is, and has adamantly refused to accept the verdict and will not relinquish its claim to any of the South China Sea.

And as their craven sycophancy at recent regional meetings showed, none of its rival ASEAN claimants nor even the United States is going to try to force China to honour the tribunal's decision.

Of course, since that decision signalled that the other claimants also have no sovereignty rights to large areas of the sea, it can be argued that everyone lost—or that everyone won.

But China, the biggest claimant by far, rejects that view. Its president, Xi Jinping, said recently that his nation's "territorial sovereignty and marine rights" over the South China Sea will not be affected by the ruling.

In response, everyone else has backed down. Even the Americans, who had earlier said Beijing risked "terrible" damage to its reputation if it ignored the verdict, have done nothing.

Given that situation, the US Secretary of State John Kerry was pointedly asked last month, "If you don't mention the ruling publicly, if nobody admits it, then are you not afraid that it could become irrelevant?"

He replied, "It's impossible for it to be irrelevant. It's legally binding. It's obviously a decision of the court that is recognised under international law and it has to be part of the calculation."

Legally binding. Recognised. Part of the calculation.

Sure, it is so binding and recognised that Beijing has declared it "null and void", while Kerry and his regional cohorts have been too petrified to even mention it publicly in their recent meetings.

As Greg Poling at Washington's Center for Strategic and International Studies said, "We should all be worried that this case is going to go down as nothing more than a footnote because its impact was only as strong as the international community was going to make it."

And they have chosen to sidestep it and make no noise. So China wins the whole sea. Game over.[6]

Activity 6

Refer to document 1.

1 Is document 1 an argument? If not, what sort of writing is it?

2 How effectively does the author support the proposal of making Te Reo compulsory in schools in New Zealand?

3 Do you think that it would be better for New Zealand students to learn Te Reo or an additional international language? Why?

Research and discuss

1. Should Americans learn a native American language?

1. What are the benefits of learning a language native to your own country, even if it is not your mother tongue?
2. Everyone can learn a second language, but some people won't try. Do you agree?
3. What is the relationship between language and thinking? In what ways can this be a globally relevant question?

6 http://www.mmtimes.com/index.php/opinion/21765-south-chinasea-decision-is-irrelevant.html

Activity 7

Refer to document 2.

1 Is document 2 an argument? If not, what sort of writing is it?

2 How effectively does document 2 show that, in many ways, today's young people are the luckiest group of young adults ever to have existed?

3 How effectively does document 2 show that there is plenty for young people to complain about?

4 On balance, do you think this is a good time to be young?

5 What do you think of the measures suggested in document 2 to help the young? What do you think the other consequences might be?

Research and discuss

1. What options are available to young people nowadays?
2. What sort of options did young people have in your country 200 years ago?
3. Compare child labour laws in your country now and 200 years ago.

Activity 8

Refer to document 3.

1 Is document 3 an argument? If not, what sort of writing is it?

2 How effectively does document 3 use evidence and examples?

3 "What we're seeing is a push back against globalisation and free trade." How far do you think this push back will go?

Research and discuss

1. What alternative forms of international trade or global economic activity can you think of?
2. Would a return to local economies protected from international competition be a good thing? How would you decide?
3. Should politicians and governments put local interests first, even if this is not in the longer-term best interest?
4. Do current trends in Western politics demonstrate everything that is wrong with democracy? If so, can – and should – we save democracy?

Activity 9

Refer to document 4.

1 Is document 4 an argument? If not, what sort of writing is it?

2 What is Bitcoin?

3 What characteristics does Bitcoin have, according to document 4?

4 Why is Bitcoin important?

5 How effective is the reasoning in document 4 to show that Bitcoin is not ready for the next global financial crisis?

Research and discuss

1. Do you think that a system like Bitcoin could ever be an improvement on the current financial systems?
2. Should we return to an older system, such as barter, or reliance on the value of gold?
3. Do we need an alternative to capitalism and consumerism for the future? If so, what could this be?

Activity 10

Refer to document 5.

1 Is document 5 an argument? If not, what sort of writing is it?
2 What are the possible consequences of drug-resistant diseases?
3 Summarise the causes of drug-resistant disease.
4 How are fake drugs contributing to drug resistance?
5 How effective is the reasoning in document 5?
6 Examine the contrasting perspectives represented in document 5. Which of these perspectives does the author seem to have most sympathy for?

Research and discuss

1. What do you think are possible solutions to the problems of:
   - **a)** drug resistance
   - **b)** drug fakes
   - **c)** low-quality generic drugs
   - **d)** high-priced, high-quality drugs that many people cannot afford.
2. Examine one globally significant medical epidemic. How could it have been better managed? What can we do to prevent another?
3. Should we prevent epidemics, or should we accept that the world is too crowded, and that disease is likely to reduce the population?

Activity 11

Refer to document 6.

1 Is document 6 an argument? If not, what is sort of writing is it?
2 How effective is the use of evidence?
3 How effective is the reasoning?
4 What might be the consequences of trying to enforce the ruling?
5 How effective is the reasoning in the following extract from *China Daily* as a response to the international ruling?

Arbitration on the South China Sea initiated unilaterally by the Philippines is a possible abuse of international law, Cai Congyan, international law professor at Xiamen University and visiting scholar at Humboldt University told Xinhua in a recent interview.

Cai said: "The Philippines' unilateral request for arbitration on the South China Sea could be deemed as abuse of international law, at least not in good faith."

He said China and ASEAN countries including the Philippines have signed the Declaration on the Conduct of Parties in the South China Sea (DOC) in 2002 that includes a dispute settlement mechanism. However, the Philippines did not fully utilise the mechanism in accordance with the Declaration.[7]

Research and discuss

1. What are international laws? How do agencies try to enforce them?
2. Discuss this statement. "Trying to get nations to agree to uphold international laws, even though it is difficult, is still better than not even trying."

Research and discuss

1. Overall, what has most interested you in the documents?
2. What would you most like to research further?

7 http://www.chinadaily.com.cn/world/2016-07/12/content_26052312.htm

Activity 12

1 Which of the following would make good research questions or subjects for an assessed essay? Why? Use the hints on the right.

  a Are conflicts in the Middle East entirely the result of failed international interventions?

  b Bio-warfare

  c Different cultural perspectives can only have a useful global impact if they are equally powerful

  d Addressing global health inequality should be the number one priority in the twenty-first century.

  e Are lifestyle choices the biggest killers now?

2 Write two or three questions of your own. Work in a group to assess and improve the questions.

When deciding on a good research question, think about the following:

- Globally significant
- Different perspectives
- Argument and discussion
- Question to answer
- Can answer within the word limit
- Suitable evidence base
- On a Global Perspectives topic

Remember to be positive and polite about each other's questions. You are helping each other to improve!

Avoid very theoretical or purely philosophical questions. To meet the assessment criteria you need to build up an evidence base, so remember to apply theoretical concepts in practical contexts.

Activity 13

1 Which of the following would make suitable questions for the team research project? Use the hints on the right.

  a Develop a cheap, effective alternative to antibiotics.

  b How can we best preserve endangered cultures in our country?

  c Raise money to fund a campaign against a government foreign policy decision.

  d International law

  e Raise awareness of international trafficking.

2 What might be the most effective solutions to international trafficking?

When deciding on a team research project, think about the following:

- Local problem
- Global relevance
- Effective solutions possible
- Different aspects for Individual research
- Contrasting perspectives
- Argument, reflection and discussion

Practice examination paper

These articles are longer than the articles in most AS Global Perspectives examinations, but they are both worth reading and reflecting on. For this practice examination you should therefore choose one of these options.

- Do the practice examination in the normal time, but accept that you cannot comment on everything of relevance – select the most relevant aspects to comment on.
- Do the practice examination with an extended time limit.
- Do the practice examination, then return to these articles to examine the arguments more thoroughly as part of your research if you are interested in this topic.

Document 1

Death by monoculture

Stephen Pax Leonard

The twenty-first century is the make-or-break century for cultural and linguistic diversity, and for the future of human civilisation *per se*. An unprecedented and unchecked growth in the world's population, combined with the insistence on exploiting finite resources, will lead to environmental and humanitarian catastrophes as mass urbanisation meets fundamental problems such as the lack of drinking water. The actions that we collectively take over the next fifty years will determine how and if we can overcome such global challenges, and what the shape of the 'ethnosphere' or 'sum of the world's cultures' is to look like in years to come.

After having spent a year in a remote Arctic community which speaks a vulnerable, minority language and whose cultural foundations are being rocked by climate change, it is clear to me that the link between environmental and cultural vulnerability is genuine and that the two are interwoven. Cultural practices of the Polar Eskimos are based on a history of survival strategies in one of the world's most hostile environments. Their language and 'way of speaking' is a representation of that. When the sea ice disappears, their stories will eventually go with it.

We, human beings, rent the world for a period of approximately 80 years. It is our duty to future tenants to leave the house as we found it. At present, linguists predict that over 50 per cent of the world's languages will no longer be spoken by the turn of the century. Instead of leaving the house in order, we are on the road to the fastest rate of linguistic and cultural destruction in history. Languages die for many reasons, but the current trend is driven by the juggernaut of the homogenising forces of globalisation and consumerism which seems unstoppable and whose language tends to be the new universal tongue, English.

I am a romantic and romantics are nowadays always disillusioned because the world is no longer how they had hoped it to be. I had gone to the top of the world and had wished to find elderly folk sitting around telling stories. Instead, I found adults and children glued to television screens with a bowl of seal soup on their lap, playing exceedingly violent and expletive crammed Hollywoodian video war games. Time and time again, I discovered this awkward juxtaposition of modernity meets tradition. Out in the Arctic wilderness, hunters dressed head to toe in skins would answer satellite phones and check their GPS co-ordinates.

Consumerism has now made it to every corner of the world. Some Polar Eskimos may live in tiny, wind-beaten wooden cabins with no running water, but Amazon delivers. Most 8 year-olds who live in Qaanaaq and the remote settlements have the latest smartphones. Media entertainment will, however, never be produced for a language of 770 speakers because it is loss-making. Technology, be it mobile phones, DVDs or video games may support the top 50 languages maximum, but never more than that. Some languages are not suited to these technologies: Greenlandic words are too long to subtitle and to use in text messaging. Polar Eskimos tend to send text messages in Danish or English because it is easier.

As the world embraces the synthetic monoculture of populism and consumerism, linguistic and cultural diversity risk being erased right across the world. For consumerism to operate efficiently, it requires as few operating languages as possible. That way, the message is consistent and the producer's cost is minimised. This globalised consumerism is the product of a system which is based on an addiction to economic growth. Growth for the sake of growth is the ideology of the cancer cell, and yet it is difficult to hear US presidential candidates or EU officials talk about anything else. Some politicians speak oxymoronically of 'sustainable growth' but the combination of a rocketing world population and finite resources is the recipe of 'unsustainability' *par excellence*. Growth has become an abstract imperative that is driving humanity to destroy the ecosystem upon which life depends. If we can shake off the growth habit and focus on the 'local' and sustainability for its own sake, minority languages will have a chance to prosper providing they engage with new digital media technologies. The Internet represents surely the best opportunity to help support small or endangered languages and yet 95 per cent of Internet content appears in just 12 languages. The Internet offers also a chance to move away from television which is largely responsible for the spread of a phoney, idiotic form of entertainment culture where production costs are too high to support minority languages. ...

When languages die, we do not just lose words, but we lose different ways of conceptually framing things. For the Polar Eskimos, there is no one concept of 'ice', but over twenty different ways of referring to various forms of ice. Through different distinctions in meaning, languages provide insights onto how groups of speakers 'know the world'.

A language is a collection of statements about the world delivered in a multitude of voices set to a background of music. ...When we lose a language, we lose an orchestra of voices that permeate the mind. As well as knowledge and perceptions of the world which are built into local language varieties, we lose the music and poetry of words and speech which elicit so much pleasure. There should be no need to defend linguistic diversity. It and the power of language is something to be celebrated. Without it, the world would be utterly dull. …[8]

Stephen Pax Leonard is a Research Fellow at Trinity Hall, Cambridge. He is primarily interested in sociolinguistics and linguistic anthropology.

8 http://www.cam.ac.uk/research/discussion/death-by-monoculture

Document 2

Let them die

Campaigners for linguistic diversity portray themselves as liberal defenders of minority rights, protecting the vulnerable against the nasty forces of global capitalism. Beneath the surface rhetoric, however, their campaign has much more in common with reactionary, backward-looking visions, such as William Hague's campaign to 'save the pound' as a unique expression of British identity, or Roger Scruton's paean to a lost Englishness. All seek to preserve the unpreservable, and all are possessed of an impossibly nostalgic view of what constitutes a culture or a 'way of life'.

The whole point of a language is to enable communication. As the renowned Mexican historian and translator Miguel Leon-Portilla has put it, 'In order to survive, a language must have a function'. A language spoken by one person, or even a few hundred, is not a language at all. It is a private conceit, like a child's secret code. It is, of course, enriching to learn other languages and delve into other cultures. But it is enriching not because different languages and cultures are unique, but because making contact across barriers of language and culture allows us to expand our own horizons and become more universal in our outlook.

In bemoaning 'cultural homogenisation', campaigners for linguistic diversity fail to understand what makes a culture dynamic and responsive. It is not the fracturing of the world with as many different tongues as possible; it is rather the overcoming of barriers to social interaction. The more universally we can communicate, the more dynamic our cultures will be, because the more they will be open to new ways of thinking and doing. It is not being parochial to believe that were more people to speak English—or Chinese, Spanish, Russian or Hindi—the better it would be. The real chauvinists are surely those who warn darkly of the spread of 'American culture' and 'Japanese technology'.

At the core of the preservers' argument is the belief that a particular language is linked to a particular way of life and a particular vision of the world. 'Each language has its own window on the world', write Nettle and Romaine. 'Every language is a living museum, a monument to every culture it has been vehicle to.' It's an idea that derives from nineteenth century Romantic notions of cultural difference. 'Each nation speaks in the manner it thinks', wrote the German critic and poet Johann Gottfried von Herder, 'and thinks in the manner it speaks.' For Herder, the nature of a people was expressed through its *Volksgeist*—the unchanging spirit of a people. Language was particularly crucial to the delineation of a people, because 'in it dwell the entire world of tradition, history, religion, principles of existence; its whole heart and soul.'

The human capacity for language certainly shapes our ways of thinking. But particular languages almost certainly do not. Most linguists have long since given up on the idea that people's perceptions of the world, and the kinds of concepts they hold, is constrained by the particular language they speak. The idea that French speakers view the world differently from English speakers, because they speak French, is clearly absurd. It is even more absurd to imagine that all French speakers have a common view of the world, thanks to a common language.

But if the Romantic idea of language has little influence, the Romantic idea of human differences certainly does. The belief that different peoples have unique ways of understanding the world became, in the nineteenth century, the basis of a racial view of the world. Herder's *Volksgeist* developed into the notion of racial makeup, an unchanging substance, the foundation of all physical appearance and mental potential, and the basis for division and difference within humankind. Today, biological notions of racial difference have fallen into disfavour, largely as a result of the experience of Nazism and the Holocaust. But while racial science has been discredited, racial thinking has not. It has simply been re-expressed in cultural rather than biological terms. Cultural pluralism has refashioned the idea of race for the post-Holocaust world, with its claim that diversity is good in itself and that humanity can be parceled up into discrete groups, each with its own particular way of life, mode of expression, and unique 'window upon the world'.

The contemporary argument for the preservation of linguistic diversity, liberally framed though it may be, draws on the same philosophy that gave rise to ideas of racial difference. That is why the arguments of Popham, Crystal, Nettles and Romaine, on this issue if not on anything else, would have found favour with the late Enoch Powell. 'Every society, every nation is unique,' he wrote. 'It has its own past, its own story, its own memories, its own ways, its own languages or ways of speaking, its own—dare I use the word—culture.' Language preservers may be acting on the best of intentions, but they are treading on dangerous ground, and they carry with them some unpalatable fellow-travellers.

The linguistic campaigners' debt to Romanticism has left them, like most multiculturalists, with a thoroughly confused notion of rights. When Nettle and Romaine suggest, in *Vanishing Voices*, that 'the right of people to exist, to practice and produce their own language and culture, should be inalienable', they are conflating two kinds of rights—individual rights and group rights. An individual certainly has the right to speak whatever language he or she wants, and to engage in whatever cultural practices they wish to in private. But it is not incumbent on anyone to listen to them, nor to provide resources for the preservation of either their language or their culture. The reason that Eyak will soon be extinct is not because Marie Smith Jones has been denied her rights, but because no one else wants to, or is capable of, speaking the language. This might be tragic for Marie Smith Jones—and frustrating for professional linguists—but it is not a question of rights. Neither a culture, nor a way of life, nor yet a language, has a God-given 'right to exist'.

Language campaigners also confuse political oppression and the loss of cultural identity. Some groups—such as Turkish Kurds—are banned from using their language as part of a wider campaign by the Turkish state to deny Kurds their rights. But most languages die out, not because they are suppressed, but because native speakers yearn for a better life. Speaking a language such as English, French or Spanish, and discarding traditional habits, can open up new worlds and is often a ticket to modernity. But it is modernity itself of which Nettles and Romaine disapprove. They want the peoples of the Third World, and minority groups in the West, to follow 'local ways of life' and pursue 'traditional knowledge' rather than receive a 'Western education'. This is tantamount to saying that such people should live a marginal life, excluded from the modern mainstream to which the rest of us belong. There is nothing noble or authentic about local ways of life; they are often simply degrading and backbreaking. 'Nobody can suppose that it is not more beneficial for a Breton or a Basque to be a member of the French nationality, admitted on equal terms to all the privileges of French citizenship… than to sulk on his own rocks, without participation or interest in the general movement of the world.' So wrote John Stuart Mill more than a century ago. It would have astonished him that in the twenty-first century there are those who think that sulking on your own rock is a state worth preserving.

What if half the world's languages are on the verge of extinction? Let them die in peace.[9]

Questions

1 Explain how the author of document 1 sees the link between environmental challenges and cultural challenges. [3]

2 a How effective is the use of evidence and examples in document 1 to show the negative effects of consumerism? [5]

b What assumptions underlie the author's perspective? To what extent do you share this perspective? [8]

3 Is the reasoning stronger in document 1 or document 2? Justify your answer. [14]

Extension activity

Documents 1 and 2 come from particular perspectives. Can you find a more solid evidence base for these perspectives?

Research and discuss

1. Can endangered cultures survive without their languages?
2. Are endangered cultures worth saving, even if the people want a Western education and a standard of living which goes with education and technology?
3. There seems to be a growing trend of de-globalisation in the world. Find out more. Debate the relative merits of globalisation and de-globalisation.

9 http://www.kenanmalik.com/essays/die.html

SECTION C
Research report

In your Research Report, you will apply the skills you developed at AS Global Perspectives and Research. You will work independently, from choosing your own research area, through selecting a research methodology, to researching, writing and producing accurate references for your bibliography.

Of course, you can discuss your progress with your teacher, but the work and the way you manage the workload will be up to you. This can be daunting, but if you implement the simple project management strategies covered in this chapter – and stick to them – you can produce a strong Research Report as well as succeeding in your other studies.

This chapter talks you through the processes involved in planning and managing your Research Report. It covers:

- revising and refreshing Global Perspectives and Research skills
- choosing your topic
- keeping a research log
- setting a research question
- the Plan-Do-Review approach to managing your project
- strategies for planning
  - breaking tasks down
  - prioritising
  - sequencing and scheduling
- strategies for doing
  - avoiding procrastination
  - selecting research methodologies
  - avoiding plagiarism
  - getting started with writing
- strategies for reviewing your plan, progress and writing.
- Meeting assessment requirements
  - Research report
  - Bibliography
  - Research log
  - Oral discussion

Working on your research report

Introduction

There are only three fundamental things to remember when you are working on your research report.

1 Revise the Global Perspectives skills.

2 Choose a topic that thoroughly interests you.

3 Apply the Global Perspectives skills.

Activity 1

1. Go through the assessment criteria for the research report, mapping the required skills to the Global Perspectives skills.
2. Which of these skills do you feel that you need help with?
3. How can you get this help?
   a. What actions can you take?
   b. Who can you ask for help?
4. Are there any skills on the marking criteria that you didn't cover in the Global Perspectives part of the course?
5. Make a plan of action. Give yourself specific tasks and deadlines.

Start a research log. Update it regularly. Include, for example:

- thoughts on research
- sources, plus comments on the use and reliability of the sources
- comments on the issues discussed
- questions for yourself
- ideas about possible counter arguments
- any difficulties you are having and how you could manage them, as well as any other relevant issues.

Choosing your topic

Choose a topic that you genuinely find interesting.

Strong independent research reports are usually:

- individual to the writer
- interesting to the writer
- based on passionate engagement
- built on existing academic ideas and research
- based on argument and discussion.

They are often:

- related to later studies.

Activity 2

1 Which of the general topics in the list below do you think are:

- interesting
- individual
- academic?

a Footballers' pay

b Abortion

c Design of fighter jets

d Chocolate

e The best car ever

f The psychology of food

g What is art?

h The role of artists in social change

i Greek literature used in modern children's literature

j Is the Internet affecting our brains?

2 Consider this diagram. Add to the diagram. Think of possible questions prompted by the diagram's content.

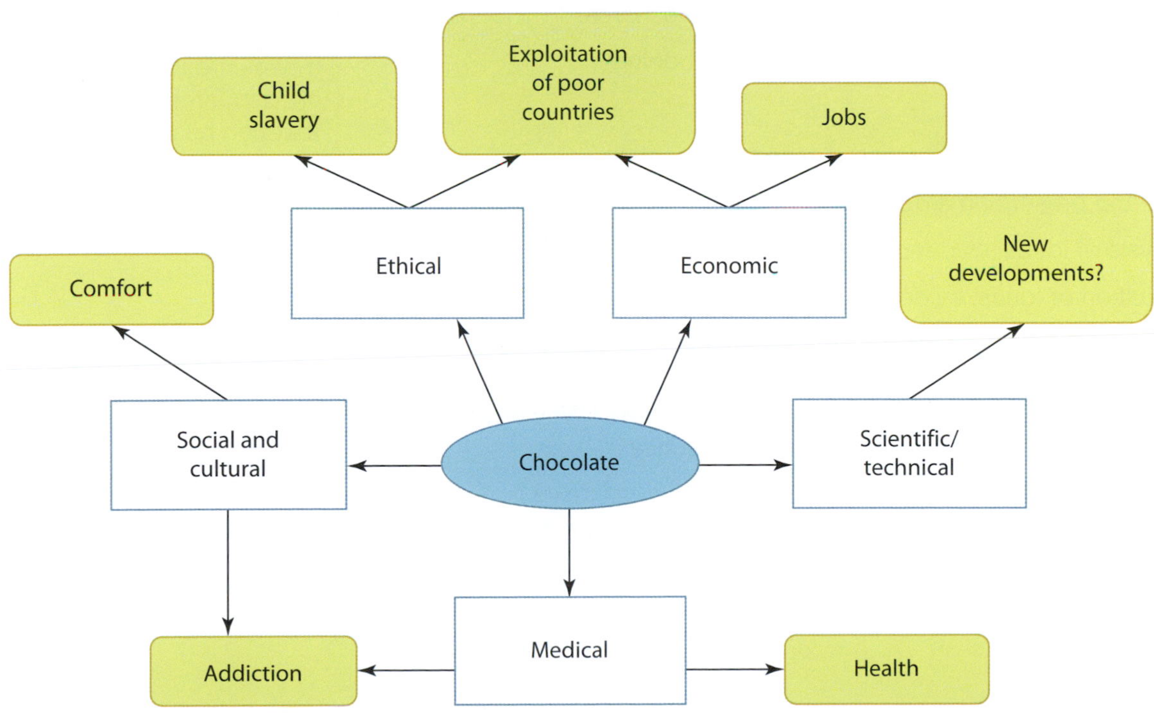

3 Do you think any of the following would make strong research areas? Why?

a A brief history of chocolate

b The cultural significance of chocolate in modern Europe

c Ways of overcoming problems of child slavery in chocolate production

d The cultural history of chocolate in Mesoamerica

e The best new chocolate bars

f The long-term effects of chocolate branding in childhood

g Herschey, Milka or Cadbury? Which is best?

h The dangers of obesity

i The economic importance of chocolate in [specific part of] Ghana and [specific part of a Western country].

j Single grower chocolate – snobbery, marketing or a beneficial development?

4 Choose two or three general areas that you care about intensely. Use diagrams to consider different aspects of each area that might lead to rewarding research areas.

5 What research areas does your thinking lead you to?

6 Use quick Internet searches, library searches and database searches to establish whether there is enough secondary material to form a base for your study.

Make sure you spend time planning, then carrying out initial reading and exploration of your research area, before you set a specific research question.

Activity 3

1 Look at section A and revise how to set a research question.

A strong research question will allow you to do the following.

- Research
  - There must be existing material to aid your research.
  - You will need to think about research methodology.
- Respond
  - It **must** be possible to answer a research question.
- Reason and present an argument, demonstrating:
  - analysis of ideas, evidence and arguments
  - evaluation of ideas, evidence and arguments
  - reflection on ideas, evidence and arguments.

Snappy titles and research questions

Snappy titles can be clever and entertaining, but don't confuse a snappy title with a research question. You must make sure that you have chosen a research question that can be answered.

2 Are the following likely to be effective research questions? Why or why not? Can you change any to make them more effective?

a The cultural history of horse racing.

b 'Football as a game for the people'. To what extent was this a phenomenon limited to the 20th century?

c To what extent are footballers paid too much?

d To what extent does the cultural significance of chocolate differ in Switzerland and the United States?

e To what extent can new truths come from Einstein's theories of relativity?

f Exploration of the relationship between patriarchy and rebellion in *Sturm und Drang* drama.

g 'Shake Spear': sword fights in Shakespeare's comedies.

h To what extent is obesity a threat to modern society?

i Is behaviour irrelevant in economic prediction?

j Geek culture: Japanese anime as a locus of identity formation in young European males.

3 Write two or three questions relating to your research.

a How effective are your questions?

b Do they match the research you are doing?

c If not, do you need to change the question? Or do you need to change the research?

4 Work with a partner to improve your possible research questions.

a Talk through the reasoning behind each of your possible research questions, focusing on the advantages and the disadvantages of each.

b Ask each other questions to help improve the focus.

1. Be prepared to amend your research question during the course of your research – **but** try not to amend your question too often! Keep an effective focus.

2. Listen to each other carefully, and answer each other's points in a helpful way – the aim is to improve questions rather than to win an argument or defend a position.

Managing your research report

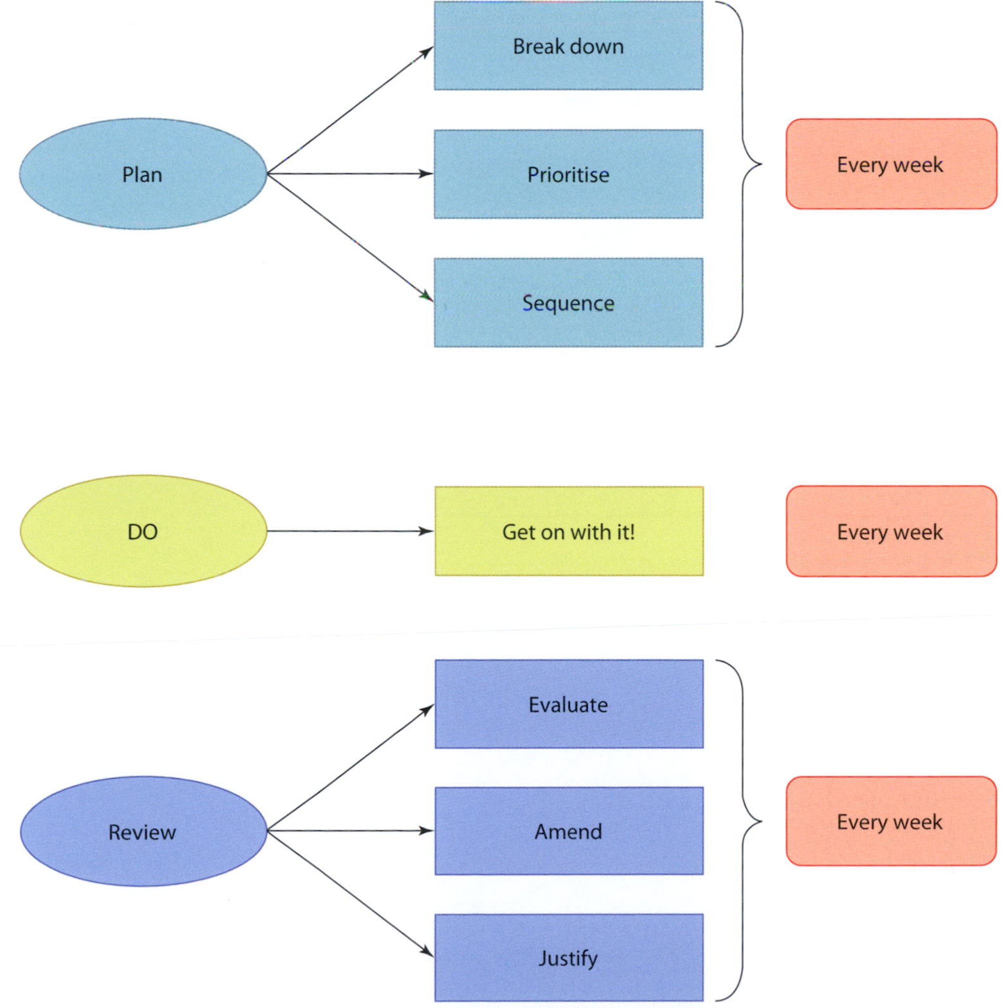

Planning

"What's the point of planning? It takes forever and we don't get marks for it."

"We get marks for managing our research, and planning is part of managing."

"Planning makes you more effective in all the things that are assessed. It helps me to use my time well, so I don't panic at the end."

Plan, do, review is an iterative process. You will need to keep repeating it.

Activity 4

1 Make a list of everything you **need** to do this week. Include:
 a lessons
 b homework
 c independent work, such as your research
 d other!

2 Make a list of everything you **want** to do this week. Include:
 a cinema trips
 b visits to friends
 c parties
 d other!

3 Which tasks need to be done first?

Scheduling rest is as important as scheduling work!

Some studies show that we do our best thinking between 4 p.m. and 10 p.m.

4 Schedule the week using a planner like this. (You can add columns if you are an early morning person or a 'night owl'.)

	09:00–10:00	10:00–11:00	11:00–12:00	12:00–13:00	13:00–14:00	14:00–15:00	15:00–16:00	16:00–17:00	17:00–18:00	18:00–19:00	19:00–20:00	20:00–21:00	21:00–22:00
Monday					L								
Tuesday					U								
Wednesday					N								
Thursday					C								
Friday					H								
Saturday													
Sunday													

a In the planner block out times for eating and resting. In these times you can put activities such as talking to friends, but avoid working.

b Work in a group. Discuss **how** you decide what to do when, and what you do if there seems to be too much to fit in.

c Does everyone in your group agree? Why or why not?

Breaking tasks down

Examples	
Do some research	☹ This is a big, vague task. How will you know when you have done this? How will you know whether you have succeeded?
Go to the library	😐 This is a start. It is an achievable target – but what are you going to do when you get to the library?
Search the database for books and articles that might be relevant to my topic	☺ This is much better. It is a specific task, with a criterion for success (relevance). As a first step to seeing whether there is enough research material, this is useful. Later, you will need to select specific search terms to select an aspect of the topic.

Break big tasks into short manageable tasks. You need to be able to tick it off a list quite quickly, and you need a criterion for success.

Activity 5

1 Which of the following tasks are suitable, well broken down tasks? Remember that you need to be able to tick them off a list quite quickly, and there needs to be a criterion for success.

a Do some research on an aspect of my topic.

b Read [specific book].

c Check the contents list and note which chapters are most relevant to me.

d Check the index for relevant content.

e Read Chapter 3 and make notes.

f Copy out relevant pages from Chapter 3.

g Summarise the key ideas in Chapter 3 in my own words.

h Photocopy four journal articles to read later.

i Write notes on a library book, underlining useful passages and adding comments where I disagree.

j Write notes on a photocopied article or chapter, underlining useful passages and adding comments where I disagree.

k Discuss my topic with my teachers.

l Prepare specific questions or problems for discussion with my teacher.

2 Look at this case of a student known as S. How can S break down her tasks over the next week?

> S is having a bad week. It is now Friday. She needs to discuss her survey results next Thursday with her tutor but hasn't actually designed the survey. She has two books and four articles on the psychology of advertising to read, as well as three on the economics of advertising. She has essays due in for Psychology (Tuesday) and English Lit. (Friday), and a Maths GCSE re-take on Wednesday that she must pass. It's also her grandmother's 75th birthday at the weekend, and S wants to give her a meaningful present.

Do you think that planning is a task that should be timetabled?

3 What do you think are the most important tasks for S? Why?

4 Decide whether there are any tasks S should defer or not do.

5 Are there any tasks that need to be done before others?

6 Write a timetable for S, showing how she can maximise her time.

Prioritising

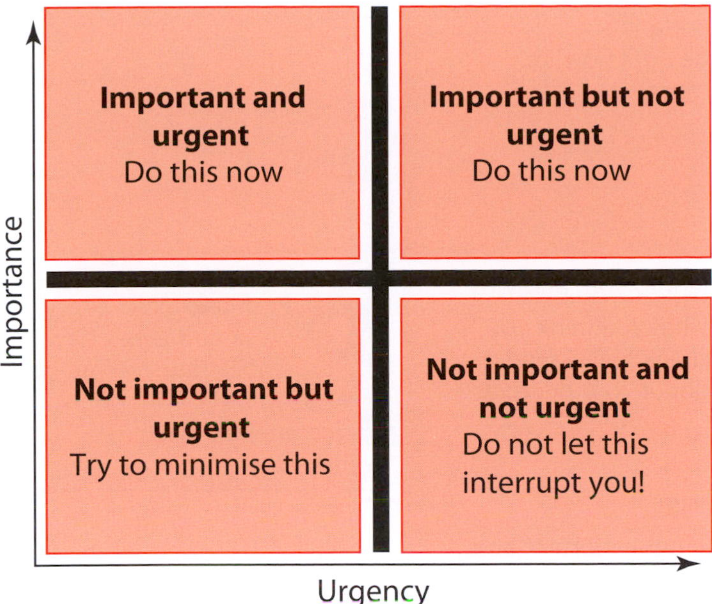

Activity 6

1 Using the diagram above, categorise these tasks.
   - a Doing research for a report due in six months' time.
   - b Answering a phone call from your friend.
   - c Answering a phone call from an elderly relative.
   - d Going to a meeting about the school play.
   - e Checking notifications on social media.
   - f Posting statuses on social media.
   - g Responding to messages from friends about nothing much.
   - h Dealing with friends who think you hate them because it took you 20 minutes to respond to their messages.
   - i Doing an essay for tomorrow.
   - j Going to the cinema with friends.
   - k Turning up to the study skills session.
   - l Reading a magazine.
   - m Buying a new pair of jeans.

2 Add at least five other activities that you do often, and categorise them using the diagram above.

3 Take the items you have categorised as 'important' and categorise them again as follows.

a

Academically important	Personally important	Socially important	Other type of importance

b

Long-term important (will further my long-term goals)	Short-term important (important to me right now, but not in the long term)

4 Think about which of these categories is most important to you, and why.

5 Think about what is genuinely important to you, and what you think you are *actually* prioritising. For instance, do you always check social media statuses when you are working? What does this say about your priorities?

6 Track everything you do for a day or a week. Note how much time you spend on each activity. Be honest!

a How much time are you spending on important tasks?

b How much time are you spending on tasks that are not important and also not urgent?

c How would you like to change this? Be precise. The table gives examples.

I should spend less time texting.	☹ Too vague.
I'll turn my phone to silent when I'm working, and tell my friends that if I don't answer quickly, it's because I'm working.	☺ Specific. You will be able to tell whether you have done this, and see whether it helps.

Prioritise tasks every week and every day. Check that you are on course to meet your goals. If you are not, prioritise differently.

Activity 7

"I know I want to go to a good university. I want to succeed. But I don't want to upset my friends, so I end up texting and chilling when I know I should be working."

Kamal

"I am really driven. I want to go to Cambridge so I always put work first. Sometimes I think my friends hate me, and I'm just so tired. I'm not sure I'll survive till exams."

Amali

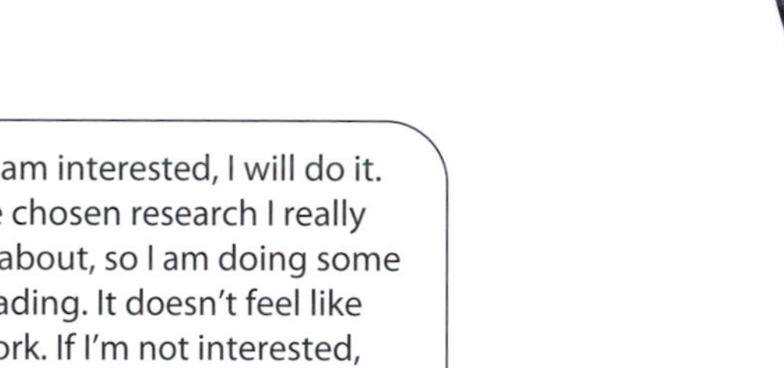

"If I am interested, I will do it. I've chosen research I really care about, so I am doing some reading. It doesn't feel like work. If I'm not interested, I won't do it, even if it is important and urgent. Like my English coursework ☹."

Joelle

1 What is each of these people prioritising?

2 How would you advise each of these people to change? Why?

3 Which of these people are you most like?

4 What advice would you give to yourself?

"On Mondays, I get ready to plan my week. On Tuesdays, I plan my week. On Wednesdays, I revise my plan for the week. On Thursdays, I put my plan for the week into my computer. On Fridays, I think about starting my plan for next week."

Source: http://www.glasbergen.com. Copyright 2003 by Randy Glasbergen

You can change the way you work to become more efficient. Separate yourself from your behaviour. Saying 'I am bad at getting on with things,' makes it sound as if you are stuck with being bad. 'I am spending too much time watching TV,' leads you to think about changing.

Planning is possibly the most important task you can do. Don't forget, though – it is important to actually carry out your plan!

Sequencing tasks

Activity 8

1 These tasks relate to work on a research report. In what order do they need to be done? Number them 1–14.

a Write the first draft of my research report.

b Check databases for relevant research material.

c Check citations.

d Read book A.

e Refine my research question.

f Go to the library.

g Locate and copy relevant articles.

h Think about issues.

i Identify areas where more research is needed.

j Find book A.

Sequencing tasks means thinking about the order in which tasks need to be done. Which tasks must be done before other tasks can start? Which tasks are so important that they should be done very soon?

k Revise research report.

l Identify research area.

m Reflect.

n Do some research.

2 Are there any tasks in the list that must be done before others can start?

3 Are there any tasks that can or must overlap?

4 Are there any tasks that should be done several times during the course of your research?

5 Are there any tasks that are ongoing over a period of weeks or months?

When there are tasks that overlap, or that are ongoing over a period of weeks, it can be useful to use a diagram to help you see the overall process (see below).

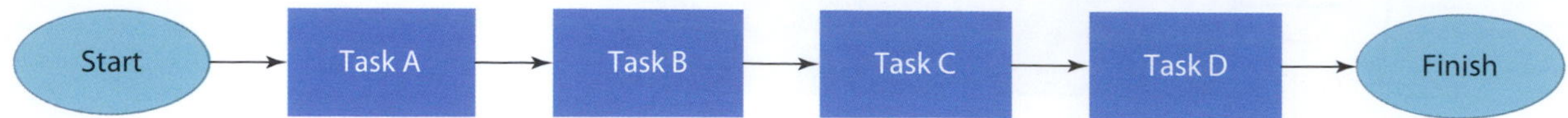

The diagram above represents a simple chain of tasks. Each task must be completed before the next task begins.

The diagram below shows a more complex set of tasks.

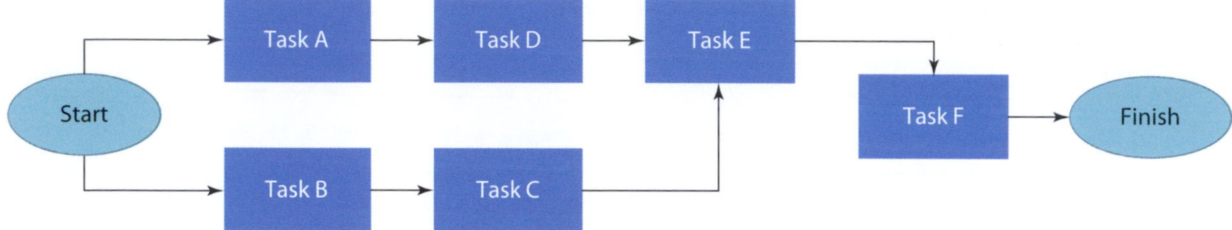

In this case task A has to be completed before task D can start. Task B can happen at the same time as task A, but it must be finished before task C can start. Both task D and task C must be finished before task E can start.

Diagrams like these are known as network analysis diagrams or critical path diagrams. They are tools used in project management. You do not need to use them, but they are helpful in sequencing tasks. If you are interesting in finding out more, you can find information online.

You should regularly think about how you sequence your tasks in the short, medium and long term. Is your short-term sequencing helping you to meet your medium- and long-term goals?

Activity 9

1 Number these tasks from 1–5 to show the order in which they need to be done.
   a Return book A.
   b Go to the library.
   c Find book A.
   d Check the library database.
   e Read book A.

2 Draw a network analysis diagram for the tasks in question 1.

3 Now add the following tasks to your diagram.
   a Make notes.
   b Summarise key ideas.
   c Reflect on issues.
   d Update the research log.

4 How long do you think each task will take? Add timings to your diagram.

5 How long will the whole process take?

6 Let's say it will take ten hours to complete the whole process. Given the other demands on your time (lessons, homework, eating, sleeping, resting, etc.), how long will it realistically take you to fit in the ten-hour process?

7 Effi has a meeting with her research mentor on 25 October to discuss her progress. It is September 27th now. Effi thinks that she can realistically spend four hours a week on her research. She wants to read two important academic books, both around 200 pages long, to discuss with her tutor.
   a How much time does Effi actually have?
   b How long is it likely to take Effi to read the two academic books and make notes?
   c When should Effi start?
   d What should Effi do to help herself work more efficiently?

Another useful tool that you can use to help you schedule your time on a long project is a Gantt chart. You should use your analysis of which tasks have to be completed before others to help you.

Gantt Chart - Project Schedule

Task Name	ID	Start	Finish	Duration	January (1–31)
Task 1	1	1/2/2016	1/6/2016	5 days	
Task 2	2	1/9/2016	1/13/2016	5 days	
Task 3	3	1/14/2016	1/18/2016	5 days	
Task 4	4	1/8/2016	1/12/2016	5 days	
Task 5	5	1/8/2016	1/25/2016	18 days	

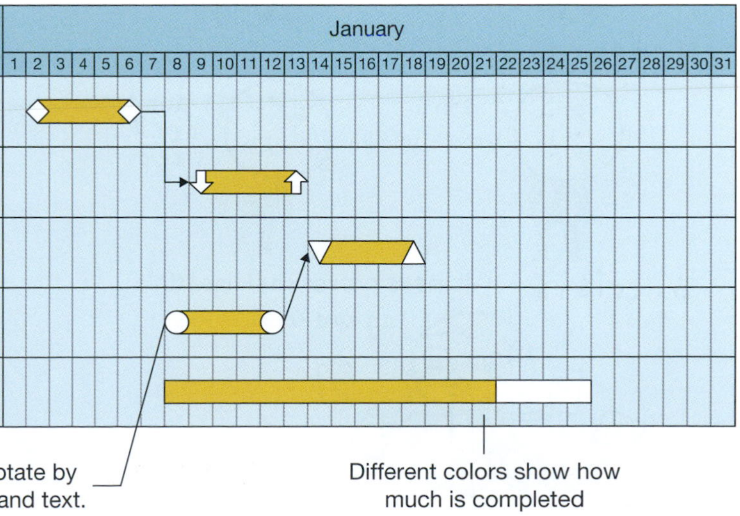

You can annotate by drawing lines and text.

Different colors show how much is completed

Activity 10

1 Make a Gantt chart for your project.

2 Make sure you think about:

- what must be done by when
- the time each task requires
- other things that take time, such as holidays, coursework, mock examinations and work experience
- unexpected things you might have to do, such as: extra research you discover you need to do during the course of your thinking; responding to difficulties such as your survey not working as you intended; or personal difficulties.

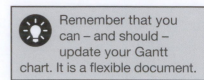

> Remember that you can – and should – update your Gantt chart. It is a flexible document.

'Do': Taking action

Source: chibird.tumlr.com

Activity 11

It is important to think about how you will avoid getting into a crisis with your research report. These points should help you.

- Remember that you need to work on things that are important but not urgent – such as doing research every week—*before* they become important and urgent. This will stop them turning into crises.
- Getting into a regular routine of working on your research will enable you to take any necessary action to prevent a crisis.
- It will be easier to motivate yourself to work on your research regularly if you care passionately about your research area. If you are struggling to motivate yourself, ask yourself whether you are working in the right research area.

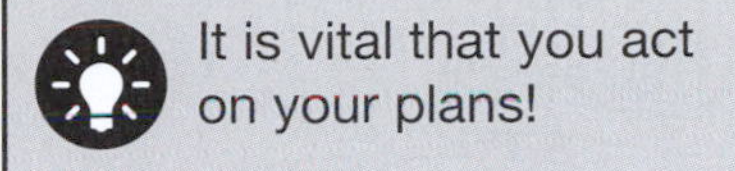

It is vital that you act on your plans!

Methodology

A

87% OF THE 56% WHO COMPLETED MORE THAN 23% OF THE SURVEY THOUGHT IT WAS A WASTE OF TIME

B

LOOK, HALF THE WORK IS DONE! ALL YOU NEED TO DO IS FILL IN THE TOP PART SO WE CAN LEGALLY SAY THE BOTTOM PART
CHOCOLATE CO-OP INC.
RESEARCH AND DEVELOPMENT
DATA:
CONCLUSION: EATING CHOCOLATE WILL MAKE YOU LOOK YOUNGER AND THINNER

Activity 12

1 The scientific method is often held to be the best research method.
   a Do you agree that the scientific method is the best research method? Discuss in groups of students with mixed areas of interest.
   b What points or concerns did your discussions raise? Make a class list.
   c Is the scientific method appropriate for your study?
      – If yes, what kind of experiments and data collection do you need?
      – If no, why not? What kinds of methodology do you think you will need?

2 Look at the cartoons above.
   a Which research methodologies are represented by each of these cartoons?
   b What problems with these research methodologies do the cartoons highlight?
   c How will you avoid the pitfalls?

Activity 13

1 What kinds of knowledge or understandings can we can gain from:
   a a survey of views on the most recent presidential debate
   b an in-depth interview with a care worker
   c an analysis of census data
   d a comparative review of news broadcasts in 1960 and 2010
   e an examination of gendered characteristics in Japanese Manga and UK cartoons
   f an experiment in the Large Hadron Collider, CERN, Switzerland
   g a computer simulation of fuel systems in a new engine
   h mathematical proof of special relativity
   i producing artworks in response to a humanitarian crisis
   j reflecting on the nature of existence?

2 In which subjects—or areas of knowledge—would you expect to see each of these methods?

What are you aiming to do in your research? Your aim might be to:

- generate a hypothesis
- test a hypothesis
- discuss an interpretation
- examine the usefulness of a theory.

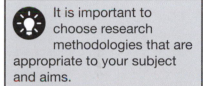

It is important to choose research methodologies that are appropriate to your subject and aims.

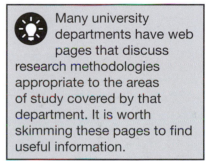

Many university departments have web pages that discuss research methodologies appropriate to the areas of study covered by that department. It is worth skimming these pages to find useful information.

Activity 14

Use online and dictionary resources to find definitions for the following types of research.

Term	Definition	
1.	Quantitative	
2.	Qualitative	
3.	Theoretical	
4.	Experimental	
5.	Primary	
6.	Secondary	
7.	Case study	
8.	Interview	
9.	Dataset analysis	
10.	Small-scale ethnographic study	
11.	Literature review	
12.	Focus group	
13.	Structured observation	
14.	Mathematical modelling	
15.	Computer simulation	
16.	Philosophical	
17.	Practice-based art research	

1. In which subjects—areas of knowledge—would you expect to see each of these types of research?
2. Which of these types of research are common in your subject area?
3. Which of these types of research do you think you will use in your research? Why?
4. Which of these research methods are likely to help you to:
   - a generate a hypothesis
   - b test a hypothesis
   - c discuss an interpretation
   - d examine the usefulness of a theory?

You must be able to justify why you have chosen a particular method of research. You should be able to link it to a research methodology. It is useful to read—or skim—an introduction to research methodology in your area of study.

You need to decide on your research methodology fairly early in your research process. If you are carrying out a survey and consulting a focus group, you will need time to set these activities up, conduct them, and analyse the results.

Make sure you choose a research methodology that is appropriate to your limits—think about your own abilities and the resources you have access to.

Activity 15

1 How effective and realistic are the research methodologies students a–d have chosen?

   a I want to build a computer simulation of the fuel systems in the Eurofighter jet. I'm also going to interview my Dad's cousin who was involved with designing the Eurofighter.

   b I'm studying 19th-century French poetry—I'm mainly looking at interpretations of sex in Baudelaire's poetry. I am mainly going to read poetry, and also some secondary research—I've got an introduction to French poetry, and a few difficult articles. My teacher says that I have to do some primary research, so I'm going to design a survey to get the opinions of other students of French poetry.

   c I'm researching gender roles in Hollywood blockbusters. I'm going to watch a lot of films and call it work.

   d I'm researching the reasons why people stick to bad habits, even though they know the dangers—for example I might focus on overeating or procrastination. I'm still unsure whether to take a scientific view, and use secondary research on the chemical reactions in our brains, or a psychological view—this would require some surveys and analysis of datasets created by other people.

2 What advice would you give each student?

Activity 16

Start to fill in this table with details of your research. You may need to return to this record several times.

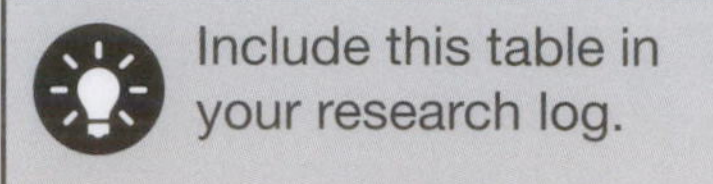
Include this table in
your research log.

Research area	
Why this area?	
Research aim (e.g. to generate a hypothesis)	
Research question	
Why this question? How does it arise from the reading I have been doing? Will it help me to meet my research aim?	
General research methodology	
Why this research methodology? How it will help me to meet my research aim?	
Specific research methods	
How will these research methods help me to meet my research aim?	
Other relevant thoughts	

Research ethics

'All of the following are considered plagiarism:

- turning in someone else's work as your own
- copying words or ideas from someone else without giving credit
- failing to put a quotation in quotation marks
- giving incorrect information about the source of a quotation
- changing words but copying the sentence structure of a source without giving credit
- copying so many words or ideas from a source that it makes up the majority of your work, whether you give credit or not.'

Source: http://www.plagiarism.org/plagiarism-101/what-is-plagiarism/

Follow these rules to avoid plagiarism

Your writing must be your own work. Plagiarism is serious academic misconduct.

Activity 17

Carry out this activity whenever you produce written academic work.

1 Check that where you have quoted (cited) any material, you have referenced it properly.
2 Check that you have not cut and pasted someone else's material into your work without including a reference giving its source.

If you keep a record of all the details of a book, journal article or webpage as you read it, citing will be much easier.

Writing

When you are writing your research report, you should think about the following:

Use your own language.
Use your own reasoning.
Make sure that your reasoning leads to a conclusion. This conclusion should answer your research question.
Everything in your final draft must help you to answer your research question.
Think of the sections in your research report as branches on a tree: each contributes to your overall argument and is an important part of the whole. The sections should not be totally independent of each other.
Use quotations from other sources to support your own ideas and reasoning.
Write something every day. You may have to delete it, but it is always better not to be staring at an empty page, wondering how to start.
Accept that you will have to write, rewrite and rewrite again. It's part of the process.
Use section headings, paragraphs and signposting language to structure your research report.
Don't worry if you don't know how to start writing. Even published authors sometimes spend hours staring at an empty computer screen, wondering what to write. Find strategies that help you to make a start.

Activity 18

1 Which of these 'getting started' strategies do you think are most likely to be effective for you? Why?
   a Put 'Write something here' on the page. Then carry on writing. Come back and edit your writing later so that it makes sense.
   b Start in the middle, and write the introduction and conclusion last, when you know what they are.
   c Decide on the conclusion first.
   d Outline the main points of each section and each paragraph, then fill in the details.
2 Work in a group to share strategies for getting started.

Reviewing

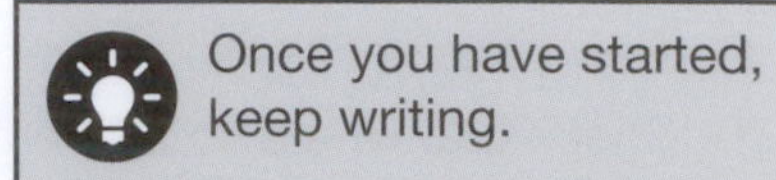
Once you have started, keep writing.

The review process involves the following tasks:

- Evaluate according to the criteria for success.
- Amend
- Justify.

This review process applies to your plan, your ongoing research and your writing.

Time how long each activity takes you. If everything is taking longer than you thought, you will need to update your plan. You may need to find ways of working more swiftly.

Activity 19

1 Evaluate the effectiveness of the planning and research carried out by each of the students below. What criteria are you using?

   a Sophie's research question is about sex in Baudelaire's poetry. A lot of the reading she has done has been about changing gender identities in French literature.

   b Paul had planned to write and distribute a survey. He had a lot of trouble phrasing the survey, which delayed the writing. There are now only two months until the deadline.

   c Adebowale has read approximately 20 books and 50 journal articles, but he cannot decide what to think—his opinion changes depending on which author he is reading. They all seem very persuasive to him.

   d Iqbal has done the reading for sections 1 and 2 of his research report, and has written those sections.

   e Suyi has written 5500 words. She has not used paragraphs or section headings in her work. She thinks that she needs to do more reading, because she believes she has only answered half of her research question. Her deadline is four weeks away.

2 Suggest amendments each student could make to their planning and/or research.

3 Justify these amendments.

Complete the next two activities as ongoing tasks over the next few weeks.

Activity 20

1 Every week, evaluate:

   a how effectively you have acted on your plan

   b how effectively you are meeting your research aims.

2 Every week, consider how you might need to amend:

   a your short-term planning

   b your long-term planning.

3 Justify your suggested amendments. Refer to your research aims, your research question and your criteria for success.

Remember that the final deadline is fixed. If you are falling behind, you need to take action, and not merely reschedule.

Activity 21

1 When you have written your draft report, review it using these questions.
   a Does every single part of your report help you to answer your research question?
   b Have you clearly answered your research question?
   c Does your report have an overall argument and direction?
   d Does your report have themed parts but no real direction?
   e Have you used quotations without citations?
   f Are there areas that need more research to improve the argument or supporting evidence?
2 What actions do you need to take to improve your draft report?

Assessment

A clear focus on the form of assessment and the criteria by which you are judged will help you to achieve as highly as possible.

For the Cambridge Research Report, you must submit:

- A 5000 word research report, which synthesises ideas, arguments and opinions, and which considers different perspectives in response to a research question.
- A bibliography which must be part of the research report, although it does not count towards the word limit.
- A research log which must 'help plan, monitor and review progress and thinking throughout the research process'. The research log must be submitted electronically. It should include your planning and your thinking.
- Evidence of an oral discussion with your teacher, which covers research methods and methodology, a justification of any conclusions and reasoned reflection on learning.

Tracking your progress

You will find it useful to keep track of how well you are progressing on a regular basis. You can consider your progress in terms of:

- the extent to which you have completed each element for submission
- the extent to which you are meeting the assessment criteria
- what you need to do to improve.

Extent to which you have completed each element

When you are engaged in such a long task as writing a research report, it is important to think in terms of 'how much' and 'how well'. You should judge your success by how much you have achieved and how well you have achieved it since the last review, rather than in terms of which bits you have completed.

Sometimes, students are tempted to measure progress by writing sections of the research report each month. This is not always the best measure of progress, because synthesis is such an important criterion in the assessment grids. Students who treat each section of their essay as totally separate are unlikely to synthesise evidence and arguments, or to consider argument and counterargument effectively.

It is better to break down the tasks in a way that will help you to bring the essay together as a whole in the end. It is important to remember that writing is an iterative process. You have to read, think, write, think, review and rewrite. The tables in Activity 1 will give you one possible way of tracking your progress towards completion of the Cambridge Research Report.

Use the following tables to help you to monitor your progress in terms of completing each element for submission.

A

Research Report

Date:

	Not yet started	Just starting	In progress; going well	In progress; having trouble	Nearly done	Done
Question						
Reading						
Thinking						
Outline structure						
Draft 1						
Peer/self-review						
Draft 2						
Peer/self-review						
Proofread						
Final draft						
Ready for oral discussion						
Comments:						
Steps to progress:						

B

Bibliography

Date:

	Not yet started	Just starting	In progress; going well	In progress; having trouble	Nearly done	Done
Making a list of possible sources						
Selecting the most important sources						
Keeping a record of sources as I find them						
Keeping a list of possible quotations with indication of where I found them						
Learning the appropriate referencing convention						
Compiling the bibliography appropriately						
Ensuring all citations are referenced in the body of the research report.						
Peer/self-review						
Revision						
Comments:						
Steps to progress:						

C

Research Log

Date:

	Not yet started	Just starting	In progress; going well	In progress; having trouble	Nearly done	Done
Planning						
Evidence of review						
Research question						
Rationale for research question						
Justifications for any change in the research question						
Notes on reading plus a record of sources						
Critical consideration of sources						
Critical consideration of ideas and arguments						
Critical consideration of different perspectives and counter arguments						
Personal responses and reflections						
Notes and comments on methodology						
Comments on any difficulties you are having and possible solutions						
Comments:						
Steps to progress:						

D

Oral interview/viva

Date:

	Not yet started	Starting to think	Can discuss in writing	Can talk about this a little bit	Can talk about this confidently	Done
Justify choice of research methodologies						
Review choice of research methodologies						
Evaluate choice of methodologies						
What conclusions have I come to?						
The reasons why I have come to these conclusions						
Opposing arguments and different perspectives						
Reasons why I don't accept the opposing arguments and different perspectives						
Reflection on what I have learned and achieved						
Comments:						
Steps to progress:						

Progress in meeting the assessment criteria

Your progress towards meeting the assessment criteria is likely to be uneven. For instance, you might read around your general topic for a month before finding a research question. After that, the more you read, the more you might realise that you need to revise your research question. This is a sign of progress, although at times it might feel as if you are failing.

Maintaining and using a research log, on the other hand, is a criterion that you should be able to make more even progress towards, so long as you do include plans, reviews, notes and thoughts on a regular basis.

As a third example, providing an oral justification is a criterion which may seem quite distant until you are suddenly able to meet it. Here it is important to recognise that everything you are doing will help you to talk about your work.

Because of this uneven progress, it is important to undertake regular reviews, and to think about the small steps which count towards success. Make sure that you reward yourself for any progress you make.

In the next sections, we are going to talk through each of the criteria, with examples. We will use grids like this one to measure progress:

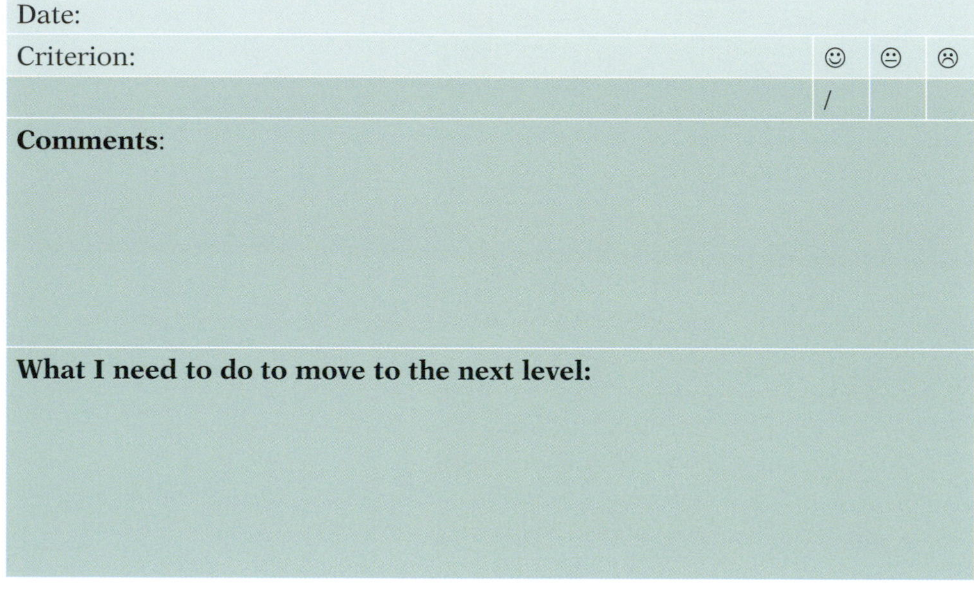

Date:			
Criterion:	☺	😐	☹
	/		
Comments:			
What I need to do to move to the next level:			

Each grid contains a smiley face, a non-committal face and a sad face. Think about these in relation to your progress:

☺ means: I am happy with the progress I have made. I feel that I am closer to meeting this criterion to my satisfaction than I was last time. This might include having dealt well with a problem.

😐 means: I am neither happy nor unhappy with the progress I have made (since last review). I might be a bit closer to meeting this criterion, but it is hard to tell. This might include feeling generally unenthusiastic.

☹ means: I am unhappy with my progress. I feel that I am further away from meeting this criterion than I was last time. This might include facing problems that you do not know how to resolve, or possibly feeling anxious.

Remember to discuss your progress reviews with your mentor and with your peers. Lots of smiley faces might mean that you are doing really well and making good progress, or it might mean that you are overconfident. Similarly, lots of sad faces might mean that you are making poor progress, or it might mean that you are underestimating your progress and being too hard on yourself. Lots of non-committal faces might mean that you are not doing enough work, or that you have picked a research question that is not motivating you. In this case, you might need to consider revising or changing your question.

Let's look at some examples of student self-evaluations using these grids:

Student A:

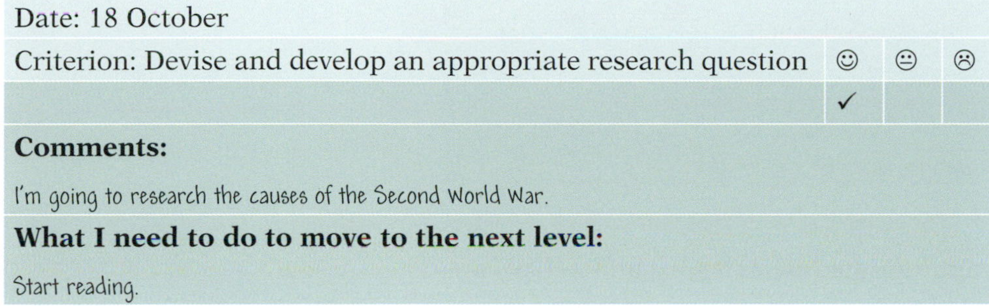

Date: 18 October			
Criterion: Devise and develop an appropriate research question	☺	😐	☹
	✓		
Comments: I'm going to research the causes of the Second World War.			
What I need to do to move to the next level: Start reading.			

Commentary on Student A:
This student is over-confident. They may be feeling happy because they have decided on a research area, but the research question is not appropriate, and it needs a lot of development. This is a fairly standard A Level history topic, so the student is not really going to be developing a deeply personal interest, or going beyond an A level essay. In addition, it is not a question. Furthermore, the student really should have started reading earlier, in order to come up with a research question. So there is also a lack of awareness about how to get to the next level.

Student B:

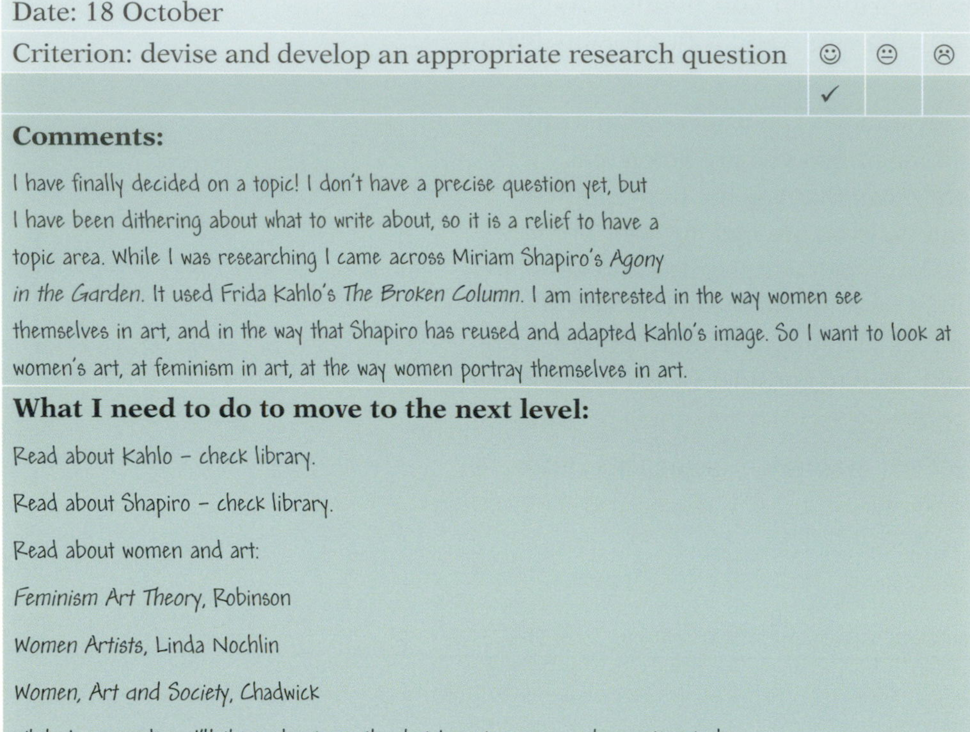

Date: 18 October			
Criterion: devise and develop an appropriate research question	☺	😐	☹
	✓		

Comments:

I have finally decided on a topic! I don't have a precise question yet, but I have been dithering about what to write about, so it is a relief to have a topic area. While I was researching I came across Miriam Shapiro's *Agony in the Garden*. It used Frida Kahlo's *The Broken Column*. I am interested in the way women see themselves in art, and in the way that Shapiro has reused and adapted Kahlo's image. So I want to look at women's art, at feminism in art, at the way women portray themselves in art.

What I need to do to move to the next level:

Read about Kahlo – check library.

Read about Shapiro – check library.

Read about women and art:

Feminism Art Theory, Robinson

Women Artists, Linda Nochlin

Women, Art and Society, Chadwick

While I am reading, I'll think about exactly what I want my research question to be.

Commentary on Student B:

Student B seems to have chosen an appropriate research area, and to have a reasonable plan of action, with targeted reading leading to a revision of the research question. They have reasonably judged that they have made good progress.

Student C:

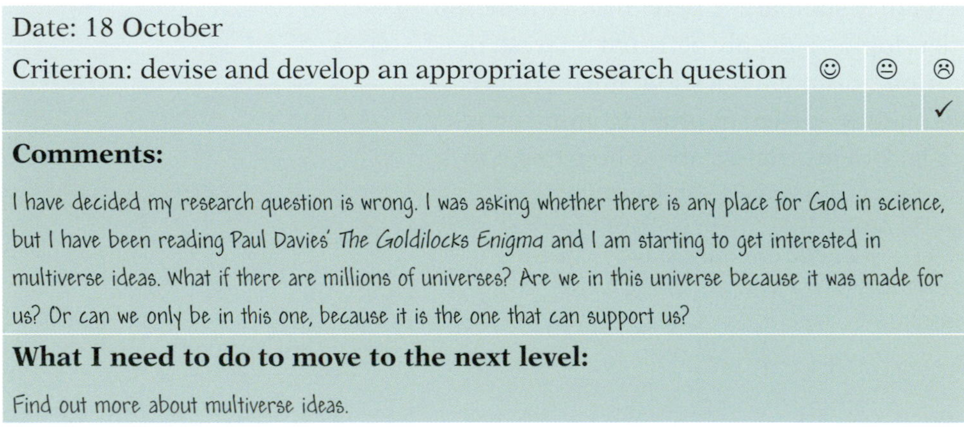

Date: 18 October			
Criterion: devise and develop an appropriate research question	☺	😐	☹
			✓

Comments:

I have decided my research question is wrong. I was asking whether there is any place for God in science, but I have been reading Paul Davies' *The Goldilocks Enigma* and I am starting to get interested in multiverse ideas. What if there are millions of universes? Are we in this universe because it was made for us? Or can we only be in this one, because it is the one that can support us?

What I need to do to move to the next level:

Find out more about multiverse ideas.

Commentary on Student C:

Student C is possibly being unfair to themselves. It is only October, so there is time for a rethink. It sounds as if they have probably made progress. They are moving away from a fairly general idea to a more specific one which is more personal to them and based on reading. It is normal for there to be some confusion about the research question while you are reading, thinking and encountering new ideas. It's almost more worrying if you never question your original research concept! Student C is right to consider finding out more about multiverse ideas, but much more specific suggestions are necessary. A quick Internet search or library search would come up with a range of reading material, for example.

Design and develop an appropriate research question

An appropriate research question will be academic, personal and challenging. There will be indications that you have thought about it carefully, developed it in response to your reading, and engaged in a constructive discussion with your mentor about the question. Remember that it must also be a **question** and not just a general topic.

Activity 22

1 How realistic is Heike's assessment of her own performance, in your opinion? Justify your answer.

Date: 22 March (Deadline 15 April)			
Criterion: Devise and develop an appropriate research question	☺	😐	☹
	✓		
Comments: I have changed my research question from, 'Were Henry VIII of England's wives really about religion?' to 'How important were spies in Tudor England?' I have ended up reading more about spies than about religion. I feel happier now.			
What I need to do to move to the next level: Redraft my essay with spies at the centre. I wish I had made this decision much earlier.			

2 Complete the form for yourself. You should repeat this activity once a week or once a fortnight until you have a clear and appropriate research question which reflects your interests and your reading.

Date:			
Criterion: Devise and develop an appropriate research question	☺	😐	☹
Comments:			
What I need to do to move to the next level:			

Design and manage your research project

The work you have been doing through the 'Plan, Do, Review' process should help you to evaluate your progress against this criterion effectively. If you are regularly planning and reviewing, and if you are thinking about appropriate research methodologies, you should be making good progress here, and you should be aware of any problems.

Aside from making sure that you are regularly planning, taking action and reviewing, the most important part of this criterion is to ensure that you are using the most appropriate research methodologies for your subject. You also need to think about what you are aiming for, and what kinds of conclusions you can draw from your research.

The most common errors that examiners see in research projects at this level include the following:

- Inappropriate research methodologies. This may be surveys used in philosophical or literary research projects from a misguided belief that 'primary evidence is necessary'. Alternatively, it may be too great a reliance on secondary research in circumstances in which surveys, experiments or focus groups would be relevant.
- Poorly designed research. This may be surveys with six participants all from the same school, or it might be an over-reliance on one or two sources in a literature review. Alternatively, it could be a poorly designed experiment.
- Conclusions which do not (cannot) follow from the research. This includes generalising from a small survey to a wider, more varied population, or drawing too strong a conclusion from a single experiment (for example, that X is *always* the case, based on one experiment). It also includes treating a single author's work as representative of an entire perspective or movement, such as post-modernism or abstract expressionism.

Activity 23

1 How realistic is Doshan's assessment of his own performance, in your opinion?

Date:			
Criterion: Design and manage your own research project using appropriate research methods and methodology	☺	😐	☹
			✓
Comments: I have been trying to think of a survey so that I can demonstrate my ability to use primary research. Our GPR teacher has been putting a lot of emphasis on survey design recently. But my research report is on the relative importance of geopolitics and local tensions in Kashmir in the nineteenth century. The opinions of ordinary people won't give me any useful information, and I can't think of a survey that will help. I feel a bit of a failure to be honest.			

What I need to do to move to the next level:

First of all, I am going to give up on the survey, and go back to reading. I have found some newspaper articles from 1863 and 1885 that report on the effects of major earthquakes. I am finding this really interesting.

I am going to search university research methodology sites for methodologies in history. I really don't understand why people's opinions today matter.

Then I am going to talk to my mentor.

2 Complete the form for yourself. You should repeat this activity at least once a month.

Date:			
Criterion: Design and manage your own research project using appropriate research methods and methodology	☺	😐	☹
Comments:			
What I need to do to move to the next level:			

Maintain and use a research log in support of the research process

Your research log should show evidence of your research process. It **must not** extend the essay beyond the word count. It **should** include your notes on your reading, records of your sources, your critical thoughts and reflections, your planning, your notes to yourself on what to do next, thoughts about possible perspectives or other lines of inquiry. Your research log will be submitted electronically.

The examiner will be able to use your research log to reassure themselves that you have done the work yourself, and not plagiarised someone else's work. They might also be able to find evidence to help them decide how effectively you are meeting some of the other assessment criteria. For instance:

> Criterion: Select and analyse appropriate concepts, arguments, perspectives and evidence from a range of source material.
>
> The examiner will look in your research log for evidence that you have considered a range of source material and selected only what is relevant. Your research report will show what material you have used, but your research log will give much more indication of how you have selected the most appropriate arguments, perspectives etc. Alternatively, it will also show the examiner if you do not have sufficient material to select from.

Students are often unwilling to leave material out of a report when they have spent time reading and thinking about it, even if it does not help to answer the question. Using a research log can therefore be useful, because it allows you to show work you have done which you have decided not to include in the research report.

Activity 24

1 Look through the assessment criteria with a partner or in a small group. Which assessment criteria can you give evidence for in the research log?

2 How do you need to change the ways in which you are using your research log in order to meet these criteria?

3 Look at the extracts from Zane's research log and her self-evaluation. How realistic is Zane's assessment of her own performance, in your opinion?

Zane's research log extracts:

October 17th

Mrs M was talking about research methodologies. She talked about literature reviews. These are evaluative reports of information on what other people have written in the area. They should:

- describe
- summarise
- evaluate
- clarify
- provide a theoretical basis.

I don't want to do that much reading. I don't really like reading.

October 24th

Mrs M was talking about research methodologies again. She talked about focus groups and interviews and surveys. You can get lots of different sorts of information about what people think. That's really interesting.

Date: 24 October			
Criterion: Maintain and use a research log in support of the research process	☺	😐	☹
	✓		
Comments: I have been keeping my research log up-to-date every week.			
What I need to do to move to the next level: Keep writing in my research log.			

4 Complete the form for yourself. You should repeat this activity at least once a month.

Date:			
Criterion: Maintain and use a research log in support of the research process	☺	😐	☹
Comments:			
What I need to do to move to the next level:			

Analyse and use relevant and credible evidence in support of arguments and overall perspectives

Here, evidence should be taken as 'evidence base', including concepts, arguments, information, perspectives, underlying assumptions etc. You should be familiar with this idea of evidence from AS Global Perspectives and Research.

'Analyse evidence' means think about the evidence and break it down into its parts. Depending on the precise nature of the evidence, this might mean identifying reasons, conclusions and unstated assumptions in an argument, or it might mean looking at how a survey was constructed to decide whether the questions were appropriate and the sampling representative. In the case of a perspective, analysing evidence can mean identifying the different lines of reasoning and different arguments that are used in that perspective, and the underlying beliefs. Analysing can also mean putting these components back together, possibly with a new interpretation. This is especially important for your research report. You need to interpret the evidence and use it to support your own reasoning.

Relevant evidence is evidence which helps you to answer your research question. As we discussed above, you can use your research log to show your thinking about what is relevant and what is not. Your research report should only include relevant material.

Credible evidence comes from reliable, expert sources. In the context of an academic essay, credible evidence comes from academics with strong reputations, and was probably published in a peer reviewed journal or book.

You might find it useful to record your thoughts about the credibility of your sources in your research log. You could use a table like this:

Author				
Title				
Found at:				
	☹	😐	☺	Comments
Reliable?				
Academic?				
Peer Reviewed?				
Reputation?				
Expert?				
Use?				

However, you should **not** generally include your thoughts on the credibility of your sources in your research report. You should select appropriate, credible material, and then focus your evaluation on the quality of argument, and how you can use the arguments and other evidence to support your own line of reasoning.

Let's look at the assessment criteria in more detail:

For 16–20 marks, in the top band, the criterion reads:

> Evaluation and synthesis of evidence is consistently well supported, developed and used effectively to draw reasoned conclusions.

For 6–10 marks, the criterion reads:

> Some evaluation and synthesis of evidence to reach reasoned conclusions. There may be overreliance on generalised comment on the origin of evidence rather than on the validity of its arguments.

Activity 25

1 Consider the extracts from Harshitha's and Abbie's research reports. How effectively do you think they analyse and use relevant and credible evidence in support of arguments and overall perspectives?

Harshitha:

Although Adamson (reference) argues effectively that craft does not count as art, because it does not meet the criterion of autonomy, he fails to observe that art does not meet the criterion of autonomy either. As Derrida (reference) and Bhabha (reference) argue, art is always the product of a particular culture. It does not stand outside of culture, totally separate. Art is the product of a mind, which arises from a particular culture in a particular time and place. In this respect, then, it has not yet been distinguished from craft.

Abbie:

Glenn Adamson is a Professor at Yale. He argues in his book that craft does not count as art because it does not meet the criterion of autonomy. Glenn has high credibility because he is a Yale Professor and he is an expert. He says that craft is always in the frame. It is craft which acts as the frame to separate art from the world.

2 Consider Abbie's self-assessment. How realistic is her assessment of her own progress, in your opinion?

Date: January 22			
Criterion: Analyse and use relevant and credible evidence in support of arguments and overall perspectives	☺	😐	☹
		✓	
Comments: I can see that I am below half marks in the assessment criteria, but I don't understand why. Mrs M has taught us to evaluate the credibility of the sources, and I am doing that. It feels like I can never do the right thing.			
What I need to do to move to the next level: I don't really know what synthesise means so I am going to talk to Mrs M.			

3 Refer again to the assessment criteria, and use the form below to assess your own progress.

Criterion: Analyse and use relevant and credible evidence in support of arguments and overall perspectives	☺	😐	☹
Comments:			
What I need to do to move to the next level:			

Use appropriate referencing and citation techniques

You should already have covered referencing and citation conventions. You will need to select a convention appropriate to your subject and use it consistently. The most important points to consider are:

- **Always** keep a note of where ideas come from. If you don't, you won't remember. You can waste a lot of time looking for an idea if you do not make a note.
- When you take notes, make sure that you include at least the author's name and title on the first page of your notes. Put the author's name on each subsequent page. When you note down a significant idea or something you might want to quote, include the page number. This is because you will have to include it in your citation, and because you may need to refer to the page to check the author's exact words. Here you can see a page of notes with the title, the author in the top right hand corner, a page reference and a diagram showing key ideas.
- Take a photograph of or scan the reverse side of the title page, or at the back, of any book that you use. This will usually include all the information you need for a reference. It does not need to be a particularly good photograph, just clear enough for you to read the information. It is possible to get apps which will allow you to manipulate the information in a scan or photograph, but you can also copy it from a photograph.
  - Regularly archive any photographs or scans you have taken.
  - It might be worth building up a list of references in the appropriate convention as you read. When you write the final research report, you will only need to delete the references you do not need, which is much easier than producing the whole list. It is also less tedious this way.

Activity 32

1 Check that you have a record of all the important details from the source material that you have used so far.

2 Write reference entries in the convention appropriate to your subject for the following sources:

a https://www.quantamagazine.org/20150604-quantum-bayesianism-qbism/

b http://people.virginia.edu/~ecd3m/1110/Fall2014/The_Character_of_Physical_Law.pdf

c Extract from Aristotle's Poetics in *Western philosophy an anthology*, Ed John Cottingham, Second edition, Blackwell Publishing, 2008

d *Splendour of Mughal Painting* by Asok Kumar Das, published in Bombay in 1986 by Vakils, Feffer and Simons Limited.

e *The Spaces of Contemporary Jewelry*: Page, Bench, Plinth, Drawer, Street, Body, World by Monica Gaspar, Benjamin Lignel, Kevin Murray, Damian Skinner and Namita Wiggers, found in the book *Contemporary Jewelry in Perspective* edited by Damian Skinner, published by Lark Jewelry and Beading in New York in 2013

3 Write a sentence showing how you would reference each of these sources when you quote from them, for example:

According to Das (1986), Mughal Painting is, '…'.

4 Choose two or three of the sources you are working with at the moment.

a Write reference entries in the appropriate convention.

b Write sentences or paragraphs showing how you would quote from them with in text citations.

5 Use the grid below to help you to monitor your ongoing progress.

Date:			
Criterion: Use appropriate referencing and citation techniques	☺	😐	☹
Comments:			
What I need to do to move to the next level:			

Provide and oral explanation and justification

You will have an oral interview, or viva, with your teacher. The main purpose of this is to ensure that you have done your own work and that you have not plagiarised someone else's work. If you have done your own research, then you will be able to talk about it, even if you find the process a little nerve wracking.

A second purpose of the oral interview is to check your understanding of your research. Your teacher will ask you about:

- your research methods and methodology
- how you justify any conclusions
- your reflections on your learning

You will need to answer freely and spontaneously, and you won't know exactly what questions are coming. However, there should not be any big surprises, so you can prepare effectively.

Some strategies you could use include:

- Every week, talk to someone about a part of your research. This will ensure that you are used to talking about it as well as writing about it. You could talk to a friend, a family member, a pet or even the mirror.
- Ask a friend or family member to pose questions for you to respond to, relating to your research. Two really useful prompts are, 'Why?' and 'Can you explain that a bit more?'

- Write out a list of all the questions you can think of relating to your methods, your conclusions and your personal reflections. Practise answering them in speech.
- Make notes to help your structure what you are saying. **Do not** write speeches to learn. This will make you sound stilted and unconvincing.
- Remember that the oral interview is not worth very many marks, and that everyone gets nervous.

Activity 33

1 Use the grid below to help you to monitor your progress.

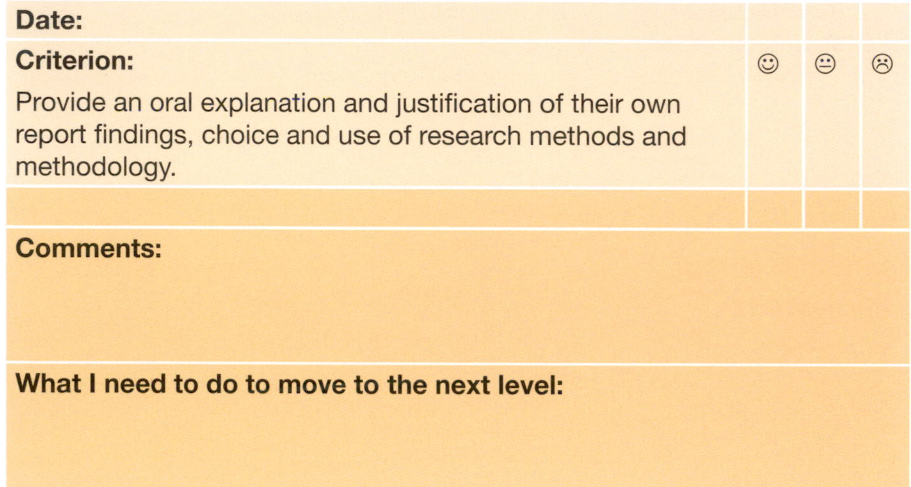

Date:			
Criterion: Provide an oral explanation and justification of their own report findings, choice and use of research methods and methodology.	☺	😐	☹
Comments:			
What I need to do to move to the next level:			

Index

A LeVaux: 'Economics and ethics of locally grown food' from http://www.denverpost.com, December 23, 2015. Reproduced by permission of the author.

Carlos Lopes: 'African Migrants: Is it payback time?' Copyright © 2015 United Nations. Reproduced with the permission of the United Nations.

Roger Mitton: 'South China Sea decision is irrelevant' http://www.mmtimes.com/, 4 August 2016. Reproduced by permission of the author.

Richard Muller: 'Is global warming a hypothesis or a theory?' from https://www.quora.com/Is-global-warming-a-hypothesis-or-theory, 9 December, 2015. Reproduced by permission.

Bob and Roberta Smith and RA and Kelly Grovier: https://www.royalacademy.org.uk from the spring 2015 issue of RA Magazine. Reproduced by permission.

Camille Parmesan & Gary Yohe: A globally coherent fingerprint of climate change impacts across natural systems from *Nature* 421, 37-42 (2 January 2003). Reprinted by permission from Macmillan Publishers Ltd.

Vivienne Parry: Extracted from *The Truth About Hormones* published in 2005 and reproduced with the permission of Atlantic Books Ltd.

Momo Kano Podolsky & Monique Hutson: 'Q&A with Joseph Carens: The Ethics of Immigration', 26 January 2015. Reproduced by permission.

Jeffrey D. Sachs: '3 reforms the UN needs as it turns 70' from https://www.weforum.org, 24 August 2015. Reproduced by permission.

Allen Scott: 'Is Bitcoin ready for the next global financial crisis?' from https://news.bitcoin.com/bitcoin-ready-global-financial-crisis/ August 6, 2016. Reproduced by permission.

Rory Stott: 'How Migration Will Define the Future of Urbanism and Architecture', 5 July 2016, ArchDaily from http://www.archdaily.com. Reproduced by permission of the author.

Datuk Zaid Ibrahim: 'There's no life if you're poor' from http://www.thestar.com.my/. Reproduced by permission.

'Are we living inside a cosmic computer game? Elon Musk echoes the Bhagwad Gita (and The Matrix)' from http://scroll.in. Reproduced by permission.

'Bangladesh clamps down on social media after cafe attack, Dhaka, Bangladesh, AFP, 7 July 2016 © Agence France-Presse. Reproduced by permission.

'Checklist of worst-case scenarios could help prepare for evil AI' from https://www.newscientist.com. © 2016 Reed Business Information - UK. All rights reserved. Distributed by Tribune Content Agency.

'Ethical Issues of The Future of Medicine: The Top 10' from https://medicalfuturist.com. Content is licensed under a Creative Commons Attribution 4.0 International license.

Extract from http://www.fathers-4-justice.org. Reproduced by permission.

'Gender equality, health, and environment' from http://www.wen.org.uk. Reproduced by permission.

Extract from 'Traditional beliefs, Western values in the workplace: Strange bedfellows?' from https://www.newsday.co.zw/, October 11, 2011. Reproduced by permission.

'The Jewelry Industry's Role in Illegal Amazon Destruction' from earthworksaction.org Reproduced by permission.

'Millennials prefer booking holidays through travel agents' from the Relaxnews Editorializer Platform https://editorializer.relaxnews.com. Reproduced by permission of Relaxnews.

'Unhappy New Year: The 10 Geopolitical Risks to Watch in 2016' from http://foreignpolicy.com/1 July 2016. Reproduced by permission.

Source of extract D: http://www.artscouncil.org.uk/how-we-make-impact/international-development. Contains public sector information licensed under the Open Government Licence v3.0.

'What is the New Order?' from http://www.theneworder.org. Reproduced by permission.

'Why marrying ecology and economics is essential' from https://www.newscientist.com. © 2015 Reed Business Information - UK. All rights reserved. Distributed by Tribune Content Agency.

Quote from http://www.un.org/en/globalissues/internationallaw/.

Quote on trafficking of people from http://www.un.org.

'Are dictators ever good?' from https://www.theguardian.com/. Courtesy of Guardian News & Media Ltd.

Extract from http://www.plagiarism.org/plagiarism-101/what-is-plagiarism/.

The World's Muslims: Religion, Politics and Society" Pew Research Center, Washington, DC (April, 2013) http://www.pewforum.org/2013/04/30/the-worlds-muslims-religion-politics-society-overview/. Reproduced by permission.

We have made every effort to trace and contact all copyright holders before publication, but if notified of any errors or omissions, the publisher will be happy to rectify these at the earliest opportunity.

Links to third party websites are provided by Oxford in good faith and for information only. Oxford disclaims any responsibility for the materials contained in any third party website referenced in this work.